I0640733

Forestry
and Its
Career
Opportunities

THE AMERICAN FORESTRY SERIES

HENRY J. VAUX, *Consulting Editor*

WALTER MULFORD WAS CONSULTING EDITOR OF THIS SERIES FROM ITS INCEPTION IN 1931
UNTIL JANUARY 1, 1952.

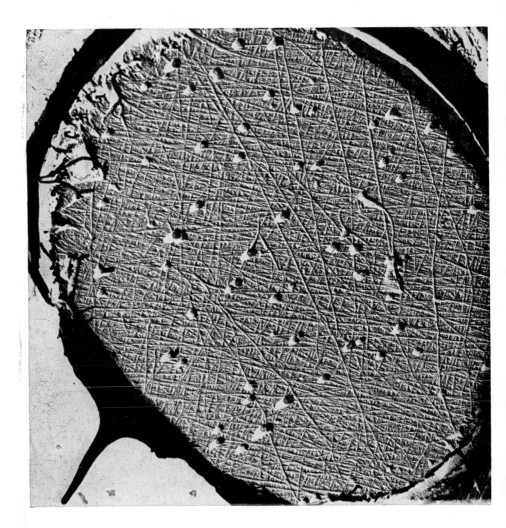

The fascinating pattern of tissue in the pit membrane of a basswood fiber. The filmy strands are microfibrils made up of longitudinally oriented cellulose molecules.

Forestry and Its Career Opportunities

Second Edition

Hardy L. Shirley

Dean, State University of New York
College of Forestry at Syracuse University
Syracuse

McGraw-Hill Book Company

New York   San Francisco   Toronto   London

3 4 5 6 7 8 9 10 – MP – 1 0 9 8 7

Forestry and Its Career Opportunities

Library of Congress Catalog Card Number 63-16468

56971

Preface

THE SECOND WORLD WAR marked the end of an epoch for citizens of the United States. No longer could the individual American stand four-square before humanity and declare himself to be unconcerned with the vicissitudes that beset the rest of mankind. No longer could he "look the whole world in the face because he owes not any man." He realized that for good or ill his own fate is inextricably interwoven with the fate of humanity throughout the world, that the bountiful resources his own country possesses and the prodigal use he has made of these in the past will not save him in the future. No open frontier lies to his west, and no unexploited or unoccupied section of the world remains that he may colonize or exploit. Henceforth his economy and his welfare must depend upon the skill with which he develops and utilizes those resources that his own land can permanently supply. He may trade with the rest of mankind, but this trade must be on a mutually helpful basis.

The purpose of this book is to present a broad picture of forestry in relation to its historic development and its place in national and world economy. Technical forestry is treated lightly, as good books covering the several phases individually are available. This book is written to help beginning students understand the many facets of forestry and to give them background for deciding whether forestry is to be their life career. It should also prove helpful to vocational-guidance counselors and the general reader interested in the scope and magnitude of forestry.

Forestry at present is in a highly dynamic state. In the eastern and western sections of the United States great emphasis is being placed on outdoor recreational use of forest lands. At the same time, increased demands are being made upon forests for their water resources, forage resources, game resources, and timber. Timber remains the product of major economic value from most of the forest lands of the United States.

Forestry is receiving increased attention in newly developing countries, for in many of these timber is of high importance in their export trade. Work outside the United States has become an important part of United States and UN assistance programs. Many foresters spend a portion of or their whole professional career in foreign service.

Forestry makes a variety of demands on its practitioners, and none is more complex than the judgment required to fit multiple use to the land so as to maximize benefits.

The author is indebted to a host of people for valuable contributions and suggestions. These include the instructors who have assisted him in the general forestry course at State University of New York, College of Forestry, at Syracuse; also many people in the federal and state forest services; the various forestry agencies in the Department of the Interior, including the Park Service and Bureau of Land Management; the American Forest Products Industries; the Society of American Foresters; and other agencies. They have furnished up-to-date information on forestry, forest employment, and forest products and photographs and other material used in the text. The author has received much help from members of the faculty and staff of the college.

Individuals deserving special mention for material furnished or critical review include Henry Clepper, Otis F. Hall, V. L. Harper, James C. McClellan, R. D. Hostetter, Francis H. Eyre, Douglas G. Haring, John W. Barrett, Gerald H. Smith, George J. Albrecht, Edwin C. Jahn, C. Earl Libby, Paul F. Graves, S. Earll Church, Charles C. Larson, Robert A. Zabel, and Genevieve Reidy. The author is especially indebted to the Misses Dorothy Reynolds and Shirley Bratt for handling the editorial and clerical work.

To all these and many others the author expresses his gratitude. Final responsibility for material included, presentation, and opinions expressed rests with the author.

Hardy L. Shirley

Contents

CHAPTER 1. *Man and His Home*

FORESTRY, in common with other professions, is an activity of men for men. The forester is concerned with the welfare of the forest because the forest contributes to the welfare of men. Men must have food, shelter for themselves and their perishable possessions, and clothing to keep them warm and dry. Without these men perish.

Man's Nature and Activities

Man has made amazing progress in meeting basic needs. Long ago he learned to domesticate plants and animals and to preserve and store food supplies. He learned to build shelters and to transport himself and his goods by water, land, and, more recently, by air. His great transportation network, together with a complex commercial system, makes it possible to move products and people long distances and to support them in cities. Man has also developed great technologic capacity which has enabled him to organize industrial production so as to increase greatly the output per man-day of labor.

All these advances help to improve man's standard of living and, hence, his potential for survival. He has needed to do these things, for, biologically speaking, he is a puny creature. In physical strength and endurance, reproductive capacity, ability to endure extremes of heat and cold or long periods without food and water, he is a poor match for the camel, rabbit, terrapin, or insect. Only through use of his intellectual powers is he able to dominate other forms of life. It is also through exercising his intellect that he experiences the highest pleasures of which he is capable. Man's curiosity and his devotion to scientific inquiry are insatiable. This has led him to explore the earth from pole to pole, to plumb the depths of the oceans, and to probe outer space with telescope, spectroscope, and now with rocket-launched satellites. All this is leaven to man's spirit and a catalyst to his constructive curiosity.

These very achievements impel man to give expression to his inner yearnings in literature, art, and music; lead him to build temples and

1

other public buildings, and to hold great religious meetings. Man's spirit is responsible for his finest achievements, yet it is delicate and, hence, to be carefully nurtured. Neglect leads to incapacity of the individual or group to respond effectively to the pressures of life.

Man's Home Is the Earth

The earth is man's dwelling place. Its major features are the atmosphere, the sea, and the land.

Air is man's most precious resource. Though he can live for hours without water and days without food, he can live but minutes without the oxygen of the air. The atmosphere is a great reservoir of oxygen, nitrogen, carbon dioxide, and water vapor. There is a ready and continuous exchange of these between air and sea and between air and land surfaces. The air has become one of the most important media for conveying messages and transporting humans. Its purity, long unquestioned, is now threatened as radioactive material is added to noxious gases and particles from chimneys, industries, and motorcars. Concern for air must henceforth be added to man's other concerns for his home.

Water is the second most useful and most abundant resource on the surface of the earth. Oceans, seas, and lakes cover 71 per cent of the earth's surface; land, but 29 per cent. Water makes up some 63 per cent of the human body and from 20 to 90 per cent of man's principal foodstuffs. It is a major element in breaking down rock into soil particles and in wearing away mountains to create plains. Water is widely available in generous quantities because of circulation from sea to land through the energy of sun and wind. Where it is absent, in deserts, man cannot dwell. Water is an increasingly urgent element for cities and industries. For this reason man should guard the stability and purity of his water supplies most zealously.

The great mass of the earth is solid material, having a mean density of about 5.52 times the density of water. It is the land surface, however, with which man is mostly concerned. Just as there is an exchange between the atmosphere and the land and sea, so there is an exchange of water between the oceans and the land. Water vapor from the oceans condenses and falls on the land. As it runs from the land it carries soil and minerals to the sea. If it were not for periodic upheavals in the earth's crust throughout geologic time and the uncovering through erosion of new unleached solid material, the earth's surface would ultimately become as sterile as the sands of the seashore.

Land Areas and Land Use

The land area of the world was originally made up as follows:

Regions	Area, million square miles	Per cent of total
Polar............	6	10
Desert...........	18	31
Grassland........	13	23
Forest...........	21	36
Total..........	58	100

The 41 per cent of the land area that is arctic and desert has been little used by man; nor is it likely to be used, because it can support but meager plant and animal life that is necessary for human existence.

Of the land outside the arctic regions man's current use is as follows:

	Per cent
Cropland...................	9
Permanent pastureland.......	16
Forests and woodlands........	34
Waste and other............	41

The most valuable land from the human standpoint is cropland, for it is here that man can concentrate his numbers, build his cities and factories, conduct his commerce, and develop his culture. Unfortunately, cropland makes up the smallest division of the earth's surface. It is, therefore, all the more precious and is to be guarded against loss by soil erosion, injudicious cropping, and alienation through too extensive encroachment by man for cities, highways, airfields, and factories. Grassland for grazing has supported the nomadic peoples of the past and present. It is suitable for an extensive type of animal husbandry such as that found in our own western states, the pampas of the Argentine, and the grasslands of Asia. Wastelands are mostly arctic or arid. Man has created some wastelands himself through injudicious cropping or pasturing. Mining, smelting, and other industrial activities may also destroy land for use by trees or crop plants.

Forest Land

There remains the 34 per cent of the land area that supports forests. Forests occupy about 11 billion acres (Fig. 1). About half the forest land is still so remote as to remain relatively untouched. About one-eighth has been so badly denuded as to be virtually useless. Only a relatively small percentage of the total, some 750 million acres, has been placed under intensive forest management. The remainder is used by man for timber or grazing, for a dwelling place, as a source of water supply, and for many other purposes, with relatively little care or thought being bestowed upon it.

Wood. Forests afford United States citizens five major products or services: wood, water, wildlife, forage, and recreation. Of these, wood is generally of the greatest commercial importance. It is through sale of wood that private landowners obtain the revenue to protect the forest, pay their taxes and interest, and build their roads and other improvements.

Wood serves mankind for a variety of purposes, but chiefly as timber

FIG. 1 Virgin Douglas-fir, Rogue River National Forest, Oregon. (*U.S. Forest Service photo.*)

for general construction, as fuel, and as fiber for pulp and paper manufacture. The total use of wood is increasing in the United States and the
world as a whole. This is particularly true of wood used for paper products, veneer, plywood, and special industrial uses. Wood is, in fact, such
a highly versatile and usable product that substantial quantities must
be used if man is to enjoy a high standard of living and a high level of
industrial production.

Wood is also a raw material for chemical processing. The leaves of
the tree manufacture foodstuffs from carbon dioxide and water by using
the energy of the sun for power. This food in the beginning is in the form
of simple sugars which the tree synthesizes further into cellulose and
lignin. Cellulose is a large complex chemical closely related to starch.
In the form in which it is found in the woody stem it is chemically rather
inert. Through treatment with various chemicals or enzymes, however,
cellulose can be broken down ultimately into its individual glucose units
and, as such, serve as food for cattle, fungi, bacteria, and other organisms.
In fact, man can make from wood a sugar suitable for human consumption. This, in turn, can be converted into alcohol, and from alcohol a
variety of industrial products can be manufactured. The other major
component, lignin, is likewise subject to chemical transformation. It
can be broken down into substances suitable for chemical use or actually
converted into a base for plastics and other chemical products.

The harvesting and processing of wood for structural and chemical
use is a huge industry in the United States and furnishes employment for
over 1,375,000 workers. The lumber, pulp and paper, plywood, cellulose-
plastics, and wood-processing industries together employ also about half
the professional men educated in forestry colleges. They perform such
tasks as technical supervision and control, planning, research, and sales.

Water. Second only to wood as a forest product is water. Forests clothe
the mountain slopes where rainfall intensities are high. They protect the
soil from erosion and streams from silting. Forested watersheds, therefore, are sought after for irrigation and municipal and industrial water
supplies.

Use of water, even more than use of wood, tends to increase greatly
with increase in urbanization, industrialization, and living standards.
Direct human use has increased sharply in recent years for sanitary
disposal, for laundry, for automatic dishwashers, and for air conditioning.
Industrial use is astounding. To manufacture 1 ton of rolled steel requires
32,000 gallons of water; 1 ton of sulfite paper, up to 90,000 gallons; and
1 barrel of aviation gasoline, 1,050,000 gallons of water.[2]

Expressed somewhat differently, the annual water consumption per
employee for certain industries in 1954 was as follows: [3]

Industry	Water consumption, gallons
Steel....................	6,765,000
Pulp and paper...........	6,700,000
Copper..................	3,300,000
Food and beverage........	900,000
Chemical................	505,000

Man will, therefore, be obliged to give increasing attention to water supplies if he is to maintain his industrial civilization.

Wildlife. A forest product of special concern to sportsmen is fish and game. Except on public and private shooting preserves, wildlife seldom takes precedence over wood or water in determining the major land use. Fish and game and furbearing animals are, however, as much a constituent of the forest as timber and can yield yearly crops of value to man. The forester, in fact, is concerned with having a proper balance of animal life in the forest both for the enjoyment of sportsmen and for the services the animals themselves perform. The forest, for healthy growth, is just as dependent upon a porous, well-aerated soil as is a farm crop. The farmer tills his field with plows, harrows, and cultivators. The forester must rely almost entirely on the work of earthworms, mites, insects, centipedes, and other soil-inhabiting life forms to break down the leaf and twig litter and incorporate it into the mineral soil, thereby opening channels for penetration of water and roots. Mice, shrews, and other small mammals play a part in maintaining a proper balance among soil-dwelling organisms. These, in turn, are food for foxes, mink, weasels, and other furbearers. Rabbits and deer tend to keep down the weed crop of the forest that might crowd out new tree seedlings. They may also, if overabundant, consume the seedlings themselves; hence, the checks provided by hawks, owls, foxes, and hunters are important.

The forester, therefore, whether he wills it or not, must be a wildlife manager as well as a timber manager. Wildlife can be encouraged chiefly by those measures that make the forest a good home for wildlife. Food, water, and cover for resting and raising young are the prime requisites of wild creatures. To the extent that man can provide these in abundance by manipulating the forest vegetation and the construction of water holes, he can increase the carrying capacity of his forest for wildlife. Wildlife management consists mainly in such manipulation (Fig. 2).

Forage. Forest lands of the South and West and some of those in other regions afford forage for domestic livestock—cattle, sheep, and to a limited extent swine and goats. This use of the forest, even more so than wildlife, requires proper supervision if it is not to lead to soil compaction, overbrowsing of tree seedlings, erosion along animal paths, and interference with production of wood, water, and wildlife and with recreational use.

All the more credit is, therefore, due to the western stockmen and foresters who have successfully combined stock grazing with other uses of the forest.

Recreation. Man, as his daily activities become more and more constricted to office and factory work in urban areas, needs the out-of-doors for relaxation and play. His physical and mental health are dependent upon it. Forested areas are particularly attractive because they provide seclusion, an opportunity to observe shy creatures in their natural habitat, and a sense of serenity and tranquillity that tends to calm jaded nerves. Special provisions must be made for concentrated human use—motor parking areas, picnic grounds, play fields, and bathing beaches with essential sanitary facilities are needed.

Public recreational use of forests is increasing rapidly and so is the need for facilities. When properly planned and supervised, public use need conflict but little with other forest uses.

In an extensive study of the changes in use of land in the United States, Clawson, Held, and Stoddard came to the conclusion that large shifts in land use from one major use to another are unlikely to occur up to

FIG. 2 The forest is a community of trees, shrubs, and herbs, and the animal life these support. A large beaver house on Deer Pond, Huntington Forest, New York.

the year 2000. There will be local changes as cities, highways, and airports grow and take land from farms and forests. They do expect that substantial changes will occur within each land use. For example, recreational use will make increasing demands upon forest lands. Also, they expect that there will be a growing demand for the products from forest land but that the potential productivity of the forests is such that this demand can be met provided intensive forest land management is practiced.[1]

The 1963 study by Resources for the Future * reflects less optimism about meeting our nation's timber requirements for the year 2000. The authors project an increase in potential timber use from 11 billion cubic feet in 1960 to 31 billion cubic feet in the year 2000. The authors express doubt that this potential will be reached from domestic supplies and imports combined. Attainment might be possible if the highest standards of forest management and forest-products use now known were extensively adopted.

Multiple Use. Wood, water, and wildlife are products of all forest land whether the timber is cut, the water used, or the wildlife harvested. All are likewise subject, within a degree, to manipulation by man. Highest human values are generally realized when the same forest area provides all these products and recreation in addition. Just as a farmer must manage the total resources of the farm—crops, pasture, livestock, barns, and farm machinery—so must the forest land supervisor manage the total resources of the forest—timber, water, wildlife, forage, and recreation. The forester is a multiple-resource manager rather than a single-resource manager. It is because the forestry profession, especially in America, was receptive to this overall responsibility that foresters are in demand by the National Park Service, Fish and Wildlife Service, and, to a lesser extent, by the Soil Conservation Service. It is for this reason also that they have been successful as managers of rubber plantations and other properties involving integrated use of multiple land resources.

The forester, therefore, bears a multiple responsibility and is to some extent answerable to several diverse interests in his management of forest land. He must give heed to the needs of local industries for timber to support the economy, to the needs of nearby and distant water users, to forage users, and to the wishes of hunters, fishermen, and recreationists.

Above all, he must so conduct his management task that the capacity of the forest to provide continuously all these products and services is not impaired. Broad training, deep understanding, and considerable wisdom are required to achieve harmonious results.

* H. H. Landsberg, L. L. Fischman, and J. L. Fisher. 1963. "Resources in America's Future," Resources for the Future, Inc., The Johns Hopkins Press, Baltimore. 987 pp.

LITERATURE CITED

1. Clawson, Marion, R. Bernell Held, and Charles H. Stoddard, 1960. "Land for the Future," The Johns Hopkins Press, Baltimore. 570 pp.
2. Select Committee on National Water Resources. United States Senate, 1960. "Future Water Requirements of Principal Water-using Industries," Committee print no. 8, 86th Cong., 2d Sess.
3. Water Resources Activities in the United States. "Future Water Requirements of Principal Water-using Industries," 86th Cong., S. Res. 48, April, 1960, 101 pp.

CHAPTER 2. *Forestry throughout the Ages*

THE ATTITUDES of man toward the forest and the laws he has established to govern its use have their roots deep in his biologic needs and social makeup. Rights of use and land-ownership patterns are conditioned by practices dating back beyond the dawn of recorded history.

Primitive Man and the Forest

Prehistoric man's relation to the forest can only be surmised from the relics he has left and from the use primitive tribes today make of forests. The following is an attempt to weave certain known facts into a plausible account of this relationship.

The earliest known men were ground dwellers rather than tree dwellers. But they did use wood. Both the Peking man and Java man used wood for fire 750,000 or more years ago.

In the forest primitive man found shade from the heat of the midday sun. He found it warmer to sleep in the forest at night than under the open sky. Beneath leafy crowns, under leaning trunks, and in hollow trees, he found shelter against rain. Fallen trunks provided a reflector for his fire and a shelter against wind. He learned to use the berries, nuts, roots, the fruits of the forest, and the forest-dwelling animals as food to sustain his life and as medicines to soothe him when ill. He learned to use wood directly for his tools, weapons, and traps. Trees also provided means of escape from aroused animals for which man with his rude weapons was no match.

The earliest known organized communities were found along watercourses that flowed through arid lands in Egypt, Mesopotamia, and India. Here sod huts were erected and cultivation of heavy-seeded grasses, the cereals, began. Scattered trees and shrubs probably occurred along the river banks and furnished fuel, handles for tools, and timber for construction. As these were used up, man probably sent expeditions farther and farther upstream to obtain wood, which could be floated down to his villages.

Cereals were the basic element which permitted organized society to

10

develop. They provided a concentrated food, easily cultivated and capable of storage. The river borders that supported grasses attracted birds and animals useful for food, and man later learned to domesticate animals as well as plants. Thus a civilization arose.

Early separation of the forest dweller and plains dweller occurred. The former lived a more primitive life but developed considerable skill in use of his forest environment. He, too, frequented the stream borders. It was only natural that watercourses became man's arteries of travel. At first he kept to the banks, but as he learned to use logs, then rafts, and finally dugout canoes, he used the stream to float himself and his belongings from one place to another. As his skills developed in hunting, in use of tools, and particularly in use of fire, he dared to penetrate into the forest areas, where he made crude openings by girdling and burning trees. He also took advantage of natural openings caused by windthrow, insect attack, or other destructive agents. Here he planted small fields and so extended his dominion over forest as well as plains.

Various types of litters were made on which man could carry food, animals he had killed, clothing, and other human beings who were unable to walk or who had risen to positions of authority and could command others to provide their transportation. When animals had been domesticated, litters were devised that could be drawn by ox or donkey. Short logs were used as rollers under heavy objects man wished to transport. Some brilliant inventor of prehistoric times conceived of combining the log and litter to form a type of cart. By chipping away wood in the center of the log, he made his cart roller into two wheels and an axle. The true wheel, consisting of hub, spokes, fellies, and rim, was developed in India.

As the river villages prospered through use of grain and domestic animals, their need for wood increased. They desired, in addition to fuel, wood for workshops, trading centers, temples of worship, and council chambers. Woodcutters were sent into the hills to procure timbers needed by ancient civilizations. We find this well described in the biblical account of Solomon's temple. Organized societies found ever-increasing uses for timber. Larger buildings were erected; more homes constructed. Boats became numerous and larger in size. Eventually they were made large enough to cross the oceans.

Man came to see in the forest a source of material for his welfare and livelihood. As timber became scarce, efforts were finally made to restrict use of forests.

Stages in Use of Forests

Primitive man was largely content to accept his food and shelter from the forest with little effort to modify his environment to suit his needs.

Fig. 3 Virgin old-growth timber with scattered openings being invaded by young growth. Primitive man made few inroads against such a forest. (*U.S. Forest Service photo.*)

The forest was, in fact, too strong for him to conquer (Fig. 3). Only by use of fire could he weaken the forest's hold on the land; and when fires burned vast areas, he was obliged to migrate.

With the beginning of agriculture man began a struggle against the forest to clear land for his crops and domestic animals. As one cleared area became infertile, he abandoned it for another. The abandoned fields soon were reclaimed by woody growth. The cycle was often repeated, giving rise to a system of shifting agriculture that may be found in certain tropical countries today. It was in common use by North American Indians and other primitive peoples. Some primitive people have, in fact, come to appreciate that their lands are too infertile for continuous cultivation and look to shifting agriculture as the only method of maintaining soil fertility.

As skill in husbandry increased, men sought to avoid the heavy labor involved in clearing new land. By application of natural or artificial fertilizers and by various cropping techniques, they attempted to maintain the land in continuous cultivation. Surplus products were exchanged in villages for other products.

Permanent occupancy and cultivation of the land often led to development of property rights both in the villages and on the land. Forest land was at first held as communal property where any man might harvest such timber products as he required. Villages provided a permanent market for fuel wood. When fuel wood became scarce, property rights were extended to the forest. These took two forms: small individual holdings and community forests in which the village authorities or ruler exercised control over the use of the land.

The growth of communities into cities and the development of agriculture increased the use of forest products for construction so that even higher values were assigned to the forest. Lumber and other timber operations solidified the rights of ownership, and exploitation of the forest was carried out with no regard for future productivity. Unrestricted cutting led to local wood shortages. Gradually such shortages spread. Timber shortages in China probably occurred as early as 5,000 years ago; in Egypt, 4,000 years ago. The Greeks and Romans felt timber shortages more than 2,000 years ago, and the central Europeans 1,000 years ago.[2]

Timber shortages caused farsighted rulers and landowners to regulate cutting in efforts to perpetuate the timber supply. Such regulations were made by the Chinese priests, by the Roman emperors, and by the Egyptians before the time of Christ. They were carried out in France, Germany, and Great Britain before the time of the Crusades. The Chinese philosopher Mencius, who lived from 372 to 289 B.C., stated the case for conservation eloquently in his advice to King Hwuy of Leang.[1] *

If the seasons of husbandry be not interfered with, the grain will be more than can be eaten. If close nets are not allowed to enter the pools and ponds, the fishes and turtles will be more than can be consumed. If the axes and bills enter the hills and forests only at the proper time, the wood will be more than can be used. When the grain and fish and turtles are more than can be eaten, and there is more wood than can be used, this enables the people to nourish their living and bury their dead, without any feeling against any. This condition, in which the people nourish their living and bury their dead without any feeling against any, is the first step of royal government.

The stages mentioned above have not always occurred in sequence; nor have all stages appeared in every forested area. They are well exemplified in the history of the Cedars of Lebanon as it is reconstructed by Lowdermilk.[4-6] †

King Solomon is recorded to have made a bargain with Hiram, King of Tyre, to exchange wheat and olive oil out of his Kingdom, including Palestine, for

* Quoted from Robert O. Ballou, ed., "The Bible of the World," The Viking Press, Inc.

† Quotation courtesy of *American Forests*.

timber of fir and aromatic Cedars of Lebanon for the construction of the Temple at Jerusalem. According to the record Solomon furnished 80,000 lumberjacks as hewers of wood for the wood operation in the forested mountains and 70,000 burden bearers to skid out the timbers. The forests that covered the lofty shoulders of the Lebanon Mountains must have been extensive to keep such a force of 150,000 workers busy.

The forests of Lebanon were incorporated into a state forest under the reign of Emperor Hadrian, and efforts were apparently made to stop indiscriminate cutting. Throughout Roman times the forests were used to build great temples and ships that sailed in the Mediterranean. After the Roman Empire fell, the lands were invaded by Arabs, who neglected the conservation works of the Romans and let them fall into disrepair. The forests dwindled and were further exploited during the Turkish period that followed. Today the forests are all but extinct. Only four groves remain. Grazing by goats and sheep has completed the destruction. "Since the Arab invasion, thirteen centuries ago, the forests of Lebanon have been exploited and neglected until the slopes have been rendered barren, gray, and rocky, making impossible the restoration of forests equal to the original stands." [6] Lowdermilk concluded from his extensive travels in the Mediterranean area, Far East, and the Caribbean: "I find that where man has lived the longest in organized societies, there the land is in worst condition." [5] Forests are destroyed, and peoples are reduced to the lowest states of general well-being. The destruction of the Cedars of Lebanon that took place over a period of some 2,000 years has been duplicated in forests of the Andes in a period of less than two generations. Here the Indians had developed terracing to a high degree. But the Spaniards found such agriculture unprofitable. Gradually one piece of land after another was abandoned and more and more virgin forests cleared for cultivation. Here the steep soils unprotected by terraces eroded rapidly under the heavy tropical rainfall so that serious gullying and complete soil exhaustion have been brought about at a rapid rate. [7]

Early Forestry Measures in Asia, Europe, and the Americas

The wholesale destruction of forests in China has probably been due primarily to two influences: first, the dividing of the land into small-sized parcels owned by individuals, and second, the general press of the population on the land. Freehold units in China reached about 2½ to 3 acres in size. These had to be intensively cultivated and irrigated to support the Chinese families. Whole mountainsides, particularly in the Yunnan Province, were cleared for many thousand feet above the valley floor and terraced for agriculture. Eventually drought caused widespread starvation of the inhabitants. As the terraces were neglected, the hillsides became badly eroded and stunted pines occupied the depleted, uncultivated soil.[2]

The Chinese Communist government reports that it is increasing tree planting to stabilize mountain soils. It has also sought through nationalization of cropland and through communal farms to increase the efficiency of food production and release labor for industry.

Forests fared somewhat better in India than in China. The Buddhist religion, as well as the activities of Indian monarchs and Hindu priests, encouraged tree-planting programs.[2] The unappropriated forests were held by the Indian princes, who harvested such rare woods as rosewood, ebony, teak, and sandalwood for export to other countries.

Forestry entered the Mediterranean region before the time of Christ. The Egyptians imported a number of trees for forest planting and had a chief forester as early as 3500 B.C. Reference is made to keepers of the king's forest and to actual foresters in Assyria, Palestine, and Asia Minor. A number of sacred groves were maintained in Lebanon and elsewhere. The Romans took a lively interest in trees, importing tree seedlings from the Indias, Africa, Spain, and Germany.[3] Greeks and Romans alike maintained sacred groves of trees comparable to those in Carthage, Lebanon, and elsewhere.

The Aztec king Nezahualcoyotl, who reigned in the fifteenth century,[2] mitigated the severe penalties imposed on citizens who trespassed on the chieftain's forest. He allowed the tribes to gather wood from the ground, but harvesting of standing timber was punished with death.

By the eighth century kings of England forbade trespass on royal property under fine of 60 shillings and thereby established the banned forests. By the tenth century English kings extended the royal right to chase over fields, pastures, waters, villages, and woods. Ordinances were passed by the princes and barons governing the amount of wood that might be cut for family use and the uses to which such wood might be put, including charcoal making and burning for potash. Reforestation was practiced by Henry VII of England and by the medieval city of Nuremberg in Germany.

During the Middle Ages clearing of land for agriculture had gone so far that decrees in both Austria and Germany forbade further land clearing. The purpose, in part, was to protect hunting privileges of the nobility, but it was also to ensure a fuel-wood supply for local industries and home use.

The first laws to prohibit the clearing of forests appeared in 1165. These were followed by ordinances in 1177, 1226, 1237, and 1291. A great number of laws were passed thereafter. The early regulation laws were simple and designed primarily to prohibit clearing of forests. Later regulations forbade pasturing newly cut areas. Some regulations even went so far as to direct that buildings be erected of stone to conserve wood.

Early community forests in France go back to the time of the Gauls in A.D. 500 to 510. Clovis in the sixth century took over royal and state forests. Eventually church property became royal property. After 1791 royal property was declared national land, which, with the addition of church property, brought the total up to 4.3 million acres. Forest officers were appointed as early as 1291, and by 1669 the first regulations governing timber cutting on public and private lands were established.[3]

In Switzerland, community forest ownership has dominated forest property throughout its history. The first forest ordinance regulating use dates around 1304, and the first working plan—made for the Sihlwald near Zurich—has, with revisions, remained in effect for more than 600 years. Special regulations governing cutting of the steep Alpine region were introduced early and were rigidly enforced.

In Austria the city forests were placed under a form of management as early as A.D. 1100. Various regulations governing the felling of timber were adopted from time to time. A comprehensive forest ordinance adopted in the reign of Empress Maria Theresa in 1754 revised many of the restrictions on private landowners and on the management of communal forests.

Regulations of timber-cutting operations in Scandinavia date back to 1638. A forest-planting law was established in 1647. In Norway, attempts were made to stop forest devastation in 1500, and a forest survey was authorized in 1600 by Christian IV. By 1725 a forest and sawmill commission was established, and export restrictions were imposed in 1795. Danish forest laws date back to 1557, and the state forests were placed under organized forest management as early as 1781.

European Forestry up to 1900

The rise of revolutionary movements and the downfall of feudalism in Europe caused a pronounced change in the attitude toward forest properties. Feudal holdings were seized in many countries and made a part of the public domain. Church property was confiscated. At first, some states sought to liquidate these lands by sale to increase state revenue. Germany adopted such a course but early in the nineteenth century appointed Hartig as chief of the forest administrative branch of the treasury department. Hartig curtailed further dismemberment of state land and instituted forest management. Since the Swiss had most of their lands in communal ownership from the beginning, little change occurred there. France had a difficult time in stopping the overcutting and abuse that followed the French Revolution. However, early in the nineteenth century regulations were established governing forest use.

Concepts of forest management developed rapidly in Germany, France, and Scandinavia during the nineteenth century. Forest properties were subdivided into compartments, and working plans established governing cutting rates and cutting areas in efforts to obtain the highest return from the soil. In France, special attention was paid to protecting watersheds against landslides and erosion, and to stabilizing sand dunes.

Regulation of cutting on both public and private land was introduced by most European states during the late nineteenth century, if not before. State forests were placed under intensive management, and efforts made to extinguish long-established rights of users, such as collecting litter and grazing livestock that reduced the yield of the forest. Important strides were made in private forestry during this period, in part because of state regulation and in part because forest properties became sound investments for their owners. Forests constituted the base of family wealth for a number of aristocratic owners. Entailed estate was established whereby the owner contracted to operate on a sustained-yield basis and to bind his heirs to do likewise in return for certain technical aid and tax inducements offered by the state.

Formal education in forestry began about 1825 when private forestry schools were established. These were an outgrowth of the old master schools that had existed before that time. In 1816 the Cotta Master School grew into the forestry college at Tharandt, which became one of the leading forestry schools in Germany. The French school of forestry was established at Nancy in 1825. It has been in continuous existence since that time. Other colleges of forestry were established during succeeding years of the nineteenth century.

Forest research began almost as early as forestry education and has been carried forward since that time.

Europe maintained its leadership in forestry until the outbreak of the Second World War. By this time the United States had developed forest technology on a high level. The war caused a temporary setback to forestry in Europe. Wartime cutting was under less strict silvicultural control than normal. Immediately following the war, local people cut fuel wood with little restriction. Occupation forces tended to impose practices aimed at supplying immediate rather than long-term needs. The national forestry authorities were, however, soon restored and the war damage was rapidly repaired.

Forest Practice in New Countries

Wasteful use of forest resources is still widespread in the world today. It is especially prevalent among nations formerly under colonial administration and among those having rich forest resources that have heretofore been only lightly used. A rich timber stand represents readily harvestable and exportable wealth that can supply foreign exchange for needed industrial development. Moreover, timber cutting clears land for agricultural use. New governments are quick to realize this. An example is the Philippine nation. This country was under Spanish domination for almost three centuries, under the United States for half a century, and under Japan during the Second World War; since 1946, it has been independent. Under Spanish rule, much of the fertile, level lands along the seacoast became incorporated in large haciendas operated for sugarcane, rice, and other high-yield agricultural crops. This ownership pattern was continued under United States rule and was accepted by the new Philippine government. When independence came, strong pressure was exerted by the Huks and other dissident elements to launch a land reform program that would enable the great mass of agricultural workers to acquire ownership of land. President Magsaysay resisted the pressure to break up the existing large land holdings but did adopt a policy, under the slogan "Land for the Landless," of opening publicly owned land to settlers. Homesteads up to 50 acres in size could be acquired by landless people on tracts declared open for settlement. Most of the publicly owned land was virgin forest. As it was cut over, certain tracts were designated for entry.

Landless people from crowded islands were soon swarming over Mindanao, Basilan, and other islands where good soils existed. They soon took up all lands opened for entry. They then began to move in behind the loggers as the superb virgin dipterocarp forests were cut, not awaiting permission from the understaffed Bureau of Forestry. Local political powers, favoring land development, encouraged the settlers by defending them against ejection by forest officers.

Soon the situation was completely out of hand. Squatters and kaingineros move in following partial cutting of virgin timber. They girdle and burn the trees left for a second cutting to plant corn, sweet potatoes, and other crops on the steep mountain slopes (Fig. 4). Within two years' time the fertility of the soil is exhausted through cropping, erosion, and exposure to sun. A coarse native grass, cogongrass, invades the land and holds it against both agricultural crops and reinvasion of forest. The kainginero then deserts the land and moves again behind the loggers to repeat his act of forest destruction.

Thus, by an uncontrolled land program, political forces have been unleashed that are leading to destruction of forests, soils, and social fiber. These superb forests are capable of yielding annually upward of 1,500 board feet per acre of the finest hardwood timber to be found in the world. These virgin mountain lands could support at a high level of prosperity a permanent population of at least one-third as many people as the equivalent area of the best agricultural land of the nation. Instead,

Fig. 4 A kainginero with his wife and daughter putting in his first sowing of upland rice. (*Photo by Martin Hurwitz, Peace Corps volunteer.*)

they are being rendered virtually useless for decades, if not for centuries, to come.

LITERATURE CITED

1. Ballou, Robert O., ed. 1939. "The Bible of the World," pp. 429–430, The Viking Press, Inc., New York.
2. Caldwell, David H. 1949. Unpublished manuscript, New York State College of Forestry, Syracuse, N.Y.
3. Fernow, Bernhard E. 1911. "A Brief History of Forestry in Europe, the United States and Other Countries," rev. ed., University of Toronto Press, Toronto, Canada, and *Forestry Quarterly*, Cambridge, Mass. 506 pp.
4. Lowdermilk, Walter C. 1941. "Conquest of the Land," U.S. Department of Agriculture, Soil Conservation Service, Washington. 34 pp. mim.
5. Lowdermilk, Walter C. 1946. "Soil Science in Wildland Management," *Journal of Forestry*, 44:788–798.
6. Lowdermilk, Walter C. 1941. "The Cedars of Lebanon—Then and Now," *American Forests*, 47(1):16–20, 34.
7. Meyer, H. Arthur. 1945. "Conuqueros—Forest Destroyers of the Andes," *American Forests*, 51(4):178–179, 200.

CHAPTER 3. *The Development of Forestry in the United States*

THE STORY of forestry in America is inseparable from the story of the early pioneers and their indomitable struggle to make a home in the wilderness they found in the new world. It is also a part of the story of those great spirits that rose up among the pioneers to create a new nation on American soil. On the one hand, it reflects the actions of a vigorous people surging eagerly forward to exploit for personal profit the rich resources of the new land. On the other, it deals with cooperative action to build churches, schools, villages, and states, and with community-imposed restraints to equalize opportunity for achievement.

Two great struggles characterize America: the struggle to occupy the land and use its resources and the struggle in the hearts of men to free the creative spirit of individualism while guiding it in the common interest. The first struggle was won with the passing of the frontier; the second will continue as long as we remain a free people.

Forestry in Colonial Times

The early American colonist found on the eastern coast of our country an almost unbroken forest that stretched west to the prairie region. Extensive forests also existed in the Rocky Mountains and in the West Coast region. Hardwood forests occupied some 403 million acres; coniferous forests, 419 million acres. Woodland in the prairie region and semidesert regions of the West occupied 93 million acres, making a grand total of 915 million acres of forest and woodland. This was 48 per cent of the total land area of the United States.

It is small wonder that the early colonist considered the forest his enemy. The forests were dense, the trees large in size, and many of them of hard and durable wood that he could dispose of only by burning. The virgin forests contained windfalls and tops of trees broken by storm. They occupied the land so completely that only by heroic effort could the pioneer wrest from the forest wilderness a few acres of land that he might cultivate. Fire was his natural ally in the land-clearing process.

20

Fig. 5   Replica of old French fort erected in colonial days near present site of Syracuse, New York.

The forest, to be sure, provided the settler with fuel, game, nuts, useful bark, and poles for erecting cabins and forts (Fig. 5). But timber to the early American colonist had largely a negative value. It was something to be rid of so that he could free the land to grow crops and to pasture his livestock.

Yet even in colonial days farseeing citizens advocated forest conservation measures. Iron foundries and glass factories of colonial days depended upon wood for fuel to smelt the ore and melt the glass. Frequently they ran short of the local supplies. Cities such as Philadelphia and Providence were short of fuel even before the Revolution. Benjamin Franklin in his article describing the Franklin stove stated in 1774: [4] * "Wood, our common fuel, which within these hundred years might be had at any man's door, must now be fetched near one hundred miles to some towns, and makes a very considerable article in the expense of families."

Perhaps the first attempt at forest conservation was a provision written into land-purchase contracts by William Penn in 1681: ". . . that in clearing the ground care be taken to leave one acre of trees for each five acres cleared, and especially to preserve oak and mulberry for silk and shipping." The charter creating the province of Massachusetts Bay in

* Quoted by permission of Gilbert Chinard.

1691 reserved the best trees, particularly white pine for shipmasts, for the Royal Navy. Such trees were to be marked with a broad arrow. This restriction was extended to New York and New Jersey later on. Because the officers of the crown were slow to mark the trees that might not be cut, and because the colonists had left Europe to escape from numerous regulations, the broad-arrow policy was difficult to enforce. Trespass was common even though severely punished when apprehended. These punishments only encouraged the colonists to go even further in defying the King's authority.[10] During the Revolution patriots in Maine, Massachusetts, and New Hampshire did their utmost to prevent the British Navy from getting control over mast and spar timbers from American forests. Their efforts in the end had a considerable effect in crippling that navy.

During the colonial period no foundation was laid for good forest practice in America. Independence removed the restrictions of the mother country and led to more reckless use and abuse of the forest. By this time sawmills had been established and the forest was being exploited for its own worth. The forest was no longer merely an encumbrance of the soil but a source of vitally needed raw material for the rapidly growing cities and villages in the new country.

Commenting on his observations in the Confederation between 1783 and 1784, Johann David Schoepf observed: [13]

> In America there is no sovereign right over forests and game, no forest service. Whoever holds new land, in whatever way, controls it as his exclusive possession, with everything on it, above it, and under it. It will not easily come about therefore that, as a strict statutory matter, farmers and landowners will be taught how to manage their forests so as to leave for their grandchildren a bit of wood over which to hang the tea-kettle.

His words were singularly prophetic.

Timbers from the forests of North America played a very important role in the rapid development of the country. Much timber was cut by ax and fashioned with whipsaws, broad axes, adzes, and froes to supply squared logs, beams, framing members, and shakes for construction. With the coming of sawmills, lumber became available. Almost 90 per cent of the one-family dwellings in the United States are of wood-frame construction. Heavy construction was also of wood in the earlier days. Masonry was used for exterior walls and general supports, wood for partitions. Railways used enormous amounts of wood for crossties, bridge timbers, stations, fuel, and other purposes. Formerly, large amounts were used for car construction. Mines have always been important users of wood in the form of timbers to support the roof, lagging for sidewalls, mine ties, and other products that are essential for safe mining operation and efficient handling of coal and ores. Farmers use wood in farm buildings and for fuel, fence posts, and corrals.

Federal Forestry Measures

The Public Domain and Its Disposal. An important source of conflict among the colonies even before they had won their independence was the ownership of the lands. Virginia's original charter embraced "Land, throughout from Sea to Sea, West and Northwest." Massachusetts claimed land beyond the Delaware.[11] Connecticut and Pennsylvania disputed control over the rich farming land in Wyoming Valley, Pennsylvania, where Wilkes-Barre now is situated. Actual armed conflict broke out. To remove this cause of disunity, the Continental Congress in 1780 passed a resolution urging the states to cede their western lands to the Union. From 1781 to 1802 the state lands ceded to the federal government totaled some 260 million acres.[8]

Through the various land-purchase acts, including the Louisiana Purchase, the Florida Purchase, the various purchases and cessions of land from Mexico, and the Alaska Purchase, the federal government acquired a vast public domain. It included three-fourths of continental United States and all of Alaska, a total of 1,800 million acres.[19] The public domain became both a source of wealth and a source of embarrassment to the federal government. It was sold for public revenue, granted to soldiers in lieu of cash payments, granted to companies to promote the building of railways, and granted to states to further education. It became a source of embarrassment, because our young nation had no trained land administrators nor any police force to prevent trespass. Squatting on the public lands was forbidden by an act of 1807. The early policy for this vast estate was to preserve it for public revenue and national development.

This attitude on the part of the Congress and federal officers in Washington was in striking conflict with the desires and actions of the frontiersmen. They occupied land wherever it was not occupied by another and used it for their own purposes. A strong demand arose to open the public lands for private settlement. The Preemption Act, passed in 1841, gave homesteaders the right to squat on land and later to purchase it. During the administration of Abraham Lincoln, the Homestead Act was passed. This opened the public domain for entry by homesteaders who desired to settle upon it and authorized the granting of 160 acres free to settlers who lived upon the land and developed it. The law was later liberalized by a series of additional laws. The Timber Culture Act permitted the government to grant 160 acres of land to anyone who would plant trees on 40 acres and keep them in healthy condition over a period of 10 years. The Timber and Stone Act, the Desert Land Act, and the Carey Act all liberalized the conditions under which settlers were able to acquire title to public land through homesteading.[19]

The Swampland Grant Act permitted the federal government to grant lands chiefly covered by swamp to the states in which they were located to be used for state purposes.

Railway land grants in alternate sections on either side of the railway resulted in a checkerboard pattern of ownership embarrassing to forest land management from that day to this. The Forest Lieu Act of 1897 [10] permitted railway companies and other land grantees to select lands outside their original grants in lieu of lands within that had already been appropriated. Some of our nation's best timberlands passed from public ownership under this act. Administration of all these acts was weak; hence fraud was widespread. Little attempt was made to determine whether homesteaders lived up to the regulations.

STEMMING THE LAND BOOM. The disposal of the public domain created the greatest land boom in history. Its momentum was tremendous. Early attempts toward restrained use received scarcely passing attention. Still, these are worthy of recall because they encouraged those who did successfully stem the tide.

François-André Michaux, who in 1819 published in English "The Sylva of North America," wrote in his introduction: [4]

I have also endeavoured to impress on the American farmers the importance and pecuniary advantages which would result to them and to their families from the preservation of different species of timber of which they ought to ensure the growth, and on the contrary I have noted those which ought to be destroyed; for I am of opinion that a bad tree ought not to be suffered to exist where a better could grow.

Private societies in Philadelphia and Massachusetts offered premiums for tree growing. As early as 1795 a New York agricultural society recommended that inferior agricultural land be devoted to trees, a recommendation that was not carried out on a large scale until 1929.

A definite federal effort was made to acquire land supporting live oak for ship timbers. At first $200,000 was set aside to purchase such land.[15] This was followed by granting the President authority to reserve public lands bearing live oak and cedar in Florida, Alabama, and Louisiana, and to conduct experiments in planting and cultivating live oak. In 1831, Congress passed a law prohibiting the cutting of live oak from naval reservations or any other lands belonging to the United States. The law was never enforced.

Carl Schurz, Secretary of the Interior, 1877 to 1881, strongly advocated proper care of the public domain and attempted to enforce the law of 1831 preventing trespass on public land. This he was stopped from doing by Congress in 1880. The Reverend Frederick Starr in 1865 predicted a timber famine within 30 years and advocated immediate research to determine how to manage forests and how to establish plantations. Secretary of Navy Woodberry during Andrew Jackson's administration tried to determine the amount of oak ship timbers that would be needed by the Navy and estimated the amount of land that would be needed to provide such timbers on a sustained-yield basis.[1] New York in 1872 set up a special commission to study the preservation of Adirondack forest for its influence on the Hudson River and the Erie Canal. In 1872, Jay Sterling Morton, Governor of Nebraska, inaugurated the first Arbor Day; and in 1873 the Timber Culture Act, which provided land grants to settlers for planting trees in the prairie states, was passed. This law had considerable influence on the planting of groves and shelterbelts in the prairie regions during the early days. It was the forerunner of the vast shelterbelt program of the 1930s.

By the late 1890s the end of free land was definitely in sight. What remained was, for the most part, poorly suited for agricultural use. Loose administration aroused the nation to the need for saving at least some land for permanent public use. Of even more concern was the rapid inroad being made on the timber resources.

Cutting of timber for lumber proceeded at a moderate pace during the colonial period and the early life of the republic. Sawmills were primitive in design and could be operated successfully only where water power was available. By 1811 the first steam sawmill was introduced, and by 1840 lumbering got under way at a very rapid rate. Maine led all other states in lumber production up to 1850, but in that year New York State took the lead; in 1860, Pennsylvania; and by 1870, peak production had shifted to the Lake States. The Northeast, which produced 55 per cent of all lumber in 1850, produced only 20 per cent in 1890. Local manufacturers in the East complained about the difficulties of getting good supplies of ash, hickory, white oak, walnut, and high-grade white pine.[16] The timber famine of which the Reverend Starr had so dramatically warned the country in 1865 seemed rapidly approaching (Fig. 6).

Beginnings of Federal Forestry. The real spark that started the federal government upon a permanent program of forestry grew out of a memorial by the American Association for the Advancement of Science addressed to the Congress in 1874. This memorial was prepared as a result of a talk by Franklin B. Hough of Lowville, New York. He stated:

> The preservation and growth of timber is a subject of great practical importance to the people of the United States, and is becoming every year of more and more consequence, from the increasing demand for its use; and while this rapid exhaustion is taking place, there is no effectual provision against waste

Fɪɢ. 6   Even the modern concrete, steel, and brick structure requires large amounts of lumber for scaffolding, forms, staging, fencing, and other temporary use.

or for the renewal of supply. . . . Besides the economical value of timber for construction, fuel, and the arts . . . questions of climate . . . the drying up of rivulets . . . and the growing tendency to floods and drought . . . since the cutting off of our forests are subjects of common observation. . . .[15]

Congress, at the Association's urging, provided in 1876 for a survey of the existing forest resources and the demands that were being placed upon them by consuming industries. Inquiry also was to be made into the influence of forest on climate and the best methods of forest practice used in Europe. Dr. Hough was employed by the Department of Agriculture at the salary of $2,000 a year. He prepared three voluminous reports that contained the best information then available on America's forest resources and forest industries. Dr. Hough was succeeded by N. H. Egleston in 1883, who prepared a fourth report. By 1881 Congress had established a Division of Forestry under the Commissioner of Agriculture.

Two new organizations to promote forestry came to the front at this time: the American Forestry Association and the American Forestry Congress. They merged in 1882 to sponsor an American Forestry Congress. This gala affair [3] was held in Cincinnati. Hough, Egleston, and B. E. Fernow, a forester with technical training in Germany, took an active part. Governors of many states participated. The meeting was climaxed by a huge parade and tree-planting ceremony. In a later congress held in Denver in 1886, the new association urged that public lands necessary for the preservation of water supply be granted to the several states in which they lay and be kept by these states in perpetuity to protect the headwaters of all rivers. It also advocated national and state forest-fire control.

PUBLIC FOREST RESERVES. Carl Schurz during his term as Secretary of the Interior repeatedly urged reserving public-domain timberland for long-term management. Numerous bills were introduced from 1876 on but were defeated by special-interest groups. A rider was attached to the act of March 3, 1891, "for the repeal of the Timber and Stone Act and for other purposes," authorizing the President to set apart from time to time reserves of land bearing forests, whether commercial or not, from the public domain. Gifford Pinchot called this act the most important legislation in the history of American forestry.[12]

An active program of reservation was undertaken by Presidents Harrison and Cleveland. These forest reserves remained in the Department of the Interior, which had no trained personnel to administer them. Bernhard E. Fernow, who succeeded Egleston in 1886 as Chief of the Division of Forestry in the Department of Agriculture, was a vigorous man who worked hard to promote forestry in the United States. Repeatedly he advocated transfer of the forest reserves from the Department of the Interior to the Department of Agriculture and their administration under the Division of Forestry.

At the request of President Cleveland the National Academy of Sciences set up a special forestry commission to report on the forest reserves and to recommend measures for their proper use. Charles Sprague Sargent of Harvard University was chairman. The commission recommended increasing the reserve by 21 million acres but made no recommendations for managing them, an omission which Pinchot felt was a serious one on the commission's part. A storm of protest arose throughout western states over what the local people called locking up the public lands.[12]

This protest led Congress to suspend all but two of the reserves created by Cleveland. At the same time it provided for managing existing and future reserves and stated the conditions under which future forest reservations might be established. This act of June 4, 1897, stated: "No public forest reservation shall be established except to improve and protect the forest, secure favorable conditions of water flow," and "furnish a continuous supply of timber for the use and necessities of citizens of the United States." [15] This act received the support of the western people and laid the groundwork for a rational policy of managing and protecting the forest reserves.

The Secretary of the Interior, as directed in 1897, attempted to protect and to administer the forest reserves. A field force of superintendents, rangers, and others was established, and Filibert Roth was placed in charge. Roth stayed only one year, however, and the Interior Department's efforts to build up satisfactory administration languished.

THE ROOSEVELT-PINCHOT ERA. The attitude of the people toward forestry in the nineties was shaped by many outstanding personalities, among whom Fernow, Pinchot, Hough, Schurz, and Governor Morton were conspicuous. The country was ready for a huge conservation program and awaited only proper leadership in the White House.

This came with dramatic suddenness when McKinley was assassinated on September 14, 1901. Theodore Roosevelt, the new President, had become imbued with the principles of conservation through his interests in wildlife and through a friendship he had formed with Gifford Pinchot, who became Chief of the Division of Forestry in 1898. The Division of Forestry became the Bureau of Forestry in 1901. In his first message to Congress, President Roosevelt, at the urging of Pinchot, Buell, Maxwell, and McGee, asserted: *

The fundamental idea of forestry is the perpetuation of forests by use. Forest protection is not an end in itself. It is a means to increase and sustain the resources of our country and the industries which depend upon them. The preservation of our forest is an imperative business necessity. We have come to see clearly that whatever destroys the forest except to make way for agriculture threatens our well-being.

The practical usefulness of the National Forest Reserves to the mining, grazing, irrigation, and other interests of the regions in which the reserves lie has led to a widespread demand by the people of the West for their protection and extension.

The President went on to advocate that administration of the reserves be united in the Bureau of Forestry.

Final action to carry out the President's recommendations did not take place until four years later. Meanwhile, Gifford Pinchot was building up the Bureau of Forestry. By offering services to large private landowners and others interested in inaugurating forestry programs, the Bureau was acquainting influential men with the meaning of forestry. Pinchot's energy and influence caused many people, the President included, to become passionately interested in conservation of our nation's natural resources.

Year after year bills were introduced into Congress to transfer the reserves to the Department of Agriculture. Additional public sentiment

* Quoted from Gifford Pinchot, "Breaking New Ground," Harcourt, Brace and Company, Inc. 1947.

for such transfer was created through a special American Forestry Congress that met in Washington in 1905. The Department of Agriculture, the Geological Survey, the Reclamation Service, the General Land Office, the president of the National Lumbermen's Association, the president of the National Livestock and National Wool Growers Association, the Union Pacific and the Great Northern Railroads, and the Weyerhaeuser Lumber Companies all joined hands in recommending the transfer of the forest reserves to the Department of Agriculture. The Transfer Act was passed February 1, 1905, and signed by President Roosevelt on that day. A month later the Department of Agriculture was given full legal authority to regulate the forest reserves.

REGULATING THE USE OF NATIONAL FORESTS. The day after the forest reserves were transferred to the Bureau of Forestry, the name of which was at that time changed to the Forest Service, the Secretary of Agriculture, James Wilson, sent a letter to the Chief of the Forest Service outlining the administrative policies to guide the management and use of the forest reserves. This letter has become a classic in federal forest policy.*

In the administration of the forest reserves it must be clearly borne in mind that all land is to be devoted to its most productive use for the permanent good of the whole people, and not for the temporary benefit of individuals or companies. All the resources of forest reserves are for use, and this use must be brought about in a thoroughly prompt and businesslike manner, under such restrictions only as will insure the permanence of these resources. The vital importance of forest reserves to the great industries of the western states will be largely increased in the near future by the continued steady advance in settlement and development. The permanence of the resources of the reserves is therefore indispensable to continued prosperity, and the policy of this department for their protection and use will invariably be guided by this fact, always bearing in mind that the conservative use of these resources in no way conflicts with their permanent value.

You will see to it that the water, wood, and forage of the reserves are conserved and wisely used for the benefit of the home builder first of all, upon whom depends the best permanent use of lands and resources alike. The continued prosperity of the agricultural, lumbering, mining, and livestock interests is directly dependent upon a permanent and accessible supply of water, wood, and forage, as well as upon the present and future use of their resources under businesslike regulations, enforced with promptness, effectiveness, and common sense. In the management of each reserve local questions will be decided upon local grounds; the dominant industry will be considered first, but with as little restriction to minor industries as may be possible; sudden changes in industrial conditions will be avoided by gradual adjustment after due notice; and where

* Quoted from Gifford Pinchot, "Breaking New Ground," Harcourt, Brace and Company, Inc. 1947.

conflicting interests must be reconciled, the question will always be decided from the standpoint of the greatest good of the greatest number in the long run.[12]

This policy has guided the management of the national forests from that day to the present. The phrase "greatest good of the greatest number in the long run" has become the motto of the Forest Service.

BUILDING THE FOREST SERVICE. The forest reserves placed a heavy administrative responsibility on the small organization of foresters. Few precedents were available to guide them. Pinchot threw his dynamic energy into welding a strong Forest Service and building up a program of national forest administration.

The task was not easy. Cattle and sheep ranchers had been grazing their animals on the public domain without federal permit and with only the rules they were personally able to impose. Naturally they resented the federal intervention. A great deal of diplomacy and sheer courage were required of the early forest officers. The Service sought from the beginning to employ men familiar with local conditions and men who understood—and, if possible, commanded the respect of—the sheepmen and cattlemen with whom they must deal. By fairness, scrupulous honesty, and devotion to the ideals set forth in Secretary Wilson's letter, the Forest Service established itself in the western country.

While Theodore Roosevelt was president, a total of 148 million acres was transferred from the public domain to the national forests. Opposition developed in the West and soon made itself felt in Washington. Eventually Congress withdrew from the President the right to set aside new national forests from the public domain. Before signing the bill, President Roosevelt set aside a large additional area in national forest —enough, he thought at the time, to establish in federal ownership all important public-domain forest land.

A White House Conference of Governors was called by Roosevelt in 1908. It stimulated interest of the states in forestry and set up the National Conservation Commission authorized to consider the four great classes of resources: water, forest, land, and minerals.

In 1909 President Roosevelt called a North American Conservation Congress. Representatives from Canada, Mexico, and the United States assembled. A declaration of principles was set forth by the Congress in which they recognized that natural resources are not confined by national boundaries, that no nation acting alone can properly conserve them, and that all resources should be made available for the use and welfare of man.

Federal-State Cooperative Programs. Gifford Pinchot, the prime mover behind Theodore Roosevelt's conservation policies, was removed from the U.S. Forest Service in 1910 by President Taft because of a controversy between him and the Secretary of the Interior, Richard Ballinger. He was succeeded by Henry Graves. Some states had initiated forestry programs, but the federal government was not at the time authorized to support their efforts through establishing standards for work to be done and providing financial and technical assistance. The Weeks Law, passed in 1911, authorized the federal government to contribute to the states on a matching basis funds for the protection of forest lands against fire. The Clarke-McNary Act of 1924 broadened and extended the provisions of the Weeks Act. By 1960 only one state, Arizona, was without a state forester or comparable official. The total area under state protection had risen to 403 million acres.[9, 17]

National Forests in the East. The Weeks Law also authorized the federal government to acquire private land for national forests where these were necessary for the protection of navigable streams. This provided the basis for the national forests of the eastern states. The authorization was later changed to include also lands needed for growing timber. The White Mountain Forest in New Hampshire, the Pisgah in North Carolina, and the Allegheny in Pennsylvania were acquired. Later the system was extended to include 43 national forests and national-forest purchase units with lands in 23 states east of the Rocky Mountains.

Forestry during the First World War. The First World War interrupted the progress of United States forestry but presented new opportunities for foresters to serve their country. The 10th and 20th Engineer Regiments were formed to get out timber needed by our fighting troops in France.[20] Graves, Greeley, Guthrie, Peck, Kelley, and many others destined to play important roles in shaping American forestry went to France as officers. Here they became acquainted with French forestry and established a fine reputation for effective service to their country. Meanwhile, Zon and Sparhawk were preparing their classic book, "Forest Resources of the World." The Forest Products Laboratory, established in 1910, had a chance to prove its mettle by finding substitutes for scarce woods and developing standards for use.

Between War and Depression. William B. Greeley succeeded Graves as Chief Forester in 1920.

Scarcity of lumber and increasing prices during the war sharpened the nation's appreciation of the role forest products play in our national defense. The United States Senate passed a resolution directing the Forest Service to study the nation's forest resources and their adequacy for normal and emergency needs. The resulting document, known as the Capper Report, emphasized the shrinking timber supplies of the nation and pointed up the general lack of forestry measures on private timber operations. Gifford Pinchot headed a committee of foresters advocating public regulation of private timber cutting, but the Capper and Snell bills, providing for such regulation, failed of passage.

For the country as a whole the early 1920s was a period of disillusionment following the war. This gave way later to reckless optimism that nursed the boom of 1926 to 1929 and vanished in the severe business crash in 1929 to 1932.

The hectic twenties, nevertheless, saw substantial advance in public forestry. Sensing that public sentiment at this time would oppose new federal regulations, and having faith that much could be accomplished by milder measures, Greeley set his course. A special committee of industrialists and forestry leaders known as the National Forestry Program Committee was formed [7] with Royal S. Kellogg, Executive Secretary of the Newsprint Service Bureau, as chairman. Other members included E. T. Allen, Phillip Ayres, Hugh P. Baker, Ovid Butler, Wilson Compton, John Foley, William L. Hall, Charles Lathrop Pack, and J. Randall Williams. Strong ties were made with the United States Chamber of Commerce and other organizations. The decision was made to concentrate effort on noncontroversial legislation. Four important basic laws aiding forestry resulted. The General Exchange Act of March 20, 1922, permitted exchange of private lands within national forest boundaries for other public lands of equal value or for national-forest stumpage in the same state. The Clarke-McNary Law increased aid to states for forest protection and provided funds for forest extension and for supplying trees to farmers for planting. The McNary-Woodruff Law of 1928 authorized appropriations of $40 million over a 10-year period for purchase of national forests. The McSweeney-McNary Law passed in 1928 provided organic legislation for research. It authorized 12 regional forest experiment stations and the Forest Products Laboratory for carrying on research in forestry and outlined a 10-year program of financial support for these organizations.[7]

Under Greeley's administration the organization and procedures of the Forest Service were further strengthened. He resigned in 1928 to become executive secretary of the West Coast Lumbermen's Association, a post he filled with high efficiency.

Robert Y. Stuart became Chief Forester in 1928. His term marked the rapid expansion of new activities authorized under the legislation of the twenties. The national survey of forest resources was launched and vigorously carried forward. The voluminous study of forest resources prepared in response to a Senate resolution and known as the Copeland Report contained information on every phase of forestry and provided background material for subsequent forest policy. Forestry was making gratifying headway until the depression set in in earnest in 1931.

The depression rocked the country even more rudely than did the First World War. The stock market crashed, industrial production dropped precipitously, and millions of workers lost employment. The absence of consumer buying power caused further price cuts, layoffs, and business failures. Banks felt the strain, they soon began to fail at an alarming rate, and the complete bank closure came on March 5, 1933. Faith in the country's financial strength and in the capitalistic system wavered. Foresters prepared for a drastic reduction in activities. But the exact opposite occurred.

The Enlargement of Federal Forestry through Emergency Programs. The cooperative approach inaugurated by Greeley seemed to have spent its force by 1930. In the depression private industry and local and state governments all appeared feeble. Businessmen, unemployed veterans, governors, and mayors thronged to Washington to beseech aid of the federal government. In 1932 substantial appropriations were requested by President Hoover and granted by Congress to expand public works to create employment. Forestry activities shared in these funds. In 1933 President Franklin D. Roosevelt proposed a vast program of public works embracing forestry, soil conservation, river-valley improvements, flood control, and public parks, as well as new schools, post offices, highways, airports, hospitals, sewage systems, and a host of other public facilities. A number of emergency agencies were established that performed useful forestry work, among them the Federal Emergency Relief Administration, the Civil Works Administration, the Public Works Administration, and the Works Progress Administration.

CIVILIAN CONSERVATION CORPS. The most imaginative and useful to forestry was the Civilian Conservation Corps, which enrolled needy young people. Camps were established on national and state forests, in soil conservation districts, and in national parks. The men were engaged in tree planting; care of plantations; timber-stand improvement; construction of forest roads, trails, and lookout towers; and various other forestry measures on public land (Fig. 7). At its peak 2,600 camps, each organized to handle 200 men, were operating. The Civilian Conservation Corps continued until 1941 when the project was closed because of war. The corps served to acquaint many people with forestry as a major government activity. It did a great deal to improve national and state forest lands and also provided young men a wholesome life and useful training for private jobs.

THE LUMBER CODE. The National Industrial Recovery Act of 1933 set up fair trade practices among industries. Article 10 in the Lumber Code under this act specified certain forest practices to be followed by industry, which involved leaving the forest in good condition to produce

Fig. 7   Hand tree planting by the Civilian Conservation Corps. Lolo National Forest. (*U.S. Forest Service photo.*)

another crop. The act was declared unconstitutional in 1935. Lumber associations, however, urged their members to continue to comply with the code so far as forest practices were concerned, and many did so.

Stuart, who died in office in 1933, at the beginning of these programs, was succeeded as Chief Forester by Ferdinand Silcox. Silcox brought to the Forest Service a new interest in and sympathy for the people who gained their livelihood from harvest and sale of forest products (Fig. 8). Great expansion in federal activities occurred during this period. National-forest purchasing increased at a rapid rate. Lumbermen readily assented to selling their cutover lands to the federal government to reduce carrying charges. New purchase units were established in Illinois, Indiana, Missouri, Ohio, Kentucky, Alabama, Florida, Mississippi, and other states.

The vast prairie-plains shelterbelt program was launched. This led to planting 18,510 miles of windbreaks by 1942. Wind-barrier planting was resumed after the Second World War, and 35,366 acres were planted in 1960.[17] Flood-control surveys were also started.

Silcox, aided by Earle Clapp and others, called for increased cooperation with private and state forestry, expansion of public forests, and regulation of cutting practices on private forest lands. Proposals for range improvement also followed a substantial report entitled "The Western Range" that appeared in 1936.

Earle Clapp became Acting Chief of the Forest Service upon the death of Silcox in 1939. A joint congressional committee was appointed in 1938 to study the forest situation, hearings were held, and a report was issued in 1941. This recommended federal cooperation with the states in regulating forest practice on private lands. A number of bills introduced in Congress between 1939 and 1951 provided for public regulation of private forestry, but opposition by industry, farm groups, and others prevented passage of federal legislation.

Attempts at wide extension of federal forest holdings at this time were also defeated.

This period saw substantial gains in conservation in the Department of the Interior. Civilian Conservation Corps and other work programs carried out important development projects on national parks and monuments. The Soil Erosion Service was started in 1933 to work with farmers. Later transferred to the Department of Agriculture and renamed the Soil Conservation Service, it sponsored tree planting and other forest improvement measures on farms. The Taylor Grazing Act of 1934 and subsequent acts placed 147 million acres of the remaining public domain in districts to be administered for the forage resource. Legislation in 1937 provided

Fig. 8 A snag field is the ghostly reminder of the grandeur of this once heavily forested slope in southern Oregon. (*U.S. Forest Service photo.*)

for management, under a sustained-yield plan, of the Oregon and California Railroad revested lands, and regulations governing the management of Indian forest lands were revised and greatly improved. In 1939 the first appropriation was made for control of fires on the public-domain lands of Alaska.

Forestry during the Second World War. Lyle Watts became Chief of the Forest Service in 1943 just when defense activities began to dominate federal programs. Lumber, which was at first proposed as a substitute for steel, soon became critically short. The Forest Service organized the Timber Production War Project in cooperation with state forestry organizations to stimulate lumber production. Special studies of lumber prices were made. At the Forest Products Laboratory new wood products were developed by research. Special schools dealt with the packaging of materials for overseas shipment and use of wood in aircraft. Specifications for wood products for military use were prepared. From Alaskan forests Sitka spruce of aircraft quality was cut. Access roads were built to open up remote national forest lands and private timberlands.

The nation looked mainly to private forest industry, however, for the major production job during the war. The ready market for forest products during the war and prosperous postwar years effected a healthy recovery in private forest industries.

Developments since 1945. The economy of the United States was functioning at record levels in 1945 when the Germans, and later the Japanese, capitulated. In anticipation of these long-awaited days, various agencies of government, including the U.S. Forest Service, had prepared a series of plans for postwar work in the expectation that peace would be followed by a rapid demobilization of the war economy and consequent unemployment. The looked-for depression, however, did not develop, largely because of the pent-up demand of the civilian population and returning soldiers for consumer goods. Almost everything was in short supply—office and factory space, clothing, food, motorcars, and a host of other consumer products, and, above all, housing. Instead of a slump, the economy surged forward to a new boom level. Lumber, paper, and other forest products were in huge demand. The major companies, recognizing the market potential that lay ahead, began to look forward to the long-term timber supplies. As a result, forestry on a nationwide basis entered a period of the most rapid advance it had seen since the turn of the century. This time the advance was stimulated by the real need for forest products and by the conviction on the part of the major timber companies that they must protect their raw-material supply. Considerable pressure was placed on the federal government to open up the national forests to commercial logging on a scale far beyond any attained heretofore. Foresters, to handle national-forest timber sales and particularly to staff the rapidly burgeoning forestry divisions established by the various private companies, were eagerly sought after. The nation as a whole was enjoying an unprecedented level of prosperity, and the outlook for the future seemed bright. Only two clouds darkened the horizon: the rapidly developing inflation resulting from increased prices and wages that followed the removal of wartime controls, and failure to reach a working agreement with the Soviet Union. In 1950 the Korean conflict broke out, and it continued until 1953. The economy of the United States since 1950 has been strongly stimulated by military expenditures. This inevitably influenced the outlook for timber supplies and the use of forest products. The U.S. Forest Service, under the leadership of Richard McArdle, who became Chief in 1952, made a new study of the timber resources of the United States with long-range forecasts of future needs to the year 1975 and the year 2000.[18] This new study was reassuring, on the one hand, because it showed that timber growth at last was in balance with timber cutting. But it showed also that the future need for forest products was likely to increase enormously during the next 45 years, with the total potential market approximately double that of 1954. Moreover, this highlighted also the need of additional land for outdoor recreation, water supplies, and the many other products and services that forest land can provide. The Forest Service, following the lead of the National Park Service, projected a large increase in campground and other facilities for recreational use. Pressure by certain recreationists was being placed on the Forest Service to set aside large areas of national forest lands for wilderness use. A multiple use–sustained yield bill was enacted in 1960,[17] in part as a counterbalance for wilderness-area bills that had been pending before Congress for a number of years.

In 1962, as a result of the report of the President's Outdoor Recreation Resources Review Commission, a new Bureau of Outdoor Recreation was established in the Department of the Interior. This Bureau is a research, planning, and coordinating agency, not a land-managing agency. The Congress in 1962 also passed the McIntire-Stennis Bill to authorize the Secretary of Agriculture to cooperate with the land-grant colleges, agricultural experiment stations, and state-supported forestry colleges to support research in forestry and sciences basic thereto. Both actions seem destined to have significant influence on future developments in forestry.

Forest survey data in 1962 indicated an even greater excess of growth over cut than in 1955. Some foresters were predicting a timber surplus of substantial proportions. The new Chief of the Forest Service, Edward P. Cliff, was directing a restudy of the national outlook before recommending new public policies.

State Forestry

The beginnings of state forestry in the United States go back to colonial days. The early ordinances of New Sweden (which became Delaware), of Pennsylvania (by William Penn), and of Massachusetts all recognized the importance of the forest and provided regulations for its proper use. With the coming of independence the states continued to take an interest in forestry measures. Agricultural societies in Philadelphia as early as 1791, in New York in 1795, and in Massachusetts in 1804 took notice of the importance of tree planting and urged that steps be taken to encourage it. In 1819, the Massachusetts Legislature asked its state department of agriculture to promote the growth of oak suitable for ship timbers.

In 1837, Massachusetts authorized a survey of its forest conditions with a view toward determining measures that might encourage landowners to practice forestry. In 1788, New York passed laws to regulate lumber grading to protect the good name of New York lumber in national and international trade.[21]

The surge of settlers to the prairie states after the passage of the Homestead Act in 1862 made the middle western folk acutely aware of the need for trees. Sod huts for living quarters and buffalo chips for fuel were a real hardship to people used to an abundant supply of wood. Tree planting caught the public interest.

Michigan in 1867 and Wisconsin shortly thereafter created forestry commissions to investigate timber operations, land clearing, and the importance of proper care of timberlands within the state. Consideration was given to shelterbelts and to proper management of forest areas. Similar forestry commissions were set up in New York, Connecticut, New Hampshire, Vermont, Ohio, Pennsylvania, and North Carolina.[8] These states together with Kansas and Maine had state forestry organizations prior to 1885. In that year California, Ohio, Colorado, and New York established state forest administration. With the exception of New York's, these early state forest organizations were temporary, but they laid the groundwork for permanent programs to follow.

In 1872 New York set up a commission to investigate the preservation of the Adirondack forests which led in 1885 to the establishment of the Adirondack Forest Preserve. After 1894 citizens became seriously alarmed by the way in which the state preserves were managed. A constitutional amendment was passed prohibiting the cutting of trees in the preserve and has been reenacted at subsequent constitutional conventions.

New York's example of acquiring state land for permanent forest use was followed by Pennsylvania in 1895, Minnesota in 1899, and by many other states thereafter.

State acquisition of land for forestry came about, however, more from default of owners on taxes and from land abandonment than from deliberate state policy.[5] It was inevitable that American pioneers clear forests for crops. Hill lands usually had less dense forests, were freer from malaria, and hence were often chosen for settlers' homes and fields; but soils were thin and steep slopes easily eroded. Mechanization of tillage placed the hill farmer at still greater disadvantage in competing with those on fertile level lands. The agricultural depression that followed the First World War brought the problem before the country.

Land abandonment—it began in New England as early as 1850—is a painful process. As family income shrinks, savings are exhausted. Repairs to the dwelling, other farm buildings, and fences are postponed. Equipment wears out. Livestock declines in vigor, quality, and numbers. Crop yields decline from inadequate tillage and fertilizer. Severe family privation may occur. Eventually the farm as a whole is abandoned, or reduced to part-time operation, while the breadwinner engages in some other occupation.

In several counties in the Lake States more than 50 per cent of the land became tax-delinquent. Land abandonment spread at an alarming rate, and clearing forests for farmlands virtually ceased. In New York, farms once occupied 80 per cent of the land area. By 1950 this was reduced to 57 per cent and by 1959 to 44 per cent. The long-established trend of giving up cropland to pasture and pasture to woodland was still in evidence in 1963.

Farmers and rural bankers themselves recognized the economic waste in farming poor lands. In New York they obtained passage of the Hewitt Law in 1929 to purchase submarginal farmlands for forests. By 1950 the total acquired was 532,000 acres, and by 1960 it was 588,000. Other states have followed similar programs. In 1934, the Federal Resettlement Administration entered the field. Many of the lands acquired by this organization have been administered as state forests under long-term lease.

As of 1961 state forest holdings totaled 28.5 million acres. States having the largest areas were:

	Area, million acres
Minnesota	4.9
Michigan	3.7
New York	3.1
Wisconsin	2.6
Nevada	2.2
Washington	2.0
Pennsylvania	1.9

Most state forest lands, including New York's 588,000 acres of land acquired from submarginal farms, are administered for timber production, recreation, watershed protection, public hunting lands, and other multiple-use purposes.

The Weeks and Clarke-McNary laws proved a great boon to state forestry departments. In most states fire-control expenditures have remained the largest item in the budget of state forestry organizations. Federal aid has been a mainstay in providing financial support and in ensuring freedom from undue political pressure on forest officers employed in state organizations.

The program in Maryland might be taken as an example of state forestry. Maryland forestry first dealt primarily with protecting the lands from fire. Soon thereafter the state agreed to perform forestry services for landowners on a fee basis. Later a state extension forester was employed to stimulate forest care by farmers. Gradually the state acquired a number of forest properties which, though small in size, were managed both for timber production and for recreation. In 1943, the state passed a law regulating timber-cutting practices on private lands. It cooperates with the federal government in farm and other private forestry programs.

Similar service programs have developed in many other states. Laws providing regulation of forest practice on private lands have been adopted in 17 states.

Farm Forestry

Farm forestry has been largely a state function. The Smith-Lever Act, passed in 1914, allotted funds through the state agricultural colleges for extension work in forestry. Initial programs emphasized tree planting and field demonstrations.

It became evident by 1924 that considerable additional effort was needed. The Clarke-McNary Law provided for distributing forest planting stock to farmers and for strengthening extension forestry.

Largely as a result of the experience of the extension foresters, the Norris-Doxey Farm Forestry Act was passed in 1937. It authorized appropriations of $2.5 million to provide advice to farmers on timber growing and timber marketing. Farm foresters, employed by the states under this act but paid in part from federal funds, visited the farmer, estimated his timber stands, marked trees that should be cut, and referred the farmer to timber buyers who might be interested in the product. This act, which proved especially popular with farmers and with the states, brought to over 100,000 farmers a clear understanding of what is meant by good timber-management practices.

The Cooperative Forest Management Act of 1950 extended the benefits provided farmers under the Norris-Doxey Act to all woodland owners. By 1960, forty-six states and Puerto Rico were cooperating with the federal government under this act. Some 531 foresters were employed and 82,188 owners had been given aid in forest management.[17]

A number of other federal-state programs have been operative during the period from 1933 to 1961 to stimulate farm forestry. These include various programs of the Soil Conservation Service aimed at reducing soil erosion and making better use of the farmland. The Pittman-Robertson Act to improve game habitats on farms provided help in tree and shrub planting. The Prairie-Plains Shelterbelt Program encouraged tree planting to protect fields and farm buildings from wind. In addition, forestry measures were included in many of the plans designed primarily to restrict overproduction of farm commodities. The Agricultural Stabilization and Conservation Program and the Food and Agriculture Act of 1962 are the most recent and generous of these programs. In 1960, 339,000 acres were planted to trees and 256,000 acres of farm woodlands were improved at a total cost to the government of $6 million.

Private Forestry

The beginnings of private forestry in America are lost in the early history of our country. Certain it is that many private landowners took an interest in their forest and attempted to protect young growth from unnecessary cutting. Farmers, plantation owners, and even loggers and lumbermen have set aside specific forest areas where logging was kept at a minimum or entirely excluded. Some have practiced good forest management over a long period of time with little or no aid from a technical forester.

Zachariah Allen [6] in 1820 planted some abandoned farmland to oaks, chestnut, and locust and kept an accurate record of his costs and income. In various sales he removed during a 57-year period timber valued at $4,948. The enterprise showed a net profit of $2,543 or 6.93 per cent per year for the entire 57-year period. This profit is over and above 6 per cent interest on land, taxes, and planting costs.

Among the early large-scale forestry ventures in the United States were those that were begun near the turn of the century on the Vanderbilt, Webb, and Whitney estates. Gifford Pinchot was employed by George Vanderbilt as consulting forester for his 80,000-acre estate in North Carolina, later named the Biltmore Forest. Pinchot brought in a sawmill and started timber operations. The venture was successful financially and attracted the attention of other forest owners. Later Mr. Vanderbilt employed Dr. Schenck to manage the forest property.

Ne-Ha-Sa-Ne Park—owned by Dr. Seward Webb—in Hamilton County, New York, and the Whitney estate adjoined one another. Gifford Pinchot and Henry Graves were employed to work up plans for management of these two estates. The first silvicultural rules governing cutting practices that were ever written into a logging contract in the United States probably are those prepared for the Ne-Ha-Sa-Ne forest. Both properties are outstanding among privately managed Adirondack properties in the quality of timber now standing on them and in the timber they have yielded the owners over the long-term period.

The accumulation of forest lands in large family estates began in Maine as early as 1850.[14] Some of these became very large properties, of which the Coe and Pingree estate is an example. The founder, David Pingree, restricted cutting of spruce to trees 14 inches in diameter and larger. After pulpwood logging came to the fore, the estate passed to David Pingree's heirs, and cutting was carried to much lower limits. The business panic of 1907 caused many private owners who had initiated forestry programs with the help of the Division of Forestry to abandon them.

About 1912 Finch, Pruyn and Company started a forestry program on its Adirondack holdings. Trees to be cut were marked by foresters, and the cutting budget was projected on a sustained-yield basis.

More recently, interest in private forestry on the part of lumber and other companies has grown at a rapid pace. The Goodman Lumber Company in Wisconsin began its first cycle of selective cutting in 1927 and has diversified utilization in its plants.[14]

The Urania Lumber Company in Louisiana began operations on a sustained-yield basis about 1917. It has been so successful in the management of its lands that it has more timber growing on its lands than the company mills can cut.

The Crossett Lumber Company at Crossett, Arkansas, owns about 500,-000 acres of land which it manages on an intensive-forestry basis. This company operates a sawmill and pulp mill.

Other companies that began forestry programs in the 1930s or earlier include the Nekoosa-Edwards Company,[20] Consolidated Water Power and Paper Company, International Paper Company, Patten Timber Company, Von Platen-Fox Company, Dead River Company, Minnesota and Ontario Paper Company, Weyerhaeuser Timber Company, St. Regis Company, Crown-Zellerbach Company, Collins Almanor Forest, Camp Manufacturing Company, St. Paul and Tacoma Lumber Company, and Champion Paper and Fibre Company.

The interest of these and many others in practicing sustained-yield forestry has led to widespread purchase of forest land in the South, the

West, and the Northeast by large lumber, pulp and paper, and other companies.

By 1960, the better-managed industrial forests were exhibiting the most intensive silviculture to be found outside experimental areas. Practices included conversion of brushlands to forests by plowing and planting, short cutting cycles and short rotations in pulpwood forests, and management units of 20,000 acres in size for each industrial forester. Nationwide, approximately 7,500 foresters—44 per cent of the total in practice—were employed on industrial work in 1960. The shift from extensive forestry was well advanced on industrial holdings [2] (Fig. 9).

Associations of private forest landowners date back to 1911, when the Clearwater Forest Protective Association was formed. Others followed shortly thereafter. At first, these were concerned with protection of forests against fire, but later on they became interested in good forest management also.

Recent developments in forestry will be outlined in Chap. 18.

FIG. 9 Multiple-use forestry. Family camping on a Weyerhaeuser Timber Company tree farm. The forested hills in the background supply timber for plywood, lumber, and paper pulp. They also supply water to the lake for recreation and human use and shelter useful wildlife. (*AFPI photo.*)

Conclusion

The following major periods of American forestry might be recognized:

1770 to 1890. This was a period of forest exploitation, of acquisition and disposal of the public domain, and of warnings of threatened timber exhaustion, but one of little permanent progress toward establishing forest reserves and basic forest policy.

1891 to 1910. The policy of federal land ownership and management was established and implemented by creation and management of national forests. Permanent state forest programs began.

1911 to 1932. National forests were consolidated and new lands acquired in the East; states extended protection to most forest lands against fire, insects, and tree diseases. State forestry was promoted and widely developed.

1933 to 1942. Forestry was recognized as vital to the national economy. Interest in private forestry revived, stimulated first by the Lumber Code and later by the American Forest Products Industries, Inc. (AFPI) and other private associations.[20] Forestry work was recognized as a useful measure to decrease unemployment. The value of forests was recognized in control of floods and dust storms, protection of watersheds, public recreation, and stabilization of communities. Working conditions for woods labor improved.

1943 to 1962. Rapid expansion occurred in forestry programs of large timberland-owning companies. Farm forestry expanded. Growing concern was felt by the United States for forestry programs in other lands. Outstanding developments occurred in research, especially in forest-products research. State regulation of private forest practice extended to 17 states. National forest timber became a significant part of the total timber harvest. Public pressure by recreationists led to improvements on national forests and to passage of the Multiple Use–Sustained Yield Forest Law. Private companies began to adopt policies governing use of their lands by recreationists. Water supply from forest lands was becoming of increasing importance.

Foresters and forestry sympathizers have always been a minority. Forestry has reached its important place in America today because men with physical and moral courage battled against strenuous and often violent opposition. No advances in forestry met with universal acclaim. All were won by struggle. Fire control on grazing and blueberry lands, establishment of national forests from public lands, control of grazing on national forests, purchase of lands for national forests in the eastern states, planting of trees, salvage of hurricane-damaged timber, forest research, shelterbelt planting, public aids to private owners through farm foresters and others, aids to lumbermen in wartime timber production, and finally public regulation of timber cutting on private lands—all have been opposed. Many are still vigorously opposed. Vast inertia stems from public indifference. Forestry measures that require public expenditures are always opposed by economy blocks. Bitter opposition may occur from those who fear their private or corporate welfare will be impaired by public forestry measures.

Few foresters can escape these conflicts.

LITERATURE CITED

1. Allen, Shirley Walter. 1950. "An Introduction to American Forestry," 2d ed., McGraw-Hill Book Company, Inc., New York. 413 pp.
2. American Forest Products Industries. 1961. "Progress in Private Forestry in the United States," Washington, D.C. 49 pp.
3. Butler, Ovid. 1946. "70 Years of Campaigning for American Forestry," *American Forests*, 52(10):456–459, 512.
4. Chinard, Gilbert. 1945. "The American Philosophical Society and the Early History of Forestry in America," *Proceedings, American Philosophical Society*, 89(2):444–488.
5. Fontanna, Stanley G. 1949. "State Forests," *Trees*, The Yearbook of Agriculture, pp. 390–394, U.S. Department of Agriculture, Washington.
6. Holst, Monterey Leman. 1946. "Zachariah Allen, Pioneer in Applied Silviculture," *Journal of Forestry*, 44:507–508.
7. Hosmer, Ralph S. 1947. "The National Forestry Program Committee, 1919–1928," *Journal of Forestry*, 45:627–645.
8. Illick, Joseph S. 1939. "An Outline of General Forestry," 3d ed., Barnes & Noble, Inc., New York. 297 pp.
9. Kling, John B. 1951. "Cooperative Forest Fire Control–Policy Determination and Administration in the Clarke-McNary Grant-in-aid Program," New York State College of Forestry, Syracuse, N.Y. 106 pp.
10. Lillard, Richard G. 1947. "The Great Forest," Alfred A. Knopf, Inc., New York. 399 pp.
11. Paxson, Frederic L. 1924. "History of the American Frontier, 1763–1893," Houghton Mifflin Company, Boston. 598 pp.
12. Pinchot, Gifford. 1947. "Breaking New Ground," Harcourt, Brace and Company, Inc., New York. 522 pp.
13. Schoepf, Johann David (Trans. by Alfred J. Morrison). 1911. "Travels in the Confederation (1783–1784)," William J. Campbell, Philadelphia. Part I, 426 pp.; part II, 344 pp.
14. Shirley, Hardy L. 1949. "Large Private Holdings in the North," *Trees*, The Yearbook of Agriculture, pp. 255–274, U.S. Department of Agriculture, Washington.
15. Sparhawk, William N. 1949. "The History of Forestry in America," *Trees*, The Yearbook of Agriculture, pp. 702–714, U.S. Department of Agriculture, Washington.
16. U.S. Department of Agriculture. 1949. *Trees*, The Yearbook of Agriculture, Washington. 944 pp.
17. U.S. Department of Agriculture. 1960. "Report of the Chief of the Forest Service," Washington. 49 pp.

18. U.S. Department of Agriculture, Forest Service. 1958. "Timber Resources for America's Future," Forest Resource Report 14, Washington. 713 pp.
19. U.S. Department of the Interior, Bureau of Land Management. 1950. "Brief Notes on the Public Domain," Washington. 21 pp. mim.
20. Winters, Robert K., ed. 1950. "Fifty Years of Forestry in the U.S.A.," Society of American Foresters, Washington, D.C. 385 pp.
21. Wolf, Robert E. 1948. "A Partial Survey of Forest Legislation in New York State," unpublished thesis, New York State College of Forestry, Syracuse, N.Y.

CHAPTER 4. *Forest Regions*

THE FOREST regions can be better understood if a few concepts of the forester and ecologist are first introduced.

Forest Land

To the forester, forest land includes not only land that is covered with trees but land that finds its highest use and service to man in supporting woody vegetation. This concept embraces not only what the land supports today but also what it may support tomorrow if put to its best use.

Land may be considered to be forest land only if climate, topography, and soil are favorable to tree growth. Land with climates unfavorable to trees may be classed as tundra, prairie, desert scrub, savanna, or parkland but not as forest land. The more favorable the climate for vigorous tree growth, the more valuable the land for forest purposes, provided soil and other factors remain favorable.

Climate includes such factors as sunlight, rainfall, air movement, and temperature, all of which affect the rate of tree growth.

Topography determines the ease with which soil can be formed and held in place. Mountain peaks above timberline, watercourses, lakes, open swamps, and bare rock faces are not forest land, though they may be included within a large forest area. Rugged topography and steepness of slope may preclude harvesting commercial timber from mountains, but such land if tree-clad is not excluded for this reason from being classed as forest land. Commercial forest land is that capable of producing usable crops of wood that are economically available and not withdrawn from timber utilization.[15] Watercourses and lakes are a result of climate and topography and are influenced greatly by the forest, which helps to regulate groundwater supply. Streams may provide transportation systems for forest products and oftentimes attract recreationists. The scenic and recreational attractions of forests are related to the land, and from the forester's point of view are an important feature of the forest as a whole.

47

Soil quality influences the growth rate, composition, and to a large extent the value of the forest. The forester is concerned with the origin of the soil, as this affects its depth and texture. He considers the natural drainage and the presence or absence of impervious layers near the surface. He is interested in the tilth of the soil, which determines how rapidly it will soak up water and how easily it may be penetrated by roots. He is concerned with its humus content and acidity, which determine whether or not it is subject to leaching and possible hardpan formation, and with the mineral nutrient content that is essential for tree growth.

Tree

A tree is defined as "a woody plant having one well-defined stem and a more or less definitely formed crown, usually attaining a height of at least 8 feet." [5] A tree should be distinguished from a shrub, which is defined as "a woody perennial plant differing from a perennial herb by its persistent and woody stems, and from a tree by its low stature and habit of branching from the base." [5]

Trees differ in kind, size, growth rate, shape, quality of wood, growth requirements, and susceptibility to fire, insects, disease, and storm damage. The United States has 918 species of trees, 174 varieties, and 89 hybrids. Of these more than 160 have commercial value.

Forest

To a hunter, the forest is a source of game and the keen enjoyment of pursuing it. To a logger, it is a source of timber. To an ecologist, it is nature's grandest biologic community (Fig. 1). To a water user, it is a regulator of stream flow. To an artist, it is a source of creative inspiration.

To a forester, a forest means what it means to hunter, logger, ecologist, water user, and artist, and very much more. Simply stated, the forester's concept includes the trees, everything that affects their growth and value, and all that forests yield of worth to man (Fig. 9). A forest is defined as "a plant association predominantly of trees and other woody vegetation occupying an extensive area of land." [5]

The Community Concept of the Forest

The forest visitor sees particular trees of outstanding interest and form. He may notice individual animals, individual wild flowers, individual edible mushrooms, and other individual examples of life that occur in the forest. To him these trees, flowers, mushrooms, and animals seem to be individuals very much as he is an individual. He may think of them as each living its independent life as he, in turn, lives his independent life.

A man is an individual, but he is also a part of some community. The community, in turn, is a part of a larger economic and social unit in which many individuals play a part and in which all are more or less interdependent. So it is in the forest. The trees are, to a certain extent, mutually dependent upon one another (Fig. 3). But they also compete for soil, water, and light. Each tree depends upon its neighbor for shelter from wind, for protecting the soil around its roots, and for providing litter and shade to make the soil suitable as a home for small plants and animals that in turn perform useful functions in the life of the forest as a whole (Fig. 2). Seed-eating birds and mammals transport seed. Red squirrels hoard pine cones and acorns.

After performing their function on the tree, hardwood leaves drop to the ground where they become food for earthworms and other soil-dwelling animals, which chew up the leafy material and pass it through their bodies. The castings, rich in humus, are further worked over by microorganisms that break down the cellulose and lignin fractions, releasing plant nutrients from the humus. Nitrogen, calcium, phosphorus, potassium, iron, magnesium, and other plant nutrients are thus made available for reuse by the trees to form leaves, twigs, stems, and roots.

The Dynamic Forest

Just as human communities change from year to year, so also do forests. Ordinarily this change is slow. Trees crowd each other, and one by one the weaker die. Shrubs and other vegetation wax or wane as the tree canopy opens or closes. Trees may slowly invade an abandoned eastern pasture. First, hawthorn, redcedar, or gray birch gain a foothold. These may later be followed by ash, red maple, and cherry, which form a denser canopy and eventually crowd out the pioneer invaders. Gradually these in turn give way to sugar maple, beech, yellow birch, and hemlock that form the climax forest.

Even the climax forest is far from static. Examined closely, it is often found to consist of groups of trees more or less uniform in age. The history of such forests reveals that most of the trees owe their origin to forest catastrophes of the past, such as severe droughts, fires, windstorms, insect invasions, or tree diseases. Examples of such natural catastrophes are the New England hurricane of 1938, the New York windstorm of 1950, bark beetle outbreaks in the western states, and the spruce budworm outbreaks in Canada and the northern states.

The forests of the United States stand intermediate in floristic complexity between those to be found in northern Europe, which are relatively simple, and tropical forests, which present unending complexity. To make the study of American forestry comprehensible, foresters have recognized a number of forest types. Forest type is a term used to

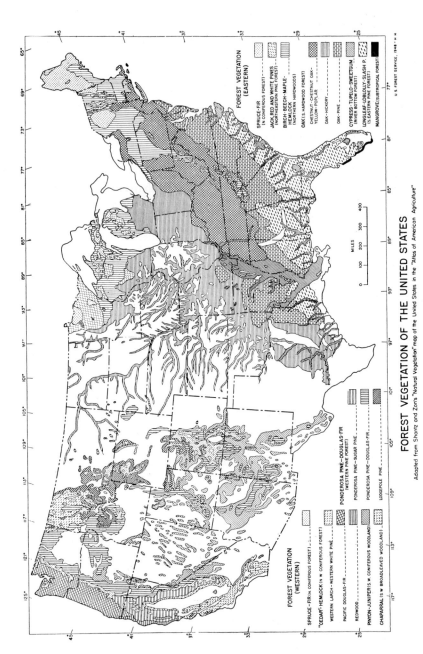

FIG. 10 Natural forest regions of the United States. (*U.S. Forest Service.*)

50

designate stands of similar composition and development. The Society of American Foresters lists 147 forest types, of which 97 are found in the eastern states and 50 in the western states. For further simplification, type groups or formations may be recognized.

The major forest formations are shown in Fig. 10. Even formations are too numerous to permit detailed discussion in a book on general forestry, especially since boundaries between formations are irregular and must be arbitrarily drawn. However desirable it might appear to follow the forest types of nature, man must work with human institutions as well. For this reason he divides the various forest regions along political lines that may be used in compiling statistics (Fig. 11) and in relating thereto other economic information. The following discussion deals with both natural forest regions and regions based on state and county lines. Characterizations of five natural forest regions will be given, along with discussions of the forest industries based on economic regions.

The Northern Forest Formations

The northern forest in the United States is characterized by sugar maple, beech, basswood, and yellow birch among the hardwoods; and by spruce, balsam fir, and hemlock among the softwoods. It includes the northern coniferous forest, the northeastern pine forest, and the northern hardwoods.

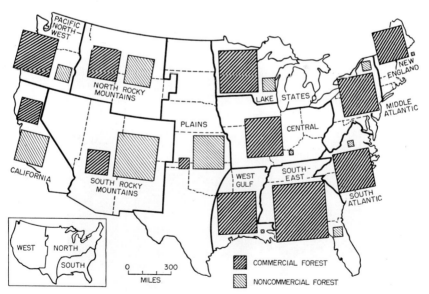

FIG. 11 Breakdown of forest regions used in reporting on forest areas and timber volumes. (*U.S. Forest Service.*)

Five tree species have ranges that correspond more or less closely to the distribution of the northern forest in the United States. These are northern white-cedar, eastern hemlock, yellow birch, northern white pine, and balsam fir. Perhaps the last-named is the best indicator of the northern forest. It is interesting that sugar maple, which more than other species gives character to the northern forest, is distributed far beyond the boundaries of the northern forest.

The northern forest is made up of a number of important forest types. The most typical are those containing beech, birch, or maple (Fig. 12). Sugar maple tends to outnumber beech and birch on the best-quality soils, and the reverse is true on thin or light-textured soils. Intermixed in the northern hardwoods forest are hemlock and, to the north and at higher elevations, red spruce, white spruce, and balsam fir. Black spruce,

Fig. 12   A second-growth northern hardwood forest with sugar maple and yellow birch.

tamarack, and northern white-cedar are found in the swamps that characterize the glaciated terrain of the northern states. White pine, red pine, and—in the Lake States—jack pine are found in pure and mixed stands in the northern forest.

The northern forest contains many species and types of high economic value. From colonial days white pine has been preeminent for lumber and remains so today. High-quality lumber is also manufactured from red pine and from red and white spruce. Hemlock, tamarack, jack pine, and balsam fir produce intermediate-quality lumber. Northern white-cedar is usually small in size but produces a durable wood suitable for shingles, boatbuilding, poles, and posts. Among the hardwoods sugar maple and yellow birch are splendid woods for furniture manufacture, flooring, and interior trim. Beech likewise is suitable for flooring, handles, and other uses requiring a hard, dense wood. White ash, black cherry, and basswood produce specialty woods suited for a variety of purposes. Ash is strong, hence useful for handles, athletic equipment, ladder rungs, and other purposes requiring high strength. Cherry is made into furniture and is extensively used for type backing because of its high dimensional stability. Basswood produces a soft, fine-grain lumber suitable for cabinetwork and is also used for veneer, cooperage, and woodenware. Paper birch that comes in after a fire is useful for dowels, stamped veneer products, and turned products such as spools. Aspen is widely used for excelsior and for meat boxes.

The most highly prized pulp species are red, white, and black spruce; and second to these is balsam fir. All may be used for both groundwood and sulfite pulp. Hemlock, jack pine, and also red and white pine may be pulped by the sulfate process successfully. Aspen is used extensively for groundwood and semichemical pulp. Since 1950 many hardwood species have been widely employed for paper pulp using the sulfate, semichemical, chemigroundwood, and cold-soda processes.

The northern forests, particularly the coniferous types, grow densely and may shade out the undervegetation. Volumes in excess of 50 cords per acre may be found on lands where the largest trees are less than 18 inches in diameter. Growth rates of individual trees are not high, but volume growth per acre often equals that of the southern and Rocky Mountain forests where wide spacing of trees results from insufficient rainfall.

White pine will grow at the rate of 500 to 800 board feet per acre per year under good conditions, though a growth rate of 300 feet per acre is more to be expected. Mixed northern hardwoods made up of maple, birch, white ash, black cherry, and beech will grow at the rate of 300 to 500 board feet per acre. Jack pine, aspen, spruces, and balsam generally grow at ½ to 1 cord per acre per year in well-stocked stands. These are goals toward which a forester might strive. The growth figures given in Table 1 are estimates of actual growth as it exists over large areas.

TABLE 1. COMMERCIAL FOREST AREAS AND
GROWTH RATES BY REGIONS [15]
(Contiguous states)

Region	Commercial forest area, million acres	Annual timber growth	
		Billion bd. ft.	Average per acre, bd. ft.
New England............	30.6	1.8	61
Middle Atlantic.........	42.2	3.2	75
Lake States.............	53.3	2.7	50
Central................	42.4	4.0	93
Plains.................	5.5	0.4	73
Total North..........	174.0	12.1	70
South Atlantic..........	46.2	6.9	149
Southeast..............	95.0	10.0	105
West Gulf..............	52.1	7.1	136
Total South...........	193.3	24.0	125
Pacific Northwest........	45.4	6.0	132
California..............	17.3	2.9	170
Northern Rocky Mts.....	33.8	1.5	45
Southern Rocky Mts.....	20.5	0.7	35
Total West...........	117.0	11.1	95
Coastal Alaska..........	4.3	0.1	30
All regions............	488.6	47.4	97

The northern forest region occupies the major area of forest land in New England, the Middle Atlantic states, and the Lake States. These are the most densely populated regions of the United States and are highly industrialized. Forest and forest products, nevertheless, make up a substantial part of the regional economy in each of these.

New England. The six New England states have a total of 31 million acres of forest land, almost all of which is commercial (Table 1). Nearly half the forest area of New England lies in Maine. Most of Maine's timberlands were cut over many years ago for sawlogs. Some have been

cut one or more times since for pulpwood. Pine and hardwoods characterize southern Maine; spruce and fir, the northern towns. Early logging
was concentrated on softwoods, as these could be floated down the
streams to mills. Companies in Maine developed the most extensive
timber-floating systems to be found in the United States.[13] Since 1955
hardwood pulping processes have come into extensive use, and with this
truck and tractor logging. Gradually Maine's remote forests are being
penetrated by public and private logging roads. Forestry in the unorganized towns of northern Maine remains on an extensive rather than
an intensive basis.

The unorganized towns of Maine are owned by large timber companies
and by family estates.[13] The major forest industry of New England is
pulp and paper manufacture. These companies have the largest forest
holdings, use more timber than other companies, and exercise a dominant
influence on forest land management.[7] The industry is primarily devoted
to specialty products, though some kraft and newsprint are manufactured.
The last few decades have seen the closing of a number of individual
mills in New England and the transfer of operations to the South. With
the widespread increase in hardwood pulping, the industry has become
more stable than it was during the period from 1930 to 1950.

New England is also noted for its wood-turning establishments and
novelty mills. These manufacture such products as ice-cream spoons,
shoe shanks, various veneer novelties, spools, bobbins, wooden heels,
brush and other handles, chair stock, small cooperage, and related
products. Furniture manufacturing also is important.

Southern New England is highly industrialized. Here timberland
holdings are mostly small in size and developed more for recreation
than for commercial forestry.

The Middle Atlantic States. The five Middle Atlantic states have 42
million acres of commercial forest land (Table 1), much of it occupied
by northern hardwoods or oak. This region, like New England, is highly
industrialized, but it also has a well-developed agriculture. Population
density is high; consequently, markets for wood products are good. Perhaps nowhere in our country is utilization of forests more intensive than
in the Middle Atlantic states. New York has many pulp mills. Pennsylvania and West Virginia have a large market for mine timbers as well as
for pulpwood. Delaware and New Jersey produce relatively minor quantities of forest products, most of which find a ready market within their
own states. The roofing-felt industry and floor-covering industry of Pennsylvania and New Jersey use substantial quantities of small-sized timber
for pulpwood. The wood-chemical industry was at one time highly developed in western Pennsylvania and New York. It declined rapidly
after the First World War and since the Second World War has become

a minor industry. A market still remains for limited quantities of charcoal for curing tobacco and for other purposes.

Only a few large timberland holdings exist in the Middle Atlantic states. These are owned by coal companies, private estates, railways, and other companies. Holdings of 5,000 to 10,000 acres make manageable properties within this region because of the diversity of products and intensity of utilization. The furniture industry, handle industry, toy manufacturing, musical-instrument manufacturing, and a host of others are found in this great industrial section of the nation.

The Lake States. The three Lake States have 53 million acres of commercial forest land [15] (Table 1). The forests of the Lake States are made up primarily of pine, northern hardwood, and oak, with limited quantities of spruce and fir. The Lake States have been cut and burned more severely than any other one region, and as a result, most of the land is seriously depleted and must be cared for over a period of 20 to 40 years before high production is restored.[2] Annual growth is estimated at 50 board feet per acre. The depletion of the standing timber naturally caused a decline in the lumber and related wood-using industries. The pine lumber industry has practically disappeared, but the hardwood lumber business is still active and probably will continue to operate on a moderate scale until young growth becomes sufficiently large to support it on a sustained-yield basis.[15]

The pulp and paper industry is well developed in Wisconsin. This industry originally depended upon spruce but now relies mainly on jack pine, aspen, and the spruce and pine imported from Canada and from the Rocky Mountain region. The Wisconsin paper industry, in common with that in the Northeast and in the Middle Atlantic states, manufactures chiefly specialty products.

Michigan is one of the foremost furniture-manufacturing states in our country. The industry centered at Grand Rapids is known throughout the land. The furniture mart in Chicago is the major furniture display and marketing center in the nation. Manufacture of novelties such as clothespins, wooden bowls, veneer products, and turned products is also important in Michigan.

The Lake States pulp and paper companies have introduced forestry programs and employ many foresters, and so have a few lumber companies. Public ownership of depleted cutover lands is well advanced in all three states. National forests total 5 million acres in area. State, county, and municipal forests that were administered by the several state forestry organizations in 1961 totaled: for Michigan, 3,700,000 acres; for Minnesota, 4,890,000 acres; and for Wisconsin, 2,568,000 acres.[3] Though Lake States forests have been badly treated in the past, they are showing a substantial comeback as second-growth stands approach merchantableness. The growth for the region as a whole apparently more than doubled between 1934 [2] and 1953.[15]

The Central Forest Formations

The Central forest is bounded roughly by the northern forest on the north, by the coastal plain on the east and south, and by the prairie on the west. The Central forest is characterized by the various species of oak, of which red oak, white oak, black oak, and chestnut oak are most common. It includes the several eastern forest types in which oak occurs as a dominant species. Associated with the oaks are various hickories, shortleaf and Virginia pine, yellow-poplar, white ash, black walnut, and, formerly, chestnut. On the wetter soils silver maple, cottonwood, elm, and sycamore are found. White pine, sugar maple, and beech occur as secondary species in the Central hardwood forest, and in certain parts of it they form important constituents of the total stand. Perhaps no other forest region of the United States contains a greater number of tree species having high technical uses than does the Central forest. Mast-producing species such as oaks, hickories, walnut, and beech afford the Central hardwood forest great potentialities for wildlife. Squirrels, wild turkey, and deer, as well as lesser game animals, fatten on the nuts from these trees.

The characteristic forest types of the Central forest are those in which one or more species of oak are common, those in which shortleaf pine occurs, and those in which yellow-poplar, beech, silver maple, and river birch occur.

The forests of the Central states furnish a wide variety of products. Black walnut, shagbark and shellbark hickories, and beech produce edible nuts prized by many people (Fig. 13). The chestnut oak produces bark of high tannin content. Hickory, ash, and oaks are used for tool and implement handles. The various oaks, of which white oak is the most valuable, are used for railway ties, tight cooperage, furniture, veneers, and other products. White oak is particularly sought for ship timbers, because it is relatively impervious to moisture, is durable, holds nails and screws well, and is very strong. It is particularly valuable for keels, framing members, and skegs.

The two most valuable woods for cabinetwork, furniture, and a variety of special uses are black walnut and yellow-poplar. Both are straight-grained, uniform in texture, easily worked, strong, and durable. Because of its high resistance to shock, decay, and warping, black walnut is the preferred wood for gunstocks. Highly figured veneer is cut from black walnut stumps. Yellow-poplar produces a veneer suitable for core stock and for highly technical uses, including aircraft veneer.

Useful lumber is also cut from gum, silver maple, beech, sugar maple, and basswood. Black locust, cottonwood, American elm, sycamore, river birch, hackberry, buckeye, and a host of other minor species have a variety of uses. Locust is valuable for posts. Elm makes a tough veneer suitable for baskets and crating.

The conifers of the Central forest include Virginia pine, eastern redcedar, and shortleaf pine. Virginia pine seldom reaches sufficient size to be valuable for use as lumber, but it is used extensively for sulfate pulp. Eastern redcedar produces a fine-grained, aromatic wood valuable for manufacturing pencils and for cedar-lined chests and closets. Shortleaf pine produces lumber comparable in quality to that of the other southern pines. In general, the conifers occupy the poorer soils on land that had been abandoned for agriculture, and none of the three can maintain itself in competition with hardwoods.

Fig. 13 The Central hardwood forests are rich in an abundance of high-quality forest trees. The shellbark hickory or king nut. Turkey Run State Park, Indiana.

The growth rate in the Central forest is somewhat more rapid than the growth rate in the northern forest, and the stand density is about the same or somewhat less. Growth rates of 300 to 500 board feet per acre can be attained annually on well-stocked stands. Even higher growth rates could be expected were it not that agriculture has crowded the forest off the most productive soils. Heavy use is made of the forest for lumber, ties, posts, and other purposes. The Central region supports a great number of wood-using industries and therefore provides a good market for the better-quality trees that are produced. Next to the more highly industrialized sections of the North, the Central forest probably provides some of the best opportunities for intensive forest management.

The six Central states have a total of 42 million acres of commercial forest land (Table 1). Small ownerships scattered through the more rugged sections of southern Ohio, Indiana, Illinois, Missouri, and Kentucky are the rule. Foresters are used as wood-procurement officers for veneer mills and sawmills looking for high-quality oak, walnut, ash, hickory, and other products.

The Southern Forest Formations

The southern forest region begins with southern Delaware and extends along the coastal plain, including all but the tip of southern Florida, and west to eastern Texas and Oklahoma. The region sends a narrow tongue up the Mississippi Valley to southern Missouri and Illinois. Primarily, the southern forest region is a pine region with swamps occupied by baldcypress, tupelo, red and black gums, swamp oaks, and various other species, including evergreen magnolia, cottonwood, willows, and bays. From the standpoint of timber production the southern region is potentially the most important in the United States.

The southern coastal plain is a relatively level, sandy plain. The inland piedmont, up which the southern forest advances, is rolling to hilly in topography and has loam and clay soils. It is characterized by the long-leaf-loblolly-slash pine type groups and the cypress-tupelo-sweetgum groups. Upland hardwoods are highly valuable, including oaks, hickories, cucumber trees, yellow-poplars, and many others useful for furniture and construction.

The Southern Pine Forest. The southern pine forest is made up predominantly of four species: loblolly, shortleaf, longleaf, and slash pines; but pitch pine and pond pine occur to a limited extent.

Loblolly pine, which is rapid-growing and the most aggressive in invading old fields, grows in moderately dense stands and attains a height of approximately 100 feet and diameters up to 30 inches. The timber is of medium quality and, when properly manufactured and seasoned, is widely used for general construction.

Shortleaf pine produces lumber similar in quality to that of loblolly pine, but the tree grows somewhat more slowly and attains slightly smaller size.

Longleaf pine, which grows all along the coastal region, extending into western North Carolina and down along the coast as far west as Texas, is one of the most interesting pines. The needles attain lengths up to 12 inches. For the first four or five years of the tree's life it may remain in the grass stage, but during this time the tree develops a deep taproot and may attain a diameter of almost 1 inch at the ground surface. The huge terminal bud remains close to the ground and well protected by thick layers of bud scales. While in this stage, the plant resembles grass and may go entirely unnoticed by someone unfamiliar with its habits. After it becomes well established, the tree begins to grow in height, shooting up at the rate of a foot or more a year, and it continues to grow rapidly until it reaches maturity. Longleaf pine may attain a diameter of 24 inches or more and a height of 90 feet. The trees tend to grow rather widely separated, as considerable soil space is needed to obtain ample moisture.

Longleaf pine is one of the most fire-resistant of all conifers. While it is in the grass stage, fires may consume the needles yet fail to kill the terminal bud. After the tree has attained a height of 20 feet or more, fires may burn through at frequent intervals with only limited damage to this tree.

Longleaf pine produces a strong, heavy, dense lumber with a high resin content. It is highly prized for general construction. Longleaf is the principal producer of gum for naval stores.

Slash pine, the most rapid-growing of all southern pines, resembles longleaf pine in many respects. Slash pine has a restricted natural distribution, but it has been successfully planted outside its natural range. It is almost equal to longleaf pine as a producer of naval stores. Both of these pines reproduce poorly after the stands reach maturity. Undergrowth of palmetto, various grasses, and resinous shrubs may exclude pine seedlings unless removed by controlled burning (Fig. 14).

The growth rate of southern forest trees is high. At 20 years of age southern pines may be harvested for pulpwood, at 40 years for piling and lumber. Plantations have given especially high yields in pulpwood. Since 1935 pulp production in the southern states has expanded at a rapid rate. High-grade kraft paper may be made from southern pines by the sulfate process. The fibers are long and the paper is very strong. It is used for bags and wrapping.

The potential growth rate per acre in southern forests is not greatly in excess of that found in the Central and northern forests. Five hundred board feet per acre annually is not unusual, though it is far above the

Fig. 14 A selectively cut slash pine forest from which a second cutting may be harvested within a few years. (*South Carolina State Commission of Forestry and AFPI photo.*)

average. A growth rate of 400 board feet per acre per year would be a good goal for the southern forest owner to work toward.

Open southern forests support grass useful for grazing livestock. Cattle can be grown along with pine trees in the South, though tree growth is generally better where grazing is excluded. Hogs are extensively pastured in southern forests. Where pasturing is moderate, the damage done is less than the value of the meat produced.

Southern Hardwood Forests. The river bottoms and adjacent uplands of the South support extensive hardwood forests. Among commercial species are ash, cottonwood, blackgum, maple, various oaks, walnut, and yellow-poplar. Associated with these in swamplands are baldcypress and white-cedar. Much of the land is subject to periodic flooding, which tends to control special composition. These forests produce some high-quality timber suitable for veneer, tight cooperage, lumber, specialty stock, piling, and other products. Growth rates are relatively rapid, 500 to 700 board feet per acre per year for good stands. Cutting cycles can be as short as eight years.

The South Atlantic States. Virginia and North and South Carolina have a total of 46 million acres of commercial forest land (Table 1). The forests occur in three topographic subregions: the coastal plain, the piedmont, and the Appalachian Mountains. These subregions support respectively the southern, central, and northern forest associations. The coastal plain region is low-lying and supports primarily pine, of which loblolly and shortleaf predominate. The piedmont region has a mixture of pine and hardwoods, with hardwoods tending to take over the land after the pine crop is harvested. The Appalachian Mountain area is high and rugged and is made up primarily of hardwoods with scattered spruce and fir at high elevations. Ownership is primarily in small holdings in the mountains and piedmont sections and in large holdings in the coastal plain.

Both lumber and pulp manufacture are major industries in the South Atlantic states. A well-developed furniture industry is centered at High Point, North Carolina. Novelty manufacture is common among the mountain folk. This section of the South is developing rapidly industrially and in forest management and forest industry. The kraft pulp mill at Georgetown, South Carolina, the world's largest, uses 800,000 cords of wood a year.[12]

The Southeastern States. Tennessee, Mississippi, Alabama, Georgia, and Florida have 95 million acres of commercial forest land (Table 1). This is the real southern pine region. It is characterized by loblolly and slash pine in the south, by hardwoods in Tennessee and the northern sections of adjoining states. This region embraces a large portion of the cotton and tobacco belt. More and more these states are looking to timber to take the place of these surplus soil-exhausting crops.

Both large and small ownerships are found in the Southeast. The small ownerships are characteristic of the more rugged sections of Tennessee, Georgia, and Alabama. The large holdings are found farther south in the coastal plain region. The Southeast has many problems in common with the South Atlantic states, for example, a tendency for the pine to be replaced by hardwoods and consequently the need for silvicultural measures to maintain the most valuable timber crops. It also has a considerable volume of hardwoods, particularly the Mississippi-bottomland hardwoods, for which only moderate use has been found. This region is growing industrially and is growing in the importance of its lumber and pulp and paper industries. The naval-stores industry is primarily a small business, which probably has reached its peak of development. Synthetic chemicals are being substituted for the natural turpentine and rosin produced from pine resin.

The Gulf States. Arkansas, Louisiana, Oklahoma, and Texas have a total of 52 million acres of commercial forest land (Table 1), made up

primarily of southern pine and hardwood. Some of the best pine-pro-
ducing lands are to be found in southern Arkansas and Louisiana.
Sustained-yield forestry has been practiced here by several lumber companies for a number of years. Much of the soil is better than that to be
found in the coastal plain of the Southeast; hence forest growth is more
rapid. Except for the narrow belt along the Gulf Coast, this section has
been only moderately industrialized. Agriculture is a major activity,
particularly the growing of cotton. Both longleaf and loblolly pine do
well in this section, but loblolly perhaps occupies a more important place
than any other one species. Though some large paper mills are found in
East Texas, lumber manufacture rather than pulp and paper manufacture is the major industry in this region. Interest in forestry has been developing rapidly in this section of the South. The value of forest land is
relatively high because of the rapid rate of growth. Since many small
investors appreciate the value of a good tract of timberland, speculation
in it has been widespread. Meager rainfall helps to maintain pine in a
region that might otherwise go to hardwoods. Development of wood-
using industries in this section is still only moderate, and good opportunities exist for future expansion.

The plains region is not a natural forest area. Trees are confined
largely to stream courses and shelter groves. These will be discussed
elsewhere.

The Rocky Mountain Forest Formations

The Rocky Mountain forest is bounded by the plains region on the
east, the Sierras and Cascades on the west, Canada on the north, and
Mexico on the south. The forests in the Rockies are located almost exclusively in the mountains. At the lowest levels, where forests are located
principally along the stream courses, aspen, cottonwood, willows, and
alder prevail. In the foothills may be found the Rocky Mountain juniper,
the bur oak, and western live oak, and in the south mesquite and the
piñon pine. These trees, growing in open groves or as scattered individuals, carry out the struggle between the true forest vegetation found
at higher elevations and the desert scrub, sagebrush, and shortgrass plains
at the lower elevation. Moisture and protection from too severe exposure to sun and wind favor the trees. Droughts, fire, and open ex-
posures favor desert scrub and grasses.

Proceeding up the mountain slopes, one encounters ponderosa pine,
blue spruce, more aspen, and oftentimes scrub oaks and maples. At
middle elevations lodgepole pine, western white pine, grand fir, western
larch, Douglas-fir, and white fir occur. Here are found the most productive forests. In Idaho and western Montana are some of the best forests
to be found anywhere in the Rockies. Western white pine, western hem-

Fig. 15   Strip cutting of lodgepole pine on the Gunnison National Forest, Colorado. (*U.S. Forest Service photo.*)

lock, and ponderosa pine form splendid stands with volumes per acre in excess of 20,000 board feet. The trees attain large size, with diameters of 3 feet or more and heights in excess of 140 feet. They produce excellent lumber. From Colorado southward the trees are generally much smaller in size and the lumber value of the timber is modest. These forests do contain many trees of pulpwood size, but water supply is generally inadequate to support pulp mills.

At higher elevations lodgepole pine becomes more common than ponderosa pine, the Douglas-fir and Engelmann spruce are more common than blue spruce, and limber pine appears (Fig. 15). At high elevations mountain hemlock, alpine fir, Engelmann spruce, red fir, whitebark pine, and bristlecone pine are the common species. Just as the forest thins out at low elevations, so also does it thin out at high elevations. Here the trees must find shelter against the high winds that sweep across the mountain crests and against the driving snow which tends to flatten them down to the ground. They must be able to perform their life functions in the short summer period when the mountain peaks are free from snow. Ravines and protected slopes where the snow does not drift too deeply are forested at higher elevations than exposed ridges. Timberline occurs at about 11,000 to 12,000 feet in the central Rockies, at 8,000 to 10,000 feet near the Canadian border.

In the intermountain or great-basin region the forests are found only on the isolated mountain ranges that occur in this area. Their distribution is limited to a relatively narrow belt varying from about 7,000 to 10,000 feet in elevation.

The chief products of the central and southern Rocky Mountain forests are water, forage for domestic livestock, and recreation. Timber operations for increasing water yield have been given serious consideration. Use for recreation interferes little with the forest. The value of these mountain forests as range for domestic livestock is often of considerable importance to local ranchers. Forage yields are low because of short growing seasons, but the grass becomes available when plains and foothill ranges have passed their productive peak. Where wisely administered, grazing in mountain forests harvests a useful resource without serious damage to water yield, timber, or recreational use.

The southern Rocky Mountain region has a total of 73 million acres of forest land, of which only 20 million acres are commercial. Most of the forest land is in public ownership, and forest industries consist primarily of sawmills and industries preparing forest products for local use.

The northern Rocky Mountain states—Wyoming, Idaho, and Montana and the Black Hills region of South Dakota—have a total of 53 million acres of forest land, of which 34 million acres are commercial. Much of this forest land produces valuable timber with rapid growth rate, and potentialities for sustained-yield forestry are good. Of the commercial forest land, the greater part, 22 million acres, is in national forests. An additional 4 million acres are found in other forms of public ownership. Private ownership totals 8 million acres, of which half is in large holdings.[15] This region is being heavily cut over so that the forest industries are declining rather than increasing in activity. The region is unlikely to develop very rapidly industrially or agriculturally. Manufacture of forest products is primarily for lumber, poles, and ties. The use of high mountain country by recreationists is almost certain to grow. Range management is a major activity of the region and will undoubtedly be intensified in the years to come.

The Pacific Coast Forest Formations

The forests of the Pacific Coast are the grandest and most awe-inspiring to be found anywhere in the world. These are exceptionally heavy timber producers. Here are found the nation's most valuable forest trees (Fig. 1): the Douglas-fir, ponderosa pine, sugar pine, western white pine, redwood, Sitka spruce, western redcedar, Port-Orford-cedar, and, in the Sierras, white fir, red fir, and the bigtree.

The most valuable commercial stands occur in the North Pacific region, where Douglas-fir and western hemlock are in mixture with Sitka spruce, silver fir, and western redcedar. Here stands of great density occur, up to 100,000 board feet an acre or even higher. Douglas-fir trees 6 to 8 feet in diameter and containing seven to twelve 16-foot logs are not uncommon. The forests of this region attain their density and impressive development because of the high rainfall and favorable temperature. Winter snows are rare along the Coast, and dry periods infrequent and of relatively short duration. Beyond the coast range are dry interior valleys that tend to be devoid of trees. As the Sierras and Cascades are approached, the forests again resume sway and hold it up to timberline, which occurs at about 12,000 feet in the South and 8,000 feet in the North.

The three Pacific Coast states together contain more than half the reserve sawtimber volume of the United States. From these uncut forests of fir, pine, and redwood comes the major volume of high-grade softwood lumber.

The forests of the North Pacific region require very heavy logging equipment for their utilization. High-lead logging equipment has been destructive, as trees not large enough to log are broken over as the huge logs are skidded out. Such logging, however, removed only about half the woody volume of the logged area. In recent years the large lumber companies have found it profitable to send in a crew with moderately heavy equipment to take out the small-sized trees suitable for pulpwood and small sawlogs before the large trees are cut. The heavy equipment is next brought in to harvest the main timber crop. Since a considerable volume of useful material may still be left in tops and broken logs, a third operation may then be carried out. This normally requires use of a portable mill equipped to saw small-dimension material from broken logs and tops and from small-sized trees that have been injured. Prelogging, logging, and postlogging are terms used to designate these three operations.

Logging and lumber manufacture represent a major item in the economy and receive important attention from legislatures and citizens. All three of the Pacific Coast states have adopted forest-practice laws which, by removing the competition of the irresponsible operator, are making the practice of forestry on private lands more economical for all owners. The pulp and paper industry is likewise developed on the Pacific Coast. Douglas-fir plywood manufacture is a unique feature of West Coast industry. The West Coast, a rapidly developing region, is perhaps closer to industrial maturity than the South. The development of the wood-using industry in the West aside from plywood, lumber, and pulp and paper manufacture has proceeded at a moderate pace. Opportunity exists for additional industries engaged in intensive wood processing in the West.

Many communities in the West that depend upon sawmills for their main source of income are destined to undergo economic decline unless some substitute industry can be found. The virgin timber resource is rapidly being depleted, and new industries to use second growth are not in all cases available to fill the gap. The next 20 to 30 years are likely to see major economic adjustments in individual companies and communities. The exploitative phase of forestry has still to run its full course.

The Pacific Northwest. Oregon and Washington have a total of 54 million acres of forest land, of which 45 million are commercial. About 26 million acres are in various forms of public ownership, primarily national forests, and the remainder is held by lumber companies, pulp companies, farmers, and nonfarmers. The total area in private ownership is 20 million acres. Special skill is required in the North Pacific forest to protect the land from fire. Nature is here more friendly to the forester than in the Sierras, but when the Pacific Coast forest does become dry, it forms a tinderbox far more difficult to control than anywhere else in the United States. The huge Tillamook fire of 1933 swept over more than 270,000 acres and destroyed 10 billion board feet of mature timber before it finally burned itself out. This fire paved the way for other serious fires in 1939 and 1945. Over 110,000 acres burned in 1945.

Some of the country's largest private timber companies are located in Washington and Oregon.[9] Favored by the rapid growth of young timber, these are progressively placing operations on a sustained-yield basis. It was here that the tree-farm movement originated, and many companies maintain large forestry departments integrated with all woods-management activities. Second-growth timberland is in high demand by lumber and pulp companies. Integrated use of wood in grouped mills manufacturing lumber, veneer, and pulp is developing rapidly. Banks and other financial institutions take an active interest in the forest-products industries and encourage commitments for long-term operation. The general outlook for forestry is very bright in the Pacific Coast states.[4]

California. California has 45 million acres of forest land of which 17 million are commercial (Table 1). About half the commercial forest land is in national forests, about 3 million acres are owned by lumber companies, and the rest by farmers and nonfarm holders. Exploitation of these forests is primarily by large companies which either own timberland or purchase stumpage from the national forests.

Along the Pacific Coast from the Oregon border down almost to San Francisco lies the redwood region, the world's most impressive forest. The sight of this evokes a feeling of awe and reverence. Here, magnificent red-barked trees from 6 to 12 feet or more in diameter lift their crowns 200, 300, and even 350 feet above the ground. Shafts of sunlight filter through the crowns like light from the lofty windows of a huge cathedral. The forest floor is covered with a deep bed of needles which cushion the step. An individual tree contains enough wood to build a modern house, and stands on a single acre would build a village. This is truly a forest of the giants.

Redwood logging is a difficult and slow operation. The huge trees must be very carefully felled if their stems are not to be shattered when they strike the ground. Oftentimes it is necessary to prepare a cradle made up of branches and small trees as a bed to break the fall of the giants. The bark on these massive trees is 5 to 6 inches in thickness. The logs must, therefore, be handled with sling equipment rather than grabhooks. After logging, a huge amount of debris is left on the ground to be disposed of, ordinarily by burning, before a second crop can be started.

Redwood trees attain ages in excess of 1,000 years. Hence, a forest once felled will not be regrown short of 500 or more years. Fortunately, redwood can be used in smaller sizes and grows very rapidly. The growth of redwood and Douglas-fir forests may exceed 1,000 board feet per acre annually under good growing conditions.

The Sierra forests contain giant Sequoia, ponderosa pine, sugar pine, western white pine, whitebark pine, Jeffrey pine, lodgepole pine, Douglas-fir, white fir, red fir, and incense-cedar. These also are impressive forests. The sugar pine may attain a diameter of 6 feet or more and contain five to seven logs 16 feet long. The Douglas-fir and ponderosa pine attain large size and have high value for timber use. The stands are considerably less dense than those along the coast. The Sierra forests are drier than those of the northern Pacific Coast. Hence, protection against fire requires the greatest vigilance. These high slopes, once burned over, are oftentimes difficult to reproduce to trees, especially if they become overgrown with mountain mahogany, manzanita, *Ceanothus,* and other shrubby species. A high degree of skill is required of the forester to maintain the Sierra forests in high productivity and to protect the watersheds from erosion and flash floods.

Alaska. The forests of the state of Alaska deserve special attention, both because of their somewhat unique nature and because of their large size. The state as a whole has an area of some 375 million acres. Public-domain forests cover about 125 million acres, and the two national forests, Tongass and Chugach, jointly occupy 21 million acres. Under the terms of the Statehood Act of July 7, 1958, the state of Alaska was granted and entitled to select 400,000 acres of open public domain as well as 400,000 acres of national forest lands for community and recreational development. In addition, it could select for state use an additional 102,550,000 acres from the open public domain. This is an area slightly larger than California.[16]

One of the major attractions for many people stems from Alaska's rugged scenery and its abundant wildlife resources. Game fish, Sitka deer, brown and black bear, mountain goats, and Dall sheep are a challenge to every sportsman who can afford the time and the cost of a trip to Alaska. For those interested in scenery alone, the trip by boat up the Inland Passage is one never to be forgotten.

The forests may be divided into two zones: coastal and interior. The coastal forests are made up largely of hemlock and spruce. The forests extend along the coast of Alaska for almost 1,000 miles, yet occupy less than 10 per cent of the area of the state. Much of the commercial timber is within 2½ miles of tidewater. Timber growth is favored by a relatively warm and humid climate tempered by the Japan Current.

The coastal timber is impressive. Stand volumes may run as high as 100,000 board feet per acre, and over extensive areas they average 35,000 board feet per acre.[1] Second-growth stands are estimated capable of producing, over a rotation of 110 years, some 70,000 board feet per acre. The Tongass Forest has some 92 billion board feet of gross volume on land that is considered to be commercially operable. Western hemlock makes up 64 per cent of the volume, Sitka spruce 29 per cent, western redcedar and Alaskan cedar 7 per cent. Cottonwood and red alder are present in minor amounts. Similar timber stands are found on the Chugach Forest, though individual trees and stand volumes are lower than on the Tongass. The timber quality on both forests is well suited for pulpwood. The Ketchikan Pulp Company, manufacturing a high grade of dissolving pulp, has a daily capacity of between 550 and 600 tons. The Japanese-owned Alaska Paper and Pulp Company opened a 450-ton high alpha-cellulose pulp mill in 1959.[1]

The interior of Alaska is cold and dry. Much of the land is underlain by permafrost. The forests are extensive, made up largely of black and white spruce with mixtures of birch and aspen. These forests at present are little utilized, but the pattern is shifting rapidly as population grows and industry develops in this forty-ninth state.

About 40 million acres may be classed as commercial forest land.[16] Growth on interior forests is estimated at 2 billion board feet annually. Some 70 small sawmills were operating in 1958, but the total cut was estimated at no more than 20 million board feet, less than 1 per cent of that allowable on a sustained-yield basis. It is estimated that some 90 per cent of the lumber used locally in the interior was imported, largely because of the poor quality of the locally produced material.[16]

Much of the land has been ravaged by fires. Lightning fires are common. Because of lack of transportation other than air and because of limited resources for fire fighting, the problem of fire control on interior forests is a staggering one (Fig. 16). Funds for control were $625,000 in 1960.[11] Although fires cause terrific damage, it is recognized that throughout the ages they have shaped the character of Alaskan forests.

Fɪɢ. 16   A local fire crew getting ready to board a plane bound for a fire on Alaska's interior forests. A scattered stand of spruce trees borders the landing strip. (*U.S. Bureau of Land Management photo.*)

Burning off a coniferous forest with its heavy layer of organic matter exposes mineral soil with its favorable seedbed for aspen, birch, and spruce. Also, exposure to sunlight increases the depth of unfrozen soil.[8]

Tropical Forests

Tropical forests in the continental United States are confined entirely to the southern tip of Florida below Lake Okeechobee. These are subtropical rather than tropical. The land is mostly swampy and covered with thickets of mangrove and other saltwater shrubs. The coconut palm is found along the coast. The tropical forest in Florida has little value for commercial timber production, though it does serve to protect the soil from erosion when heavy seas occur. Within the swampy lands of southern Florida live many large birds and animals, including alligators, crocodiles, flamingos, and other creatures that require the solitude of remote areas for their homes.

The state of Hawaii, in the subtropic latitudes of 19 to 22°N, consists of eight main islands and several islets along a 390-mile chain. The total area is 4,111,000 acres. Kauai, the westernmost of the major islands, is the oldest and has the deepest soils. Originally, the better soils on all islands were well forested with sandalwoods and koa, known commercially as Hawaiian mahogany. The level, deep soils on all islands have been taken over for cultivation of sugarcane and pineapple. Forests remain on the steep mountain slopes and the thin-soiled lava flows. A large part of the forest area is covered with desert scrub, of which mesquite is a typical species at the lower elevations. Most of the forest is found between 2,000- and 8,000-foot elevations. The forests have been badly abused through overcutting and grazing by wild goats, pigs, and cattle. Hawaiian forests are now managed mainly for watershed protection and for recreational use. A small amount of timber is harvested locally and sawed in the four sawmills found on the Islands. The rainfall on many of the Hawaiian Islands is excessive. One mountain on the island of Kauai has more than 800 inches of rainfall a year. The forest officers in Hawaii are attempting to plant burned-over areas and denuded forest lands with tree species that will be particularly valuable in maintaining the soil in condition to absorb moisture rapidly.[6, 10, 14]

The United States has real tropical forests in Puerto Rico and the Virgin Islands. Puerto Rico, an island about the size of Connecticut, has a great diversity of vegetation. At its eastern end rainfall is in excess

Fig. 17   A 48-inch tabanuco tree, Luquillo Experimental Forest, Puerto Rico. (*U.S. Forest Service photo.*)

of 200 inches annually, and dense tropical rain forests can be found. Here are giant tabanucos, guaraguaos, ausubos, and the valuable *Magnolia splendens*. The forest is highly diversified, supports large trees, and has a rapid growth rate (Fig. 17). Many of the woods are hard, heavy, durable, have beautiful figured grains, and, once properly seasoned, are suitable for cabinetwork.

In a range of mountains extending along the island from east to west are found most of Puerto Rico's forests. On the rest of the island the demands of agriculture and grazing are so heavy that space does not exist for growing timber. Coffee is cultivated at moderately high elevations under the shade of trees. Agricultural research has demonstrated that coffee can be grown without shade on Puerto Rico if the soil is properly fertilized. The yield of sun-grown coffee can be tenfold that of shade-grown. A revolution was taking place in this form of mountain agriculture in 1961.

The moderately dry sections of Puerto Rico will grow mahogany, silk cottonwood, Spanish cedar, teak, and other valuable trees. The tabanuco will also grow on moderately dry lands. On the driest sections of the island only cactus and lignum vitae will survive. The latter is one of the heaviest and densest woods that occur anywhere. It is richly impregnated with waxes and therefore is a wood valuable for making stuffing boxes for the propeller shafts on ships.

The forests of Puerto Rico have been intensively utilized for fuel and, to a limited extent, for construction timbers. It will be a long and difficult process to build up the forests to supply the needs of the local population. The Tropical Forest Research Institute maintained at Río Piedras is accumulating much valuable information on how to protect and manage tropical forests.

The three Virgin Islands—St. Croix, St. Thomas, and St. John—total only 133 square miles in area and have limited commercial forests.

LITERATURE CITED

1. Bruce, Mason B. 1960. "National Forests in Alaska," *Journal of Forestry,* 58:437–442.
2. Cunningham, R. N., and Forest Survey Staff. 1950. "Forest Resources of the Lake States Region," U.S. Department of Agriculture, Forest Resource Report 1, Washington. 57 pp.
3. Guernsey, Roger L. 1961. "State Forestry in the United States, 1961." Memorandum to Ralph Wible, President, Association of State Foresters. 5 pp. mim.
4. Guthrie, John A., and George R. Armstrong. 1961. "Western Forest Industry: An Economic Outlook," The Johns Hopkins Press, Baltimore. 324 pp.

5. Hawley, R. C., Chairman. 1944. "Forest Terminology," Society of American Foresters, Washington, D.C. 84 pp.

6. Judd, C. S. 1935. "Forestry in Hawaii," *Journal of Forestry*, 33:1005–1006.

7. Lewison, Wayne C. 1949. "What Is Private Forestry Doing in the Northeast from the Viewpoint of an Industrial Forester?" *Proceedings, Society of American Foresters' Meeting*, Boston, 1948, pp. 189–190, Washington, D.C.

8. Lutz, H. J. 1960. "Fire as an Ecological Factor in the Boreal Forests of Alaska," *Journal of Forestry*, 58:444–460.

9. Moir, Stuart, DeWitt Nelson, Michael Bigley, William H. Price, and W. D. Hagenstein. 1949. "What Is Private Forestry Doing in the West?" *Proceedings, Society of American Foresters' Meeting*, Boston, 1948, pp. 169–181, Washington, D.C.

10. Rhett, Beverly. 1947. "Sugarwater Forests," *American Forests*, 53(1): 8–10, 47–48.

11. Robinson, R. R. 1960. "Forest and Range Fire Control in Alaska," *Journal of Forestry*, 58:448–453.

12. Seigworth, Kenneth J., Ray F. Bower, Harley Langdale, Jr., and Paul M. Garrison. 1949. "What Is Private Forestry Doing in the South?" *Proceedings, Society of American Foresters' Meeting*, Boston, 1948, pp. 159–169, Washington, D.C.

13. Sewall, Joseph. 1949. "What Is Private Forestry Doing in the Northeast?" *Proceedings, Society of American Foresters' Meeting*, Boston, 1948, pp. 184–186, Washington, D.C.

14. United Nations, Food and Agriculture Organization. 1948. "National Situations: Information on Forestry and Forest Products in Asia and the Pacific Area," *Unasylva*, 2(6): 330–331.

15. U.S. Department of Agriculture, Forest Service. 1958. "Timber Resources for America's Future," Forest Resource Report 14, Washington. 713 pp.

16. Zumwalt, Eugene V. 1960. "The Alaska Public Domain," *Journal of Forestry*, 58:443–447.

FOREST TREES, in common with other long-lived plants and animals, have no fixed life span. Some, such as aspen, rarely exceed an age of 70 to 90 years, but eastern hemlock may live for 700 years and the giant Sequoia to 4,000 years. Even the most massive of all trees may be surpassed in age by the giant cypress of Mexico and the gnarled and weather-beaten ancient bristlecone pines of Arizona. Specimens of the latter have been found with over 4,600 annual-growth rings. Few trees die because of age alone. Instead they become broken by storm, are struck by lightning, are weakened by drought, are attacked by insects, or break off from the onslaughts by heart-rotting fungi.

Groups of trees growing together in forest stands also have no fixed age. But stands, like individual trees, reach a stage of maturity in which they contain the maximum of sound-wood volume. Thereafter, the stand thins out. Individual trees become defective. Fallen stems and broken tops indicate decadence. In such stands many trees weaken at about the same time, thus presenting insects and disease organisms an opportunity to build up to outbreak proportions. Open conditions favor windthrows and allow the sun to dry the surface litter so that fires, if started by lightning or other causes, spread rapidly.

The purpose of forest protection is to forestall these and other losses so that man will have plenty of trees to serve his own needs. This is accomplished by direct attack on fires, insects, and other destructive agents and by managing the forest so that conditions conducive to damaging outbreaks are minimized.

Controlling Fire

Man has always feared forest fires, and with good reason. The Peshtigo fire in Wisconsin in 1871 burned 1¼ million acres and took 1,500 lives.[9] The same year a 2-million-acre fire in Michigan took 138 lives. In 1894 the Hinckley fire in Minnesota burned over 160,000 acres, taking 418 lives. The great Idaho fire in 1910 burned 2 million acres and cost 85 lives. The 1918 Cloquet fire in Minnesota took 432 lives. The Tillamook fire of 1933 in Oregon burned 270,000 acres. Fires in the same area burned again in 1939 and in 1945, bringing the total burned-over area to 310,000 acres.[28] In 1947 a huge fire in Maine burned over 220,000 acres, destroying 1,000 homes and taking 16 lives.[4, 27] Total damage was estimated at $30 million. Even small fires have been known to take life. On August 5, 1949, Montana's 5,000-acre Mann Gulch fire killed 13 people, 12 of them experienced smoke jumpers. The crew was caught despite exercising every reasonable precaution against a disaster.[6] The same year a district ranger was killed fighting a small fire on the St. Jo National Forest.

Man's Attitude toward Forest Fires. In early days fires were generally looked upon as a benefit in that they burned off woody growth obstructing agriculture. Even today there are those who feel that fire in the woods is desirable to kill snakes and chiggers, to improve grazing, and to clean out the undergrowth. As the country became settled, however, man's attitude toward forest fires changed from tolerance to respect and fear.

Federal and state forest officers were the first to assume responsibility for protecting wild lands against fires. Expenditures by state agencies for fire prevention and control exceed those for all other forestry purposes. Federal and state expenditures for control of forest fire on state and private lands were $56,641,000 in 1960.[26] This is exclusive of expenditures for fire detection and suppression on the national forests and by the Bureau of Land Management for protecting the interior forests of Alaska.

Even so, forest fires in 1960 burned 3,856,000 acres of state and private lands and 421,000 acres of national forests. The fire year was a bad one in which 104,000 fires occurred. More than half the area burned on state and private lands resulted from 13,700 fires on 8 per cent of the land that received no protection. The progress of state and private fire-control efforts since 1945 has been good, as the following record attests: [2, 26]

Year	Protected area, million acres	Area burned, million acres
1945	302.9	17.2
1950	360.5	15.1
1955	387.1	7.4
1960	403.0	3.9

By 1960, fire control had been extended to 92 per cent of all state and private lands and to all national forest land.

Forest fires destroy wildlife, mature timber, and young growth. They strip the soil of its protective cover, thereby augmenting floods. A very destructive flood occurred in Salt Lake City in 1945 on a watershed of about 600 acres that had been burned over 11 months before the flood came. The fire itself did little direct damage, but the flood caused damage of $347,000. A 225-acre fire near San Antonio was responsible for a flood causing damage of $47,000.[10]

Notwithstanding the disastrous effects of uncontrolled fires, there are times and places where controlled fires are useful tools. In areas of the South, grass and pine needles accumulate on the forest floor, forming a heavy "rough." Burning this rough under careful control during the winter eliminates fuel that might give rise to disastrous fires in spring and fall. Such controlled burning tends to discourage hardwoods and favors the reproduction of longleaf pine, a very fire-resistant species. It also lessens damage by brown-spot needle disease of longleaf pine.

With forest management come roads, trails, working crews scattered over the forest, and detailed control plans. Fire control becomes integrated with forest management.

Causes and Prevention of Forest Fires. The objective of fire-control planning is to prevent as many fires as possible and to suppress those that do start before they get large. Only one forest fire in ten is due to lightning; nine are due to man's carelessness. Smokers, incendiaries, and debris burners cause two-thirds of all fires. Railroads, campers, lumbering operations, and miscellaneous causes account for the remainder. Man-caused fires have been reduced by shutting down logging operations during hazardous periods, installing spark arresters on locomotives, requiring permits for debris burners, enforcing state laws against incendiaries, closing forests to sportsmen in severe seasons, and by constantly calling the attention of the public to the necessity for caution with fire in the woods.[25]

PRESUPPRESSION ACTIVITIES. Presuppression activities are closely related to fire prevention. The causes of fire are analyzed, and a major fire plan is prepared to provide prompt detection and suppression. Fire lines and roads are constructed to furnish access and lines from which fires may be effectively fought. Equipment is obtained and located at strategic points. Forest fuel–types are mapped and efforts are made to reduce fuel on areas where fires are most likely to start. Fire-danger rating stations are established, at which weather readings are systematically taken and measurements made of the moisture content of forest fuel. Fire-danger meters are devised to integrate the hazards due to temperature, humidity, fuel moisture content, days since last rain, wind velocity, season, and time of day.

Fire-danger meters and burning-index meters permit calculating rate of spread of fire. The fire dispatcher, with other information available to him, can thus determine the size of crew to dispatch to bring the fire under control. Seasoned judgment must, of course, be used with these aids.[11]

The key to quick action is prompt detection. Trained watchers in lookout towers are on constant alert during hazardous periods. They spot the fire, determine its location and probable size, and telephone the information to the district ranger. Ground and air patrols may be used when visibility from lookouts is poor.

FIRE SUPPRESSION. A small fire can oftentimes be controlled by one man or by a very small crew. Small fires are fought directly with shovels, rakes, fire swatters, water from backpack pumps, and other simple tools. The crew first knocks down the hot spots, cuts off the head of the fire, and then proceeds to build a line around its flanks and rear.

On large fires camps must be established with a supply system, workshop, communication center, and fire-camp headquarters. A relatively large organization may be involved, with a thousand or more men working on the fire line. Coordination becomes a major item, and communication must be established between the fire boss and the foremen who are responsible for the several sectors. Heavy equipment may include bulldozers, heavy fire plows, and tank trucks with hose for spraying water on hot spots (Fig. 18).

Kinds of Forest Fires. GROUND FIRE. The ground fire occurs where the fire burns in a heavy layer of duff or peat such as accumulates in a swamp.[12] Such fires may burn to a depth of 6 feet or more and are extremely difficult to put out without digging out the burning material. They burn slowly and are not a serious menace in themselves, but they may smolder for weeks and then suddenly set surface material afire.

SURFACE FIRES. These fires, which are the commonest of all, burn the dry vegetation and forest litter. Where tree growth is sparse, such fires may travel rapidly. Wind accelerates rate of spread.

Surface fires can be fought with all types of equipment and by many stratagems. Small fires can be fought on the advancing front, quickly knocked down, and the flanks then extinguished. Fire fighters usually attack large fires on the flanks, working toward the head. On very large fires, lines are prepared in advance of the fire. As the surface fire approaches, backfires are set and are drawn by the draft of the head fire down toward it. The two fires then meet some distance back of the fire line and burn themselves out, but constant vigilance must be exercised to extinguish any spot fires that occur from sparks thrown over the fire line.

CROWN FIRES. These burn in the crowns of coniferous trees, are exceedingly hot, travel rapidly, and can run many rods ahead of the accompany-

FIG. 18   A Mathis fire plow is used to suppress wild fire on the Ocala National Forest, Florida. (*U.S. Forest Service photo.*)

ing ground fire. Usually the heat from the surface fire dries out the needles and heats them to the ignition point. Crown fires are very spectacular. They throw sparks for long distances, and great care must be exercised in fighting them lest the crew be entrapped in the fire. Crown fires can best be fought by putting out the surface fire during the night and early morning, when the crown fire generally dies out. The only other available method may be to fight such fires by means of backfires that burn off the surface material that would provide the heat necessary to keep the crown fire going.

After any fire has been brought under control, mop-up operations begin and continue until the last spark is out. Mop-up involves digging out burning stumps, burying logs, felling burning snags, and digging out fire in peat or heavy litter.

Use of Aircraft. Aircraft are used for patrol, observation, and transport of men, equipment, and supplies. Airplanes equipped with tanks holding up to 4,000 gallons of fire-retardant liquids have been used in squadrons to attack forest fires directly. These are effective in stopping or retarding small fires until ground crews arrive. Helicopters are also being used to spread fire retardants. Sodium calcium borate and swelling bentonite clay are used in slurry form as fire retardants.[20] Monoammonium and diammonium phosphates with and without thickeners are also reported to have given good control on going fires. Attempts have also been made to dissipate electric charges causing lightning by seeding clouds with dry ice.[4] Helicopters have been used for scouting, liaison, and landing men near the fire line. They can be used by the fire boss as a base of control. They can transport equipment and evacuate injured men. They are also being used to transport special crews that jump from the craft to the ground to attack the fire directly or to prepare spots where the craft may land with men and supplies [20] (Fig. 19).

The most spectacular use of aircraft is transport of smoke jumpers. These skilled fire fighters are flown to the fire, then parachute down, arriving fresh within a short time after the fire is detected. Thousands of jumps have been made. Even though parachuting in rugged tree-covered country is hazardous, the smoke jumpers have had a remarkable safety record.

Fig. 19 Loading a fire crew and equipment into a helicopter to take off for a fire in interior Alaska. (*U.S. Bureau of Land Management photo.*)

Fire-control Organizations. A fire-control organization is of necessity large and far-flung, and a maximum of responsibility must rest on the men on the ground. On national forests the district forest ranger is usually the fire boss. In state forest organizations the district foresters have this responsibility. The state forester backs them up with extra equipment and manpower if required but does not attempt to take over the job unless the district organization breaks down.

The northeastern states have enacted a fire-control compact with central coordination which permits states to furnish men and equipment to a neighbor state if a fire threatens both states or is too large for one state organization to handle.

Despite the great progress that has been made in nationwide fire control, there still remained in 1960 some 32 million acres without organized control.[26] On this area 13,700 fires occurred in 1960, burning 6.0 per cent of the land. This rate is six times as high per unit area as that on protected lands.

Review. After a large forest fire has been extinguished, there remains the final job of reviewing the fire. This includes determining where it started, determining the cause of its starting, and a review of the initial action taken, of all subsequent actions, and of their efficacy in hastening the time when final control was achieved.

Growth Impact

Fire is the most dramatic cause of loss of timber, but diseases and insects are even more destructive. Fire, insects, diseases, and other destructive agents cause death of live timber of merchantable size. This, however, is not their total damage. They delay restocking of damaged forest areas, and they reduce growth rate because of changes in timber site and type, by weakening trees and by defoliation. They also may kill trees below merchantable size. The combined effect has been designated as growth impact.[24] The U.S. Forest Service estimated growth impact for 1952 to be as shown in Table 2. Diseases are seen to cause 45 per cent of the total growth impact, insects 16 per cent, and fire 15 per cent. Together total losses less salvage were estimated to be 10,440 million cubic feet in 1952. The timber cut for commercial use that year was 12,274 million cubic feet.[24] These heavy losses by natural agents have caused the U.S. Forest Service, the state foresters, and private forest landowners to increase substantially their efforts to detect and control forest insects and diseases. The federal appropriation for control of diseases and insects for the fiscal year 1962 was $9,350,000. An additional $2,995,000 was spent for research on insects and diseases. However, it was not until 1947 that Congress authorized the Department of Agricul-

TABLE 2. MORTALITY, GROWTH LOSS, AND GROWTH IMPACT ON
COMMERCIAL FOREST LAND RESULTING FROM 1952 DAMAGE,
BY CAUSES, UNITED STATES AND COASTAL ALASKA [24]

(Growing stock)

Cause	Mortality, million cu. ft.	Growth loss, million cu. ft.	Growth impact	
			Million cu. ft.	Per cent
Fire.............	236	1,452	1,688	15
Disease..........	773	4,275	5,048	45
Insects...........	1,000	778	1,778	16
Weather..........	843	114	957	9
Animals..........	65	944	1,009	9
Miscellaneous *....	593	136	729	6
Total..........	3,510 †	7,699	11,209	100
Salvage ‡.........	769	....	769	
Net loss........	2,741	7,699	10,440	

* Types of damage not ascribed directly to causes listed include suppression, mortality, and growth loss due to logging injury.

† This figure represents actual 1952 mortality.

‡ Utilized from dead trees in 1952.

ture to make adequate surveys to detect incipient outbreaks and to initiate prompt control work.

Protecting the Forest from Insect Attack

Insects causing damage to forest trees may be grouped under the following types: sucking insects such as aphids and scales, defoliators, bark beetles, and insects that destroy wood. A few insects such as the pine-shoot moth and the white pine weevil destroy the terminal buds or terminal shoots and hence deform the trees.

Aphids and Scale Insects. These do not directly kill forest trees, but they may so weaken the trees that they succumb to attacks by other insects or to disease. An example is the beech scale, which, in conjunction with the Nectria fungus disease, has caused widespread dying of beech in Maine and New Hampshire. The aphids and scale insects suck plant juices from the stems, leaves, and other succulent tissue of the tree, and a few attack roots. Aphids and scale insects are subject to predation by the ladybird beetle, by other insects, and to a limited extent by birds. Reliance on control in the forest has been on natural agents and introduced insect diseases and predators.

Defoliators. The serious defoliators are the larvae of certain moths and sawflies and, to some extent, the adults and larvae of some beetles.

Examples are the tussock moth, forest tent caterpillar, larch sawfly, Leconte sawfly, gypsy moth, brown-tailed moth, and spruce budworm. Most are native insects, though the gypsy and brown-tailed moths were introduced from Europe. All have caused serious damage when outbreaks occurred. In an outbreak that began in 1909 and continued for almost a decade, the spruce budworm destroyed 250 million cords of spruce and fir pulpwood in Quebec, Maine, New Brunswick, and Minnesota. A second outbreak began in Ontario in 1935. By 1947 most of the mature fir and a considerable part of the white spruce stands had been killed over an area of over 20,000 square miles. The amount of timber killed was enough to supply the pulp mills of Canada for more than three years. This outbreak reached New York in 1945 and Maine in 1946. Considerable defoliation occurred in New York in 1946, but the budworm population dropped off during 1947 and 1948 so that serious damage did not occur. The spruce budworm larvae show a preference for feeding on balsam fir buds that develop the pollen cones.

The 17-year locusts, or cicadas, may sweep over considerable areas of forest, feeding heavily on leaves and damaging branches in which they deposit eggs. May beetle adults cause some defoliation, though this is rarely serious. The larvae, white grubs, feed on roots and cause heavy losses in nurseries and young plantations.

Bark Beetles. These beetles are the most destructive of all the insects in terms of the quantity of timber destroyed. They burrow beneath the bark, feeding on the inner bark and cambium, where they find considerable quantities of sugars and starches. Although the healthy trees oftentimes produce a vigorous flow of sap that kills the insects, trees infested in late summer, and those which have a limited moisture supply or are unable to resist the attack for other reasons, are girdled and killed. These beetles provide avenues for the entrance of fungi and bacteria and may carry spores on their bodies from infected trees to healthy trees.

Defoliators and bark beetles have a tendency to fluctuate widely in population. They may be present in the forest for a long period of time and cause no appreciable damage and then within a period of two or three years develop a huge population that causes a devastating outbreak.

The western pine beetle is estimated to have killed 25 billion board feet of timber from 1921 to 1946; the Black Hills beetle, 2.5 billion feet

Fig. 20 Bark beetles cause heavy losses in mature timber in western forests. A ponderosa pine tree under heavy beetle attack. (*U.S. Forest Service photo.*)

from 1895 to 1946; and the mountain pine beetle, working in California, has caused damage to sugar pine, western white pine, and lodgepole pine totaling 20 billion board feet.[3, 21] The Engelmann spruce beetle killed 4 billion board feet of spruce timber during the period 1942 to 1948 (Fig. 20).

Wood-destroying Insects. Wood in service is attacked by various wood-destroying insects, the most serious of which are termites, carpenter ants, and powder-post beetles. The powder-post beetles will work in tool handles, furniture, flooring, and barn timbers where the moisture content is considerably below that required by termites. No insect can work in wood dried to 6 per cent moisture content.

Degrade caused by insects attacking the green log results in annual losses in lumber of $63,200 in New York.[22]

Preventing Insect Damage. Insect damage is controlled by preventive measures brought about by good forest management, reduction of favorite foods or habitat conditions, introduction of parasites and predators, and direct control. Pure plantations of trees over large areas are an open invitation for insect or disease outbreaks. Severity of white pine weevil attack can be reduced by planting pine in mixture with hardwoods, but, unfortunately, the hardwoods oftentimes prove to be a more serious menace to the pine than the weevil. A more successful practice is to plant the pines close together. Spruce budworm damage can be minimized by removing the mature balsam fir before the insect reaches outbreak proportions.

Good forest management has proved to be the most effective overall method that we have of combating both insects and diseases. Control of western bark beetle damage has been possible by learning to recognize the types of trees that the beetles will attack and removing these in early logging operations.[18]

Damage to wood in service can be prevented largely by keeping the wood dry and preventing direct contact between the wood and the soil. Certain timbers which must be located closer to the soil than 18 inches can be protected by impregnating them with various preservatives.

DIRECT CONTROL OF INSECT OUTBREAKS. Attempts to control insects by direct methods have proved costly in the past.

When DDT (dichloro-diphenyl-trichloro-ethane) and other powerful insecticides became available, airplane spraying proved effective in reducing insect damage.

Control of the tussock moth outbreak in Idaho was effected by aerial spraying in 1947. A total of 413,000 acres was covered at a cost of $1.57 per acre.

Widespread use of DDT, Sevin, chlordane, and other chemicals highly toxic to insects is looked upon with disfavor by many biologists. They rightfully pose the question, if you distribute enough chemical to kill the destructive insect, how much damage do you do to other life that plays a role in balancing natural populations? Birds, fish, and reptiles have been killed by DDT applied as a spray to kill insect pests. If the spray drifts onto plants grazed by dairy cows, DDT shows up in milk. Standards are currently in use that greatly minimize untoward effects.

A relatively new advance in chemical insecticides is use of systemics —chemicals that are highly toxic to insects and that can be injected into tree stems or absorbed by roots and carried throughout the tree.

As more is learned about the life history, physiology, and toxicology of insects, new methods of control appear. Studying introduced insects in their homeland has led to discovery of disease organisms, parasites, and predators. These have been reared in large enough numbers to provide a considerable degree of control over certain introduced and a few native insects.[26]

Tree Diseases

Various diseases of trees kill or damage seedlings, young timber, and mature forest trees. Diseases are of two main types: nonparasitic and parasitic. The nonparasitic tree diseases include those caused by drought, sunscald, winter injury of various types, improper nutrition, injuries from smoke or gases, and injuries resulting from flooding. Some nonparasitic diseases such as sunscald and smoke injury are of local occurrence. Others such as drought damage and wind burn may be widespread.

Few soils of the United States are so deficient in mineral nutrients that trees cannot survive. Many are infertile, however, and support only small-sized trees, as do the sand plains of New Jersey. Glacial outwashed sands of sections of the Lake States and New York, following cultivation, have been seriously reduced in their capacity to support vigorous tree growth. The poorest soils are often found on rocky ridge tops and along lands recently elevated from the sea.

Locally, trees may be damaged by chemical wastes, such as the acid water from mines, smokes, and smelter fumes, and by other toxic chemicals in heavy concentration. The outstanding example is the copper basin of Tennessee. Here smelter fumes, mainly sulfur dioxide, have resulted in the death of all trees for a distance of about 8 miles from the smelter.[15,16] Trees are also readily killed by flooding caused by dams. Unfavorable weather will be discussed later.

Parasitic Diseases. Parasitic diseases of trees are caused by bacteria, fungi, viruses, nematodes, and mistletoes.[1,7,13,17,19,23] Fungi cause more losses than any other type of disease, particularly in the larger trees. Nematodes are destructive of seedlings and of newly germinated seed. The phloem necrosis disease of elm and brooming of black locust are caused by virus infections. The parasitic organism causing a disease is called a pathogen.

FUNGAL DISEASES. Many tree diseases, of which the chestnut blight is a good example, are spread by spores carried by the wind. The chestnut blight, which was first reported in New York City in 1904, spread rapidly, killing all trees as it went. No effective control for the disease has been found. Consequently, the chestnut has been wiped out as a commercial tree throughout its range.

The rusts are highly specialized fungi. A classical example is the white pine blister rust fungus, which was first found in North America at Geneva, New York, in 1906. It occurred on cultivated gooseberries and currants, which were promptly destroyed. By 1909 a new infestation was found on eastern white pine seedlings which were imported from Europe and shipped widely over the Northeast and the Lake States. Attempts to destroy these were unsuccessful. By 1915 all hope of eradicating the fungus from the United States was abandoned, since it was learned that new infections had been introduced on the West Coast. These have spread on the western white pine and sugar pine.

The fungus attacks all five needle pines. It enters the trees through the needles, spreads down the twigs to the main branches, ultimately to the main stem,[14] and kills the tree by killing all the bark and thus girdling the stem. The rust cannot spread directly from pine to pine but must spread from pine to currants or gooseberries. On these it causes only moderate damage and may spread from one currant bush to another. In the fall of the year spores are produced which can infect only pine. The white pine blister rust may, therefore, be controlled by eliminating currants and gooseberries which enable the infection to spread to pine stands. Approximately 28 million acres in the eastern and western states are within the white pine blister rust control areas. This rust is one of the most seriously destructive diseases of forest trees in our country.

The Dutch elm disease, an excellent example of a disease in which the causal agent is carried by an insect, broke out in Europe and was found in the United States in 1930. The fungus is parasitic on living trees and saprophytic on dead trees. Its yeastlike spores produce toxins which are carried by the sap stream throughout the tree and so cause death. The disease organism is carried from diseased to healthy trees by the elm bark beetle. Beetles were introduced at the same time as the disease in various importations of elm logs used for producing high-grade furniture veneer. Efforts have been made to control the disease by destroying infected trees and by protecting healthy trees through spraying with DDT to control the beetles.

Year in and year out heart rots are responsible for more damage to timber than other diseases. The fungi are spread by wind-borne spores that infect the tree through injuries caused by logging, ice breakage, fire scars, insect attack, or through other injuries that expose the heartwood of the tree. The fungi causing heart rot are of several types, but the group known as the polypores are the most common and widespread. They produce bracket-shaped, spore-bearing conks on the tree trunk. Heart rot has caused heavy damage in western stands and is particularly prevalent in eastern stands where the best trees have been removed (Fig. 21).

No feasible method has been found for preventing heart rot in forest trees. The only effective control is the practice of intensive forestry. Care should be taken to eliminate fire, since much heart rot gets its start through fire scars. Where selective logging is carried out, care should also be taken to avoid injuring the base of trees. The annual loss from heart rot is estimated at 1.5 billion board feet.[13]

The fungi that cause heart rot in trees also cause decay of slash and fallen trees. This is a valuable function in the forest. If the wood did not decay promptly, we would soon have the forest cluttered up with highly inflammable debris making the growth of future trees impossible.

Wood-rotting fungi cause considerable loss to wood in service as well. It has been estimated that approximately 10 per cent of the annual production of lumber in the country is used each year merely to replace wood which has decayed in service.[1] Control of decay in wood is obtained by keeping it dry. Many uses of wood, such as for railroad ties, telephone poles, and piling, necessitate its location in places where it becomes wet. In these cases, wood decay is impeded by treatment of wood with toxic chemicals such as creosote, zinc chloride, or pentachlorophenol.

MISTLETOES. The eastern mistletoe and, to some extent, the western mistletoe are carried by birds. These are parasitic seed plants that grow on the branches of pines and hardwoods, sending their rootlike haustoria down into the conductive tissue of branches. The eastern mistletoe at-

FIG. 21 Fungi take a heavy toll of timber, especially of trees injured by fire or logging. (*U.S. Forest Service photo.*)

tains fairly large size. It produces seed covered with a sticky, gelatinous material that adheres to birds' feet, thereby spreading the infection from one tree to another. The dwarf mistletoe causes witches'-brooms and other damage to conifers, particularly to ponderosa pine. The seeds of this plant are forcibly ejected for a distance of 20 to 40 feet horizontally.

No effective control has been found for the dwarf mistletoe.

Federal Aid in Pest Control

The federal government takes many steps to prevent introduction of tree pests and to control introduced and native pests that damage forests. The maintenance of a plant quarantine and inspection service at all ports of entry has been helpful in keeping to a minimum the number of serious diseases that have been introduced.[8] Plants to be imported should be grown under quarantine until such time as it is clear that they are free from disease.

Protecting the Forest against Animals

Domestic Animals. No measure is available of the total damage caused to American forests by domestic animals. Grazing is practiced the least in the Northeast and in the heavy forests of the Pacific Coast since these regions produce little forage in the forest. Wood lots are commonly grazed throughout the Middle Atlantic and central states, the South, and all the West except in the heavy forests along the coast.

Grazing is defensible in the West where timber stands are of low density and a considerable amount of grass can be found between the trees. This is true to a certain extent of the pine forests of the South also. Throughout the rest of the United States little grazing value would exist in the woods, provided the trees were growing as densely as they are capable of growing.

Cattle, sheep, horses, hogs, and goats compact the soil, reducing infiltration of water, inhibiting root growth, and reducing aeration. Erosion is a particularly serious menace in western forests subject to heavy grazing by sheep and cattle.

Hogs consume seed when it first falls, and they continue to destroy young seedlings until these have passed the cotyledon stage. Hogs may destroy seedlings of longleaf pine by eating the roots.

A study in Ohio revealed that grazing caused a substantial reduction in the flow of maple sap which, when translated into terms of maple-syrup production, amounted to $10.67 per acre annually.[5]

BENEFICIAL EFFECTS OF GRAZING. If properly regulated, grazing has some beneficial effects. Grazing animals can consume much of the grass and other herbaceous vegetation that would otherwise become a serious fire hazard, and grazing can control the composition of a forest by killing out unwanted hardwoods.

Protection against Wildlife. It is a maxim that any animal that lives in the forest must get its food from the forest, and this often comes in part from the woody vegetation, either directly in the form of leaves, twigs, buds, and bark or indirectly in the form of nuts, fruits, and fungi that grow on the live or dead trees.

Where squirrel populations are dense, they may destroy an entire seed crop. Mice, chipmunks, and birds eat tree seed in large quantities. Grosbeaks have destroyed the entire seed crop of certain southern pines. Birds also eat the young seedlings when they first emerge. In coniferous nurseries seedbeds must be screened lest the birds destroy every emergent seedling.

Rabbits, mice, deer, and other browsing animals will eat young tree seedlings. Deer and rabbits both tend to browse more heavily on hardwoods than on softwoods, thereby influencing the reproduction of conifers. Where they are overly dense, however, they effectively keep down seedlings of both hardwoods and softwoods.

The bark of trees is eaten by rabbits, mice, squirrels, porcupines, deer, and elk. Mice are particularly destructive of sugar maple, working beneath the snow during winter.

Porcupines, where abundant, may cause extensive damage to both hardwood and softwood trees by gnawing bark. They may girdle trees at almost any height, and they also cut off twigs.

Elk gnaw the bark from young aspens and alders during the winter.

Ruffed grouse, squirrels, porcupines, deer, rabbits, and many other animals feed on the buds of trees. The actual damage caused by this feeding is difficult to appraise. Squirrels cut off terminal shoots and may later return to the ground and eat the buds. Such cutting during the winter and late spring months is beneficial to animals that cannot reach the high branches in the trees. It is believed that none of the animals do serious damage through destruction of the buds once the trees have passed the sapling stage.

Beaver are the only animals that fell large-sized trees. They may also girdle trees that they do not completely cut down. Beaver cutting is normally limited to trees of 2 to 4 inches in diameter, but they have been known to cut down trees as large as 18 inches and even larger. Beaver eat the bark from felled trees and store branches underwater for winter food. Dams erected at the outlet of a low or swampy area may back up water, flooding several acres of land. Most trees thus inundated die. Beaver damming universally promotes water storage, thus serving to maintain water tables and regulate stream flow.

CONTROL OF WILDLIFE DAMAGE. Wildlife-damage control can best be effected through good wildlife management combined with good forest management. The wildlife population is likely to be most destructive during those periods of the year when food is least plentiful. If timber-cutting operations are carried out at this time, deer, rabbits, and other animals that inhabit the forest may collect to browse on the branches of felled trees.

From time to time wildlife populations in local areas may become excessive and result in severe damage to the forest. This will require direct action. Hunting and trapping are usually the most effective for game and fur animals. Live trapping and transport to other areas has rarely succeeded in reducing population. Fencing is costly. Nature eventually will bring about an adjustment through predators, disease, and starvation, but such adjustments are often delayed until severe damage to the wildlife range occurs. Furthermore, natural adjustments may severely deplete the seed stock.

Unfavorable Weather

Native forests, though not immune to injury, withstand normal vicissitudes of weather. They may be seriously injured by abnormal weather. Plantations of exotics are likely to be particularly susceptible. Drought injury can be minimized by planting drought-resistant species, by eliminating vegetation that competes for soil moisture, and by preserving moderate overhead shade. Tree seedlings hardened in the nursery by exposure to soil dryness and not overfertilized are likely to survive better on dry sites than unhardened stock.

High temperature sometimes causes loss to tree seedlings, particularly in nurseries. This can be prevented by watering the seedlings during the hottest part of the day. Heat loss is rare in forest plantations but has been known to occur on occasions. Usually it is spotty and confined chiefly to places where air drainage is poor. Air temperatures that kill seedlings must be as high as 120 to 130°F, and such temperatures rarely occur in regions where trees normally grow.

Frost action on heavy soil may heave fall-planted trees from the soil or lift them so far out that they die. Frosts may also stunt growth and actually exclude trees from "frost pockets," which have poor air drainage. A frost pocket results not from cold air flowing in from the outside, but rather from radiation of heat from the soil to the sky. On clear still nights, air thus cooled is impeded from flowing away, and accumulates until it overflows the obstruction to air drainage. Once air drainage has been blocked, it is almost impossible to restore a good tree cover. Frost that extends over wide areas may also cause severe damage to trees, especially late spring frosts after the buds have opened and vegetative growth has started.

Sunscald and winter burning of forest trees occur on unusually warm days with bright sunshine while the ground is still frozen. Winter burning is due to severe loss of water from needles when the roots are unable to replace it. Sunscald appears to result from freezing of tissue newly activated by solar heating.

Wind. High winds will uproot trees or break them off. Moderate winds will break the tops. Cyclonic storms of tornado type will sweep through a forest, leveling trees in their paths. Hurricanes cause severe damage to forests (Fig. 22).

FIG. 22 A windstorm in July, 1940, left this badly bent survivor of a beautiful virgin red pine stand, Chippewa National Forest, Minnesota. (*U.S. Forest Service photo.*)

Although forests cannot be completely protected against damage by windstorm, damage can be minimized by proper density and by maintaining good borders at the edge of the forest to prevent the wind from sweeping under the crowns.

Rain. Heavy rainfall sometimes causes land slips, gullying, flooding, and heavy washes that may wash trees out by the roots. Most forests, however, keep the soil sufficiently open so that the water soaks in and causes little erosion or damage. Snowslides or avalanches may harm forests in high mountains. Only limited steps can ordinarily be taken to prevent these, such as keeping vegetation on the upper slopes and promoting the growth of woody vegetation wherever possible. Hail may strip the leaves from trees, but such storms are generally of local occurrence, and recovery from such damage usually is rapid.

Snow and Ice Damage. Wet snow, and particularly rains in freezing weather, may overload tree crowns and cause extensive breakage. A single ice storm may damage trees over thousands of acres. Trees planted out of their natural range are especially susceptible. Hardwoods are usually damaged most by ice, conifers most by wet snow. Trees with narrow crowns usually resist damage better than broad-crowned trees. Trees in stands that are neither too dense nor too thin usually have sturdy stems which enable them to resist snow breakage.

Diastrophism. Locally forests may undergo damage resulting from earthquakes and volcanic action. In 1959, a severe earthquake occurred in the upper Madison River Valley of Idaho. Extensive faulting resulted that tilted Hegben Lake, thus creating some new land and inundating other land. Minor damage occurred to the forest because of diversion of streams and falling boulders. The most spectacular event, however, was a huge slide that sent trees, boulders, and soil cascading into Madison River Canyon, creating a natural dam almost 500 feet high. A lake formed behind the dam, killing the trees that were flooded. Tidal waves resulting from earthquakes may damage low-lying forests along the seacoasts but seldom penetrate far inland.

Lava flows and deposits of volcanic ash have destroyed considerable areas of forest in Hawaii and in Alaska. The Mt. Katmai eruption in Alaska in 1912 buried thousands of acres, killing the tree growth. Fine ash, in fact, drifted all the way around the earth from this eruption.

The forester should look mainly to intensive forest-management measures as his first and major line of defense against damage from fire, insects, tree diseases, and weather.

Combined with game management, forest management will keep the forest free from excessive wildlife damage. Poorly planned operations cause a progressive decline in forest yield, wildlife yield, water yield, and the services of the forest. They tend to make fires more frequent and devastating and open the forests to attacks by destructive insects and diseases. Intensive management with a well-developed road system is essential to good protection and salvage of damaged trees.[12]

LITERATURE CITED

1. Boyce, John Shaw. 1961. "Forest Pathology," 3d ed., McGraw-Hill Book Company, Inc., New York. 572 pp.
2. Brown, A. A. 1949. "Progress, but Still a Problem," *Trees,* The Yearbook of Agriculture, pp. 477–479, U.S. Department of Agriculture, Washington.
3. Craighead, F. C., and John M. Miller. 1949. "Insects in the Forest: A Survey," *Trees,* The Yearbook of Agriculture, pp. 407–413, U.S. Department of Agriculture, Washington.
4. Crocker, Clayton S. 1949. "Fighting Fires from the Air," *Trees,* The Yearbook of Agriculture, pp. 508–516, U.S. Department of Agriculture, Washington.
5. Dambach, Charles A. 1944. "Comparative Productiveness of Adjacent Grazed and Ungrazed Sugar-maple Woods," *Journal of Forestry,* 42:164–168.
6. Forbes, Robert H. 1949. "The Smoke Jumpers Carry On," *American Forests,* 55(10):18–19.
7. Gill, Lake S., and Jess L. Bedwell. 1949. "Dwarf Mistletoes," *Trees,* The Yearbook of Agriculture, pp. 458–461, U.S. Department of Agriculture, Washington.
8. Gravatt, G. F., and D. E. Parker. 1949. "Introduced Tree Diseases and Insects," *Trees,* The Yearbook of Agriculture, pp. 446–451, U.S. Department of Agriculture, Washington.
9. Guthrie, John D. 1936. "Great Forest Fires of America," U.S. Forest Service, Washington. 10 pp.
10. Hammatt, R. F. 1949. "Bad Business; Your Business," *Trees,* The Yearbook of Agriculture, pp. 479–485, U.S. Department of Agriculture, Washington.
11. Hardy, Charles, and Arthur P. Brackebusch. 1960. "The Intermountain Fire-danger Rating System," *Proceedings, Society of American Foresters' Meeting,* San Francisco, Calif., 1959, pp. 133–137, Washington, D.C.
12. Hawley, Ralph C., and Paul W. Stickel. 1948. "Forest Protection," 2d ed., John Wiley & Sons, Inc., New York. 355 pp.
13. Hepting, George H., and James W. Kimmey. 1949. "Heart Rot," *Trees,* The Yearbook of Agriculture, pp. 462–465, U.S. Department of Agriculture, Washington.
14. Hirt, Ray R. 1933. "Blister Rust, a Serious Disease of White Pine," New York State College of Forestry, Syracuse, N.Y. 5 pp.
15. Hursh, C. R. 1932. "The Forest Legion Carries On," *American Forests,* 38:16–19.
16. Hursh, C. R., and C. A. Connaughton. 1938. "Effects of Forests upon Local Climate," *Journal of Forestry,* 36:864–866.

17. Hutchins, L. M. 1949. "Diseases and the Forest," *Trees,* The Yearbook of Agriculture, pp. 443–445, U.S. Department of Agriculture, Washington.
18. Keen, F. P. 1949. "Pine Bark Beetles," *Trees,* The Yearbook of Agriculture, pp. 427–432, U.S. Department of Agriculture, Washington.
19. Martin, J. F., and Perley Spaulding. 1949. "Blister Rust on White Pine," *Trees,* The Yearbook of Agriculture, pp. 453–458, U.S. Department of Agriculture, Washington.
20. Phillips, Clinton B. 1960. "Fighting Forest Fires from the Air," *Proceedings, Society of American Foresters' Meeting,* San Francisco, Calif., 1959, pp. 137–140, Washington, D.C.
21. Rohwer, S. A. 1949. "The Key to Protection," *Trees,* The Yearbook of Agriculture, pp. 413–417, U.S. Department of Agriculture, Washington.
22. Simeone, J. B. 1949. "Damage by Wood Borers in Lumber and in Buildings," unpublished manuscript, New York State College of Forestry, Syracuse, N.Y. 3 pp.
23. Swingle, R. U., R. R. Whitten, and E. G. Brewer. 1949. "Dutch Elm Disease," *Trees,* The Yearbook of Agriculture, pp. 451–452, U.S. Department of Agriculture, Washington.
24. U.S. Department of Agriculture, Forest Service. 1958. "Timber Resources for America's Future," Forest Resource Report 14, Washington. 713 pp.
25. U.S. Department of Agriculture, Forest Service. 1950. "Report of the Chief of the Forest Service," Washington. 69 pp.
26. U.S. Department of Agriculture, Forest Service. 1960. "Report of the Chief of the Forest Service," Washington. 49 pp.
27. Wilkins, Austin H. 1948. "The Story of the Maine Forest Fire Disaster," *Journal of Forestry,* 46:568–573.
28. Woods, John B., Jr. 1950. "The Rehabilitation of the Tillamook Burn," *Journal of Forestry,* 48(5):362–364.

CHAPTER 6. *Forest Care and Use*

MAN IS WILLING to care for what he expects to use. He will care for a forest provided such care is necessary for his use of it. The use he makes of a forest determines the care needed. Watersheds need forest cover that keeps the soil porous and receptive to water infiltration and retention. Game forests should provide abundant game food, water, and coverts. Forests used for recreation should have parking lots, picnic areas with sanitary facilities, trails with inviting vistas, impressive and picturesque trees, and, preferably, a stream or lake. Forests for timber production should contain species of high timber value and individual trees with tall, straight, clear stems.

To use a forest, man must protect it, care for it, harvest its products, and process them for use. This is true whether its products be water, wildlife, timber, or human recreation.

Needs of the Growing Tree

Most forest trees start out as seedlings. The seed of a forest tree may be very small and light. Tiny seed such as that of the trembling aspen may be carried miles by the wind and must germinate within four or five days or the seed dies. Other seeds are large, such as those of the oak, chestnut, walnut, and, largest of all, the coconut. These fall directly to the ground. They may roll a short distance, but unless transported by man, animals, or water, they germinate near the mother tree. Large seeds may also be short-lived. They can be killed by excessive drying; consequently, if they are to germinate, they must find a moist place on the forest floor. Rarely do these seeds live through the first summer unless they germinate. Seed of hawthorn, basswood, and junipers are long-lived, rarely germinating before the second summer following ripening.[8]

Each seed has stored within it reserve food to support the life of the seedling—for three or four days in the case of aspen, as long as one year in the case of oak. As soon as the reserve food in the seed is exhausted, the seedling is strictly on its own. It must manufacture its own food in its leaves and absorb through its roots water and the mineral

95

elements necessary for its livelihood. The organic food which is converted into stem, root, branch, and leaf tissue must come from the photosynthetic activity of the leaves. Photosynthesis is the process by which the leaves use the energy of sunlight to combine carbon dioxide from the air with water from the soil to form a carbohydrate-like substance. Simple sugars, starches, oils, lignin, and cellulose are formed from the primary and secondary products of photosynthesis. Simple sugars are combined with nitrogen to form proteins. All are used by the tree for growth. The seedling must, therefore, have access to water, carbon dioxide, and light to provide its food substance. Its roots must take up a number of mineral elements that are essential to the life of the tree. These include nitrogen for protein synthesis; phosphorus for nucleoproteins and energy transfer; potassium apparently for enzyme action and translocation of carbohydrates; sulfur for amino acids and growth substances; calcium for cell walls; magnesium, a constituent of chlorophyll; iron to promote chloroplast synthesis and respiration; manganese for chlorophyll synthesis; zinc for synthesis of growth regulators; copper for enzymes; boron for sugar translocation; molybdenum for nitrogen metabolism. Other elements in trees include aluminum, sodium, and silicon found in relatively large amounts and others found in smaller amounts. What role, if any, these play in the tree's living processes is still to be determined.[5] Favorable temperature is also essential for photosynthesis and growth.

The rate at which a tree grows depends largely on the rate at which it can be supplied with its basic growth needs—mineral nutrients, water, carbon dioxide, and light. If any one is absent, growth slows down or ceases entirely; and if it remains absent for long, death will ensue. Fortunately, throughout the moist tropical and temperate zones most elements are available in adequate amounts for satisfactory tree growth. The one that is most likely to be limiting is moisture supply. The mineral elements needed by the trees are abundant in the earth's crust and are usually present in ample concentration to support vigorous growth. Occasionally, a soil is found that is deficient in calcium, potassium, sulfur, or some other one element. Tree growth can be improved on such soils by applying a small amount of the deficient element. An interesting case of deficient supply of potassium occurred on formerly heavily farmed sand soils on the Pack Demonstration Forest at Warrensburg, New York. A red pine plantation badly stunted quickly resumed normal growth where pine or hardwood slash from healthy trees was distributed and allowed to decay. This led to a series of experiments applying various individual and combinations of mineral salts until the deficient element, potassium, was revealed.

Nitrogen in the form of nitrates, nitrite, or ammonium compounds, which trees can use, may also be below the optimum for maximum tree growth. Experiments have shown that trees may make substantial response where nitrogen is applied to poor soils. Carbon dioxide is always present in the air in sufficiently large amounts to support tree growth. Sunlight is always ample in the temperate and tropic zones except beneath the shade of a dense forest overstory. If the sunlight that penetrates to seedlings is much below 15 per cent of full sunlight, they will not grow satisfactorily.

When any one element necessary for the growth of trees is present in minimal supply, the rate of growth is determined largely by the supply of this one element. Optimum growth requires a complete supply of all the several elements.

Many tree seedlings survive best if protected from the hot rays of the sun that heat and dry the soil. Usually, seeds that germinate best in the shade produce seedlings that are capable of surviving for a considerable period of time in low light intensities. These are said to be shade-tolerant. Those that germinate best in the open may require abundant sunlight if they are not to weaken and die. These are said to be shade-intolerant seedlings.[1]

Hazards to Survival. From the very beginning the young tree seedling must face conditions that tend to destroy it. A dry hardwood leaf that is blown accidentally over a tender pine seedling may, if packed down by rainfall, be sufficient to cause its death. A small insect may clip the stem or destroy the growing point before it can form leaf tissue to support life. An animal may tread on the seedling or a bird may eat it. A hailstone may break it off, and even rain may beat it into mineral soil. Literally hundreds of seedlings must start for each tree that grows to maturity.

When the seedling gets larger, a rabbit may eat it, a disease may strike, or insects may consume it.

When the seedling reaches sapling size, it must compete with its fellow trees and sometimes with older trees that shade it and send their roots into the same soil areas. Wind, lightning, fungi, or insects cause death of the older trees, and so the sapling gets its chance to go ahead. When it attains pole size or larger, wind, sleet, snow, and ice all present hazards to survival.[7]

Climates for Trees. In the temperate zones trees must have at least 15 to 20 inches of rainfall each year to survive; in tropical regions, 25 to 30 inches. Trees require generally a minimum growing season of approximately 100 days free from frost. Those adjusted to northern climates, however, can complete their growth in a shorter period, and many northern trees are capable of surviving satisfactorily in climates where frost may occur any month in the year. Active growth may take place at temperatures above 40°F, though the most rapid growth generally occurs at 60 to 80°F. Evergreen trees may carry on photosynthesis at temperatures as low as 21°F.[5]

The length of daylight affects tree growth in that it tends to limit the range over which an individual species will extend. It may determine the times at which buds open in the spring and leaves are dropped in the fall. By this means tree functions are regulated.

The growth of leaves, stems, and roots is regulated by plant-growth substances called plant hormones, or auxins, which are complicated chemical substances that tend to inhibit growth in one region and stimulate it in another. Growth substances are largely responsible for the expression of dominance in terminal buds and in the main root system.

Maturity and Death. As the tree grows to maturity, it reaches the period when it begins to produce flowers and fruit containing seeds that serve to perpetuate the species. Seed production is generally favored by an abundance of sunlight and moisture. Consequently, after partial cuttings remaining trees tend to develop a larger crown and to produce abundant seed. Good seed years may occur annually in some species, biennially in others, and at irregular intervals of three to nine years in many species.[5, 8]

Seed production becomes more bountiful as the tree approaches maturity. When abundant seed is formed, less food reserves remain to support the growth of the tree. When growth rate declines, the tree is unable to extend its root or crown system fast enough to meet its needs. So, gradually, the overmature tree weakens. Heart-rotting fungi grow in wounds caused by broken limbs, fire scars at the base, or injuries by man or animals. Eventually, the weakened tree is either thrown by wind or dies where it stands (Fig. 22).

Establishing Forests on Open Land

Extensive fire-swept areas of the Lake States and the South, badly eroded fields, and other lands cleared for agriculture but unsuited for such use are destined to remain nonproductive for decades unless rehabilitated by tree planting. Unclothed with woody growth, they may become a source of flood runoff, silt, and debris that menaces other lands. Protective tree plantings are needed on denuded mountain slopes and on the prairie-plains region to minimize wind erosion and exposure of farm homesteads. The total area in need of forest planting was estimated by the U.S. Forest Service to be 52 million acres in 1952.[9]

Extensive tree planting has been carried out by the U.S. Forest Service and by Michigan, New York, and other states. Counties and municipalities, and even school districts, have engaged in tree planting. Stimulated by extension foresters and various crop-reduction programs, farmers have in the aggregate planted considerable areas to trees. Since 1945 Christmas-tree growers have greatly expanded their activities. Of

special significance have been the large areas of private planting es~~
lished since 1945 by many pulp and paper and other timber compan~~
These plantings are strictly for commercial wood production. Many have
shown outstanding returns on the capital invested. More than that, these
plantings have caught the imagination of top management in the industry. This has led such companies to employ forest geneticists, tree
physiologists, and other scientists and to establish extensive experimental
programs in search of means for increasing the timber yield from forest
land.

Tree seed may differ radically from agricultural seed. It is borne high
in the trees where it is difficult to observe and collect. It must be collected as soon as ripe but before wind dispersion occurs. Tree seed is
adjusted to germinating in the natural forest habitat and also is adjusted
to many different means of dispersal. Some of it is well protected against
destruction. Basswood, for example, must lie for one to two years on the
forest floor while the seed coat is softened up by action of microorganisms before sufficient water will penetrate to enable the embryo to
swell and emerge. Cottonwood, willow, elm, maple, and most of the
seed that ripens in early spring is short-lived. The forester must know
how to collect cones and fruit, how to extract the seed, how to hold it in
storage until ready for use, and how to pretreat it so as to get satisfactory
germination in his nursery beds (Fig. 23). Under proper conditions many
kinds of tree seed can be stored for several years without serious decline
in vitality.[8]

Seed may be sown directly in the forest where the seedlings are to
grow. This is desirable practice for heavy-seeded species such as oaks,
walnuts, and hickory. Care must be taken to protect such seed against
rodents, lest they dig up and devour every seed. If a proper seedbed
can be prepared, the seedling will spring up in the place where it is to
grow permanently.

This is a decided advantage in that it avoids root disturbances that
occur during planting. But special care is necessary in seed protection,
seedbed preparation, and oftentimes in weeding and thinning if a forest
is to be established directly from seed. It is generally cheaper and more
successful to provide such initial care in a tree nursery.

Seed and Nursery Practice. The majority of tree seeds are so small
and the seedlings so delicate that if sown directly on the planting site,
survival is exceedingly low. To plant successfully such species as northern white-cedar, white spruce, hemlock, many of the pines, larch, and
fir, it is desirable to grow the seedlings for one to four years in a nursery.[6]

Seedbeds are carefully prepared, and the seed, after appropriate pre-
treatment, is sown in rows or broadcast in the beds, covered to protect
it against soil drying, and watered daily until germination occurs. The

Fig. 23 The modern tree-seed extraction plant is fitted with automatic temperature and humidity controls. Cass Lake Extractory. (*U.S. Forest Service photo.*)

nursery beds must be weeded, watered, and properly fertilized to produce a satisfactory crop of tree seedlings suitable for forest planting. The nursery must also be protected against diseases and insects, birds, mice, and other destructive agents. The job of a nurseryman is an exacting one. He must be on duty daily to discover early and correct promptly any unfavorable factor that may be operative in his nursery. The task of the nurseryman is not to grow fine-looking seedlings, but to grow seedlings that are vigorous and rugged enough to stand up under field conditions (Fig. 24).

Field Planting. Field planting of tree seedlings requires proper preparation of the planting site to receive the seedlings. This can be done by furrowing, scalping, burning, or complete cultivation of the soil. The latter has proved the best way of converting lands invaded by brush to forest.

Each seedling must be carefully set in the ground at the proper time of the year so that it has good opportunity for survival. Spring is normally the best time to plant, but trees can be successfully planted in the fall in many parts of the country. The modern tree-planting machines have greatly facilitated field-planting operations on sites on which such machines can be used efficiently. Two men with a machine can plant 8 acres a day, and on favorable sites even more. This is about four times as fast as hand planting. It has also been found that good machine planting is better than average hand planting.

Plantations must be protected against fire and browsing animals during the first two or three years of their life.

Competition from herbs, shrubs, and weed trees must not be excessive. Protection of newly planted trees by an overhead canopy tends to enhance first-year survival, but if older trees are left standing after the seedlings once become established, they will stunt the growth.

Plantations may require thinning at least once before the trees are of sufficient size to bring in enough income to cover the cost of the thinning operation. Where a market for Christmas trees and other small-size products is available, such thinning operations may be made at a profit.

The Tree and the Forest

A forest, as stated earlier, is much more than a group of trees occupying an area of land. It is a community made up of trees, shrubs, herbs, birds, mammals, and myriads of lower forms of plants and animals. All play an interdependent part in the life of the forest as a whole.

Fig. 24 Modern nursery operations are highly mechanized. A root pruner in operation, Chittenden Nursery, Michigan. (*U.S. Forest Service photo.*)

Shrubs use space not occupied by trees. Many produce valuable food for wildlife. They protect the openings and forest borders against sweeping winds. When dense, they may impede the growth of seedlings, but shrubs, like trees, tend to go through a life cycle. Groups get overdense as they reach maturity. They may then die out over wide areas and make the land available for tree seedlings and other vegetation.

Herbs also serve as food for wildlife. Many of them such as the wild vetches and peas serve to nitrify the soil. They provide foods for insects many of which burrow in the soil, opening up channels for roots and water. These, with burrowing mammals, earthworms, millipedes, mites, and other forms of life, break down leaf litter and cultivate the forest soil.[10]

Animals browse on shrubby thickets, preventing them from getting too dense; they also help to keep insects in check. The insects, in turn, break down wood and kill weak trees, thereby preparing the way for drastic changes which will occur in time. Bacteria help to store up nitrogen in the soil. Bacteria and fungi also break down wood, leaves, and other plant material to the basic inorganic compounds usable for new plant growth.

Climax and Virgin Forests

Change occurs in the forest from year to year, decade to decade, century to century.

The forest is a splendid builder of soil. As soil accumulates, conditions favor more and more complex forms of forest. Pioneer plants such as lichens, mosses, algae, and ferns prepare the way for grasses, other herbs, and small shrubs. These prepare the way for trees. The first trees may be light-demanding trees such as redcedar, juniper, gray birch, or piñon pine. Gradually, the forest passes through various stages in a succession toward a climax forest vegetation that will occupy the soil for an indefinite period.

The climax forest needs to be distinguished from the virgin forest. We may have a virgin forest of paper birch, white pine, or Douglas-fir, but these are not considered climax forests. They owe their origin to some fire or other catastrophe in the past. A virgin forest is one that has not been disturbed by man's activities or heavily grazed by domestic livestock. It may represent almost any stage in the succession from the pioneer trees to the climax forest.

The climax forest, on the other hand, is composed only of those species that have the capacity to maintain indefinitely possession of the land without the aid of man, fire, windstorm, or other major destructive agents. Neither the climax forest nor the virgin forest is necessarily ideal for man's use. Examples will make this clear. On Star Island in Cass Lake, Minnesota, no commercial timber cutting has been permitted. The soil is essentially uniform throughout. On the island can be found every stage in natural forest succession for the region. The pioneer jack pine forest occupies the lands most recently burned, but even though this forest is near maturity, few jack pine seedlings and even fewer poles can be found. The longer-lived red pine, where mixed with the jack pine, is taking over instead. The red pine also reproduces only moderately well so it is replaced by the still longer-lived white pine. The white pine forest is grandest of all. The trees reach heights of 120 feet or more and ages of 400 years or more, and they produce a forest of high aesthetic value and utility. But white pine also is giving way to a maple-basswood climax. These trees, being ill adapted to the sandy soil, attain a height of only 40 to 50 feet and ages of barely 150 years. This hardwood forest is not impressive to look upon, nor does it offer any temptation to the logger. It can, however, hold the soil against the pines and other species and therefore represents the climax.

The virgin forests which our ancestors discovered in America were estimated to average but 6,300 board feet per acre. Stands of this density represent good merchantable timber, but they are far from the ideal. Good pulpwood stands oftentimes run 30 to 50 cords per acre, and saw-timber stands in the eastern states may run as high as 20,000 to 40,000 board feet per acre.

In the virgin forests heavy stands were interspersed with open areas, burned areas, windfall areas, and areas where the timber died from attack by insects, tree diseases, or other causes. Droughts undoubtedly had a great deal to do with the dying of timber over substantial areas. Practically all our pine forests in the South, the Douglas-fir forests of the West Coast, and the jack pine and the red pine forests of the Lake States owe their origin to fires or to other destructive agents.

Making the Forest Useful

The forester's job involves more technical work than planting trees and protecting forests from fire and other destructive agents. He must mold the forest stands so that they grow into forms that best serve his purposes. To produce valuable timber, he should make certain that the forest growing space is used by straight, clean-boled trees of useful kinds. He will take advantage of markets for small-sized material to dispose of injured, defective, crooked, diseased, and poor-quality species. Thereby he diverts the growing potential of the soil from poor to valuable trees.[4] Even in well-managed forests, at least half the timber grown is of small size and medium to poor quality. Rehabilitating cutover lands, which is the task in which most foresters in the East and South are now engaged, produces a very small percentage of premium material. Harvesting and marketing low-grade forest products, therefore, is the major challenge of the present-day forester. He is usually expected to do this at a profit to the landowner at least sufficient to meet taxes and other carrying charges.

Caring for Seedling and Sapling Stands. Stands of natural seedlings and saplings, like those of plantations, improve with care. They may require weeding, cutting out undesirable trees and shrubby growth that is tending to choke out good trees; release cutting from older trees, after these have seeded in the area and protected the seedlings during initial establishments; and thinning so as to favor those seedlings which will make the best crop trees. If dense stands are not artificially thinned, they will be thinned by nature through extensive blowdown, snow and ice breakage, or other natural means. Rabbits, deer, porcupines, and other animals sometimes participate in the thinning operation, but the type of job they do is far from perfect.

Pole-size Timber. When the timber stand reaches pole size, thinning becomes more necessary than with saplings. From this size onward the trees have merchantable value if markets exist for pulpwood, fuel wood, or charcoal wood. For each timber type and site a certain crown density is attained beyond which further increase results in no additional growth of woody material per acre. This is attained when the crown density permits only 1 to 2 per cent of sunlight to penetrate to the forest floor. At such densities a timber stand actually converts something less than 2.5 per cent of the total solar energy received into chemical energy in the form of woody tissue.[5] The forester's aim is to concentrate the realizable growth on the most useful tree stems. He may either pick out the small-sized trees—this method is called a thinning from below—or select the large-sized trees, a thinning from above. Usually it is best to combine the two methods, taking some of the large limby trees and some of the small ones that would die naturally if not removed. The growing space can then be made available for full use of the trees that will produce the highest values in subsequent cutting operations. Best results are obtained if thinnings can be made lightly and frequently. The Danish stands that yield as high as 500 cubic feet per acre annually are thinned at about three-year intervals.

Management of Sawtimber Stands. Stands of sawtimber size may still be thinned and improved by cuttings. Improvement cuttings remove the poor-quality trees and those injured by wind, falling trees, fungi, or other causes. If damage has been severe, such operations are called salvage cuttings. Salvage cuttings should be made, if possible, before the tree dies, as the lumber may otherwise be low in value.

Harvest cutting may be on either a clear-cutting or a partial-cutting basis. Clear-cutting is done by strips or by patches or blocks, which may be regular or irregular in size; or it may extend over very large areas. Clear-cutting large areas of timber is usually bad practice in that it exposes the soil to the drying action of sun and wind, creates a huge fire hazard unless the slash has been disposed of, and removes all source of seed for natural restocking. Strip cutting and cutting in blocks has been widely adopted in the Douglas-fir region. It has also been used successfully for lodgepole pine (Fig. 15).

PARTIAL CUTTING. The simplest type of partial cutting is the seed-tree cutting. From one to ten or more trees are left per acre to seed up the surrounding land. This method works well with species, such as southern pines, that require plenty of light and soil space for establishment and growth. The trees left standing after logging should be sound, wind-firm, good seed producers, and well distributed. Seed trees should also be of good genetic strain so that they produce desirable offspring.

A shelterwood cutting resembles seed-tree cutting, but usually more trees are left standing. These provide seed and light shade to protect the young seedlings from direct sunlight and frost injury. Once seedlings are well established, the final cut removes the old trees, and the new forest takes over the area. The shelterwood system has been used for the reproduction of northern white pine.[4]

The selection system promotes an all-aged forest in which trees are harvested on an individual basis as they reach financial maturity. Young seedlings take over the space relinquished by the veteran (Fig. 25). A

FIG. 25 Marking a mature Jeffrey pine for cutting. Plumas National Forest. (*U.S. Forest Service photo.*)

type of selection forestry known as *Dauerwald* (continuous forest) was advocated in Germany and practiced for many years prior to 1940. The true selection forest, however, is not adapted to trees that grow best in even-aged stands, of which pines are an outstanding example. The selection system is best adapted for long-lived trees that endure shade, such as the northern hardwoods. Some foresters think it unsuited even to these.

REPRODUCING FOREST STANDS. After harvest of the mature timber crop, the forest may be reproduced by artificial planting or seeding or by favoring natural reproduction. Because of the expense involved in planting, American foresters normally try to get natural reproduction. This may require preparation of the seedbed by burning, scarification of the soil, or other measures. Sometimes woody shrubs and undesirable trees must be destroyed.

Improving Value with Use. The more intensively man uses the forest, the more rapidly he may shape it to fit his needs, provided his use is properly guided. It is by judicious use of the ax that the best individuals and species are favored, that overdense stands are thinned, and that adequate light is admitted to the forest floor. This is necessary to maintain vigorous activity by the soil fauna and flora that break down litter, converting it to useful humus, and release mineral elements needed by trees.

The extent to which the individual tree species will respond to release from the competition of their neighbors and the rapidity with which the thinned forest closes ranks so as to put on high wood volume are a measure of the response to management. This response in turn determines the type of silviculture that may be used, the length of the cutting cycle, and the monetary yield that can be expected from efforts expended on the forest.

Silvics, Silviculture, and Forest Management

The forester uses the term silvics to include those phases of soil science, botany, zoology, and protection that deal with the fundamental nature of forest plants and their relationships to one another, to soil, and to the animals that live in the forest.[7]

Silviculture draws upon all fields of knowledge included in silvics for its basic scientific information. It is not, however, a science in itself, but rather the art of using these sciences so as to produce high yields of valuable crops from the forest whatever the nature of these crops may be. Silviculture is limited by the physical and biological factors of environment, by the genetic capacity of trees, and by the expenditures man can afford to make to favor tree growth.

Practice of silviculture is an art in that it requires shrewd compromise between what is lowest in cost and what science shows to be the best practice. It is an art also because it must combine knowledge of many sciences in a way that can be skillfully done only through exercise of well-informed judgment.[4]

Forest management is the application of silviculture to the business of growing timber. Management, therefore, embraces not only silviculture but the other factors that must be combined to make the growing of timber a successful venture in terms of the owner's desire, whether this be for money, protecting watersheds, recreation, or game. The silviculturist is guided in his plans and activities by the aims of management, which reflect the wishes of the owner. There can never be a perfect compromise between the desires of the landowner and the needs of the forest trees for best growing conditions. It is for this reason that it will always require men of thorough training and keen understanding of potentialities to manage forest properties and to mold forest vegetation so as to achieve the ends desired by the timber owner.

Units for Buying and Selling Forest Land and Timber

Forest land is measured in terms of *acres, sections* or *square miles,* and *townships.* In countries using the metric system, *hectares* are used as units of area.

An *acre* of land is 43,560 square feet or 10 square chains. (A chain is 66 feet.) An acre is roughly equivalent to a square 208 feet on a side.

A *section* of land is a subdivision of a township of the national land survey system. It includes the land as originally surveyed, no matter how accurate that survey happened to be. An accurately surveyed section, except where correction lines for the earth's curvature are made, is a square 1 mile on a side and contains 640 acres.

One *township* is a square of 36 sections.

One *hectare* is a plot of land containing 10,000 square meters. It is equivalent to 2.47 acres.

A *board foot* is a unit of lumber measuring 1 inch in thickness and 12 inches in length and breadth or the equivalent thereof. It may be determined by multiplying the length and breadth of a piece of timber in feet by its thickness in inches. A piece of lumber 12 feet long, 6 inches wide, and 2 inches thick contains $12 \times \frac{1}{2} \times 2$, or 12 board feet.

Pulpwood, fuel wood, chemical wood, and wood used in tanning are usually sold by the *cord.* The *standard cord* is a stack of wood 4 feet high, 8 feet long, and made up of sticks 4 feet in length. It contains a gross volume of 128 cubic feet. The net volume may vary from about 70 to over 100 cubic feet, depending upon the size and straightness of the wood in the cord and the way in which it is piled.

Crossties, posts, poles, shoe-last blocks, blanks for baseball bats, and a host of similar products are sold by the *piece.* Piling is sold by the linear foot. The value of piling varies with its length and diameter. Price per linear foot for a 50-foot piling is considerably more than for one 40 feet long. Railway ties, likewise, vary in price with the size. Since switch and bridge ties are longer, they are worth more than the standard ties.

Mine timbers may be sold either by *piece* or by *weight*. Heavy mine timbers bring a higher price per unit weight than small mine timbers and lagging.

Veneer bolts may be sold on the log-scale basis. If of small size, like birch bolts, they may be sold by the cord.

Measuring Lumber. As most lumber is cut square-edged with parallel faces, the number of board feet in any board, plank, or timber can be easily determined with lumber rules.

Log Rules and Log Scaling. To measure the contents of logs in terms of squared lumber, log rules have been devised. Many types exist. In common use are the Doyle, the Scribner, and the International. The Doyle rule underscales the lumber volume that can be cut from small logs. The Scribner rule underscales the volume to be cut from large logs. A combination of the two, the Doyle-Scribner, underscales both small and large logs. The International rule gives accurate volumes for any diameter of log. As the log buyer or sawmill man is usually the one who determines the unit on which he will buy, the Doyle rule is in widespread use in the small timber of the eastern states. Inasmuch as the value of logs increases as their size increases, the Doyle rule, when used to buy ungraded logs, is not so unfair as it might at first seem.

Determining the volume of a log in board feet is called log scaling. The log scaler must make appropriate deductions for defects such as crook, sweep, decay, checks, or splits. The usual method is to scale the log as if sound and then scale the defects and subtract this from the gross scale (Fig. 26).

Neither the board foot nor the cord is an exact unit of measure when applied to round products. For this reason the cubic foot and cubic meter are substituted when precise measurement is desired. It is often useful to be able to convert from one unit of measure to another, but this can never be done with any degree of exactness unless size of product is known. For general purposes it is assumed that 1,000 board feet of lumber can be cut from approximately 204 cubic feet of logs, which is the equivalent of about 2.5 cords. One cord is about the equivalent of 400 board feet.

Estimating Standing Timber

Volume estimates of standing timber are important to those who buy or sell it, operate it, or appraise it for taxes or damage.

Timber estimating requires determining the volume to be found in trees of various sizes, the number of such trees per unit area, and the total area of trees of the given forest type and condition class. A first step, therefore, in preparing to estimate timber is to obtain tables that

Fig. 26 Scaling logs on the Eldorado National Forest, California. (*U.S. Forest Service photo.*)

will show for trees of various sizes the number of units of product they contain.[2,3]

Volume Tables. Volume tables have been prepared that give for trees of various sizes the volume in commercial units such as board feet, in cords, in cubic feet, in ties, and residual board feet, in other piece products, and in tons of such products as mine props. The volume tables are prepared by cutting sample trees, measuring their diameters, heights, and merchantable length, and computing the units of products they contain.[3]

Volume tables formerly were based on the diameter and total height of the trees. James Girard determined that more accurate estimates can be made by basing volume on the tree form class and the merchantable length of the tree. The form class, as defined by Girard, is the ratio between the diameter inside bark at the top of the first 16-foot log and the diameter at 4½ feet from the ground, where it can readily be measured by means of calipers.

Estimating Timber Volumes on Small Tracts. A forester usually takes with him tables of tree volumes and bark thicknesses, calipers or tapes for measuring tree diameters and distances, a hypsometer to measure tree heights, tally forms and holder, and possibly chalk to mark lines and a device to measure diameters at the top of the first 16-foot log. On small tracts the timber cruise may be 100 per cent, especially for such high-value trees as black walnut, white oak suitable for veneer and tight cooperage, ash, yellow-poplar, and cherry (Fig. 27).

After all trees have been measured and tallied in the woods, the volumes are determined and summarized. A stand table may be prepared that shows for each species and diameter the number of trees and total merchantable volume.

Estimating Timber Volumes on Intermediate-sized Tracts. For timber tracts over 100 acres in size, it may be too costly to measure and tally each tree, particularly if the timber is small in size or low in value. Some method of sampling the timber then becomes necessary. Two new tasks then must be performed by the timber cruiser: He must determine the area of the timber tract and of each stand on it, and he must decide on a method for sampling the trees on each.

If a map exists, the area can readily be determined. If no map exists,

Fig. 27   Estimating timber in a central New York woodland. (*U.S. Forest Service photo.*)

it may be necessary to make a survey of the property and from this construct a map.

The next task is to divide the timber tract into timber size or condition classes and into forest types. Condition class indicates the size of timber on an area as seedling and sapling, pole, or sawtimber in size; and if of sawtimber size, as light stands or heavy stands. If aerial photographs and a good road system are available, it may be possible in the field to delineate on the photographs these types and condition classes for later sampling. This is the system now used by most men who are obliged to estimate timber on large areas. When photos are not available, condition classes and types are determined on cruise lines.

For the areas that are to be sampled on the ground, the forester must determine the intensity of cruise he will need; that is, how many plots of definite area (⅕- or ¼-acre plots are usual) he must measure and where these are to be located. This requires experience with similar timber or preliminary sampling and statistical computations to determine variability. He then goes on the ground, following a compass line, and, stopping at regular intervals, he lays out square or circular plots of definite area. On these he records all trees by diameters and some by heights. From the latter he determines an average height to apply to trees of each diameter class. After sampling one plot, he moves on to the next. Usually a cruiser works with a helper who runs the compass line and tallies the trees. Separate tallies may be kept for each forest type and condition class.

It is desirable to keep the tallies on the individual plots separate, or at least in groups of five or ten plots. These then can be worked up as units and used to determine the variability of the timber stands. From this it is possible to calculate the probable accuracy of the timber estimate for any intensity of cruise that is used. Field tallies are worked up in the office. The volumes summarized are multiplied by the appropriate area factor to convert the sampled volume into total volume in the type and condition class.

Cruising Large Forest Tracts. For estimates of large areas it usually pays to use aerial photographs. A system of timber cruising is adopted that involves dividing the area up into types and condition classes and determining the degree of sampling needed in each to arrive at a satisfactory overall estimate. Careful statistical control should be used throughout. A competent survey party will include a man familiar with statistical and sampling procedures. It is his task to design the survey so that the greatest overall accuracy results for the effort expended. Skilled photo interpreters are employed, equipped with stereoscopes and special measuring devices that enable them to measure crown width and tree-shadow lengths on photos and from these to compute tree diameters, heights, and volumes. By a proper combination of extensive and intensive use of photos and by field checking on estimates of volumes, species distribution, and cull, estimates of timber volumes on vast areas can be made with surprising accuracy and a minimum of field work. Cost of such surveys is correspondingly reduced.

Tree Grades. A refinement that is being introduced into timber cruising is to estimate timber volumes by tree grades. Tree grades are based on the percentage of high-grade lumber that may be cut from them. As lumber values vary widely with grade, tree grade is essential to determine tree value. The change in tree grades within a managed stand over time is one of the best indexes of the success of forest management. Tree grades are usually developed from log grades and these, in turn, from the lumber grades produced. Log grades are coming into increasing use, especially where veneer and other high-quality grades are in demand. Up to 1962 only limited use had been made of tree-grade estimating.

Estimating Timber Growth. The simplest way to determine the growth rate of a forest property is to compare the growth rate with that existing on a similar property bearing the same types of timber and having similar soil and climatic conditions. This is the method generally used in Europe where records have been kept over a long period of time. These values are corrected for the density of stocking, and yield tables are made up which show the volumes that may be expected at any 10-year period in the life of the stand.

Such yield tables are available only for restricted regions in the United States, primarily because of the greater degree of variability in stand density, tree sizes, and tree species. "Normal" yield tables have been prepared by measuring stands of varying ages, all of which contain a full stocking of trees. These tables also are difficult to apply to field conditions.

A new approach, called the "continuous forest inventory," has been widely used on industrial forest holdings and has been adopted as standard practice in the nationwide forest survey. Permanent $\frac{1}{4}$- or $\frac{1}{5}$-acre plots are established on which all trees are identified and measured carefully for diameter, height, and tree quality. The plots are reexamined some 5 to 10 years later and the measurements repeated. If enough plots are used, an accurate estimate of growth rate over a wide area is obtained.

For immediate determination of growth rate on specific forest areas, the radial growth for the past 10 and 20 years may be determined for trees of various sizes from increment cores. This growth rate may then be projected forward for a like period of time with corrections, if needed, for diameter growth decline with increasing stand density.

How Forest-management Practices Affect Forest Growth

The growth on a given forest area will vary widely with the intensity of forest practice.

The more frequently timber stands can be cut over, the better. Weakened trees—those that have been damaged by wind, ice, or other causes—can thus be harvested to augment the total yield from the property. If the trees to be removed are carefully selected each time, the stand remaining will keep thrifty and grow rapidly.

Trees will thin out naturally when the volume, according to normal-yield tables, is at about 115 per cent of normal. Such stands can be thinned down to about 60 per cent of normal volume without seriously decreasing the total growth rate. Because of judicious and frequent thinning, the forest at Friesenburg in Denmark has stands yielding as high as 500 cubic feet per acre annually. The average for the whole of Denmark is but one-fifth this amount.

LITERATURE CITED

1. Baker, F. S. 1934. "The Theory and Practice of Silviculture," McGraw-Hill Book Company, Inc., New York. 502 pp.
2. Bruce, Donald, and Francis X. Schumacher. 1950. "Forest Mensuration," 3d ed., McGraw-Hill Book Company, Inc., New York. 467 pp.
3. Chapman, Herman H., and Walter H. Meyer. 1949. "Forest Mensuration," McGraw-Hill Book Company, Inc., New York. 522 pp.
4. Hawley, Ralph C. 1946. "The Practice of Silviculture," 5th ed., John Wiley & Sons, Inc., New York. 354 pp.
5. Kramer, Paul J., and Theodore T. Kozlowski. 1960. "Physiology of Trees," McGraw-Hill Book Company, Inc., New York. 642 pp.
6. Toumey, James W., and Clarence F. Korstian. 1942. "Seedling and Planting in the Practice of Forestry," 3d ed., John Wiley & Sons, Inc., New York. 520 pp.
7. Toumey, James W., and Clarence F. Korstian. 1947. "Foundations of Silviculture upon an Ecological Basis," 2d ed., rev. by C. F. Korstian, John Wiley & Sons, Inc., New York. 456 pp.
8. U.S. Department of Agriculture, Forest Service. 1948. "Woody-plant Seed Manual," Miscellaneous Publication 654, Washington. 416 pp.
9. U.S. Department of Agriculture, Forest Service. 1958. "Timber Resources for America's Future," Forest Resource Report 14, Washington. 713 pp.
10. Wilde, S. A. 1946. "Forest Soils and Forest Growth," Chronica Botanica Company, Waltham, Mass. 241 pp.

CHAPTER 7. *Harvesting Timber Crops*

LOGGING IS A dramatic operation, fraught with many hazards to life and limb. No one can watch a giant tree crash to the ground without a feeling of awe at the tremendous force released. Equally impressive is watching a cable skidder swing such logs to a landing as if they were matchsticks and watching a log loader pick up a 32-foot log, 3 feet or more in diameter, and place it on a logging truck. Because of the heavy, hazardous work they must perform, loggers feature in song and legend for their brawn and daring. The aim, however, of the logging operators has been to substitute machines for human brawn and to develop safety practices that minimize hazards to workers.

Logging embraces those activities involved in harvesting timber crops and transporting them to the place of manufacture. While strictly speaking it might apply only to the cutting and transporting of products in log form, it is used as a broad term to cover the cutting of pulpwood, veneer bolts, crossties, piling, poles, and many other products.

A major aim of silviculture is to produce crops of timber. The major aim of logging is to harvest such crops. Both silviculturist and logger desire to perform their jobs at minimum cost. If their activities are uncoordinated, the silviculturist may insist on operations that increase logging costs unduly, and the logger may so damage the forest as greatly to increase the costs of silviculture. The only sound approach is to coordinate both activities so that combined costs are minimized.

Logging changes the forest drastically. Under the skillful hand of a competent forester, logging is a means of molding the forest from one of mediocre quality to one of high quality. The character of logging, therefore, furnishes one of the best indexes to the level of forestry being practiced. If care is taken to preserve young growth, if seed trees and immature trees are left to restock the area, if heavy accumulations of slash are disposed of, and if the area generally is left in condition for producing a good second forest crop, it is evidence that conscious effort to practice forestry is being exercised.

Stumpage, the price of trees standing in the woods, made up in 1948 only 10 to 22 per cent of the lumber price f.o.b. mill,[1] and logging costs made up 30 to 50 per cent of lumber price. Labor represents the major item of expense in logging.

In 1956, stumpage represented 46 per cent of the wholesale price of Douglas-fir lumber; logging costs, 22 per cent. Nationwide there was a sharp increase in stumpage prices between 1945 and 1957 and a slight decline between 1958 and 1961.

The Evolution of Logging in America

Logging has gone through four stages in the United States. Early logging was primitive. It was done with the simplest of tools—the ax, the prypole, and the swing dog, a forerunner of the peavey. Horses or oxen skidded logs to water, whence they were floated to the mill as individual logs or attached together in log rafts.

The crosscut saw, peavey, and other improved tools and equipment helped usher in the second stage, characterized by winter sledding of logs in the North and wagon hauling where snow for sledding was undependable. Huge lumber camps were operated to house workmen and horses.

The third stage was the introduction of railway logging, the dominant system used in the Lake States. Logs were loaded on huge sleds that were drawn by horses over iced winter-haul roads across swamps and lakes to railway spurs. There the logs were loaded on cars and hauled to the mill. Where large lakes or streams were involved, many of the logs were driven after they reached the main watercourse. Railway logging reached its peak on the West Coast, where it was combined with high-speed cable skidding.

This high-lead system of cable logging has proved very destructive in that small trees that stand in the path of the onrushing logs are badly scarred or broken off completely. Where the logs are drawn along the ground, huge furrows are made. This method of logging is still used, however, particularly in rugged topography where tractors can be worked only with difficulty.

The fourth stage of logging, which in 1962 was widespread, was truck and tractor logging. The logs are skidded by tractor to a landing along a woods road and there loaded onto trucks that transport them to the mill. The great network of public highways throughout the country has greatly stimulated truck logging. A good truck road is more expensive to build than a logging railway spur, but it is also more permanent and admits of greater flexibility in the logging operation. When timber is smaller in size and scattered in location, as is the case throughout the eastern states, railway logging becomes far too expensive. Here truck and tractor logging is almost universal.

The fourth stage has also been marked by the introduction of power-driven saws for felling and bucking. Power-driven drills, road-building and maintenance equipment, loading devices, and small power skidders have also been introduced. The bulldozer, power shovel, dump truck, and other heavy road equipment are essential items in a modern logging operation.

The key machine in truck and tractor logging is the bulldozer. It clears the campsite, performs much of the heavy work in road building, prepares the landing sites, swamps out the skid roads, bunches the logs, and may skid them to the landing. It performs countless other chores, such as helping to rig a cable skidding operation, and it is the machine to lend a helping hand when truck, grader, or loader loses its footing.

Planning and Layout

Logging operations may be grouped under four headings: planning and layout, log making, skidding, and hauling. For logging a woodlot or some other small area, relatively little attention needs to be given to planning; but where large areas are to be logged, planning is very important. Planning a large western logging operation may involve these steps: (1) The head cruiser explores the timber area and decides whether or not it can be logged profitably. (2) Other cruisers or timber estimators determine the volume of timber and the locations of the heaviest stands. (3) The logging superintendent plans the location of his main haul road and sends in a survey party to stake it out. (4) Secondary roads or logging spurs are laid out and construction begun. (5) Spar trees and landings are located, sidings and turnarounds established. (6) The entire road system or railway system is built, or at least enough of it for logging operations to start. (7) The area is divided into cutting blocks to be assigned to individual cutting crews. (8) Repair shops, logging stores, and a logging camp are established if necessary. (9) Spar trees are rigged, logging equipment moved in, and the actual operations begun. While these steps are listed in sequence, they are actually carried on concurrently in most logging operations. While one area is being logged, the cruisers and surveyors are preparing for the next year's operation. While road making is going on at one end and logging operations are in active progress farther back, cleanup crews are taking out equipment and railway steel where logs have been removed. Relogging or other cleanup operations complete the logging job (Fig. 28).

The logging foreman must understand the cost of the several operations. It is his obligation to plan each phase so that the total cost will be minimized. He must know how far logs can be skidded before it pays to build additional road. He must lay out the operation in such a way that it moves in an orderly fashion without bottlenecks and without one

Fig. 28 It takes little capital to buy a small sawmill, but skill is required to saw lumber accurately. A Connecticut State Park Commission Service forester is instructing the young owner in sawing technique. (*U.S. Forest Service photo.*)

crew's endangering or being in the way of another. Coordinating all these activities and supervising them is a difficult task calling for special knowledge and administrative skill.

Logging Operations

Felling and Bucking. Timber is felled by using the ax or the ax and saw. First, the undercut is made perpendicular to the direction in which the tree is to fall. Skillful timber fallers can drop a tree almost anywhere they wish unless the tree is decayed, leans badly, or has a one-sided crown. Even then considerable latitude exists as to where the tree can be dropped. The fallers begin to saw on the opposite side of the tree parallel to the undercut until approximately 1 to 3 inches of wood remains, depending upon the size and species of tree. Usually, the tree will then start to fall. If necessary, wedges are used to start it tipping in the direction of fall. As the tree starts to fall, the saw is removed and the fallers step back out of the way to avoid being struck by debris or being injured by the butt of the tree, since it may jump back should the crown lodge partway down.

Limbs must be cut flush with the stem from the merchantable portion.

Bucking, that is, cutting the tree into measured log lengths, is done with a saw. Formerly the ax and crosscut saw were used for felling and bucking, and the ax alone for limbing. The one- and two-man power chain saws were used for most of these operations in 1962.

Power chain saws are operated by compressed air, electric motors, and gasoline motors. The more popular types are the gasoline motors inasmuch as these may be transported around the woods without the necessity of dragging cables or air hoses. Efforts are being made to mechanize further the operations of felling trees and bucking them into logs or pulpwood billets. Various types of tractor-mounted saws have been developed.

Active experimentation on timber-harvesting machines was under way in Canada and the southern section of the United States in 1962. These included machines that could limb, debark, and buck whole trees. Others could delimb, top, and debark a standing tree, snip it off at the stump, and load it onto a skidding tractor. Such equipment was still in the developmental stage, but experimenters were enthusiastic as to its future possibilities.[3] Similar experiments have been carried out in the U.S.S.R.

Skidding. After the logs have been cut, they must be moved to a landing for loading on railcars or trucks. This operation is called skidding, if done along the ground, or yarding, if done by overhead cable. Greater diversity is to be found in the methods by which logs are moved from the stump to the deck than in other phases of logging operations. The simplest method is to loop a chain around the log and drag it in by horse or tractor. At the landing the chain is unhooked and the logs are rolled by hand tools onto a deck.

To lighten the load on horses or tractor, various supports are used to hold the front end of the log off the ground. The "go-devil" consists of a bunk attached to two runners. A simple sled may be used. The "dray" is a type of bobsled. The logging arch is a device that straddles the logs holding the front end up. It may consist of high wheels attached to an axle and drawn by horses or of elaborate track-laying or rubber-tired sulkies with elevated fair leads through which choker cables attached to the logs can be connected to the tractor winch (Fig. 29).

A modification of the logging tractor is a combination tractor and arch all built together. Such a tractor usually is wide and has wide treads to facilitate winching logs in from the side and to give greater traction in soft ground. Having the arch and tractor as a single unit greatly increases maneuverability. Logging tractors of somewhat similar design have been in use since 1948 in the U.S.S.R.

The track-laying tractor, though unsurpassed for traction and pulling power, has certain disadvantages. The tracks are subject to heavy wear,

Fig. 29 An integrated rubber-mounted tractor and skidding arch. (*LeTour-neau Company photo.*)

and replacement is expensive. The machine can travel only at modest speeds. It is forbidden on asphalt-paved highways. It damages roots of uncut trees and it consumes considerable fuel. It is, therefore, unsuited for long hauls. The modern trend is to replace track-mounted equipment by rubber-mounted equipment where possible. A type of skidding tractor has been developed modeled after the heavy 7-yard self-powered earthmovers. The two forward wheels carry the engine. They are driving wheels equipped with a power transfer differential. The arch is hinged by universal joint mounted high so that the front wheels may turn under it. Each of the arch wheels has a separate drive. The result is a heavy four-wheel-drive articulated tractor and arch with a very short turning radius (Fig. 29). Comparable tractors have been developed for skidding small logs.

Where topography is too steep or where the ground is swampy so that neither horses nor tractors can work, various types of cable logging may be used. In the high-lead system logs are dragged along the ground by cable that leads through a block on a tall spar tree or portable spar. This provides enough lift to clear normal obstructions such as stumps.

The skyline system has a heavy cable suspended between two spar trees with a carriage riding on the cable. The skidding cable runs from the winch to the carriage and down to the ground, where logs are attached by choker cables. This system is useful in removing logs from steep canyon walls. A modest-sized version known as the Wyssen cable, which can be set up for small volumes of logs, has been developed in Switzerland.[1] Details on cable and other logging methods are given in textbooks and pamphlets on logging.[1, 2, 4, 5, 7, 8]

Various modifications on the high-lead and skyline systems of cable logging are used throughout the United States and Canada. The heavier and more elaborate systems are used in the big timber of the West, and the simpler systems are used in the East.

A gravity skyline system has been developed for large timber. In this case a 2-inch cableway is suspended with or without intermediate supports from the top to the bottom of a steep slope. A car containing a radio-controlled engine rides on this cable. The car is hauled up the slope and lowered by a power skidding winch and cable. The car itself has a powered winch from which cables can be let down on the slope. The system may be used for distances of 150 feet on either side of the main cableway.

In recent years, experiments have been made with full tree logging in both Canada and the U.S.S.R. The trees are felled, yarded to the landing area, and there limbed and bucked by power chain saws. The branches are piled and burned and the logs loaded on trucks for transport to the sawmill or pulp mill.

Hauling. At the log landing the logs may be placed on a rollway whence they are rolled onto trucks or freight cars for hauling to the mill. Various types of log loaders are also in use, including jammers, gin poles, skyline loaders, swinging booms, self-loading trucks, and crosshaul loading by means of a team or tractor (Fig. 30). Mechanical loaders include types that pick up the logs in huge iron fingers (air tongs) and place them on the truck. Hand loading is done with pole skids and peavey. Oftentimes conveyors are used for loading pulpwood.

The logging trucks may be conventional motor trucks fitted with special bunks on which the logs rest, or they may be the tractor and trailer combination, if used for heavy loads. All sorts of modifications exist, depending on the heft of the load to be hauled, the type of road over which it is to be drawn, and the skill and ingenuity of the manufacturer or builder who has prepared the truck for logging use. For soft ground, special wagons equipped with track-laying tread and drawn by a crawler-type tractor may be used. Pulpwood is usually hauled on conventional trucks or special trucks with long racks on which the wood is piled. In railway logging the logs are loaded on gondola-type cars, or

Fig. 30 A heel boom loader placing a huge hardwood log on a truck of an Aguinaldo Development Company operation in the Philippines. (*Photo by Martin Hurwitz, Peace Corps volunteer.*)

on flatcars. Special pulpwood boxcars, developed by a Maine railway, can be unloaded by unfastening one side, which is hinged, and tipping the entire car. Pulpwood may also be bundled to facilitate handling in the woods and at the mill yard.

Logging in the Northeast

The northeastern section of the United States has very little large sawtimber left. Much of the cut comes from farm woodlands and other small holdings of second growth. Consequently, logging operations are on a small scale and use relatively simple equipment. The common operation involves a one- or two-man crew with chain saws. These men fell, limb, and buck the logs. A tractor is used to skid the logs to a landing where they are rolled by hand onto the logging truck or loaded by a modified power shovel, forklift, overhead loader, or other device.

Trucks are usually unloaded by removing binding chains and stakes and rolling the logs off onto the ground or onto a rollway by use of a peavey. Various types of power devices are sometimes used to remove the logs from the truck (Fig. 31).

Pulpwood logging is similar to and, in fact, often carried on concurrently with sawtimber logging. Camps are operated in some remote areas of Maine and the Adirondacks but are rare elsewhere in the East. Hand peeling of pulpwood has been largely replaced by drum or other power peeling at the mill, or by chemical debarking in the woods. In pulpwood production one man will produce 2 to 4 cords per day. Production of sawlogs runs 2,000 to 4,000 board feet per man-day, depending on the species and size of the logs, on the skill of the men, and on the equipment available for their use.

A considerable amount of tree-length logging is being done in the Northeast. The trees are skidded in and bucked at a landing by power saw. This has increased the production of pulpwood cutters by ¼ to ½ cord per man-day.

River driving, though declining, was still in use in 1962 in Canada and Maine. Logs to be river-driven are landed on the river ice or along the banks of the stream, whence the logs can be pushed into the river by means of a bulldozer. River driving often requires heavy capital outlays for construction of splash dams, special flumes to carry the logs around rapids, booms to prevent the logs from being stranded along swampy

FIG. 31 Unloading pulpwood at the Northwest Paper Company mill, Cloquet, Minnesota. (*AFPI photo.*)

sections of the river, and various other improvements to avoid log jars or loss of logs through stranding on bars. Log floating, where it is feasible, remains the cheapest form of log transportation.

Both pulpwood and logs are transported by water in barges, on rafts, and in booms. Barges are used mostly for coastwise shipping and, to a limited extent, on lakes. Booms towed by tugs are used to move pulpwood and logs across inland lakes.

Logging in the South

Many southern operations are relatively small in size. The chain saw is widely used in felling and bucking. Logs are usually bunched and skidded to the landing by tractor. Logging of pine on the coastal plain is more highly mechanized than hardwood logging in the mountains and small woodlands. Production per man-day may be as high as 5,000 board feet. Where the stands of timber are large in size and operations are conducted by large companies, tractors and logging arches are used. Cable logging is used in swamps. At the landing the logs are usually loaded on trucks or tractor and trailer combinations by using power loaders. A number of new devices have been put on the market recently to facilitate the handling of logs at a landing.[5, 7, 8]

Western Logging

Logging techniques are highly developed in the West. The West has the largest trees, heaviest stands of timber, and roughest topography. Here logging is a major industry, methods are complex, and equipment is highly mechanized. It is here that a new profession, that of logging engineering, has been developed to cope with the multitudinous problems of logging occasioned by rugged topography and large timber.

Power chain saws are in common use. In the California pine region fallers work in pairs and may do no limbing or bucking. One pair of fallers may cut from 60,000 to 100,000 board feet per day, and one limber can usually keep up with a pair of fallers. Buckers are able to cut from 30,000 to 50,000 feet per day and usually work alone. The logs are bunched and hauled in by huge tractors equipped with logging arches. A large tractor may yard as much as 60,000 board feet per day in 32-foot logs. Loading is done with specialized log loaders. Formerly, railway hauling was usual in the pine region, but by 1962 had been replaced primarily by tractor and trailer hauling.[7, 8] Ponderosa and western white pine logging is similar, though logs and equipment are smaller.

Rugged topography, dense undergrowth, and fallen logs add to the difficulties of logging in the Douglas-fir region. The felling crew in the Pacific Northwest may cut from 25,000 to 30,000 board feet per day;

those using power saws, 75,000 to 80,000 board feet. Tractors equipped with logging winches are used in bunching, and arches are used in skidding. High-lead logging and skyline logging are still in use in certain areas where other types of logging are difficult because of topography. Almost all loading is done by power loaders. A great deal of the transportation is by truck.[7, 8]

The capacity of western logging equipment is astounding. Winches on skidding tractors can exert a line pull of 35 tons. Loaders can lift logs up to 40 tons. Logging trucks may haul up to 40 tons in one load. A log stacker at the yard may lift up to 50 tons. The trend is toward even larger equipment so as to increase the output per man-day and to reduce the breakdowns caused by the overloading often necessitated by the heavy logs.

Waste in Logging

Waste occurs in logging because of careless felling, which may break the log or injure valuable trees that otherwise would be left standing. Trees may also be injured or destroyed in skidding and slash disposal. The Forest Service estimated that in the year 1952, 13 per cent of all timber cut in logging operations was wasted.[6] The logging waste or residue referred to in this case does not take into consideration cull trees that were left standing or the waste in stumps.

Much progress has been made in reducing logging waste since 1944. In the West, the operation has been divided into prelogging, logging, and postlogging.

In Chap. 5 the "growth impact" of fire and tree diseases was discussed. Logging also has a "growth impact." This occurs where cull trees remain to occupy soil, when injured trees are left to become culls before the time of next logging, and when the forest is in such condition that young trees do not promptly become established to replace those harvested. Waste occurs if camps and other improvements needed to carry on logging are immediately removed or allowed to deteriorate. Because the entire costs of improvements must be met anew, this prolongs the time during which trees become unhealthy and die before loggers return for a second operation.

Growth loss occurs if logging is carried out too early or too late in the life of the stand. If timber is harvested before the stand is mature, the total volume cut is small and the value of products is low.

At the time of logging there are often many defective or cull trees in forests. These may contain as much as 50 per cent sound material, but it is so expensive to harvest and process such trees that they are left standing in the woods. The stumps and tops of trees are seldom harvested in logging operations. Exceptions are black walnut stumps and those of other highly figured woods that are useful for veneer and cabinet purposes, as well as pine stumps used for recovery of naval stores in the South.

The Place of the Forester in Logging

Careful logging is indispensable to intensive forest practice. The forester who understands logging is likely to hold a far stronger position in his company than one who does not. Logging is the first step in the chain of operations by which the product of the forest finds its way to the ultimate consumer. It cannot be bypassed; therefore, logging jobs exist whenever timber is utilized.

When forestry is integrated with the timber operation, roads built for fire protection can also be built to serve for logging. Timber cruising and management activities can be integrated with the logging program of the company. The woodlands-manager positions in large corporations are well paid. The men occupying these exercise a high degree of authority and spend vast sums of money for labor, equipment, and technical services.

Planning logging activities on a large operation requires a great deal more than simple woods experience. It requires knowledge of timber volume and quality, of engineering to survey and build roads, of the uses and limitations of logging machinery, and of cost control so as to minimize overall expenditures. It is a job for the fully trained forest officer who has been well seasoned by several years of practical experience.

Logging involves training the various men who take part in the operation. This training must emphasize care in protecting the forest, skill in the various operations, and, above all, safety. On operations where intelligently planned safety training has been given and safety constantly stressed, accidents have been no greater than in industries considered to present only normal industrial hazards.

LITERATURE CITED

1. Brown, Nelson C. 1949. "Logging: The Principles and Methods of Harvesting Timber in the United States and Canada," John Wiley & Sons, Inc., New York. 418 pp.
2. Bryant, Ralph C. 1923. "Logging: The Principles and General Methods of Operation in the United States," John Wiley & Sons, Inc., New York. 556 pp.
3. Clepper, Henry. 1961. "Thomas N. Busch and the Buschmaster," *Journal of Forestry*, 59:126–130.
4. Koroleff, Alexander M., and C. R. Silversides. 1948. "Transport of Wood by Gravity over Suspended Wire," Pulp and Paper Research Institute of Canada, Woodlands Research Index 43, Montreal. 8 pp.

5. Simmons, Fred C. 1951. "Northeastern Loggers' Handbook," U.S. Department of Agriculture, Agriculture Handbook 6, Washington. 160 pp.
6. U.S. Department of Agriculture, Forest Service. 1958. "Timber Resources for America's Future," Forest Resource Report 14, Washington. 713 pp.
7. Wackerman, A. E. 1949. "Harvesting Timber Crops," McGraw-Hill Book Company, Inc., New York. 437 pp.
8. Whisnant, A., ed. 1959. *Loggers Handbook*, 19:269.

CHAPTER 8. *Lumber Manufacture and Sale*

LUMBER manufacture is the process by which round logs are converted into square-edged pieces of uniform width and thickness. These pieces, if 2 inches or less in thickness, are called lumber; if over 2 inches, planks, deals, or squared timber. The terms are used loosely. The process of lumber manufacture involves the application of power to a tool that cuts a channel through the log. In simplest form this may be a whipsaw or sash saw with power applied by men. In modern sawmills, many power-driven machines and processes are used to complete the conversion. It may take days to convert a large hardwood log to lumber by hand sawing, but only minutes are required in a modern sawmill.

Lumber manufacturing is an important industry in the national economy. In 1958 the lumber and wood-products industries employed 586,000 workers, had payrolls of $1,997 million, and added $3,089 million to the value of their raw material as a result of manufacturing. The lumber industries outranked—in both employment and values created—the tobacco, furniture and fixtures, petroleum and coal products, rubber products, leather and leather products, and instrument industries.[14]

Of wood products harvested from the forest for the period from 1934 to 1952, logs for lumber represented more than half the total volume.[2] Of all the many products and services forests provide, timber for lumber manufacture has by far the greatest direct monetary value. It brings tangible returns to the timberland owners that far surpass returns received for watershed protection, wildlife, and recreation, important as the latter may be. Ignoring this basic fact leads to misunderstanding of the entire basis for private forest management in our country.

To speak of lumber manufacture only in terms of workers employed, values created, and timber consumed gives an entirely inadequate picture of what a generous lumber supply has meant to the American people. It has meant homes for families. Who can estimate the value of homes in satisfactions, family harmony, thrift, mental composure, and loyalty to country? It has helped to make possible independent farmsteads on which single families could pursue their livelihood unbeholden to a

127

landlord class. It has helped to make possible the creation of a host of small business enterprises from the crossroad stores to toy manufacturers. And it has provided a cheap and easily worked material suitable for the expression of man's creative urge, whether for a bookshelf, a pigeon cote, or a fine wood carving. These intangible values cannot be expressed in dollars, but they are high among those things that give meaning to human life.

Lumber also plays an indispensable role in our country's military defense. Poles, logs, and lumber were used in frontier blockhouses in colonial and early post-Revolutionary times (Fig. 5). During the First World War the 10th Engineer Regiment was engaged in cutting logs and sawing lumber to supply our fighting forces in France. Lumber was also in high demand at home.

In the Second World War lumber in huge amounts was used for barracks, military shops, overseas warehouses, bases, and docks, and to repair bomb damage in cities. Over 16 billion board feet of lumber, half the lumber cut that year, were used in 1944 to crate and box military supplies and equipment for shipment overseas.

Development of Lumber Manufacture

The use of wood for houses, boats, fences, and barricades began in America with the arrival of the first white man. Leif Ericson is said to have built ships from timbers harvested along the New England coast. Lumber manufacture was under way at Saint Augustine before the arrival of the Pilgrim Fathers and began at Jamestown, Virginia, in 1625 and at Berwick, Maine, in 1631. The early use of wood was in the form of twigs, small poles, and bark such as the Indians used for their baskets, tepees, long houses, and canoes. When white men brought in the ax, poles and hewn timbers were used to construct cabins, churches, trading posts, and forts. The first lumber was probably cut with the old-fashioned whipsaw. The first power sawmill was a modification of the whipsaw, substituting water power for human power. This gave way to steam power early in the nineteenth century. With the application of power came the development of the circular saw, which increased the speed with which logs could be converted into lumber. Toward the end of the nineteenth century the band saw was introduced in the larger and more efficient sawmills.[1, 2, 5]

The Trend in Lumber Production

Trends in lumber production for the United States as a whole and for four states are given in Fig. 32. It was not until 1905 that peak production in Maine occurred. The peak lumber production in New York State occurred much earlier. The graphs of lumber production for Minnesota and Mississippi show even more interesting trends. Production rose rapidly to a sharp peak in 1895 in Minnesota and in 1925 in Mississippi. From this peak, production in Minnesota dropped to less than one-tenth that at the peak; in Mississippi the drop was only one-half. The contrast indicates that Minnesota forests were more severely depleted by logging and fire than those of Mississippi.

All four states cut their old-growth timber when the market was first good. Production declined rapidly after this initial cut. All showed an increase to a secondary peak at the close of the Second World War. The decline was resumed after this peak.

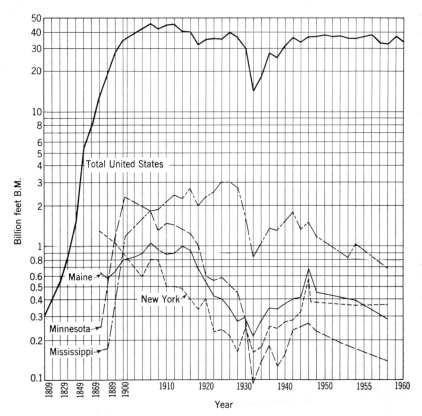

FIG. 32 Lumber production in four states and in the United States from 1799 to 1960. (*Data from* "*Lumber Production in the United States 1799–1946*," *by Henry B. Steer, U.S. Department of Agriculture Miscellaneous Publication 669, October, 1948; U.S. Department of Agriculture, Forest Service, "Historical Forestry Statistics of the United States," compiled by Dwight Hair, Statistical Bulletin 228, 36 pp., 1958; and National Lumber Manufacturers Association, "Lumber Industry Facts 1960–61.*")

Two other factors have influenced lumber production to some extent: the decline in per capita consumption of lumber and an increase in lumber prices. In Figs. 33 and 34 are shown indices for wholesale prices of lumber, of all building materials, and of all commodities. It is seen that all building materials have increased in price more rapidly than all commodities and that lumber has increased in price far more rapidly than all building materials. At the same time consumption of lumber per capita, though showing considerable fluctuations, has on the whole declined. The lumber price index continued to rise since 1949 and in 1960 stood at 121 per cent of the 1947 to 1949 level. Peak use of lumber per capita corresponded to the period of peak lumber production.[6,11]

The United States uses per capita more than four times the amount of lumber used in western Europe, three times that used in Russia, and 7½ times the amount used in Central and South America and in the world as a whole.

Some of the decline in per capita lumber consumption from the peak of 1,030 board feet per year in 1907 is due to the substitution of products definitely better suited than lumber to the specific purpose. An example is replacement of boardwalks by concrete sidewalks. Between 1945 and

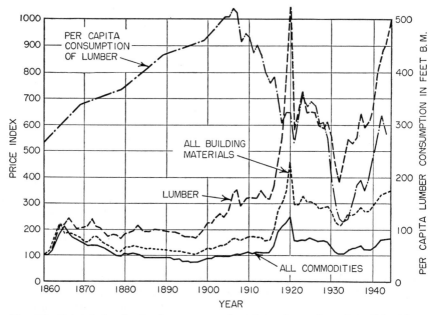

FIG. 33 Price index for lumber compared with similar indices for all building materials and all commodities, 1860 to 1944. The chart also shows per capita lumber consumption for the same period. (*Data on prices from "The Trend of Lumber Prices," by Lee M. James, Journal of Forestry, 45:646–659, 1947.*)

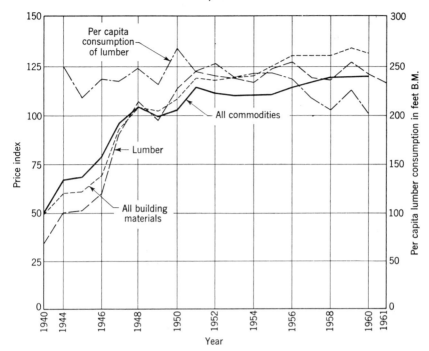

Fig. 34 Trends in per capita lumber consumption and price indices of lumber, all building materials, and all commodities from 1940 to 1961. 1947–1949 = 100. (*Data from U.S. Department of Agriculture, Forest Service, "Historical Forestry Statistics of the United States," compiled by Dwight Hair, Statistical Bulletin 228, 36 pp., 1958; U.S. Department of Commerce, Bureau of the Census, "Statistical Abstract of the United States," 1961; and National Lumber Manufacturers Association, "Lumber Industry Facts 1960–61."*)

1958 annual per capita consumption has varied between 193 board feet in 1958 and 270 in 1950, with a tendency toward low values since 1953.

That all is not well with the lumber and wood-products industry is borne out by changes in United States manufacturing industries between 1954 and 1958. Among 19 industry groups the percentage increase was 21 in value added by manufacture, but there was about a 1 per cent decline in total employment. For the lumber and wood-products industries, which stood at the bottom of the list, there was a decline of 5 per cent in value added by manufacture and of 9 per cent in number of employees.

Lumber Production by Species

The most important timber species used in lumber production in the United States for the year 1958 are as follows:

	Production, million bd. ft
Softwood species:	
Douglas-fir.......................	9,329
Southern pine......................	6,420
Ponderosa pine.....................	3,233
Western hemlock....................	2,475
Redwood...........................	917
Other softwoods....................	5,005
Total softwood production............	27,379
Hardwood species:	
Oak...............................	2,882
Yellow poplar......................	615
Sweet gum.........................	412
Maple.............................	572
Cottonwood and aspen...............	176
Other hardwoods....................	1,349
Total hardwood production............	6,006
Total softwood and hardwood production......	33,385

SOURCE: National Lumber Manufacturers Association. 1961. "Lumber Industry Facts 1960–1961," Washington, D.C. 57 pp.

The Sawmill

Lumber manufacture includes those operations that take place from the time the log is unloaded at the sawmill until the lumber, either seasoned or green, finished or rough, is loaded on the car for shipment to the consumer. A typical stationary, medium-sized sawmill has a log pond into which the logs are dumped directly from the truck. From the pond the logs are carried into the mill by means of a power-driven chain running in a V-shaped ramp. Here the logs are rolled onto a sloping log deck. From the deck they are placed directly on the saw carriage either by hand or by a mechanical loader. The log is pushed on the headblocks of the carriage and held against the knees by heavy pointed dogs while it is passed successively through the headsaw.

The headsaw may be either a circular or a band saw, but in either case, the saw will have swaged teeth. The first pass by the headsaw removes a slab. The second pass may remove a 1-inch board. After the second cut the log is normally turned, so that the flat face is either down or placed up against the knees. Additional slabs and boards are then removed, and the log re-turned for cutting off the third slab and boards. A fourth turning is made to remove the last slab, and the remainder of the cant is then sawed into lumber (Fig. 35).

The slabs go to a slasher or swing saw, where they are cut into short lengths for fuel wood. The round-edge lumber passes through an edger which trims the two edges square. The squared boards pass to the trim

FIG. 35 Sawyer operating a band headsaw, Webster Hardwood Lumber Company of Dixie, West Virginia. (*AFPI photo.*)

saw, where the ends are cut square, and then onto the green chain, where the lumber is graded and sorted (Fig. 36).

Power may be furnished by steam or a stationary diesel-power unit, or the machinery may be driven by individual electric motors. A large sawmill must have a burner or other waste-disposal unit for handling sawdust, slabs, edgings, and other waste material. Much of this may be converted into cattle bedding, pulp chips, and other useful products. If this material is used for pulp, the bark must be removed. This is usually done in log form. The slabs and edgings may then be chipped and sent directly to the pulp digester. Use of such chips increased rapidly in all forest regions during the decade 1950–1960.

The lumber may go directly from the green chain to the dry kiln or from the green chain to an air-seasoning yard. Usually the better grades are kiln-dried and low grades are air-seasoned.[7,9] In the dry kiln the lumber is dried in a period of two to four weeks. It may then be surfaced, regraded, and shipped, or graded and shipped directly.

Fig. 36 Grading freshly cut lumber on the green chain. (*K. S. Brown and AFPI photo.*)

Large sawmills commonly saw the lumber into thicknesses of 2 inches or more on the headsaw and then send it through a resaw for further cutting. A few sawmills in the United States have adopted gang saws for sawing small logs. Either one pass may be made through the gang saw to cut round-edge lumber, or the logs can be passed through one frame of gangs that flatten the surface on two sides. The cant is then turned down and sent through a second gang saw which removes the other two slabs and saws the cant into 1- and 2-inch lumber.[1,2] The gang saws are highly efficient for sawing small logs of uniform size. Insofar as possible, handling is mechanized. Rubber-tired timber carriers straddle small lumber piles, then lift and carry these bodily to the seasoning or storage yard, where mechanical cranes or other hoisting machines lift them to the yard piles. The forklift truck can pick up a bundle or small pile of lumber, carry it to the pile, and stack it up to heights of 12 feet or more. The same forklift can take the pile down, carrying the lumber to the planing mill or loading platform. Seasoned lumber may be handled in similar ways. Methods vary widely from mill to mill (Fig. 37).

The Portable Sawmill. The description given above of medium-sized sawmill operations is vastly different from that of typical portable mills. These may consist of only a headsaw rig. Usually an edger and a swing saw that serves to trim and cut up slabs are added. Power is furnished by a tractor or stationary power unit. Logs are delivered to the mill by truck and rolled directly onto deck and carriage. The lumber may be yard-piled or loaded directly onto a truck for sale. Such mills may be moved frequently, and some can be set up to saw as little as 100,000 board feet (Fig. 28).

Truck- or trailer-mounted sawmills using circular or band headsaws have been manufactured that can be set up to saw as little as 5,000 board feet. Many are as efficient as small stationary mills in terms of output per man-day.

Size of Mills in Relation to Lumber Production. The small portable sawmill common in the eastern section of the United States cuts about

Fig. 37 Modern lumber handling in a dry storage shed. (*AFPI photo.*)

5,000 to 8,000 board feet of lumber per day and employs from four to eight men. Many such mills operate intermittently. In contrast, the large mills of the Pacific Coast cut from 100,000 to 1 million board feet per day.[2]

The total number of sawmills operating in the United States probably exceeds 40,000. It was estimated that there were about 1,700 in New York State in 1948. The small mills, however, account for only a small percentage of the total production. Approximately 3 per cent of American sawmills produce over half the total output of lumber. Gradually, however, the small- and medium-sized mills are assuming increased importance as the supplies of heavy stands of virgin timber are depleted.[2]

Technical and Skilled Jobs in Lumber Manufacture. The most important workman in the mill is the head sawyer, for it is he who sets the pace in the mill and who decides how the log is to be cut up. He stands beside the headsaw and works the lever that controls the movement of the log past the saw. On the carriage may be a "dogger" and a "setter." Both men operate the dogs that hold the logs on the carriage; and the setter, on signal from the head sawyer, sets the log forward for the proper width of cut and, upon further signal, turns the log as the sawyer directs (Fig. 35). Lumber machinery manufacturers in 1960 offered fully automatic carriages by which the head sawyer alone may control the air dogs and set feed as well as the movement of the carriage. The tail sawyer catches the slabs and boards as they come from the headsaw and drops them onto rollers whence they are carried to the swing saws and edgers.

Lumber is sold by grade; the higher the grade, the higher the price it brings. The grade of lumber that can be sawed from a log depends on log defects and on the skill of the head sawyer. He will usually place the log on the carriage with the poorest face down. This face is sawed last after he has removed as much high-quality lumber as he can from the other three faces.[10]

The machinery in the sawmill is kept in shape by the millwright, whose task it is to oil and service the various pieces of equipment in the mill. The machinery consists of the jack ladder, the headsaw rig —which includes the headsaw, the carriage, and the driving mechanism for the carriage and log-turning machinery—the edger, the trim saw, and the slab saw. In addition, there are various power-driven rolls, dead rolls, chain conveyors, waste conveyors, sawdust blower, and sometimes resaws.

The saws are kept in shape by the saw filer, whose job ranks second only to that of the head sawyer. In large mills saw filing is done with complicated machines. Band headsaws must be changed about three times each eight-hour shift; other saws require less frequent changing. Each type requires a special filing machine.

Softwood lumber is commonly graded on the basis of its suitability for structural purposes, i.e., its strength. Hardwood lumber is graded on the basis of the yield of clear material above specified minimum sizes that may be obtained by ripping or crosscutting the board one or more times. Although grades are highly standardized, the lumber grader has no time to lay out cuttings or make other detailed inspection. He must quickly determine and mark the grade of each board as it passes by him, turning each one in the process (Fig. 36).

Freshly sawed lumber must be seasoned to reduce moisture content and prevent deterioration. This is the responsibility of the yard foreman and dry-kiln operator.

Lumber seasoning is a technical operation requiring careful control to avoid degrade due to warping, staining, checking, splitting, or case hardening.[2,4,7,9] Whether to be air-seasoned or kiln-dried, the lumber must be carefully piled, and "stickers" must be used to separate the courses for free air circulation.

The dry kiln is a chamber in which prescribed rates of lumber drying are maintained by control of temperature and humidity.

Moderate-sized mills must also have accountants to keep books and analyze costs. Lumber prices are set in the large market places rather than at the sawmills.

Supervision is required for mill operation, handling lumber in the yard, and finishing and loading. Constant care is necessary to keep each operation moving with a minimum outlay for labor. Mill layout must therefore be periodically scrutinized for minor improvement in flow of material and economy of labor.

Concentration Yards

The concentration-yard operator performs a valuable service in collecting lumber from widely scattered mills, grading it, seasoning it, holding it until he has carload lots of the types consumers demand, carefully grading it, and shipping it out. Concentration-yard operators oftentimes finance portable-mill operators.

Others run financing and jobbing operations without moving the lumber to central yards. Such businesses tend to thrive in the eastern states where small mills operated by owners with limited capital abound.

Wholesale Selling

Much of the lumber may be sold by manufacturers directly to large retail dealers. Even medium-sized retail dealers can use a full carload of lumber at a time. Lumber trade associations, of which there are many, establish standards and furnish information to manufacturers and customers that facilitates the lumber trade.

Exporting of lumber is carried out by large manufacturers, particularly those having port facilities. The British trade sets standards for international lumber dealing. Tropical timber and special veneer logs are imported for distribution to furniture and other manufacturers throughout the United States.[1, 8]

Retail Lumber Handling

The construction industry uses more lumber by far than all others. Lumber is the chief material used for erecting one- and two-family dwellings, garages, farm buildings, small stores, and warehouses. It is widely used for fences, scaffolding, concrete forms, temporary flooring, and other purposes in heavy construction of steel, concrete, and brick (Fig. 6). The agency furnishing lumber to builders is the retail lumberyard.

The country's average annual lumber production from 1950 to 1960 was about 37 billion board feet. Almost half of this reached the ultimate user through the retail yard. About 25,000 retail yards are found in the United States. Their principal business is supplying the needs of residential construction. The United States census lists more than 55 million dwelling units, mostly one- and two-family size and mostly of wood-frame construction for the year 1956.[12]

New dwelling construction in 1959 approximated 1.4 million units. The median postwar cost per unit was in excess of $8,000, and realtors estimate an annual cost of 5 per cent for maintenance and repairs, probably a generous estimate. Even so, it is easy to appreciate the importance of building materials and the retail lumberyards that supply them.

The retail yard is, generally speaking, small business. Usually the owner serves as general manager. His principal customers are light-construction contractors. He usually handles builders' hardware, cement, roofing, paint, and other builders' supplies as well as lumber.

In order to progress very far, the retailer has to be familiar with general construction practices as well as with the technical facts about his own merchandise. He must be prepared to sell "packages" for complete buildings as well as pieces. Traditional methods of construction are constantly being modified to fit changing demands. Different living habits bring about different needs. Although wood as a basic material for residential construction will not soon be replaced, new and more efficient uses for the same material are daily developments. Many new materials reflect sound advances in all the sciences. The task of promoting better means to good homes represents an economic obligation which may not be adequately met by the traditional lumberyard. The field is always open for improvements when the handling costs amount to 22 per cent of the cost to the consumer.

The successful retailer must be able to handle all the management details that affect a corporation by himself. A sound understanding of the principles of economics, finance, accounting, marketing, and salesmanship is useful.

Retail lumber dealers are often called on by both builders and the public to work up a bill of materials from simple blueprints. They may be asked to estimate costs of a garage or dwelling. Some engage directly in the contracting business as a sideline.

Designing and constructing homes is important work and should be done well. Planning is the key to success in the contracting business. Through application of engineering principles to house design, materials may be saved.

Almost anyone who has worked on a house can learn how to put in a foundation, erect framing, and build strong, watertight walls. It is quite another task, however, to combine materials and labor into an attractive home designed for functional living.

Perhaps no basic need in America has been less satisfyingly met than housing. With the population growing at more than 1.5 million per year and with a heavy increase in new families, opportunities for imaginative builders appear bright.

Prefabricated Buildings. The principle of prefabrication is used to some extent in almost all construction, as, for example, in window and door framing. The degree of prefabrication employed varies from such uses to complete precutting and section assembly. In 1948 there were 34,000 housing units built through use of ready-made sections of floors, walls, and roofs.

Although the industry seems to be permanently established, there are many problems yet to be solved which cause instability. Large business has the problems of overhead, shipping, and storage. The small operator lacks purchasing power and proper advertising, engineering, and architectural services.

Waste in Lumber Manufacture and Use

Waste in Manufacture. Sawmill residues consist of sawdust, slabs, edgings, trimmings, shavings, and of lumber too low in grade to be utilized. Additional waste occurs in seasoning, and a certain amount occurs in mill yards, wholesale yards, and retail yards. Sawdust, shavings, and other fine material make up 18 per cent of the total wood volume harvested, and this figure includes only that waste which occurs in primary manufacturing. The ordinary circular headsaw in the sawmill cuts a $\frac{1}{4}$-inch saw kerf. This means that if the lumber is sawed into 1-inch boards, 20 per cent of the wood volume is converted into sawdust. If headsaws are improperly aligned, they cut inaccurately. This results in a heavy loss of lumber in the planing mill, where boards must be planed to uniform thickness. The planing mills usually remove about ⅛ inch from each surface planed.

Slabs and edgings are often reworked for lath, small-dimension stock, and other wood products. Inasmuch as slabs and edgings come from the outside of the log, they contain the highest grade of lumber. It is, therefore, often profitable to spend considerable effort in salvaging this material. Trimmings account for considerable waste in sawmills because softwood lumber is usually trimmed to even 2-foot lengths and hardwood lumber to 1-foot lengths. The waste that occurs at the sawmill totals 48 per cent and is distributed as follows: [1, 12]

	Per cent
Saw kerf	11
Slabs	10
Edgings	9
Bark	9
Seasoning	4
Remanufacturing loss	4
Miscellaneous	1

Seasoning loss occurs because of checking, splitting, warping, cupping, internal collapse, and other defects that may occur when lumber is improperly seasoned. Such defects may be of a minor nature, or they may be so severe as to render the entire board useless except for fuel.

One means of reducing waste and of upgrading low-quality lumber is to cut it into small-dimension sizes at the mill. Hardwood small-dimension products include turning squares, blanks for such products as gunstocks, and precut pieces for chairs and other furniture parts. This is normally a highly competitive field but does result in close use of lumber at the mill.

Softwood small-dimension stock may likewise be prepared in sizes suitable for a variety of uses.

Waste in Lumberyards. Fungi and insects will attack lumber in storage, mills, concentration yards, and retail lumberyards if it is improperly piled and has a high moisture content. Green lumber sawed during warm weather is subject to sap stain unless it is treated with a stain-preventive solution and rapidly dried.

The powder-post beetle causes considerable damage to oak, ash, and hickory in lumberyards of the Northeast. Accurate estimates on the amount of damage are not available, but the overall waste due to decay and insect damage to wood in service and in yards is estimated at approximately 10 per cent of annual lumber use. Termites are said to cause $40 million worth of damage to wood in service throughout the United States.

Waste of Wood in the Construction Industry. Wood waste in the construction industry is considerably less than it formerly was, because lumber is trimmed to standard lengths used in construction. Unnecessary use occurs when specifications for structures require heavier timbers than are actually needed to support the weights involved.

Waste of Wood in Use. Wood-destroying insects and fungi attack untreated fence posts, poles, piling, ties, and other products that must be exposed to moisture or used in contact with the ground. Porches, and other portions of the house that are exposed to moisture, are particularly subject to decay.

Faulty construction is responsible for most of the decay hazard in houses. Any type of construction which results in collection of moisture —in the form of rainwater, snowmelt, or condensed moisture vapor—subjects wood to a decay hazard. This can be overcome by avoiding all types of leaks, by providing adequate ventilation, and by placing moisture barriers between the insulation and the interior wall surface.

Wood may give unsatisfactory service because of the use of green lumber, the wrong grade, or improper species, or because of shoddy design and workmanship. The use of poor fastenings, poor finishing, and poor glued joints reduces the service life of furniture and wood in other uses.

Decay in wood that must be in contact with the soil, such as posts, poles, and greenhouse flats and benches, and in wood in vegetable-storage houses that must be kept moist can be minimized by treatment with suitable preservatives.

Stabilizing the Lumber Industry

Lumber production for the country as a whole has fluctuated widely in the past, and the fluctuations have been closely related to business and building cycles. Only insofar as our nation succeeds in controlling business cycles can lumber production be stabilized (Fig. 32).

Even greater in significance than these major cycles, however, are fluctuations in production by regions, states, and individual companies (Fig. 33). Here depletion of standing timber supply has been a major factor. With a declining supply of raw material, business volume may be maintained by increasing the intensity of processing and by expanding operations to include manufacture of pulp, veneer and plywood, shingles, and other wood products.

Seasons and Cycles in Light Construction. The building industry fluctuates widely in activity with seasons and with building cycles. Such fluctuation intensifies the business problems of the retail lumber dealer, the independent builder, and the prefabricator. Unless each maintains flexibility in organization and business volume, he will fail to take advantage of good times or will take heavy losses during slack periods.

Building cycles are especially hazardous to prefabricators. Business may virtually disappear for months at a time. The individual builders may lay off hands and thus survive a period of low activity with minimum loss. This is one reason that many small builders characterize the light-construction field today.

Outlook for Lumber Production

The outlook for lumber production is not by any means as optimistic as that for plywood and paper products. In contrast to the growing consumption of these two products, lumber consumption in the United States has declined since 1908 in both absolute and per capita amounts. A slight upturn in consumption has occurred since 1945 because of the upsurge in residential construction, but the proportion of lumber used in home construction has continued to decline.[15] While some of this decline can be attributed to lower prices for competing materials, price relationships alone do not account for it all.[3] Lumber use has declined during periods when other building materials were increasing in cost more rapidly than lumber (Fig. 34). The per capita consumption of lumber was showing a decline during the decade 1950–1960, while softwood plywood increased by 156 per cent, fiberboards by 38 per cent, and structural steel by 5 per cent.[13] During this decade, the price index of lumber increased from about 114 to 116; of structural steel, from 120 to 200; and of structural clay products, from about 110 to 160. Lumber even showed a favorable price relation to construction materials in general during this decade.

Consumer dissatisfaction has been one element of importance due to the cost of painting and other upkeep. Also, brick and stone exteriors have a prestige value in some regions that wood does not command. Another unfavorable factor has been the cost of wood in place compared with that of competing materials. Lumber distributors, generally, have been slow to develop packaged selling, such as a completely erected house exterior or room units ready for installation, though a few have supplied such service.

Lumber costs also remain high because of the considerable amount of handling required between the headsaw and the finished product in place in a home.

But there is reason for optimism also. The lumber industry has launched a large-scale research and promotion program designed to discover and correct practices that lead to consumer dissatisfaction and prejudice. Lumber was winning back some of the markets that it had previously deemed lost to metals—window frames, for example, and kitchen cabinets. Real family income has been increasing, and with it an increase in the use of wood in homes occurs.[16] Most important of all, the number of families has increased, and this seems likely to continue for decades to come. The U.S. Forest Service—after considering expected future population, gross national product, housing, and other factors —estimated that residential construction may be between 2½ and 3 million units by the year 2000, roughly double the rate of construction in the decade 1950–1960.[12] Total future lumber demand is projected as follows:

	Demand, billion bd. ft.
Consumption in 1952	41.5
Consumption in 1975:	
Lower projection	47.6
Medium projection	55.5
Consumption in 2000:	
Lower projection	54.8
Medium projection *	79.0

* The latest projection by Resources for the Future for the year 2000 is 97.6 billion board feet.

As lumber use between 1952 and 1962 remained essentially the same, doubt has been expressed as to the likelihood that the upper and medium projections will be realized. Much will depend upon the availability of suitable sawtimber, the cost of lumber in place in buildings, and the ability of the industry to keep lumber competitive in the construction field.

LITERATURE CITED

1. Brown, Nelson C. 1947. "Lumber: Manufacture, Conditioning, Grading, Distribution, and Use," John Wiley & Sons, Inc., New York. 344 pp.
2. Brown, Nelson C., and James Samuel Bethel. 1958. "Lumber," 2d ed., John Wiley & Sons, Inc., New York. 379 pp.
3. Dickinson, Fred E. 1960. "Wood at Its Apogee," *Proceedings, Society of American Foresters' Meeting,* San Francisco, Calif., 1959, pp. 41–44, Washington, D.C.
4. Henderson, Hiram L. 1946. "The Air Seasoning and Kiln Drying of Wood," 3d ed., published privately, Albany, N.Y. 332 pp.
5. Holbrook, Steward H. 1938. "Holy Old Mackinaw," The Macmillan Company, New York. 278 pp.
6. Lumber Survey Committee. 1959. "National Survey of Lumber Demand and Supply," 113th Quarterly Report, Sept. 17, 1959.
7. Mathewson, J. S. 1930. "Air Seasoning of Wood," U.S. Department of Agriculture Technical Bulletin 174, Washington. 56 pp.
8. Steer, Henry B. 1948. "Lumber Production in the United States, 1799–1946," U.S. Department of Agriculture, Miscellaneous Publication 669, Washington. 233 pp.
9. Thelen, Rolf. 1929. "Kiln Drying Handbook," U.S. Department of Agriculture Bulletin 1136, Washington. 96 pp.

10. U.S. Department of Agriculture, Forest Service. 1946. "Crossroads Conference for Sawmill Operators: How to Produce More and Better Lumber," Washington. 58 pp.

11. U.S. Department of Agriculture, Forest Service. 1958. "Historical Forestry Statistics of the United States," compiled by Dwight Hair, Statistical Bulletin 228, Washington. 36 pp.

12. U.S. Department of Agriculture, Forest Service. 1958. "Timber Resources for America's Future," Forest Resource Report 14, Washington. 713 pp.

13. U.S. Department of Agriculture, Forest Service, and Commodities Stabilization Service. 1960. "The Demand and Price Situation for Forest Products," Washington. 39 pp.

14. U.S. Bureau of the Census. 1960. "Statistical Abstract of the United States," 81st ed., Washington. 1,040 pp.

15. Zaremba, Joseph. 1960. "The Vanishing Lumber Market for House Exteriors," *Forest Products Journal*, 10:642–643.

16. Zaremba, Joseph. 1961. "Family Income and Wood Consumption," *Journal of Forestry*, 59(6):443–448.

CHAPTER 9. *Wood: Its Nature and Its Uses*

Wood is a material of such universal utility that, had nature not supplied it in great abundance, man would himself seek to invent such a product. Wood has high strength in relation to its weight. In tensile strength it exceeds steel by three- to four-fold. In compression its strength is one-third to one-half that of steel. In stiffness it greatly exceeds steel on a weight basis. Across the grain wood is relatively weak in tensile strength and compression, but along the grain it is very strong. Wood has low heat, sound, and electrical conductivity. It, therefore, makes warm walls, warm furniture, rooms relatively free from objectionable reverberations, and relatively soundproof walls. Wood is soft enough to be easily fashioned and worked with simple hand and machine tools into a great variety of shapes and forms. Since it has intrinsic beauty, it is well suited for the manufacture of interior trim, furniture, and other commodities in which appearance is of great importance.

It has an absorbent surface suitable for gluing, staining, or painting. Its elasticity is such as to make it suitable for long bows and for making violins and woodwind musical instruments. Its shock resistance makes it the preferred material for railway ties, baseball bats, golf-club drivers, and for shuttles and picker sticks used in weaving.

How a Tree Grows

Wood is made up of tiny cells that are formed in the two actively growing regions of the tree: the tip regions of root and stem and the cambial region. Elongation of stems and roots occurs only at the tips. Here behind a cover of protecting tissue lies the apical meristem, or region of dividing cells, and here are formed the cells responsible for all increase in length of stem and root. The apical meristem gives rise to all cells that make up the primary stem tissue. Buds that develop into branches, leaves, or flowers are formed at the tip.

The apical meristem also gives rise to the cells that form the cambium a short distance back from the growing tip. The cambium also is a region of rapidly dividing cells. It forms between the primary xylem (wood)

145

and phloem (bark) in the newly formed stem and gives rise to all secondary tissues found in the mature tree stem. The cells cut off on the inside of the cambium become woody, thereby giving strength to the main tree stem. Those cut off on the outside develop into the bark that protects the cambium and main stem and conducts fluids. Near the outer surface of the young stem is another bark-forming region called the cork cambium, which forms corky tissue. As the stem grows, the cork cambium is pushed outward, ruptures, and dies. New cork cambia are formed inside by young bark cells. This process is repeated continually as the tree grows.[2] The expansion of the main woody cylinder causes rupture of the outer bark, which eventually is sloughed off.

The wood on the tree stem is laid down each year in a sheath that extends from the root tips to the stem tips. This sheath completely surrounds the stem and, once formed, becomes lignified (woody) and develops into permanent tissue. Except during the year of its formation, the sheath does not itself increase in diameter or length. Each year a new sheath is formed on top of the old and thus the tree increases in girth. Each year also the actively growing stem tips form new cells that extend the height of the stem. Each new sheath is longer than its predecessor by the amount of total elongation that occurred during its year of formation.

Gross Structure of the Tree Stem

The mature tree stem from the center out contains a pith, a region of soft spongy cells having little lignification and therefore adding little to the strength of the tree stem. Outside the pith are the various sheaths of wood. When the stem is cut in cross section, we see these sheaths as rings, called growth rings. They extend from the pith to the cambial region that lies between the wood and the bark. Outside lies the bark, which may be made up of alternate layers of corky and fibrous tissue. Bark tissue in itself adds little to the strength of the tree stem.

If a small portion of the tree stem is broken, it tends to splinter, for the main elements of the stem are much longer than thick and are arranged parallel to the tree stem. This gives the tree stem its strength to resist bending and breaking as it sways in the breeze and bears its burden of leaves in summer or snow and ice in winter.

Between the pith and the bark there is often a zone of darkly colored wood and a zone of lightly colored wood. The dark wood is spoken of as heartwood and the light-colored wood as sapwood. This difference in color is due in part to the deposition of various chemical substances in the heartwood of the tree. The light-colored sapwood forms the main channel for movement of water and minerals up the tree trunk to the branches and leaves. Being highly permeable to water, sapwood on posts and other wood products exposed to attack by fungi decays readily. The dark-colored heartwood of most trees conducts little water, because the conducting vessels are either plugged by thin membranes, called tyloses, as in white oak, or impregnated with resin, gums, or other substances that impede water movement, as in longleaf pine. The heartwood functions chiefly as a supporting column for the crown. Generally it is considerably more decay-resistant than sapwood.

A cross section of the tree stem may also reveal a series of fine lines extending radially from the bark toward the pith. These are called rays. They are very prominent in oaks and inconspicuous in aspen and, therefore, help one to identify kinds of wood. The ray cells serve as a channel for movement of materials across the growth rings and as storage cells for reserve foods. Their function will be better understood after a description of the cellular structure of the tree stem.

Microscopic Structure of Wood

The Cellular Structure of a Coniferous Stem. When a very thin section of a coniferous woody stem such as white pine is prepared and examined under the microscope, the cellular makeup of the stem becomes evident (Fig. 38). With low-power magnification the differences between springwood and summerwood that mark the annual rings of temperate-zone woods become evident. The cells formed in the spring are large and have large central openings; those formed in the late summer are flattened and have narrow openings in the center. A cross-sectional view will reveal here and there large channels lined by thin-walled cells. These are resin ducts which serve to transport the resin up, down, or across the tree stem. The major-supporting elements of the woody stem are tracheids, which are small- to medium-sized, heavy-walled cells. When these cells are viewed in a section cut in a radial direction, it can be seen that they have small circular markings, known as bordered pits.

Running at right angles to the tracheids are the ray cells. These consist of ray tracheids and thin-walled ray cells. Since the thin-walled ray cells are weaker than tracheids, they are responsible for the wood's splitting along the line of a ray. Other types of cells in a pine stem are those that secrete resin. These are found both in the rays and in the vertical stem tissue.

The tracheids are no longer living cells nor do they perform any living function. Many of the thin-walled cells may also be dead, but those that secrete resin are living. Other living cells enter into the storing and transformation of foods manufactured in the tree leaves.

The Cellular Structure of Hardwoods. The term "hardwood" is applied loosely to all forest trees that do not belong to the group known as conifers. A more appropriate name is porous woods, because these stems,

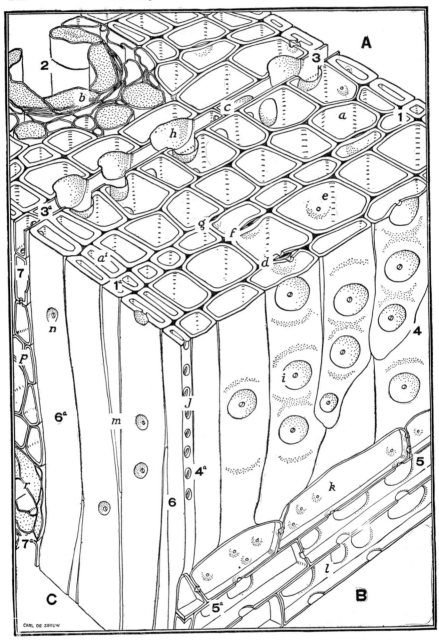

FIG. 38 Schematic diagram showing cellular structure of northern white pine wood. Face A, a cross section showing a resin canal 2, tracheids *a*. Face B, radial section. Face C, tangential section. (*From Brown, Panshin, and Forsaith, "Textbook of Wood Technology," vol. 1.*)

in contrast to those of the cone-bearing trees, are made up of small wood fibers with very narrow cavities and of large thin-walled connected tubes that serve as the main conductive channels for movement of water and other materials up and down the tree stem. These show up as pores and are very conspicuous on a cross section of the wood. Their presence can easily be demonstrated by taking a short length of red oak or some other stem, placing one end in water, and blowing on the other end. A series of minute bubbles will disclose the passage of air through the pores.

The hardwoods are divided into two groups: the ring-porous group and the diffuse-porous group. In the ring-porous species the springwood pores are very large, whereas the summerwood pores are small. In the diffuse-porous woods the difference in size of pores is far less noticeable. When sections of the hardwood stems are examined under the microscope, it is found that the wood is made up of long, heavy-walled wood fibers which bear pits, vessel segments which serve as the conducting members for transport of water, and other thin-walled cells some of which serve as gum-canal cells and others of which enter into the transformation and storage of food (Fig. 39). Rays may be very broad and conspicuous or narrow and inconspicuous. They may be made up entirely of thin-walled cells or of radially oriented thin cells and vertically oriented tracheids. As in the conifers, they serve to transport material across the tree stem. The living cells within the main woody stem transform plant foods, changing sugars into starches and, later on, starches into sugar. In this way food stored during late summer can be utilized during early spring for rapid growth of new plant tissue.

Wood Identification. The various types of cells, their shapes, and their arrangements serve as features for identifying wood. Most common woods can be readily identified by the gross features that are easily discernible to the naked eye or under a hand lens. A few woods can be identified only by a study of their microscopic structure. Here, the types of cells that are present, their markings and shapes, the number and types of pits, and the presence or absence of gums, resins, and various other features in the wood have definite value in deciding upon the kind of wood in question.

The Structure of the Woody Cell. The electron microscope reveals an even more fascinating structure than can be seen by naked eye, hand lens, or microscope. This instrument enables us to study the structure of the cell itself and the way the cell-wall layers are built up. The cell wall consists of three layers: the middle lamella, a layer of relatively weak tissue between the cells that is made up largely of lignin; the primary cell wall, a relatively thin layer that is first laid down in cell formation; and the secondary cell wall that is usually quite thick and forms the main supporting layer (Fig. 40). A warty layer is sometimes

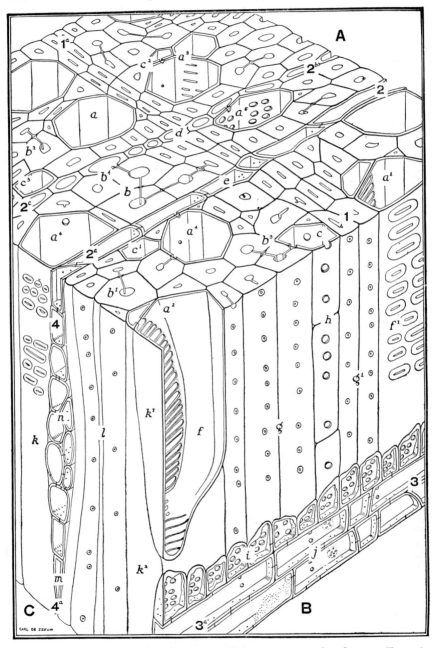

Fig. 39 Schematic drawing showing cellular structure of red gum. Face A, cross section showing vessels *a*, fiber tracheids *b*. Face B, radial section showing ray 3 and wood parenchyma *h*. Face C, showing ray cells 4 and fiber tracheid 1. (*From Brown, Panshin, and Forsaith, "Textbook of Wood Technology," vol. 1.*)

found on the inside of the secondary cell wall. The cell walls themselves are found to be made up of microfibrils that are wound around the cell in a spiral manner. These microfibrils may branch and rejoin or join other microfibrils. Hence, the cell itself is tube-shaped with walls composed of netted, spirally wound tissue of great complexity. The microfibrils are cemented together with lignin, thus making an amazingly complex, tough, and stiff system (Figs. 41a and b and frontispiece). The microfibrils are made up of longitudinally oriented cellulose molecules that are too small to be revealed by the electron microscope.

The Physical Properties of Wood

The strength, hardness, toughness, shrinking and swelling, and other physical properties of wood are dependent to a considerable extent upon the type of wood and its microscopic and macroscopic structure. Balsa

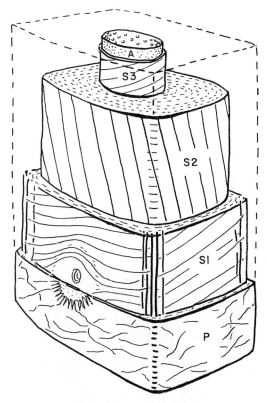

Fig. 40 Schematic drawing showing the structure of the woody fiber. (*Courtesy Modern Materials. Edited by Henry H. Hausner. Academic Press Inc. 1958.*)

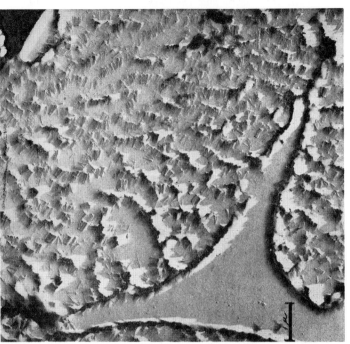

FIG. 41b Molecular architecture in a wood cell. Portion of the lumen and gelatinous (G) layer in a gelatinous fiber from the tension wood zone in bigtooth aspen, *Populus grandidentata* Michx. The methacrylate was removed from the ultra-thin cross section before shadowing with Cr. Note the microfibrillar strands which have fallen over onto the substrate when the matrix was removed. Magnification: 13,200×. (*Photos by W. A. Côté and A. C. Day, State University College of Forestry at Syracuse University.*)

FIG. 41a Molecular architecture in a wood cell. Electron micrograph, replica technique, of the inner surface (lumen lining) of a portion of a vessel segment in basswood, *Tilia americana* L. The large, ropelike bands are spiral thickenings, and the smaller, white shadows project from pit openings. The organization of the microfibrils around the pits and into the thickenings is particularly significant. Magnification: 8,400×.

wood, for example, has thin-walled fibers, making it soft, light, and easily worked. Because of the lightness, stiffness, and high degree of porosity it is especially valuable for certain types of construction and insulation. Balsa wood is excellent as a core material in sandwich construction, as it holds glue well, is stiff, and is exceedingly light.

In contrast, hickory and oak are heavy. They have large pores, but they also have a high proportion of dense wood made up of heavy-walled fibers that make the wood hard and strong. Some kinds of wood are very straight-grained. White pine and redwood are good examples. Others may be spiral-grained or have interlocked grain as elm does. In the latter case, part of the woody elements may be laid on in a clockwise spiral direction and other layers in a counterclockwise direction. Such interlocked grained woods resemble plywood in that they are exceedingly difficult to split. A tough wood is one that will bend without breaking. Ash is noted for its toughness, and because of this it is used for making tennis rackets, snowshoes, handles, ball bats, and other articles requiring bending and shock resistance. Basswood, cedar, and redwood break quickly upon bending and hence may be called brittle woods. Woods that are strong in both compression and tension are those that are dense.

The primary woody substances, cellulose and lignin, are essentially the same for hardwoods and softwoods of all species. The major differences that occur in the chemical composition of woods are due to the gums, resins, minerals, and other material that may permeate the wood but do not enter directly into its cellular structure. Certain woods, such as aspen, basswood, and white pine, are relatively free from gums and resins. Longleaf and other southern pines, and particularly lignum vitae, are heavily impregnated with gums and resins that increase weight, add to stiffness and brittleness, and give them special properties. Lignum vitae is a standard wood for stuffing boxes in steamships.

Not only does wood vary with species of tree, but it also varies within the individual tree and from one tree to another, depending upon its growth conditions. Rapidly grown pine tends to be more brash or brittle than pine that has grown at a moderate rate and is therefore little suited for pattern and cabinetwork. Rapidly grown hickory, ash, and maple are harder than slowly grown wood of the same species and are consequently used where high strength and high resistance to shock are important. For a great many uses no specifications as to the number of rings per inch are required, but for special high-grade uses, such as for aircraft structural material, this becomes of major importance. A rough measure of the strength of wood can be obtained from its specific gravity.

The hardness of the wood influences its tendency to split upon nailing. Very hard woods, such as maple, ash, and hickory, are difficult to nail without splitting. Soft-textured woods, on the other hand, such as basswood, white pine, and aspen, are easily nailed and have only moderate tendency to split.[9]

All woods when dry have good heat- and electrical-insulating properties. Most of the gums and resins that are found in woods are themselves nonconductors of electricity. Some kinds of wood have a relatively high ash content. These when wet will conduct electricity. For this reason their moisture content can be estimated by means of an electrical moisture meter which measures the resistance between two electrodes when these are pushed into the wood. The open pores and thin-walled tracheids that are common in wood give it excellent heat-insulating qualities.

A property of wood that causes considerable difficulty in use is its tendency to shrink and swell with change in moisture content. Water occurs in wood as free water in the lumina of the cells and as absorbed moisture within the cell walls. The free water can be evaporated from the wood without causing any pronounced shrinkage. The point at which all moisture has been withdrawn from the cellular spaces and yet cell walls are saturated is called the fiber saturation point. This occurs at about 25 to 30 per cent moisture content. As the wood dries below the fiber saturation point, shrinkage occurs and continues to occur until the wood is thoroughly dried. Shrinkage across the grain exceeds many times that along the grain. Equilibrium moisture content is that at which the wood neither gains nor loses moisture when surrounded by air of a given relative humidity and temperature. Wood that is to be used for furniture must be dried to about a 6 per cent equilibrium moisture content; that to be used for exterior walls, to about 12 per cent. The tendency of wood to shrink or swell can be largely prevented by impregnating the wood with certain chemicals that will hold it in swollen condition. If chemicals having the capacity to swell wood are then polymerized, they form a plastic substance with the wood that maintains the wood at the swollen dimension.

The high affinity of cellulose for water not only causes wood to shrink and swell but also results in lowering the strength properties with increases in moisture content. The lignin fraction of wood is a plastic substance that can be softened at elevated temperature. Wood heated with steam, or even dry heated, to above 100°C can be bent into various shapes and will retain this bent form. Heating wood also reduces its stiffness. If wood is compressed or held in bent condition for a long time, it tends to hold its new shape because of lignin flow.[6]

Uses of Wood

Design of Wooden Structures. Joints require major attention by the wood designer, for it is here that failures are most common. The strongest wood joints are those that are held by means of glue. The use of modern synthetic adhesives has made it possible to fabricate a large number of articles from wood which have essentially the same strength in all directions and which can be formed and bolted without any weak joints.

The stiffness of a beam varies directly with the square of its depth. Therefore, wooden members that are to support floors and heavy structures are made deep in comparison with their breadth or thickness. In designing wooden structures, it is important to bear in mind the type of loading that will be involved. Structures are strongest if the load is along the lengthwise dimension of the beam rather than at right angles to it. Other engineering principles that apply to all structural design should be followed. Trusses should be built up of triangular sections so that each section will be rigid. Use should be made of those forms and shapes that give the desired degree of stiffness or flexibility in all designs of wooden structures.

Small as well as large wooden structures need careful design. Good design takes advantage of the highly useful properties of wood and offsets its weaknesses. Furniture and many other household articles will give unsatisfactory service if designed with weak joints or improperly finished. Glued joints that loosen in time are especially troublesome. If modern design, based on an understanding of wood properties, is combined with modern machining, gluing, and finishing, wooden articles can give pleasure and satisfaction during long periods of use.

Veneer. Veneer is wood cut in sheets of thicknesses from $\frac{1}{100}$ to $\frac{1}{4}$ inch. Veneer $\frac{1}{100}$ inch in thickness is used for aircraft plywood. Veneer even thinner than $\frac{1}{100}$ inch is used for plywood novelties and is backed with paper for wall paneling. The thick veneers, $\frac{1}{8}$ to $\frac{1}{4}$ inch, are used for containers or stamped articles. Face veneer for furniture is $\frac{1}{28}$ inch thick.

Fine veneers are used in furniture and office panels; common veneers, in the manufacture of many small items that run into big-time business. Items such as medical splints, tongue depressors, fruit containers, ice-cream spoons, veneer baskets, and shipping containers all come wholly or partially from veneer. The industry is characterized by small and large operations requiring varying degrees of technical skill, depending upon the quality of the product being sliced or sawed.

Veneer is manufactured by three separate processes and is called rotary veneer, sliced veneer, or sawed veneer. Rotary veneer is made from large logs cut into appropriate lengths corresponding to the width of the veneer desired. The bolts are soaked and steamed, then placed on a huge lathe. The veneer bolt turns against a heavy knife that extends the full width of the veneer bolt.[7] The first few sheets that come off extend only partway around the bolt; but as the bolt becomes cylindrical, the veneer is unwound in a continuous sheet. It is clipped into appropriate lengths, and defective sections are discarded. After it passes through a dryer, it is ready for manufacture into plywood or other products. When the veneer is used for making baskets, tongue depressors, and novelties, the processing is carried to completion before the veneer is dried.[3]

Sliced veneer is preferred to rotary cut for most exposed furniture surfaces. The sawed flitch or crotch is steamed, fastened in a heavy clamp, and moved in an oblique direction past a huge, sharp knife that cuts off the veneer in thin slices the length of the flitch being cut. Sliced veneer is kept in the order in which the sheets are removed to facilitate matching of grain. It is dried and shipped to furniture or other manufacturers. Skill is required in matching veneer to obtain the most beautiful patterns of grain.

Sawed veneer is cut from flitches by thin circular or band saws that remove the veneer in thicknesses of $\frac{1}{8}$ to $\frac{1}{4}$ inch. Veneer sawing is not common today.

Plywood. Plywood consists of thin layers of wood glued together so that the grain of each successive layer is at an angle to the layer next to it. The finished product is strong in all directions, changes little in dimensions, and is superior to solid wood for many construction and allied purposes. The plywood industry is characterized by large corporations, large independent operators, and by highly technical problems of production. The industry is faced with the problem of maintaining production with a decreasing supply of large clear logs. Adjustments are being made so that small medium-grade logs may be used.

Veneer for plywood manufacture is usually rotary-cut unless the plywood is to be used for special furniture stock. The veneers are first separated into core stock and face stock. Core stock can be of less uniform texture and can include certain defects, provided they do not result in complete absence of woody material. Where knotholes exist, they must be patched. Knots in face stock are also removed and small plugs inserted either by hand or by modern patching machines. Core stock may be of one kind of wood and face stock of another.

Plywood is constructed of three, five, seven, or any other odd-numbered layers of veneer.[7] The two surface layers have the grain running in the same direction, but each successive layer of veneer is placed at right angles to the preceding. Crossbanded layers are coated top and bottom with glue. The laid-up panels are pressed at room or slightly elevated temperatures. When hot-presses are used, one or two panels are pressed between steam-heated platens.

Many adhesives used in modern plywood require heat for curing. Adhesives may be of the quick-setting, synthetic resins such as the phenol-formaldehydes, urea-formaldehydes, melamines, and resorcinols; or they may be made of animal or vegetable glues of the cold-setting type. After the adhesives have cured, the plywood panels are taken from the presses, the edges are trimmed square, and the surfaces are sanded. The plywood is then ready to package for shipping to the consumer.

The veneer and plywood industries are among the most rapidly growing wood industries. Production of softwood plywood in 1945, expressed in equivalent to $\frac{3}{8}$-inch stock, was 1.2 billion square feet.[12] By 1950 it was 2.7 billion; by 1955 it was 5.3 billion; and by 1959 it was 7.6 billion.

Laminated Wood. Laminated wood consists of successive laminae glued together with the grain parallel. The Second World War with its shortage of metallic structural material brought the industry into prominence. Large laminated beams, trusses, and arches make possible construction of huge, clear-floor-space buildings such as blimp hangars, armories, and field houses. Because of their beauty and ease of forming in any desired shape or design, laminated beams have been widely used for church construction and auditoriums.

Laminated timbers may be small or huge. The small timbers are used to make skis, aircraft propellers, and other products requiring high strength and uniformity. Large timbers are laminated for boat keels and skegs, beams, arches, and other purposes.

The problems in this industry are many, including high cost of production, waste in manufacture, and high wood requirements.[9] Many research and production problems still face the industry. Lamination does, however, permit fabrication from boards of timbers with greater strength ratios than solid wood members. It also permits wood to remain in the large-construction field despite scarcity of large-size timber.

Sandwich and Box Construction. Special types of structures used in aircraft and for other purposes where high strength and stiffness must be combined with light weight are sandwich construction, box beams, and laminated shapes.[7] Sandwich construction consists of inner and outer layers of strong and heavy veneer separated by a balsa wood, fiberboard, or other light core material. This principle is used in manufacturing flush doors and other products.

Box beams and shapes are hollow structures with solid or laminated wood for the two main stress-bearing members, but these are connected by glued-on plywood faces that cause the two members to act as one and greatly stiffen the beam. Glued, laminated shapes and forms may be of box construction, or they may be arranged in T's, angles, I beams, and other forms.

Particle Board. A product of relatively recent origin that is finding widespread use is particle board.[5] The process involves converting scraps into chips of rather uniform size, thin chips or flakes for faces and thicker chips for the interior of the board. The chips are screened, coated with adhesive, spread on platens in layers, and placed in a hot-press to cure the adhesive. The resulting product, usually made up in ¾- or ½-inch thicknesses, is relatively stable against moisture changes, as the random arrangement of chips gives the effect of crossbanding in plywood. A flake surface has a pleasing pattern suitable for certain decorative uses. The product has found widest use as a core material in veneered-furniture manufacture. The quality of the final product can vary widely, depending upon the quality and uniformity of chips, the amount and character of the adhesive used, the care in manufacturing, and the degree of technical control employed. Plant capacity in the United States was about 15 million square feet annually in 1950, 100 million in 1954, and 300 million in 1956.

Wood Treating

When wood is to be exposed to destruction by insects, marine borers, fungi, and fire, wood treating to prolong its service life has long been practiced. Its importance increases as wood becomes scarce and as costs of replacing wood in service mount. The quantities treated, by products, for the year 1959 are shown in Table 3. Creosote, either full strength

TABLE 3. WOOD GIVEN PRESERVATIVE TREATMENT, 1959 [1]

Material treated and unit	Quantity treated	
	Million units	Million cu. ft.
Poles, number................	6.0	78.3
Crossties, number............	16.1	52.1
Lumber and timbers, bd. ft.....	521.4	39.9
Fence posts, number..........	25.9	15.7
Piles, lin. ft.................	23.7	14.7
Switch ties, bd. ft...........	54.2	4.5
Cross arms, number..........	3.9	3.6
Miscellaneous, number........	5.7	5.7
Total volume treated........	....	214.5

or in solution with coal tar, petroleum, or other materials, was used for 69 per cent of all wood treated. Other preservatives in use in 1959 included pentachlorophenol, chromated zinc chloride, acid copper chromate, fluorochrome arsenate phenol, and various proprietary products. These products may be used for both pressure and nonpressure treatment.[1]

For treating ties, piling, posts, and poles, coal-tar creosote is cheap and effective. This may be applied as a hot dip or diluted with solvents and applied with a brush. Results with these methods are only partially successful, for the treated layer is thin, and insects, fungi, or marine organisms will enter through cracks, checks, and abrasions. Far more effective protection is provided by treatment with preservative under pressure. Piling, which requires heaviest treatment, is first heated and evacuated. Treatment technique determines the degree of penetration and amount of preservative retained.

Commercial wood-treating plants operating in 1959 totaled 358. Of these, 277 were pressure plants, 55 were nonpressure, and 26 used both methods of treatment.[1]

Wood may also be treated with dyes or other chemicals to modify its appearance and properties. Of considerable importance is the treatment of wood with chemicals that reduce inflammability. Wood cannot be made fireproof, i.e., treated so that it will not oxidize when heated to high temperature; but it can be treated so that it will not support combustion. Effective fire-retardant chemicals are diammonium phosphate, monoammonium phosphate, and phosphoric acid. Other chemicals that will stop combustion are aluminum sulfate, ammonium bromide, ammonium chloride, boric acid, and monobasic zinc phosphate. Still others may reduce either flaming or glowing.[8,9] Wood treated with fire retardants in 1959 totaled 919,000 cubic feet, of which lumber made up 78 per cent.[1]

Wood-processing Industries

Wood processors include those manufacturing novelties, furniture parts, handles, boxes, crating, cars, boats, musical instruments, trunks, baskets, fixtures, and burial caskets.[4] They vary in complexity from nailing a few boards together to make a loading pallet to the manufacture of piano movements and hand-carved shoe lasts.

The 1954 United States census classified wood processing under 25 categories. A few of the more important are shown in Table 4, which gives the number of establishments, men employed, and value added by manufacturing. Together, the wood-processing industries employ more workers and create greater values than sawmills and planing mills.

Furniture manufacture exceeds all other wood-processing industries in value of products. The industry is centered in the eastern section of the United States. Important producing states with percentage of total output attributed to each are: North Carolina, 12.0; New York, 10.5;

TABLE 4. STATISTICS ON SOME IMPORTANT WOOD-PROCESSING
INDUSTRIES FOR THE YEAR 1954 *

Type of industry	Number of establishments	Number of men employed	Value added by manufacturing, dollars
Veneer mills................	261	12,825	59,250,000
Plywood plants.............	255	39,201	246,250,000
Wooden containers..........	1,513	52,304	208,116,000
Wood household furniture (not upholstered)...............	2,785	124,898	592,714,000
Wood office furniture........	112	5,509	28,757,000
Miscellaneous wood products...	2,103	38,600	172,961,000

* U.S. Bureau of the Census. 1957. "Census of Manufacturers: 1954," Bulletins MC 24 A-D, MC 25 A, B, Washington.

Illinois, 9.0; Indiana, 8.5; Virginia, 7.0; Pennsylvania, 6.5; California, 6.0; and Michigan, 5.5.[7]

The wood-processing industry is primarily a small-business field. Only a few companies are sufficiently large to have their securities listed on the great national exchanges. Many are family-owned. Because they are small, they offer both the advantages and the limitations of small industry.

Broadly speaking, wood goes through the following operations as it is manufactured into commodities: sawing, seasoning, resawing, machining, gluing or fastening with metal fastenings, finishing, and packaging. These might be departments in a manufacturing plant. Most require technical control by an engineer, chemist, or wood technologist for best results.

Conditioning Wood for Manufacture. Wood to be fabricated must first be properly conditioned. If the wood is to be bent or cut into veneer, it must be soaked and steamed. Soaking in chemicals that have mild plasticizing action facilitates bending. Many wood products, particularly those made from veneer or turned on a lathe, may be completely processed before drying occurs. Each industrial plant is likely to own and operate its own dry kiln, observing the precautions mentioned earlier.

Machining of Wood. Woodcutting operations include ripping and crosscutting, planing the surface with jointers and planers, molding the wood by the use of variously shaped high-speed cutterheads, turning wood on various types of lathes, boring by the use of bits, and carving of wood either by hand or by use of mechanical routers.

Each operation has its own technical problems. Rough lumber is resawed, ripped, and crosscut very much as these operations are carried out in the sawmill. To cut wood along curved lines, narrow-bladed band saws are used. For very intricate work the jigsaw is required.

Jointing, planing, molding, turning, and routing require careful workmanship and technical control to avoid splitting, roughened grain, and overheating of wood or cutter.

Fastening of Wood. The weakest parts of products manufactured of wood are likely to be the joints. Joint weakness is accentuated by the weakness of wood across the grain. Various mechanical devices have been constructed to facilitate and improve wood fastening: wooden pegs or dowels; nails of various sorts, including rosin-coated, cement-coated, and roughened galvanized nails; corrugated metal fastenings; wood staples; screws, including lag screws; bolts; rods; and various forms of timber connectors. The effectiveness of all these mechanical fastenings varies with the way in which they are used and with the wood on which they are used.

Gluing. Gluing is one of the most satisfactory means of fastening two pieces of wood together. A good glued joint is as strong as the wood itself. It avoids the removing or crushing of woody substance. Modern glues and adhesives are made from a great variety of raw material. Some can be used on wood that is to be subject to repeated wetting and drying; others are moisture-resistant; some have little or no resistance to moisture. Some glues are subject to crazing or other forms of breakdown after prolonged use.

Sanding and Finishing. Sanding is a relatively simple operation that requires but ordinary care for good results. It should be well done, because it is very difficult to cover up a rough surface by paints and varnishes.

Final finishing involves applying various seals, stains, lacquers, varnishes, paints, or other coatings to the wood surface. Many of these must be sanded or rubbed between coats and buffed after the application of the final coating.

Modern wood finishing is of two types: the penetrating oil seals, stains, varnishes, and resins; and those finishes applied to the surface of the wood, such as shellac, varnish, lacquer, paint, and related products. The penetrating seals, and particularly the penetration of wood with chemicals that form a hard resin upon curing, give a surface of maximum resistance to marring.

Few of the modern finishes applied to the surface of wood are as resistant to wear as the wood substance itself. This is especially important in flooring. Varnishes are readily worn away.

Research and Quality Control. Every large manufacturing plant must have its inspectors and testers to maintain quality of product. Oftentimes such a plant has a special research staff whose responsibility it is to test the products of the company and of its competitors and to determine means by which products can be made more cheaply and better. Wood-products engineers are employed in practically all research organizations of the wood-processing industries, but only the larger companies feel that they can afford a research organization.

Packaging. Packaging the finished product is the work of an important division in many plants. The packaging industry for the United States as a whole does an estimated $5 billion business yearly. Modern packaging involves not only mechanical protection but also protection against moisture and fumes that might mar or destroy the product during transit. During the Second World War a vast research and training program, which involved designing of packages for special products, was undertaken. The result was a technique that made it possible for packages to be immersed in salt water or to stand unprotected for two or three months on the shores of tropical islands without damage to the contents.

Plant Layout and Design. Small wood-fabricating plants as a group might profit much from adopting modern plant layout and design in their operations. Men who have specialized in layout of woodworking plants have been able to perform important services in improving flow of materials and output of factories.

Management, Sales, and Administration. The wood-processing industries and those servicing them require sales management, production management, and general administration. Men with technical background who understand how to apply modern technology and administrative techniques so as to increase output, improve quality, and lower costs are being sought.

Wood-processing Residues

All wood processing creates residues, or waste products. The most common are sawdust, shavings, defective pieces, and short or narrow pieces.[10] These represent a substantial source of wood for profitable use, provided such material in usable sizes and volume can be collected at reasonable cost. Integrated industries that include sawmills, planing mills, particle-board mills, veneer mills, and pulp mills located on a common site can reduce waste to a minimum. Other companies may contract their residues to nearby plants. Small plants in dairy regions can usually dispose of shavings, sawdust, and fine chips for cattle bedding.

The total residues from wood-processing plants in 1952 are given in Table 5. Certain types of mills create large volumes of residues in proportion to the product being manufactured—cooperage, 54.5 per cent;

TABLE 5. PLANT RESIDUES IN THE UNITED STATES
AND COASTAL ALASKA, BY KIND OF MATERIAL
AND BY INDUSTRY SOURCE, 1952 *

Industry	Material, million cu. ft.			Per cent
	Coarse	Fine	Total	
Lumber †.....	1,466	1,484	2,950	86
Veneer.......	67	138	205	6
Pulp ‡.......	82	88	170	5
Cooperage....	23	17	40	1
Other ¶......	23	26	49	2
Total......	1,661	1,753	3,414	100

* U.S. Department of Agriculture, Forest Service, 1958. "Timber Resources for America's Future," Forest Resource Report 14, p. 171, Washington.

† Includes planing mills integrated with sawmills.

‡ Plant residues at pulpmills relate only to wood losses in storage and in preparing the wood for pulping. Losses incurred in the pulping processes are excluded.

¶ Includes small-dimension and turnery plants, shingle mills, chemical and excelsior plants, and similar establishments using roundwood.

lumber, 47.9 per cent; veneer, 47.2 per cent; and miscellaneous manufacturing, in aggregate, 29.4 per cent.[11]

Wood Turning. The wood-turning industry has very heavy waste. Most of the material that is turned is first sawed square or split and seasoned before it is turned. Losses in turning of squared blanks often run as high as 75 per cent of the wood material. The loss is particularly heavy in turning such products as bowling pins, shoe lasts, spools, spindles, bobbins, shuttles, gunstocks, handles, ball bats, and related products.

Veneer. Veneer manufacture produces residues from 47 per cent of the raw material. Short unusable lengths of veneer are produced by the rotary process in truing up the veneer bolt before continuous sheets can be taken off. The central core of veneer bolts is sometimes sawed into small-dimension lumber. Veneer scraps are produced by trimming to remove defects. Veneer loss also occurs during seasoning when the veneer may crack and check.

Secondary-wood-processing Waste. The amount of waste that occurs in secondary wood processing varies widely from product to product. In products such as ladder rungs, turned furniture, and handles, the waste runs as high as 75 per cent. In furniture manufacture it may run even higher. A high degree of waste is inevitable in products that must be turned, molded, and shaped by various means. Waste also occurs as a result of cutting out defects and of buying improper lengths of lumber for the product to be made. Total waste is estimated at 463 million cubic feet, all of which is probably used for fuel or other purposes.

A special form of waste is due to overspecification by lumber buyers. Much high-grade lumber is used for purposes for which low-grade would do just as well. Elimination of this type of waste awaits the development of an intensive market for small-dimension material.

LITERATURE CITED

1. *Proceedings, American Wood-Preservers' Association, 56th Annual Meeting,* p. 257, Washington, D.C., 1960.
2. Brown, H. P., A. J. Panshin, and C. C. Forsaith. 1949. "Textbook of Wood Technology," vol. 1, McGraw-Hill Book Company, Inc., New York. 626 pp.
3. Brown, Nelson C. 1950. "Forest Products," John Wiley & Sons, Inc., New York. 399 pp.
4. Deckert, R. C., and R. J. Hoyle. 1957. "Wood-using Industries of New York," State University College of Forestry at Syracuse University, Technical Publication 27. 124 pp.
5. Johnson, E. S., ed. 1956. "Wood Particle Board Handbook," The Industrial Experimental Program of North Carolina State College, Raleigh, N.C. 303 pp.
6. Kollmann, F. 1955. "Some Aspects of Wood Technology (being a series of lectures delivered at the Forest Research Institute, Dehra Dun, in 1951)," Office of Geodetic and Research Branch, Survey of India, Dehra Dun, India. 192 pp.
7. Panshin, A. J., E. S. Harrar, W. J. Baker, and P. B. Proctor. 1950. "Forest Products—Their Sources, Production, and Utilization," McGraw-Hill Book Company, Inc., New York. 549 pp.
8. Steer, Henry B. 1949. "Wood Preservation Statistics 1948," *Proceedings of the American Wood-Preservers' Association,* 45:407–450.
9. U.S. Department of Agriculture, Forest Products Laboratory. 1940. "Wood Handbook," Washington. 326 pp.
10. U.S. Department of Agriculture, Forest Service. 1947. "Wood Waste in the United States," Report 4, from "A Reappraisal of the Forest Situation," Washington. 45 pp.
11. U.S. Department of Agriculture, Forest Service. 1958. "Timber Resources for America's Future," Forest Resource Report 14, Washington. 713 pp.
12. U.S. Bureau of the Census. 1960. "Statistical Abstract of the United States," 81st ed., p. 702, Washington.

CHAPTER 10. *Wood Chemistry, Paper, and Plastics*

IN CHAP. 9 it was stated that microfibrils of wood fibers are bundles of linearly oriented cellulose molecules cemented together by lignin. Wood chemistry deals with the study of cellulose, lignin, and other wood constituents; their molecular structure and properties; their chemical behavior; their use in industry; and their breakdown by microorganisms and other means.

Both cellulose and lignin belong to a family of chemical compounds known as polymers. A polymer is made up of a number of simple units chemically linked to form long chains or networks.

Composition of Wood and Occurrence of Components

Chemically, wood contains two types of components: those that are insoluble in neutral solvents, or nonvolatile [10] with steam, or both; and those that can be removed by such solvents or steam.[9] The latter are spoken of as extractives, or extraneous substances, and include tannins, waxes, oils, resins, gums, sugars, pigments, and other substances. The former, called the wood substances or cell-wall substances, are made up of lignin and the polysaccharide system termed holocellulose, which is made up of cellulose and the hemicelluloses together with minor amounts of pectic materials. Hemicellulose is the name applied to the alkali-soluble portion of holocellulose. The hemicelluloses may be broken down by weak acids. Wood contains about 20 to 30 per cent lignin. Temperate-zone hardwoods contain less lignin than the softwoods. About 50 to 60 per cent of the cell wall of wood is composed of cellulose, and about 20 to 30 per cent is comprised of hemicelluloses. In wood the individual fibers are held together with an amorphous material in the middle lamellae which is primarily lignin together with a certain proportion of hemicellulose and perhaps some cellulose. The lignin in the middle lamellae not only cements the cells together but adds rigidity and strength to the wood. The primary and secondary cell walls contain a relatively small amount of hemicellulose and lignin and a large amount of cellulose, though, actually, both lignin and hemicellulose are found

165

together with cellulose in all portions of cell walls throughout the woody stem.

Since both cellulose and lignin are inert to ordinary chemicals, wood is not easily corroded in the air or in salt water. Cellulose and lignin both, however, can be decomposed to yield foodstuffs that will support the life of fungi and various other wood-destroying organisms. For this reason wood decays. Neither pure cellulose nor pure lignin contains ash. Wood ash contains a fairly high percentage of potassium and calcium. The ash content of wood is due largely to the deposition of chemicals in the tree stem from the water that is transported from the roots. A small part of the chemicals enters into the live tissue, in the rays, cambium, and bark. Consequently, wood ash contains all those elements that are essential for plant growth, except the carbon, hydrogen, oxygen, nitrogen, and sulfur that are lost during combustion.

The Chemical Nature of Cellulose

Cellulose is the major component of the cell wall of woody and other plants. Cellulose is a chemical compound of high molecular weight made up of units of anhydroglucose, that is, glucose from which a molecule of water has been subtracted. The empirical formula for cellulose is written as $(C_6H_{10}O_5)_n$, where n equals the number of glucose anhydride units combined in the molecule. Native cellulose has 5,000 to 7,000 anhydroglucose units per molecule; wood pulps, 600 to 1,000; and commercially regenerated cellulose, such as rayon, 200 to 600 units.[4, 10] The cellulose molecule is large enough to be classed with colloids. Cellulose can be quantitatively hydrolyzed to yield glucose.

Cellulose molecules are linear or threadlike in form. Most of them are organized parallel to each other and more or less parallel to the fiber axis. In a highly organized parallel condition, these molecules form microcrystals, whose existence can be proved by X rays. It is the linear nature of the cellulose molecules, together with their packed parallel organizations, which gives cellulose fibers their strength.

Cellulose from all plants has the same chemical composition. Cellulose is closely related to starch chemically and has the same empirical formula. The difference lies in the linking of the glucose units. These are believed to be cup-shaped. In starch, the linkage is with the cups all concave upward so as to form a spirally coiled chain. In cellulose, the linkage is with the cups alternately concave upward and concave downward, thus forming a linear chain. This small difference in structure is responsible for vast differences in physical properties and chemical behavior. When treated under controlled hydrolysis, starch breaks down into maltose and cellulose into cellobiose. These are identical in composition but differ in stereochemical configuration. Cellulose can be arbitrarily divided into three groups—alpha-, beta-, and gamma-cellulose. Alpha-cellulose, which contains the longest molecular chains, remains undissolved when treated with 17.5 per cent aqueous sodium hydroxide; beta-cellulose dissolves but may be precipitated by acidification of the alkaline solution; and gamma-cellulose, which is made up of the shortest molecular chains, remains in solution. Cotton has about 98 per cent alpha-cellulose. Wood pulp has a much lower alpha-cellulose content and is higher in amounts of beta- and gamma-cellulose.

Plant cell walls contain other substances known as hemicelluloses. These have been loosely defined as those portions of the cell wall that may be extracted by dilute alkalies or by mild hydrolysis. However, portions of the hemicelluloses are quite resistant to chemical action and remain in the purified wood pulp. The hemicelluloses are made up of long chains of sugar units quite like the cellulose, but the nature of the simple sugars may differ from that of cellulose. Hemicelluloses when hydrolyzed may yield glucose, galactose, or mannose (all six-carbon sugars called hexoses) and xylose or arabinose (pentoses). Hemicelluloses which are made up mainly of pentose sugar units are known as pentosans. These upon hydrolysis yield pentoses that cannot be converted directly into alcohol by yeast. However, certain yeasts have been discovered that convert pentose sugars into proteins and fat usable as fodder for animals. The pentose units can also be converted to furfural.

It is possible, by appropriate treatment of wood with chlorine and 95 per cent alcohol containing 3 per cent monoethanolamine or by other chemical means, to dissolve away the lignin and leave the total polysaccharide fraction. This product is called holocellulose and is the non-lignin portion of the cell wall, or the total cellulose plus hemicelluloses. Woody plants contain 70 to 80 per cent holocellulose.

Cellulose is separated from most of the other constituents of wood by the industrial chemical pulping processes: the sulfate, the sulfite, and soda processes.

Properties and Derivatives of Cellulose. Cellulose has high affinity for water. Even after cellulose has been dried in a vacuum oven over phosphorus pentoxide, it still retains 0.35 per cent water. It is, therefore, one of the most powerful dehydrating agents. Dry, fibrous materials are good electrical insulators, but it is almost impossible to keep woody material dry. The electrical conductivity of wood increases over 100,000-fold in the range from 7 to 30 per cent moisture.

Wood pulp or cellulose fiber may be mechanically "hydrated." This is one of the actions that takes place when wood pulp is beaten. The fibers hold more water because of the increased area of the finely broken fibers. The pulp tends to become gelatinous. The glassine grades of paper pulp are made by "hydrating" the pulp in the beater. Since such pulp gives up its moisture very slowly, it can be run only at a slow rate on a paper machine. It is said to have a low freeness. After prolonged beating, the fibrous nature of wood pulp almost completely disappears, and the whole becomes a gelatinous mass, which, upon drying, becomes a horny, amorphous substance.

Cellulose can be dispersed in a cuprammonium solution known as Schweizer's solution.[4] From such a solution the cellulose can be recoagulated in a dilute acid bath. Rayon manufactured by the cuprammonium process is known as Bemberg rayon. The viscose process of manufacturing artificial silk is more widely used today. In this method cellulose is combined with caustic soda and the alkali cellulose is reacted with carbon disulfide to give a product, cellulose xanthate, soluble in dilute sodium hydroxide. From this cellulose xanthate, cellulose can be regenerated by acidification. If the viscose solution is forced through a spinneret and the cellulose regenerated in the acid bath, a thread or filament is formed. If the viscose solution is extruded through a long slit, it forms a sheet, which, upon drying, becomes cellophane.

Cellulose treated with a mixture of nitric and sulfuric acids forms nitrocellulose, which has high explosive properties.[10] Nitrocellulose containing less nitrogen than guncotton is used for lacquers and plastics. Cellulose forms esters with acetic acid known as cellulose acetate, which, being thermoplastic, may be softened by heat. Various plastic materials are made of cellulose acetate, including rayon, films for photographic work, and various other products. Lacquers are made of mixed esters of cellulose acetate and butyrate. Ethyl and methyl ethers can also be made from cellulose. Plasticized ethyl cellulose may be used as an insulating coating for wire and may be extruded in strips for the manufacturing of materials for furniture seats. It is flexible, tough, and dimensionally stable; has low moisture absorption; can be easily fabricated; and takes printing.

The affinity of cellulose for water, due to the formation of weak hydrogen bridges, is useful for many products, particularly underclothing. In wood, it gives rise to dimensional instability which is undesirable. Chemists have recently been able to graft various chemicals with polymeric properties onto the cellulose molecule. This can then be polymerized to form graft polymers. This process offers intriguing possibilities for combining the tensile strength and toughness of cellulose with water-resistant properties of other plastics, thereby opening entirely new fields for plastic materials. Already experiments are under way to develop graft polymers on paper.

Lignin

Lignin is more difficult to separate from woody cell walls than is cellulose. Lignin is not known to be a discrete chemical compound. The term denotes a system of high-molecular, amorphous compounds chemically closely related. It has been defined as "that incrusting material of the plant which is built up mainly, if not entirely, of phenylpropane building stones." [10] Whether the material, after it is extracted from the cell wall by various chemical methods, is the same that occurs in the cell is not known, but it is generally conceded that certain modifications occur during the extracting process. For these reasons and others the molecular weight and structure of lignin remain unknown. When lignin is chemically broken down by various methods, it yields a number of compounds that are believed to be present in modified form in the lignin molecule. Among these are vanillin, cyclohexylpropane, acetoguaiacone (derivative of material found in lignum vitae), beta-vanilloyl ethyl alcohol and acetyl vanilloyl, and hydroxybenzoic acid and isohemipinic acid.[2] Vanillin is manufactured from lignosulfonic acid formed during the sulfite cooking process of making wood pulp.

The structure of lignin is known to be very complex. In its major part it is composed of phenyl propyl units which may be uniform or not. The lignin of conifers differs from that of hardwoods in the higher methoxyl content of aromatic rings in hardwoods.[10] A property of lignin highly undesirable for the paper manufacture is its tendency to give color reactions with various chemicals. To form a sheet that will remain white upon aging, lignin must be removed. In the process from 40 to 60 per cent of the weight of wood is lost. Efforts are currently being made to determine the nature of these color reactions with a view toward preventing their occurrence. Lignin in itself has plastic properties and may ultimately prove to be a valuable agent in the wood-plastics field. It will react with certain other plasticizing and polymerizing agents to form new plastic materials. Lignin, in common with coal and other products, can be hydrogenated, that is, treated with hydrogen under elevated temperatures and pressures to yield various petroleum-type derivatives. These include products resembling gasolines and lubricating oils.

Making Paper Pulp from Wood

The largest wood-chemical industry by far is the pulp and paper industry. It is important because of the wide and growing use of paper and paper products and because pulp preparation is the first step in the manufacture of cellulose-based plastics.

The Chinese made paper in A.D. 105, using bark from the mulberry trcc and old linen and fish nets. The Arabs learned papermaking from the Chinese and improved and perfected the process. It was not until early in the eleventh century that paper was first made in Europe (in Spain) and not until 1690 that the first mill was established in the United States. During most of this period, paper was made from linen rags. Because of the scarcity of raw material the production of paper did not keep pace with the demand.

Paper was not made successfully from wood until the middle of the nineteenth century. Limited amounts of paper are still made from rags, straw, cane bagasse, bamboo, and marsh grasses. These materials, though important locally, taken together contribute only a small percentage to the total paper manufactured. Wood is now the predominant paper-making fiber.

Scope of the Pulp and Paper Industry. The two important major operations in making paper products are pulp production and paper and paperboard manufacture.

Closely related to paper manufacture is the manufacture of paperboards for shipping containers, paper insulating felts, paper building

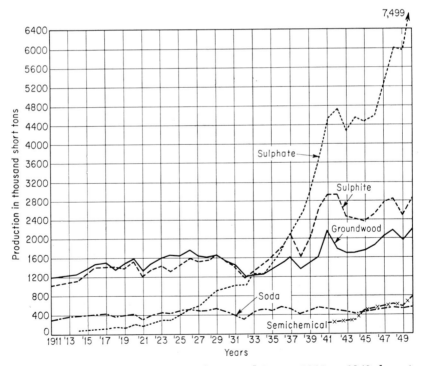

Fig. 42a Wood-pulp production in the United States, 1911 to 1949, by principal processes.

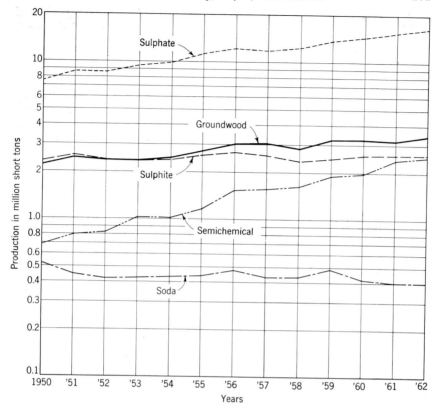

Fig. 42b Wood-pulp production in the United States, 1950 to 1962, by principal processes. (SOURCE: *U.S. Department of Commerce, 1961. Pulp Paper and Board Industry Report* 17, *p.* 12.)

boards, and paper-base plastics. Converting plants for making boxboard, corrugated board, paper cups and plates, building boards, and other products are sometimes operated in conjunction with the paper mill. Some of the operations which may be carried out in the converting plant include laminating, saturating, coating, printing, and fabricating.

Pulp companies sometimes operate by-product chemical plants to convert pulping waste liquors into useful products, such as lignin, alcohol, vanillin, and fodder yeasts.

Pulp is manufactured by treatment of wood or other fibrous raw material in such a way that the fibers are separated into a pulpy mass. This can be done by either chemical or mechanical means or by a combination of chemical and mechanical means. A number of different pulping processes in use [6] are described below. The amount of pulp produced by major processes is shown in Figs. 42a and b.

In all processes except those for pulps made into coarse grades of building boards, clean, bark-free wood is required. Most of the bark removal is done at the pulp mill.

Groundwood. The making of groundwood is a purely mechanical operation. The wood billets are forced against the face of a large grindstone at a pressure of about 40 pounds per square inch. The axis of the billet is parallel to the axis of the stone because the longest-fibered pulp is obtained in this way. The face of the stone is "dressed" or roughened so that it tears the fibers loose from the wood. Water is played on the stone to remove the groundwood as a pulp or "slush" and to maintain the temperature of grinding at the proper point (about 160°F). The pulp is screened to remove knots and lumps of wood, thickened by removing water, and then sent to a paper mill to be made into paper.

Groundwood is a low-grade, low-cost pulp, which is suitable only for the cheaper grades of paper and paperboard. The pulp consists largely of broken fibers, fiber fragments, and fiber bundles. Groundwood, which has low strength, must generally be mixed with a stronger pulp. Newsprint, for example, is made from 85 per cent groundwood and 15 per cent stronger pulp. Papers made from groundwood are not permanent. The chief advantage of groundwood is low cost, which is derived from the high yield (92 per cent) of fiber from the original wood. The groundwood process is growing in importance because of its increased use in printing papers. Recent improvements in making "bleached" groundwood have added to the number of grades of paper in which this pulp can be used. The production of groundwood in the United States in 1960 amounted to 3,247,000 tons. The price was $82 to $100 per ton in 1961.

The principal item of manufacturing cost is power. The power requirement for grinding spruce and fir is between 50 and 60 horsepower days per ton (895 to 1,074 kilowatthours). Only softwoods such as spruce and fir and soft-textured hardwoods such as aspen can be successfully pulped by the ordinary grinding process.

A mechanical pulp that closely resembles groundwood in properties and use is made by defibrating untreated chips in a disk refining mill. Again, power consumption is a major item in total cost. Spruce, fir, hemlock, and Douglas-fir may be used.

Sulfite Process. The sulfite process is an acid chemical process in which chipped wood is cooked in a liquor consisting of a solution of calcium bisulfite and sulfurous acid that contains a total of about 6 to 7 per cent sulfur dioxide. The cooking liquor is produced at the mill by burning sulfur in specially designed burners to form sulfur dioxide which is absorbed in water and reacted with limestone. During cooking, the sulfur dioxide reacts with the lignin to form soluble calcium lignosulfonic acids.

Cooking is carried out in large metal digesters lined with acid-resisting brick. These digesters hold enough chips to produce 20 to 30 tons of pulp. Wood is chipped by forcing the end of the log against a large rotating metal disk equipped with sharp knives; this produces chips about ¾ inch in length. The chips are loaded into the digester, and approximately 700 gallons of cooking liquor are added per 1,000 pounds of chips. Then the digester cover is bolted on and live steam introduced. The temperature is raised to about 260 to 300°F and held there for a period of four to fifteen hours. The time of cooking depends upon the species of wood used, the concentration of cooking liquor, and the grade of pulp desired. During cooking, the pressure continues to rise and the digester must be "relieved" at intervals to maintain a pressure of about 75 to 100 pounds per square inch. The schedule of relieving the digester is one of the most important factors in the control of the cook, since it determines the concentration of sulfur dioxide in solution and controls the temperature.

As soon as the cook is completed, the digester charge is blown into a large tank where the pulp is washed with large quantities of water to remove the dissolved lignin and spent liquor. The yield of pulp is about 45 to 50 per cent of the original weight of wood. Most of this is pure cellulose. The waste liquor, which contains most of the lignin and the remaining components of the wood, is discharged. This waste of raw material and pollution of water has encouraged research efforts toward use of waste sulfite liquor. The waste can be recovered and reused when ammonia or magnesium is used as the base of the liquor in place of calcium. Various useful products, such as alcohol, fodder yeast, and lignin derivatives, can be recovered from the waste liquor by appropriate techniques. Disposal of waste liquor still remains a major problem of this process.

Sulfite is a high-quality pulp. In the unbleached grades it is used in newsprint, catalog, glassine, paperboard, and wrapping paper. After bleaching with hypochlorite, it is suitable for white bond and ledger papers. In 1960, production was 2,579,000 tons. The price of unbleached sulfite pulp was about $120 per ton and of bleached pulp, $155 per ton. The species used for the sulfite process are the long-fibered coniferous woods such as spruce, hemlock, and balsam. In recent years some hardwood sulfite pulp has been produced.

A modification of the sulfite process involves digesting the chips in a less acid liquor. Magnesium may be used as the base instead of calcium. The acidity is about pH 4. This saponifies the resins so that pine may be used. Pine is unsuited for acid cooking. The magnesium-based liquor is suitable for chemical recovery, and thus pollution is avoided.

Soda Process. The soda process is an alkaline chemical process, using as the cooking chemical sodium hydroxide, which is made at the mill by reacting sodium carbonate with lime. This process permits the recovery and reuse of chemicals from the waste liquors. These are concentrated by evaporation and then burned in furnaces where the dissolved organic matter in the waste liquor (mostly lignin) is burned and the alkali is recovered as sodium carbonate.

The cooking operation is carried out in unlined steel digesters, which are usually smaller than sulfite digesters. The cooking liquor is a 5 per cent solution of sodium hydroxide. Enough of this is added to produce a weight of chemicals about 20 per cent of the weight of the wood. Cooking is done at a temperature of about 340°F for a period of four to six hours. The yield of soda pulp after bleaching is about 43 per cent of the original wood weight.

The soda pulping process is the only one that has not increased substantially in output since 1929. The process is used only for the pulping of hardwoods, and is the least important of the major pulping processes, but, even so, 420,000 tons of pulp were produced in 1960. The pulp is low in strength and is used in combination with stronger pulps in the manufacture of book and magazine papers. The price of bleached soda pulp was about $130 to $135 per ton in 1961. No new pulp mills using the soda process have been constructed in the United States in recent years.

Sulfate Process. The cooking liquor in the sulfate process consists of a 5 per cent solution of alkali of which about 75 per cent is sodium hydroxide and 25 per cent is sodium sulfide. Enough liquor is added to the digester to equal 20 per cent of the weight of wood. Cooking temperature is about the same as that used for the soda process (340°F). Cooking times vary from $1\frac{1}{2}$ to 7 hours, depending upon whether a coarse grade or a bleachable grade of pulp is desired. The yield of pulp varies from 45 to 55 per cent of the weight of the wood.

The chemicals are recovered from the waste liquor by evaporating most of the water, adding sodium sulfate to replace lost alkali, and burning the cake that contains inflammable lignin and saponified resins. The heat produced is sufficient to evaporate the water and to supply steam for the digesters.

The sulfate process produces a strong pulp in a short cooking cycle. The process is well suited to the pulping of pine and is widely used in the southern states. The unbleached grades, or "kraft" pulp, are used in wrapping papers, corrugated board, fiber boxes, and paper bags. The pulp is rather difficult to bleach, but improved bleaching processes have made available white grades suitable for writing and other high-grade papers. Almost any species can be pulped by the sulfate process.

The sulfate has been the fastest-growing pulping process and in 1960 was the largest. Total production of sulfate pulp in the United States in 1960 was 14,516,000 tons, and the price was $160 per ton for the bleached grades.

Semichemical Processes. The semichemical processes, also called semimechanical, use a chemical treatment to soften the wood followed by mechanical defibrating in a disk mill or on a pulpwood stone. The cooking chemicals may be any of the conventional cooking chemicals, although generally a mixture of sodium bicarbonate and sodium sulfite is used. Hardwood chips are furnished to a digester, and cooking liquor is added to a concentration of about ½ pound per gallon. The temperature of cooking is about 250 to 340°F, and the time varies from two to five hours. After cooking, the chips are discharged to a refiner consisting of one or two rotating metal disks which reduce the chips to a fibrous state (Fig. 43). The yield of usable pulp is 70 to 90 per cent of the original wood weight.

The cold-soda process involves steeping chips in caustic soda solution. These are then defibrated in a disk mill. This has been developed as a continuous process eliminating the large batch-type digesters. The method can be used in relatively small-sized operations. Hardwood chips are used. The pulp can be used in place of groundwood for con-

Fig. 43 A disk refiner for wood pulp and chips.

tainer board or bleached for lighter-colored papers such as newsprint and groundwood specialties.

The chemigroundwood process [3] involves cooking the wood in billet form in neutral sulfite or other liquors, then defibrating the billet on a pulpwood stone. The softening that occurs during the cooking process makes grinding of hardwood billets possible. The power requirement is less than half that required for grinding fresh spruce wood. The quality of the resulting pulp is intermediate between that of groundwood and that of chemical pulp. In yield, chemigroundwood approaches ground-wood pulp. The process is in use in Europe and at the Great Northern Paper Company in Maine for making newsprint.

The semichemical, cold-soda, and chemigroundwood pulps are inter-mediate grades used for paperboard and other products requiring low-cost pulps. The pulps can be bleached and refined for use in high-grade papers. Bleaching with chlorine dioxide decreases the yield from around 70 per cent for the unbleached semichemical to 55 per cent for bleached grades. Bleached semichemical pulp is suitable for glassine paper, maga-zine stock, and related grades. A problem is to get good fiber separation without lowering freeness too much. Considerable power is used by the disk mill in refining the partially cooked chips.

Whole Wood Fiber. Special pulping processes reduce wood to the fibrous state with little or no chemical. One of the most important of these is the Masonite process, in which wood chips are heated for a very short time in a special "gun" with steam at a pressure of 1,000 pounds per square inch. The chips are then discharged through a quick-opening valve where the explosive action of the entrapped steam reduces the softened chips to a fibrous state. The fibers can then be formed into a loose, porous insulating material or pressed into hard board.

Another whole-fiber pulp is made by the Asplund process. Wood chips are forced into a cylindrical reaction chamber by means of a screw feed. Chemicals and steam are added and after retention up to 20 minutes, the softened chips are fed into a disk refiner. The yield is 90 per cent. The pulp is used for coarse building boards. In 1960, 1,207,000 tons of pulp were made by these methods.

Technology of Paper Manufacture

Paper manufacture is a separate operation from pulp manufacture. Pulp received at the paper mill is mixed with water and subjected to refining in special beater or refining machines. During beating the pulp is further subjected to a rubbing or crushing action which "hydrates" and fibrillates the individual fibers. Without this treatment it would be impossible to make strong paper.

To the pulp in the beater the various materials used in making paper are added. Most papers must be sized so that they will not absorb water or ink. Sizing is accomplished by adding a solution of rosin soap to the pulp followed by a solution of alum, which precipitates the rosin on the fibers. Clay may be added to improve the smoothness and increase the opacity, starch to increase strength, and dyestuffs to color paper. If the paper must retain its strength when wet, urea-formaldehyde or melamine-formaldehyde resins may be introduced.

Modern paper mills may omit the beating process by using the Jordans to perform this function. Blending of the stock takes place by metering the several components into a stock chest. A stock chest is a huge vessel into which the diluted pulp is pumped. An agitator keeps the pulp and other components in suspension. From the stock chest the pulp goes through a Jordan refiner that substitutes for the beater and then flows directly to the headbox of the paper machine.

The thoroughly beaten pulp mixture is diluted to form a suspension of about 1 per cent fiber and pumped to the paper machine. The modern paper machine is one of the largest and most expensive individual machines used in any industry. There are two types, the Fourdrinier for making paper and paperboard and the cylinder for making multi-ply paperboard. The Fourdrinier machine consists of a horizontal, endless wire sieve on which the dilute fiber suspension is flowed (Fig. 44). The water drains through the wire and the fibers are felted and interlocked with each other on top of the wire. The wet fibrous mat is then picked up by a special felt and carried first through a series of presses which compact the paper and press out the water and then over a series of steam-heated dryers which lower the moisture content of the paper to 5 to 7 per cent. At the end of the machine the paper is passed through a series of highly polished metal rolls, called a calender stack, where the paper is given a final polish. Since all these operations are carried out in continuous sequence from the time the fiber suspension is first flowed onto the wire, close synchronization of the various paper-machine sections is necessary. Fourdrinier machines operate at speeds of 200 to over 3,000 feet per minute. A paper mill may operate anywhere from one to ten machines.

Cylinder machines differ from Fourdrinier machines in that the paper is built up in plies instead of being laid down in a single layer. A cylinder machine consists of a series of vats in each of which is suspended a hollow wire-covered cylinder. The stock is pumped into the vats and a thin layer is picked up as the cylinder revolves. The thin layer is then transferred to an endless felt which picks up succeeding layers until a multiple layer of the desired thickness is formed. This paper is then

Fig. 44   The headbox and wire of a small paper machine. The suspension of pulp in water flows from the headbox onto the continuous belt of wire cloth. The white water drains through the wire and is returned to the system. The student on the right has just taken a sample of the white water.

pressed and dried in the same manner as paper made on a Fourdrinier machine. The particular advantage of cylinder machines is that different stock can be used in the various plies.

A recent development, called an inverformer, permits manufacturing laminated paper on the Fourdrinier machine. The process involves use of top wires that pass over forming rolls just beyond the flow box. Successive flow boxes and top wires add new layers to the first. Water is removed mostly through the top wires by suction.

After leaving the paper machine, the paper may be given one or more special treatments in a converting plant. It may be run through a super-calender, embossed, surface-sized with glue or starch, or coated with pigment and adhesive.

Paper Coating. The printing characteristics of paper can be greatly improved by coating it with clay and other materials to brighten the color and to fill in the rough spots between fibers. Coated paper is widely used where fine detail in printing is desired. As the technology of coating improves, thereby making the process applicable to lower grades of paper, the use increases rapidly. Production of coated paper in the United States increased 70 per cent between 1951 and 1960 compared with an increase of 32 per cent for paper of all types.

Technology of Paper-Plastics Combinations

Closely related to the pulp and paper industry is the plastics industry. Paper, in the generic sense, is combined with plastics materials by three principal methods. The first involves the treatment of processed paper in sheet form by saturating or coating resins or both. In the saturation method the paper is brought below the level of the resin bath in a suitable trough, and the resin-laden paper is then passed between two pressure rolls in order to control the amount of resin in the paper sheet. Both sulfite and sulfate papers are used, the former with "elastic" resins and the latter with fusible thermosetting plastics. Papers treated with elastic resins (e.g., the rubbers) are subsequently coated by conventional knife coaters and used for the manufacture of many commercial objects. Papers treated with fusible thermosetting resins are generally plied up under heat and pressure to form infusible, hard, paper-resin panels.

The second method is to add a water-soluble resin or emulsion to the paper stock during the beating or refining operations. Thermoplastic resins are used to make flexible board and cover stock, such as artificial leather products. Thermosetting resins are used for paper packaging, electrical moldings, laminates, cold and hot pulp moldings, and the like.

The third method is use of filler pulps and wood flours in thermosetting resin coatings and moldings. Wet or semidry fibers are incorporated into the resin material prior to the fabrication of the plastic. The filler tends to toughen the final molding.

Importance of the Pulp and Paper Industry

The pulp and paper industry group is tenth largest in the United States. In 1958, the value added by manufacture was $5,855 million.[7] The importance of the paper industry in the national welfare is even greater because of the essential part which paper plays in every phase of modern life.

The paper industry has shown remarkable growth, particularly in view of the ancient origin of the industry. The widespread use and increasing consumption can be attributed to the low cost and versatility of paper. No low-cost substitute exists for paper as a wrapping, packaging, printing, and writing material.

Paper consumption moves up and down with the general business cycle, but the long-term trend in paper consumption has been steadily upward. In 1960 the estimated total consumption of paper and paperboard in the United States was 41 million tons. This would amount to an apparent per capita consumption of 453 pounds for the year.[5] Increase in per capita consumption coupled with a rising population spells long-term growth in paper consumption (Table 6).

TABLE 6.   UNITED STATES PRODUCTION OF
PAPER AND PAPERBOARD BY GRADES [1,8]

(Thousands of tons)

Grades	1939	1948	1962
Fine paper...................................	724	1,142	1,992
Book paper...................................	1,535	2,339	2,030
Groundwood printing and specialty paper........	568	808	914
Newsprint paper.............................	954	875	2,072
Tissue paper.................................	645	1,188	1,833
Coarse and special industrial paper.............	2,239	3,461	4,992
All other papers.............................	783	1,380	2,626
Total paper..............................	7,448	11,193	16,459
Total paperboard, including construction.......	6,025	10,773	21,121
Total paper and paperboard................	13,473	21,966	37,580

In 1960 the pulp and paper industry reported 447,000 wage earners receiving $2,230 million in wages. The total value of sales was $12,670 million. Pulp production was at an all-time high of 25,154,000 tons. The industry was operating at about 93 per cent of capacity.[5] The 1960 record was surpassed in 1961 for paper and paperboard production.

The paper industry requires heavy investment and large-scale operations to function efficiently. A single, modern paper machine costs in the neighborhood of $4 million, and the construction of a modern pulp and paper mill with a single paper machine costs $150,000 per ton of daily capacity or $45 million for an average-sized mill of 300 tons. The paper industry ranks highest among all industries in the capital invested per worker. The industry is normally highly competitive.

Raw-material Supply. The basic raw material of the paper industry is wood. In 1960 slightly over 40 million cords of wood were consumed by the paper industry. Of the total wood consumed, 1,410,000 cords, mostly spruce, were imported. The species used for pulp production vary according to the section. In the southern states nearly 90 per cent of the pulpwood is southern yellow pine. In the North, the principal species are spruce, fir, eastern hemlock, and pine. In the western states, pulpwood is chiefly spruce, true fir, and western hemlock. Hardwood species are less desirable than the softwoods, but the use of hardwoods is increasing because of the diminishing supplies of softwoods. In the North the principal hardwoods used are aspen, birch, beech, and maple. In the South the gums and oaks are used. Pulpwood accounted for about 28 per cent of the timber harvested in 1960.

The United States imports about 73 per cent of the newsprint consumed, mostly from Canada.

For the United States as a whole, ample reserves of woods suitable for pulp exist in the forest. The industry has been obliged, however, to process less spruce and more hemlock, fir, pine, and hardwoods. Integration of sawmills and pulp mills, a common practice in Scandinavia, is under way to some extent in the United States.

Domestic pulp consumption for paper in 1960 was 26,500,000 tons, of which about 2,389,000 tons were imported. About 9 million tons of waste paper were reprocessed in 1960. Consumption of waste paper showed a significant decline since the war in contrast to the increasing consumption of virgin pulp. Processes for deinking waste paper were being introduced in 1962 that should increase its use.

In order to operate effectively, pulp mills must be near their source of wood. Paper mills, on the other hand, are sometimes located near their markets instead of near their source of raw material. Paperboard mills which use waste paper as a large part of their raw material are often located in or near large metropolitan areas in order to be near their supply of waste paper. An essential requirement in the location of both pulp mills and paper mills is an adequate supply of good water. A sulfite or sulfate pulp mill requires in the neighborhood of 92,000 gallons of water daily for each ton of pulp produced, which in the case of a 400-ton mill would result in a daily consumption of about 40 million gallons of water. Chemical supply, labor supply, and good transportation facilities are also important.

World Trade. The paper industry is an important factor in world trade. In 1959, imports of pulp, pulpwood, and newsprint amounted to $1,089 million. The value of paper exports was $337 million.

Distribution of Mills and Working Conditions

Paper mills are distributed in fairly well-defined regions of the country. The principal ones are the Lake States, Ohio, eastern Pennsylvania, New York, Massachusetts, Maine, the southern states, and the West Coast states. Concentration facilitates business and professional association. Most mills are located close to their source of wood supply in small communities which are usually chiefly dependent upon the paper and pulp mill for their livelihood. Geographical regions are often associated with the production of particular grades of paper. Paper mills in the South make principally kraft papers, mills in Massachusetts are noted for their rag-content writing papers, mills in Michigan make a high percentage of all book papers, and the mills in New York State make principally groundwood specialties and catalog papers. The South in 1960 accounted for approximately 60 per cent of the wood pulp produced in the United States.

The paper industry is progressive. Although it was one of the last of the major industries to adopt modern scientific methods, once started, it made rapid progress. The industry employs a large number of well-trained chemists and engineers. The paper industry finances a graduate school at Lawrence University, known as the Institute of Paper Chemistry, where men are specially trained for the paper industry. Other schools training men for this industry are the State University College of Forestry at Syracuse University, Lowell Institute of Technology, Miami University of Ohio, University of Maine, Western Michigan University, North Carolina State College, and McGill University in Canada. Other schools have one or more courses in papermaking.

Cellulose and Plastics Industries

Industries that manufacture rayon, cellulose plastics, and cellulose derivatives are closely related to the pulp and paper industries. Much of the alpha-cellulose used for dissolving purposes is produced by companies that also manufacture papers, and closely allied techniques are used.

The plastics industries use wood in other forms also. Wood flour and finely ground charcoal are used as extenders in various plastics. Wood fiber or pulp may similarly be used, though the plastic mixture may require preforming because fiber interferes with plastic flow. Lignin is used to a limited extent as an extender and also as a plasticizing agent. Many companies in the wood-fiber and lignin-plastic fields entered this as a sideline to paper or pulp-product manufacture.

Other plastics manufacturers use wood flour or wood carbon in ways differing widely from the techniques of pulp and paper manufacture. Small companies may manufacture plastic novelties, machine parts, or household articles. Manufactures of rubber and many chemicals differ radically from pulp and paper manufacture; yet their technologists may be members of the Technical Association of the Pulp and Paper Industry (TAPPI).

The plastics industry has a bright outlook, as the products, output, and companies involved are expanding rapidly. The industry has places for both large and small companies.

LITERATURE CITED

1. American Paper and Pulp Association. 1949. "The Statistics of Paper," 2d ed., New York. 63 pp.
2. Brauns, F. E. 1948. "The Proven Chemistry of Lignin," in West, Clarence J., ed., "Nature of the Chemical Components of Wood," pp. 108–132, TAPPI Monograph Series 6, New York.
3. Libby, C. Earl, and Frederic W. O'Neil. 1950. "The Manufacture of Chemigroundwood Pulp from Hardwoods," New York State College of Forestry, Syracuse, N.Y. 42 pp.
4. Plunguian, Mark. 1943. "Cellulose Chemistry," Chemical Publishing Company, Inc., New York. 96 pp.
5. *Pulp and Paper International.* 1960. Review Number, vol. 2, p. 114.
6. Stephenson, J. Newell, ed. 1950. "Pulp and Paper Manufacture," vol. I, "Preparation and Treatment of Wood Pulp," McGraw-Hill Book Company, Inc., New York. 1,043 pp.
7. U.S. Bureau of the Census. 1960. "Statistical Abstract of the United States," 81st ed., Washington.
8. U.S. Department of Commerce. March, 1963. "Pulp, Paper and Board, Annual Review," Industry Report 19:8, Washington.
9. West, Clarence J., ed. 1948. "Nature of the Chemical Components of Wood," TAPPI Monograph Series 6, New York. 234 pp.
10. Wise, Louis E., and Edwin C. Jahn. 1952. "Wood Chemistry," 2d ed., Reinhold Publishing Corporation, New York, vol. I. 688 pp.

CHAPTER 11.   *Secondary Forest Products*

LUMBER AND OTHER sawed timbers made up 64 per cent of the timber cut from United States forests in 1954. Pulpwood was second, making up 22 per cent. Veneer accounted for 6 per cent and other products 8 per cent.[13]

Products of Wood

Crossties, Cooperage, Shingles, and Excelsior. Crossties require about 1.3 billion board feet of wood annually. Despite considerable research in both the United States and Europe, no satisfactory substitute for the wooden crosstie has been developed. Annual requirement for the period 1950 to 1955 was 35 million ties per year. The life of untreated ties is five to eight years, that of creosoted ties 20 to 30 years.[1] Oak has long been a favorite wood for crossties and accounts for almost 40 per cent of those in use, but southern pine and Douglas-fir are also widely used. Locally many other species are accepted, such as hemlock, larch, lodgepole pine, gum, hickory, beech, and ash. The heavy crosstie is 7 inches by 9 inches by 8 feet 5 inches and contains 45 board feet. The crosstie market provides a good outlet for small-sized logs of medium quality, provided the wood will hold spikes, is strong enough to withstand the impact of heavily loaded trains passing over the rails, and may be successfully treated with preservative for decay prevention.

The cooperage industry manufactures barrels, kegs, tubs, pails, and other round products for packaging both dry and liquid materials. The barrel form was particularly well suited as a package for heavy materials because it could be easily rolled on its side or bottom by a man and was strong in proportion to its weight and volume. Modern packaging and materials handling by lift trucks have caused a sharp decline in use of barrels. Also, metal drums have replaced wooden barrels for such liquid products as lubricating oil, turpentine, and alcohol. The cooperage industry has declined accordingly. The wooden barrels and tanks still play an important role in the distilling industry.

The cooperage industry in 1908 consumed 1,775 million board feet of material. By 1927 this had dropped to 1,307 million board feet; by 1947, to 558 million; and by 1952, to 355 million.[9] The future trend is uncertain. Some reversal of the decline may occur because of the use of barrels for packaging export items and the continued use of barrels for whisky and other spirituous liquors.

Slack cooperage is manufactured of southern pines, western pines, gum, and other species. The barrel or keg consists of staves, head, and hoops. Staves may be cut by a special cylindrical saw, but this is wasteful, as considerable wood is consumed as saw kerf. Larger mills steam the stave bolts and slice the staves from quartered bolts with a heavy knife in a stave cutter.[1] The staves are seasoned, jointed so as to fit closely, and beveled and grooved for the head. Heading stock is cut on special saws, seasoned, surfaced, jointed, laid up, and turned into individual barrelheads. Hoops are mostly of metal but may be made of elm, hickory, or ash. Barrels are assembled at place of use on special forms.

Tight cooperage is manufactured by similar processes. High-quality material—white oak is preferred—is used for staves and heading. All machining must be carefully done and final assembly must be accurate to make the finished barrel watertight. White oak suitable for tight cooperage brings prices in excess of those for veneer logs.

Shingles are sawed from carefully selected bolts trimmed to exact length and quartered. The shingle bolt carriage operates so as to cut tapered shingles, the thick end cut from first one and then the other end of the bolt.[1] Shingles are cut green, trimmed, baled, and seasoned, and bales are re-pressed and tied. The shingles are then ready for shipping. The preferred shingle wood is western redcedar, but northern white-cedar, cypress, and redwood also make durable shingles. The medium-grade wooden shingle has declined in use as a roof covering partly because of the greater ease of laying the asphalt-impregnated paperboard shingle. High-grade shingles have, however, become increasingly popular for siding on residences. Edge-grain western redcedar shingles may last 30 to 40 years. When used as siding on houses, they may have an even longer life. Stained shingles used as siding may show little evidence of deterioration after 45 years of use.

The volume of wood used in shingles was about 400 to 500 million board feet annually in 1945.[10]

A product of some importance is excelsior, which is used largely for packing and upholstery. Excelsior is made from 36- to 56-inch bolts of aspen, cottonwood, yellow pines, basswood, and yellow-poplar.[5] The wood is dried and shredded by special machines. Only sound, straight-grained wood is suitable for excelsior. Three main grades are manufactured. A cord of 56-inch wood produces about 1 ton of excelsior.

Pulpwood. Most pulpwood is cut by wood-pulp manufacturers operating their own crews and camps or by contractors. Pulpwood is not an active article of trade that is cut and stocked by dealers to be sold upon demand to pulp companies. Farmers and independent cutters may cut and deliver pulpwood to a mill, but rarely do they have more than one mill close enough to provide a ready market. Pulpwood specifications are determined by the mill or mills purchasing wood in a given locality. In the Lake States, pulpwood is commonly cut in 100-inch lengths and purchased by the "double-cord." In the South the 60-inch cord is used, and it is being specified for hardwood pulpwood by some northern mills.

Pulp manufacturers prefer to purchase peeled pulpwood because of the difficulty of debarking dried wood. Woods labor, however, has become increasingly expensive and scarce. Sap peeling has accordingly declined. A system of chemi-peeling has been introduced. This requires cutting a girdle around the tree in normal sap-peeling season and treating this with appropriate chemicals. This kills the tree and loosens the bark so that a year later it falls off during cutting of the pulpwood.

The greater part of the pulpwood is debarked mechanically by using huge drums in which the billets are tumbled, thereby rubbing the bark off, and various other bark peelers including hydraulic barkers that use high-pressure jets of water.

River-driven wood in Maine is usually floated with the bark on. By the time the wood reaches the mill, the bark has already been rubbed off or can be easily detached in a drum or other type of mechanical debarker. Other phases of pulpwood logging have been covered in Chap. 7. In 1960 the paper industry of the United States consumed 40 million cords of pulpwood. By the year 1975 it is estimated that 65 to 72 million cords may be required.[13]

POLES AND PILING. Poles are used to carry telephone, telegraph, and electric wires, and for limited other uses, such as supports for floodlights and clotheslines and as building material for log cabins. Piling is used for docks, wharves, abutments, and piers; for bridge foundations and trestlework; and to prepare foundations for buildings.[1] Specifications for piling usually require that a line from the center of the butt to the center of the top stay within the pile for its entire length. Comparable straightness is desired in poles.

Straight, reasonably soft, cylindrical stems are desired for poles. Western redcedar, northern white-cedar, and Atlantic white-cedar are favored because of high durability, but southern pine is also extensively used. Most poles are treated with preservatives to above the ground line. It is here that decay hazard is most acute. Piling is often treated for its entire length. Although the same species used for poles may be used for piling, harder and stronger wood is acceptable and may be preferred. All piling must withstand the shock of the pile driver.

Poles are set with the large end in the ground; piles are driven small end first. Both poles and piles are sold by length; 30, 40, 50, 60, and 70 feet are commonly used. Both poles and piling must be peeled. Together they represent an annual drain on our forests estimated to be 134 million cubic feet.[13]

MINE TIMBERS. Round timbers are extensively used in mines to support the roofs of drifts and stopes. Heavy timbers are used to carry the weight; small timbers, called lagging, to deck the roofs and line the walls. Flattened timbers are used for mine ties, and special double-pointed 18-inch pieces, called sprags, to lock wheels of mine cars to stop them. Mine timbers are specified as to size and species according to availability and the use intended. Timbers should be strong and stiff and crack to give warning before breaking. Durability is desirable in drifts and shafts but is of minor importance in places requiring protection for only a few weeks while the vein is being worked. Where durability is important, treated timbers may be used. The annual cut of round mine timbers was 77 million cubic feet in 1952.[13]

The increased use of strip and open-pit mining has lessened somewhat the demand for mine timbers since 1945.

POSTS. Posts are cut of available woods in lengths of 5 to 8 feet or more. Strong and durable woods are preferred, such as cedar, locust, cypress, oak, and tamarack. Eastern redcedar, northern white-cedar, Atlantic white-cedar, and western redcedar make durable posts. If treated, fence posts can be of any wood that takes treatment well. Posts are used in the round and split in halves and quarters, and most are set in holes. Untreated posts of nondurable woods last three to seven years under eastern service conditions; the durability of treated posts is 12 to 20 years, depending on the effectiveness of treatment. About 131 million cubic feet of wood was cut for posts in 1952.[13]

The growing popularity of electric fences in recent years has made possible the use of fewer, shorter, and smaller-sized posts than are required for woven or barbed wire not electrified.

FUEL WOOD. Wood used for fuel in the United States was 1,004 million cubic feet in 1952.[13] Because wood is heavy, bulky, and inconvenient to use as fuel, it is rapidly being displaced by coal, oil, and natural gas. Mechanized handling and manufacture are essential to low cost and competition with other fuels. The heating value of a cord of dry maple wood is equivalent to about that of a ton of coal. As a luxury for fireplaces fuel wood will have a market for years to come. It offers enterprising foresters a chance to develop local markets for low-quality trees that should be removed to favor growth of better trees. Sawmill waste is commonly used for fuel, especially slabs and edgings. Tops and limbs may be used but are laborious to work up.[11]

SHAVINGS AND SAWDUST. Shavings and sawdust are used for stock bedding, fuel, and packing. They may be burned directly or made into briquettes in special machines. Special sawdust burners have been devised for use in western states where sawdust is plentiful. In the dairy region of the Northeast, sawdust and shavings find a ready local market for cattle bedding. They are superior to straw for this purpose because of their high absorptive capacity.

Sawdust, shavings, chips, and shredded bark may be applied directly to fields as a soil amendment. They loosen clay soils, help hold moisture in sands, and break down into humus that improves both sands and clays. Usually nitrogen must be applied with fine wood to support the growth of the organisms that cause decay. Portable chippers are now in operation that can chip limb wood and light branches for application to soil.

Both sawdust and shavings are used for packing articles for shipping where less resilience is needed than that provided by excelsior. If bark-free, they may also be used for manufacture of wood flour and for hydrolysis to make alcohol. The latter use is dependent upon large quantities of waste available at one locality and at a low price.

Extractives and Derivatives. NAVAL STORES. Turpentine and rosin are obtained by distilling the resinous exudate from the tappings of long-leaf and slash pine in the Southeast.[15] The field operation consists in chipping through bark of living trees, hanging resin cups, and delivering crude gum to the still. The industry is restricted to the southern pine region and characterized by many small distilling operations.

Tapping trees for naval-stores production is a relatively slow and laborious process. A fresh streak must be made weekly. Every three or four weeks the gum is "dipped" from the cups in which it is collected and taken to the still for refining. During the Second World War, resin yields were increased by substituting bark chipping for deep chipping and by applying sulfuric acid to the freshly cut streak (Fig. 45). This keeps the resin canals open and prolongs the flow of resin. Turpentine distillation must be carefully controlled to make sure that the product is uniform and taken off only between proper boiling-point levels. If burning occurs, the quality of the product deteriorates rapidly. The gum should be kept as free as possible of dirt, water, and other foreign material.

Turpentine, rosin, and pine oil are extracted with hot gasoline from chips of the stumpwood of longleaf and slash pine. This process is called "steam and solvent extraction." The operations are on a large scale with

FIG. 45   Bark chipping for resin flow. The resin is collected in the cup beneath the apron. (*U.S. Forest Service photo.*)

elaborate equipment and trained men. Continual search is made for new products and ways to reduce costs. The products are made to exact specifications. The gum turpentine industry has not grown much since 1945. Production was valued at $29 million in 1937, at $38 million in 1947, and at $25 million in 1954.[14] Products from softwood distillation, on the other hand, have found increasing acceptance. Values of shipments of distilled products for corresponding years were: 1937, $17 million; 1947, $73 million; 1954, $89 million.[8] Although turpentine has long been the most important solvent used in paint manufacture, it has been losing ground to other organic solvents. Rosin is the most effective material for sizing in paper manufacture and is widely used in paint, varnish, and soap manufacture (Fig. 46).

Turpentine and rosin may also be recovered from the sulfate pulping process.[17] This method is used considerably in Europe where gum rosin is difficult to harvest because of low yield from native pines. In the pulping process the wood is chipped and pulped, and the saponified resins and oils which rise to the top of the digester are skimmed off. These skimmings are acidified to yield "tall oil" having about 45 per cent resin acids. These, in turn, are refined by distillation, by extraction, or by special chemical treatment to yield rosin, fatty acids, and sterols. Output of naval stores in the United States in 1954 was: turpentine,

Fig. 46   Selective cupping for naval stores, Olustee Experimental Forest. The first 10-year cycle is now in its fourth year. After 10 years of cupping, the worked trees will be harvested and a second cycle begun on the trees marked with an X. Seed trees unworked will still remain. (*U.S. Forest Service photo.*)

18,176,000 gallons; and rosin, 1,845,000 drums of 520 pounds each. The total income was $113 million.[8]

OTHER WOOD EXTRACTIVES. Other extractive substances in wood are tannins, various phenolic constituents, and various dyes and coloring matters.[16, 17] The phenolic and other resin compounds in wood may be used to a limited extent in identifying species.

Tannins occur in a great number of woody and herbaceous plants. The chief sources of tannins used in the United States are quebracho imported from South America, chestnut and hemlock from the United States, mangrove from Borneo, and wattle from South Africa.[3] Sumac leaves, scrub oaks, and the barks of red spruce and Douglas-fir can also be used as sources of tannin. The tannins vary considerably in their nature and also according to the method of extracting them from the wood. Usually tannins are obtained by steeping the chipped wood or bark in hot water.

The tannin industry made shipments valued at $14 million in 1954.[9]

Various phenolic substances are found in wood, but these normally occur in low concentrations, 0.5 per cent or less. The phenolics, nevertheless, have considerable influence on the durability of wood, for they are toxic to wood-destroying organisms. Tannins serve also to discourage wood-destroying organisms.

Woods yield a number of natural coloring materials or dye substances. These belong to four major chemical groups: the quinones, hydro-quinones, benzopyrans, and chromones.[6] Maclurin is a pale yellow dye material found in mulberry and in Osage orange. Walnut hulls contain a material, juglone, that produces a dark dye for wool and silk. Various tropical woods have been used as sources of dye materials, among them the greenheart woods of the Bignoniaceae, Caesalpiniaceae, and the Lauraceae, *Haematoxylon*, sumac, and others. The chemistry of natural dyestuffs is complicated.

WOOD DISTILLATION. When wood is heated with a limited amount of air, it breaks down into a number of products, among them methyl alcohol, acetic acid, various phenols which are found in wood tar, and other products. Charcoal is the end product from the wood itself. The gases formed upon heating wood are combustible and may be converted into liquid fuels.[4, 16] Wood gas was used extensively by Germany, Sweden, and other nations during the Second World War when they had limited amounts of petroleum fuels. It remains a potential source of fuel wherever petroleum and coal are unavailable.

The chief product of wood distillation, charcoal, must be made of wood. Charcoal is used for domestic cooking, for broiling in restaurants and dining cars, and for picnics and barbecues. It is often used on shipboard for cooking and is the main cooking fuel of the tropics. Charcoal has limited use in the steel industry for manufacturing certain grades of high-carbon steel. Because it produces a reducing flame, charcoal is used for heating soldering irons used by tinsmiths. For the same reason charcoal blankets—fine charcoal treated with a fire retardant—have been used by the steel industry to cover the molten metal while it is being poured. Activated carbon is made by treating fine charcoal with super-heated steam. This has far greater adsorptive capacity than ordinary charcoal and hence is widely used in gas masks, in city water purification, and for other purposes where high adsorptive properties are required. Charcoal is also used for curing tobacco.

Wood-chemical plants can use top and limb wood unsuited for lumber or pulp manufacture and can use heavy slabs from sawmills.

The wood-distillation industry achieved substantial prosperity between 1910 and 1920 but declined rapidly between 1920 and 1940. A sharp but short-lived revival occurred from 1940 to 1945, and an almost equally sharp decline followed. Many plants of the Northeast closed and others had ceased to recover products other than charcoal by 1950. A market for charcoal seems likely to continue indefinitely, although the industry has been one of waning importance. Coke now replaces charcoal in most steel furnaces; and synthetic methanol, acetic acid, and acetone are made more cheaply and efficiently from natural gas and petroleum than from wood. However, if new and cheaper methods of harvesting and distilling can be discovered, the industry may again become important.

The total value of products shipped in 1954 was $14.5 million.

Very little research has been done on wood pyrolysis. The original wood-chemical industry is a relatively simple one and has never been sufficiently profitable that companies could accumulate financial reserves for research to keep the industry abreast of modern developments. Had as much effort been spent on studying the by-products from wood distillation as has been spent on the by-products of coking of coal, it is probable that wood pyrolysis would be a flourishing industry in our country today.[4]

Other Forest Products

Maple Products. Maple products bring in a substantial income to farmers and others who engage in tapping the trees and refining the sap. The capital required to refine sap was about $2,000 in 1950, and a minimum-size operation was one of about 500 pails.

Production of maple syrup in the United States attained an all-time high of 6,612,000 gallons in 1860. This level was approximated in 1918, when production was 6,564,000 gallons. Since this time production has dropped markedly. In 1945 it was 1,030,000 gallons; in 1955, it was 1,594,000; and in 1959, it was 1,191,000 gallons. The price of maple syrup has averaged from $1.18 per gallon in 1933 to $5.10 per gallon in 1947. Retail prices were as high as $6 to $8 per gallon during the period 1945 to 1960. Vermont led all states in 1959, followed by New York. These two states accounted for more than half the total production.[8] Production is carried out mainly by farmers as an early spring activity before cultivation for field crops begins.[2,18] Even in communities where "sugaring" is common practice, only a small percentage of available trees are tapped.

Maple syrup is strictly a luxury commodity selling for four or five times the price of cane-sugar syrups. Pure maple syrup is used to flavor other syrups and to flavor confections, ice cream, and other products; lower grades of syrup are used in curing tobacco.

Christmas Trees and Greenery. It is estimated that approximately 28 million Christmas trees are used annually in the United States. Over 21 million of these are cut in the United States and more than 5 million are imported.[7] The northeastern and Middle Atlantic states provide about 6.5 million trees, the Lake States over 5 million, the southern states about 3 million, and the Pacific Coast and Northwest over 6 million trees. About 1.5 million trees are cut annually from established plantations and the remainder from natural stands. The most common sizes of Christmas trees are 5 to 7 feet, though they range from 2 to 20 feet or more. The value of the industry in the United States is from $20 million to $50 million, depending upon whether wholesale or retail prices are considered.

Many growers have found Christmas-tree plantations a very profitable form of land use, yielding gross returns of $30 to over $100 per acre annually. Under sustained-yield production a grower could count on no more than 100 trees per acre annually. Favored species in the United States are balsam fir, Douglas-fir, black spruce, redcedar, white spruce, red pine, and Scotch pine. Plantation-grown trees, because of their better shape and denser foliage, have increased greatly in popularity since 1950.

Holly for Christmas wreaths, mistletoe, laurel, and other evergreen material are valuable for decorative purposes. Various decorative materials are harvested from the forest at seasons of the year other than Christmas. Wood ferns are used in floral decorations. Ground pine and other club mosses are used both for Christmas wreaths and to form chains or ropes for weddings. Evergreen branches are extensively used for decorations throughout the winter period, as are pussy willow, red osier dogwood, and other tree branches in early spring. Flowering dogwood is especially sought in late spring when the floral bracts are in full display, but its collection in many states is prohibited. Redbud, cherry, and peach boughs are also used during the season they are in flower.

Tree Seed. The harvesting, extracting, and storage of tree seed is becoming an increasingly important business in the United States. Vast quantities of seed are used by state and federal nurseries engaged in tree-planting programs and by private nurseries as well. Seed for forest planting must be of high quality and must be collected from parent trees adapted to the climate in which the tree seedlings are to be set out. The U.S. Department of Agriculture makes it a policy to use only seed of known origin in all plantations on national forests and on other plantings the Department sponsors. Suppliers must provide adequate evidence to verify place and year of collection before seeds are purchased by public nurseries.[12]

Fruits and Nuts. Many wild fruits and nuts enjoy good local and even regional markets. Black walnuts, hickory nuts, butternuts, pecans, hazelnuts, piñon pine, and various other edible nuts are collected and sold locally for human food. Beechnuts, acorns, and other nutritious fruits and nuts serve as food for wildlife and are often used by domestic animals, particularly swine. Locally, they form an important resource of the forest.

The forest also produces a variety of berries and fruits useful for human food. Many have a good local or regional market. Among these are blueberries, cranberries, persimmons, wild raspberries, strawberries, blackberries, and cherries. Little attempt is made to cultivate or control the harvest of products other than cranberries and blueberries.

Medicinal Herbs and Pharmaceuticals. In the past the forest has furnished a number of plants used for pharmaceutical purposes. Among these have been wild ginseng, sarsaparilla, yellowroot, and a host of others. Medicinal drugs are now produced mainly by drug companies through synthetic processes or from cultivated plants. Only a limited market exists for wild medicinal herbs.

Flavoring extracts may be obtained from the twigs and leaves of various forest plants. Oil of wintergreen is made from black birch twigs by steam distillation. Various other waxes, oils, and flavoring materials are obtained from the forest and enter into commercial use. Among them is the gum of the balsam, which is used as a cementing material in the optical industry and for the mounting of permanent microscope slides.

Tropical-forest Products. Cinchona bark produces the alkaloid quinine and closely related products useful in the prevention and cure of malaria and other fevers.

Rubber, chicle, dyestuffs, and tanning materials are still imported into the United States from tropical and subtropical regions. Restricted imports during the Second World War caused much concern. Efforts have been made to grow cork oak in California, cinchona in Costa Rica, and dyestuffs in Puerto Rico.

Natural rubber is used for a great variety of products for which it is better suited than modern synthetic rubbers. Attempts to produce natural rubber from guayule and Kok-saghys were successful during the Second World War but highly expensive.

LITERATURE CITED

1. Brown, Nelson C. 1950. "Forest Products," John Wiley & Sons, Inc., New York. 399 pp.
2. Cope, J. A. 1949. "Maple Sirup and Sugar," Cornell Extension Bulletin 397, Ithaca, N.Y. 32 pp.
3. Flinn, Edwin S. 1948. "Wood Tannin," in West, Clarence J., ed., "Nature of the Chemical Components of Wood," pp. 146–166, TAPPI Monograph Series 6, New York.
4. Gillet, Alfred. 1949. "The Future of Wood Pyrolysis," pp. 45–51, Fourth Meeting of the Technical Committee on Wood Chemistry, Food and Agriculture Organization of the United Nations, Brussels, Belgium.

5. Panshin, A. J., E. S. Harrar, W. J. Baker, and P. B. Proctor. 1950. "Forest Products—Their Sources, Production, and Utilization," McGraw-Hill Book Company, Inc., New York. 549 pp.
6. Shriner, Ralph. 1948. "A Review of Natural Coloring Matters in Wood," in West, Clarence J., ed., "Nature of the Chemical Components of Wood," pp. 182–219, TAPPI Monograph Series 6, New York.
7. Sowder, Arthur M. 1949. "Christmas Trees—The Industry," *Trees*, The Yearbook of Agriculture, pp. 248–251, U.S. Department of Agriculture, Washington.
8. U.S. Bureau of the Census. 1957. "Census of Manufacturers: 1954," Industry Bulletin MC 28F, "Gums and Wood Chemicals," Washington.
9. U.S. Bureau of the Census. 1960. "Statistical Abstract of the United States," 81st ed., Washington.
10. U.S. Department of Agriculture, Forest Service. 1946. "Potential Requirements for Timber Products in the United States," Report 2, from "A Reappraisal of the Forest Situation," Washington. 70 pp.
11. U.S. Department of Agriculture, Forest Service. 1947. "Wood Waste in the United States," Report 4, from "A Reappraisal of the Forest Situation," Washington. 45 pp.
12. U.S. Department of Agriculture, Forest Service. 1948. "Woody-plant Seed Manual," Miscellaneous Publication 654, Washington. 416 pp.
13. U.S. Department of Agriculture, Forest Service. 1958. "Timber Resources for America's Future," Forest Resource Report 14, Washington. 713 pp.
14. U.S. Department of Agriculture, Forest Service. 1958. "Historical Forestry Statistics of the United States," compiled by Dwight Hair, Statistical Bulletin 228, Washington. 36 pp.
15. Ward, Jay. 1949. "Naval Stores: The Industry," *Trees*, The Yearbook of Agriculture, pp. 286–291, U.S. Department of Agriculture, Washington.
16. West, Clarence J., ed. 1948. "Nature of the Chemical Components of Wood," TAPPI Monograph Series 6, New York. 234 pp.
17. Wise, Louis E., and Edwin C. Jahn. 1952. "Wood Chemistry," 2d ed., Reinhold Publishing Corporation, New York.
18. Woods, John B. 1949. "Our New Maple Sugar Crop," *American Forests*, 55(6):21, 30.

SINCE COLONIAL DAYS the American public has cherished the right to hunt, fish, and trap. Perhaps this more than any one feature of modern-day life gives us a feeling of kinship with the pioneers who settled our land.

Rich and poor men alike enjoy hunting and fishing. Success depends far more on skill, patience, and physical vigor than on expensive equipment. These sports, therefore, evoke a feeling of equality among all devotees. Even the humblest citizen may find himself the center of admiration if he excels with rod or gun.

For several decades the only measures taken to promote the welfare of wildlife were legislative acts to regulate hunting, fishing, and trapping. Decade by decade these became more restrictive while the hunters and fishermen increased in numbers and in dissatisfaction over the scarcity of game. Thus the stage was set for scientific wildlife management.

What Is Meant by Wildlife and Wildlife Management

Wildlife includes all animals that make their homes in forest, field, and wasteland, and that obtain the necessities of life from the natural environment without substantial aid from man at any time during their life cycle. Wildlife is a much broader term than game, as it includes such varied creatures as hawks, ospreys, songbirds, shrews, red squirrels, the furbearing animals, porcupines, and woodchucks.

Fish may or may not be included as wildlife, but the wildlife manager is often called upon to deal with fish as well as with land animals. The term wildlife has a further connotation. To be wildlife the animals must be free to move about in their natural environment and to obtain from their environment all their life requirements. If they are dependent upon man for one or more of their life requirements, they become, to that extent, domesticated.

Wildlife management covers those activities undertaken to increase the value of wildlife to mankind. These activities are similar in purpose to, but radically different in technique from, those the farmer engages in to care for herds and flocks. The farmer directly controls his breeding stock, feeds his herds, and confines his animals so that they can be easily cared for. The wildlife manager accomplishes his ends primarily by indirect means. Wildlife management serves the interests of fishermen and hunters; of cameramen and recreationists; of trappers and fur dealers; of those who profit directly from the sale of hunting rights, sporting goods, cameras, and binoculars; and of those engaged in the tourist trade. Wildlife management is of concern to forest and rangeland managers because of the interrelationships, both beneficial and harmful, between the wild animals and the commercial resources of forest and range.

Values of Wildlife. It is very difficult to assign direct monetary values to wildlife. Opinions vary widely from those who declare that the monetary value of wildlife is negligible to those who maintain that wildlife performs priceless services to mankind without which we would soon be overwhelmed by destructive insect pests.

Professor R. T. King defines wildlife values under the following seven headings: *

1. COMMERCIAL VALUES. Income derived from the sale of wild animals or their products or from direct and controlled use of wild animals and their progeny. This results in either the destruction of the animals or their transformation from a wild state to a domestic or semidomestic state, e.g., commercial fishes and all their products, furs, fur and game farming, game as food, domestication.

2. RECREATIONAL VALUES. Moneys expended in the pursuit of wildlife in connection with sports and hobbies such as hunting, fishing, hiking, touring, camping (to the extent that these last three are based on the attractions of wildlife), collecting (nonscientific), and photography (as a hobby). This includes sums spent for equipment, supplies, wearing apparel, license fees, transportation, provisions, board and lodging, guide service, etc. It may or may not result in the destruction of the animals.

3. BIOLOGICAL VALUES. The worth of the services rendered to man by wild animals, e.g., insect and rodent control; soil formation, enrichment, tillage, and aeration; water conservation, sanitation, suppression of diseases, recovery and conversion of materials not otherwise recoverable, pollination, etc. Some of these services could be performed by man in the absence of animals but only by increasing operating costs; for others man is totally dependent on wild animals.

4. SOCIAL VALUES. Values accruing to the community as a result of the presence of wild animals, e.g., increased opportunity for wholesome and economical outdoor recreation, hobbies, and adventure; utilization of leisure time; enhancement of interest in surroundings and required activities; increased real estate values; income from otherwise idle lands

* From special, mimeographed lecture notes of R. T. King.

and increased farm income, offsetting carrying charges incurred in other connections; creation of marketing possibilities for minor products; alleviation of monotony; and increased physical and mental health.

5. AESTHETIC VALUES. Values of objects and places possessing beauty, affording inspiration, contributing to the arts through music, poetry, literature, and painting, and possessing historical and patriotic significance. (In these last-mentioned respects native species of wild animals in their natural surroundings are similar to sites of physiographic, political, military, and biographical interest.) These values are largely purely personal but are, nevertheless, of vital concern to practically everyone spending any time in the out-of-doors. They are also the values that induce a goodly number to become interested in our natural resources and active in their conservation.

6. SCIENTIFIC VALUES. Values realized through the use of wild animals and their populations as a means for investigating certain fundamental and widespread natural phenomena that may affect man's interests either directly or indirectly, e.g., population behavior, diseases and their spread, varying virulence of pathogens, certain aspects of nutrition and reproduction, ecological relations, population dispersal, phenological phenomena, speciation, social organization, etc. These values are of particular interest to the ecologist, pathologist, epidemiologist, and sociologist, and, indirectly, to all who benefit by their worth.

7. NEGATIVE VALUES. Value of property destroyed or damaged by wild animals and costs incurred in efforts to limit or reduce wild-animal populations and to prevent their access to or use of crops, stored products, and structures. This includes losses to growing and stored crops, such as hay, grains, fruits, and vegetables; to livestock on farms; to grasses and livestock on the range; to standing, stored, and manufactured timber products; to processed and stored foods, and to manufactured goods and articles. Also included are damages to buildings, rights of way, dikes, levees, irrigation and drainage ditches, terraces, and other structures; losses from diseases harbored or transmitted by wild animals; and costs of protecting, repelling, poisoning, trapping, and other means of control.

The sum of all these several values is the total value of wildlife to mankind and is the justification for wildlife conservation. These values run into substantial sums. Data on expenditures for the fiscal year 1956–1957 show: [7]

	Expenditures, millions of dollars
Hunting licenses..	50
Fishing licenses.............................	43
Federal and states for wildlife restoration.......	22
Federal and states for fish restoration..........	7

These expenditures are modest in comparison with those for fishing and hunting gear and for transportation, meals, and lodging.

Attitudes toward Wildlife. Just as men differ in their appraisal of the value of wildlife, so also do they differ in their attitude toward wildlife. Some have no interest in wildlife nor do they feel that wildlife in any way affects their welfare. Others oppose any use of wildlife by mankind. Many people interested in wildlife are concerned with restricted use, that is, taking of fish by the rod and game by the gun. Conservationists recognize and appreciate all the values of wildlife, but they may or may not oppose direct efforts by man to manage wildlife in his own interests.

The wildlife manager is concerned with all values of wildlife and with the proper balance between wildlife and other resources present in its natural environment. Those who would burn the forest to provide food for deer take a very narrow view indeed of wildlife management. Those who would maintain pure stands of spruce over extensive areas where hardwood and other mixed species tend naturally to grow likewise have a limited understanding and appreciation of the importance of multiple use of forest land. Very little land in our country produces its highest overall returns as deer pasture or as a pulpwood forest. Balanced and integrated use of the wildlife, forest, soil, water, and recreational resources of the land ordinarily yields the highest long-term return for the benefit of mankind.

Measures to Conserve Wildlife. When the pioneers first landed on the shores of North America, they found abundant wildlife, which they took with little thought for the future. Gradually, as our country became settled, wildlife diminished. Both sportsmen and others attributed this decline in game to the toll of hunters. To check depletion, legislatures introduced closed seasons, prohibited market hunting, and established bag limits in the hope that this would protect and restore wildlife; but these measures proved only partially effective.

Certain species were removed from the list of game animals. First were the songbirds and other wild creatures of benefit to mankind but of little use as game. Species approaching extinction were completely protected. Special regulations were introduced restricting the methods that might be used in taking wildlife. Baiting game and the use of live decoys in the taking of waterfowl were prohibited. Finally, the restrictions limited the hours of the day as well as the days of the week on which wildlife might be taken.

Men sought to control predators. Some sought to destroy all hawks, owls, and eagles; some, all fish-eating birds, such as herons, pelicans, and kingfishers; some, the carnivorous animals, such as bears, wolves, and coyotes; others, furbearing animals, such as foxes, weasels, minks, and skunks; and still others, rodents, such as woodchucks, porcupines, and squirrels. All these were believed to destroy game or some things valuable to man. Unregulated destruction of predators has, in the opinion of many biologists, caused at least as much harm as good.[8] They feel that the predators perform a useful function in eliminating the weak and diseased animals and in harvesting the natural increase above that which the environment can support.

Wildlife refuges were established to conserve wildlife. The original idea was to have a few large refuges which could serve as sanctuary and provide a reserve stock of wildlife to replenish depleted territory. Such measures have been most effective when the refuges are relatively small in size, many in number, and interspersed with land used for other purposes where the creatures can find foods that do not occur in the refuge. Modern refuge programs embrace sound management of land, including forests, range, and croplands, for the purpose of protecting and increasing native wildlife. Surplus animals are removed by regulated hunting or live trapping to restock other areas.

Artificial replenishment has been widely practiced in the stocking of trout streams and in the rearing of pheasants and other wildlife for release on natural ranges. Foreign species have also been introduced. These measures have provided sport for many individuals who might otherwise have been unable to take game.

All the above-named measures have been included in the wildlife managers' techniques. Wildlife management encompasses all these and more. Productivity of wildlife depends upon the breeding habits of the animals and the productivity of their environment. Man cannot manipulate animal habits, but he can manipulate the environment.

Behavior of Species and Populations. Species of animals differ widely in their breeding habits, feeding habits, cruising radius, and gregariousness. Differences in these characteristics cause the variation found in range and distribution of species, densities tolerated, hunting pressures withstood, and the influence animals have individually and collectively on their environment. Some animals bear only one or two young annually; others may bear up to ten or more. The ruffed grouse commonly lays eight to fourteen eggs in a nest; the loon only two. The white-footed mouse may bear four to eight litters of six to eight mice each during a year. The cottontail rabbit may produce three to four litters of four to five young each in a year. The bear produces one to two young every other year.

The capacity of a species to multiply until it occupies its range completely is its biologic potential. This is remarkably high for some game species and accounts for their resistance to hunting pressure and the irruptions in population that sometimes occur. Deer on understocked range may show an annual increase of 40 to 50 per cent; elk, 21 per cent; raccoon, 50 per cent; and quail, as high as 460 per cent. For wild ducks 70 per cent of those that reach flying stage have a life span of less than one year. About 60 per cent of the ruffed grouse kill is of birds less than a year old. Several other species seem to maintain their populations with about a two-thirds turnover each year.[1, 11]

The distribution of animals in a given area naturally will depend upon how selective they are in their feeding. Animals that eat a wide variety of foods may find their life requirements within a relatively narrow area and consequently abundant, while those selective in feeding will find them sparse. The ruffed grouse, being quite selective in its feeding, requires up to 5 acres to support a single pair of birds. Other birds, such as wild ducks, geese, blackbirds, and starlings, can be seen in flocks.

Cruising radius is the distance an animal or bird will travel to meet its daily life requirements. All factors essential for its welfare must be found within its daily cruising radius, else the animal will leave the area. It is for this reason that large areas devoted to a single crop— whether this be wheat, potatoes, or spruce—tend to produce a small amount of wildlife, whereas those that are highly diversified, with woodland interspersed with pasture, clean-tilled crops, and waste areas, tend to support dense wildlife populations.

Animal cruising radii for a few species have been determined as follows:

	Radius, miles
Ring-necked pheasant	$2\frac{1}{2}$
Ruffed grouse	$\frac{5}{8}$
Bobwhite quail	$\frac{1}{4}$
Cottontail rabbit	$\frac{1}{4}$
White-tailed deer	7

Some animals tend to exhibit group behavior that is not readily discernible in the individual animals. For instance, there must be limits of density of population in both directions. The animals must be sufficiently numerous to find mates but not so dense as to overstock their range. A population must be of a certain minimum size and occupy certain minimum range if it is to survive. This is particularly true of such animals as the Rocky Mountain sheep that feed in bands and require fairly large areas to maintain themselves. Some animals have special tolerances for others of different species and for various factors of the environment. Others are limited in their tolerance and will drive out populations of other animals or leave themselves. The population should have a proper sex and age-class distribution if it is to remain vigorous and healthy. Some populations can readily be transplanted to a new location, whereas others can establish themselves in a new environment only with difficulty. All these considerations influence what the game manager can do successfully to promote the welfare of wildlife.

Range Essentials. A wildlife range must provide all the essentials for the life processes of wildlife. It must contain food, coverts, and water sufficient for all species concerned, for both sexes, for all age classes of the various species, and for all activities and life functions of these species. For example, it is not sufficient simply to have plenty of young sprouts as food for deer. There must also be well-distributed water, particularly during the period when fawns are born so that the does need not travel far from the newborn fawns to find food and water.

All essentials of the wildlife range must likewise be well distributed over the range and must be sufficiently close to one another so that an animal can meet its life requirement within its cruising radius. This naturally varies between adults and young and between nursing females and mature males.

Factors that tend to restrict wildlife population are rigorous winters; unseasonable cold or rainy weather, especially during the period when young are born; prolonged drought; failures of nuts, fruits, and forage; accidents; disease outbreaks; predators; parasites; pressure of domestic animals; land clearing for cultivation; swamp drainage; forest fires; and hunting. Man has probably done just as much, if not more, to restrict wildlife through his appropriation of wildlife range for his crops, domestic animals, roads, dwellings, and industries and by the starting of forest fires and other acts of carelessness as he has by all his hunting and trapping. Wildlife is favored by abundant food, water, coverts, and such special requirements as salt for herbivores, gravel for gallinaceous birds, and hibernating places. Not only must all necessities for life be present in the environment, but they must be within reach of the animal during his normal daily travel. Interspersion of food, water, and cover is essential to abundant wildlife population, just as interspersion of human food, water, raw materials, power, and markets is essential to dense human population [12] (Fig. 47).

Because few wildlife ranges have an ideal distribution of all the essentials for game animals, populations are correspondingly reduced. The interaction of the two factors of biologic potential of species, on the one hand, and range essentials, on the other, determines the game population and the numbers that may be harvested without depleting the breeding stock. This interaction is probably the least understood by the sportsman, yet it is this that accounts for the limited success that attends restocking and release programs, buck laws on well-stocked range, game introductions, and many other questionable practices. On a nonhunted tract of good grouse range, it was found that though the fall population varied from 29 to 55 per 100 acres over a three-year period, the spring population remained constant at 25.[12] In this case the birds are socially intolerant of heavier populations.

Many species, particularly the white-tailed deer, have the tendency to overstock their range, especially where predators are kept in check.[11] This leads to stunted individuals, low reproduction rates, and heavy losses by starvation in winter. It also leads to serious depletion of the food and cover plants that support the herd. Natural restoration of depleted game range is a slow process.[11]

Developing a Wildlife Management Program. Management of an area for wildlife, like management for timber, requires an inventory of resources. This means determining the types and populations of wildlife present and the condition of the animals. It is equally important to survey the food and cover available to support them. Next, measures are con-

FIG. 47 Saving a few "den trees" will favor forest wildlife. (*U.S. Forest Service photo.*)

sidered to improve the environment for use by wildlife. Such measures might include logging, if the area is composed primarily of mature timber; planting, if there is an excess of open land; creation of coverts through encouraging growth of shrubs and leaving large tops on the ground; and developing water supply.

If he is to avoid shortsighted measures, the wildlife manager must have a certain philosophy. All wildlife must be included within his sphere, not just game alone; he is managing environment primarily, and he must keep in mind the interests of all concerned with wildlife and the land supporting it. Man's purpose is served best if many types of animals are present where they can be seen, enjoyed, and studied. Animals, just as timber, can be managed on a sustained-yield basis. Wildlife management cannot be divorced from administration of the land on which it occurs. It is but one of many products of the land that are of value to the landowner and the community.

PUBLIC POLICIES AND PROGRAMS. Migratory birds, including waterfowl, are under federal jurisdiction. All other wildlife is considered the property of the state in which it is located, because wildlife can freely move from one man's land to another's. The owner of the land does not have the right to take wildlife as he sees fit on his own property; he must conform to the game laws established in his state. The only exception is that Indians may take fish and game at any time on reservations. Wildlife on national forests is likewise considered the property of the state in which the forest is located.

The federal government has jurisdiction over the wildlife on national parks and national monuments. Here the government attempts to maintain an abundant and vigorous population of wild animals.

FISH AND WILDLIFE SERVICE. The Fish and Wildlife Service of the Department of the Interior is the government's expert agency for management of fish and wildlife resources. This Service is responsible for managing 261 national wildlife refuges totaling 17,371,000 acres. Of these, the 13 big-game refuges totaled 5,625,000 acres; 5 game refuges, 4,640,000 acres; 44 migratory-bird refuges, 3,705,000 acres; and 198 waterfowl refuges, 3,398,000 acres.[7] A number of the reserves are located on land administered by other agencies, but 10,987,000 acres are under the sole or primary jurisdiction of the Fish and Wildlife Service.*

Other major responsibilities of the Fish and Wildlife Service include research in wildlife management, administration of federal aid to states for the protection and management of wildlife, maintenance of inland fisheries, conservation of salmon, expert service on river-basin development plans, marine-fishery research, utilization of fish resources, control of predators and rodents, administration of Alaskan fisheries, adminis-

* Personal communication from Arthur A. Davis, 1950.

tration of federal statutes for the protection of wild fowl, cooperation with the American republics in the enforcement of the migratory-bird treaties and other wildlife work, research on whaling, and various international fishery problems.[3, 6]

In addition to its regular activities, the Fish and Wildlife Service serves as an expert agency for other government land-managing agencies such as the Bureau of Land Management, Indian Service, National Park Service, U.S. Forest Service, and the Soil Conservation Service.

STATE CONSERVATION DEPARTMENTS. The major activities in game management are centered in the state conservation departments. These issue licenses, protect game against illegal hunting and fishing, operate hatcheries, advise legislatures on seasons and bag limits, manage state refuges and public fishing streams and shooting grounds, and conduct research in game production. The last-named activity is often shared with or delegated entirely to the state agricultural colleges. By far the largest number of wildlife specialists are employed by the states. It is estimated that the states employ approximately 4,000 men engaged as game protectors and a total of some 400 biologists. The biologists are commonly stationed at the headquarters of the state fish and game departments, where they assist in administration and planning and carry on research. State work in fish and wildlife management is supported by federal grants made possible through sale of duck stamps for hunting licenses and through taxes on sporting arms and ammunition and on fishing equipment. During the fiscal year 1959, federal aid to states in wildlife restoration totaled $16,526,000; in wildlife research, $4,590,000. Additional grants were made for fish management.[17]

The states have need for men who can write about wildlife and who can deliver talks before schools, sportmen's clubs, and other groups interested in wildlife. There is an especially attractive field for biologists with a flair for popular writing.

OTHER AGENCIES. Forest and other wild-land owners have implied responsibility for wildlife. The owner should cooperate with public agencies to carry out operations so that they favor wildlife. Care in forest management, distributing operations over a wide area and over a number of years, and avoiding needless destruction of wildlife dens, coverts, and breeding areas are helpful.

The farmer has responsibility, because he owns a substantial area of land that produces wildlife. More than other landowners, he may find that wildlife interferes with his activities. Game requires food, and the farmer feels that he has certain rights to the game he has fed. He has the right to control hunting on his land. Farmers have planted waste areas to game food and have taken other measures to promote the welfare of game. It is only fair that they receive some consideration from the public and the sportsman for their contribution to the welfare of wildlife.[8, 12]

Sportsmen's clubs have a major responsibilty in wildlife management. It is their members, more than any other group, who determine public policy and who contribute funds for wildlife research and wildlife management. It is they, also, who lease land for special hunting privileges. The sportsmen's clubs are ideal organizations for the dissemination of information on wildlife and for enlisting the interests and energies of people in taking needed steps to improve wildlife habitats. Through sportsmen's magazines an excellent opportunity is available to interest a wide group of individuals in scientific game management.

The general public also has responsibility, because wildlife has values that go beyond those realized by the landowner and by the sportsman. It is to the American public as a whole that we must look for appropriate legislation to prevent indiscriminate destruction of valuable wild creatures and for review of proposals made by landowners and sportsmen. The public also will have the responsibility for providing some of the funds for carrying on wildlife work. The wildlife manager, in turn, has a responsibility to the public to provide accurate, unbiased information on wildlife questions and, particularly, to help the public to appreciate the values inherent in the wildlife resource. Only as he serves the public well and is appreciated by it can the wildlife manager expect to see his profession grow to full fruition.

Human Factors and Wildlife Management

In no phase of forest land management are diverse opinions and interests more widespread or responsibilities less clearly enforceable than in wildlife management. Conflict of interest is widespread. Perhaps few sportsmen stop to analyze their own reasons for enjoying hunting and fishing. Certainly, for modern man, there are far more economical ways to provide food and clothing. He can enjoy outdoor exercise in other less expensive ways. Few think of their sport as providing a service to the landowner in harvesting his surplus wildlife, and only the sadist derives pleasure from the killing of wild creatures.

Most people while hunting and fishing feel a freedom from the restrictions that organized society imposes upon them. It is this desire for freedom of action that poses the fundamental conflict, for lethal arms must be used with great caution if danger to other men and to buildings and livestock is to be avoided.

Thoughtless acts of sportsmen, such as leaving gates open, scattering lunch papers and tin cans, using trees for target practice, trampling on growing crops, and shooting near buildings are all annoying to the landowner and cause him economic loss. Beyond this are downright acts of vandalism. As a consequence, many owners have closed their lands to public hunting. Others lease their land to game clubs that, in turn, post it against public use.

In densely populated states the question naturally arises, can public hunting be maintained? Posting increasingly reduces the land areas available, and growth of highways and rural residences carry legal restrictions on areas where firearms may be discharged. The federal Food and Agriculture Act of 1962 provided for aids to farmers to provide fee hunting and fee fishing.

Certain states are enacting cooperative fish and wildlife management legislation. Such laws provide minimum protection and services to landowners for keeping their lands open to public hunting. They depend primarily on educational efforts to improve landowner-sportsmen relations. If they fail, public hunting in densely settled areas will be increasingly restricted to publicly owned lands.

Good hunting can be maintained for restricted numbers of individuals, as game-management practices in Europe have abundantly demonstrated. Whether free hunting can be maintained for the many under the American tradition is still to be determined.

The Job of the Wildlife Manager. The typical wildlife manager is a state employee having responsibility for the protection and well-being of wildlife over an area of some 30,000 acres or more. His responsibility carries little authority. How then does he get results? The imaginative protector is one who knows his landowners and encourages them to plant game food and cover plants with aid from Pittman-Robertson funds, who addresses sportsmen's clubs on wildlife requirements, who enlists the interests of school children in studying wild creatures and improving nesting areas, and who promotes good sportsmanship among the public. He is, in fact, more a teacher than a warden.

WORKING CONDITIONS. Working conditions for the wildlife manager are demanding. The wildlife manager must be alert to prevent trespass, especially during hunting seasons and during those periods of the year that are critical for wildlife. This means that he must often be in the field during the stormy weather of winter and during the period when young are born in the spring and summer. As wildlife do not observe an eight-hour day, the wildlife manager must often be in the field before dawn and work until after dark. This is particularly true of the wildlife research man. The field is certainly not one for the man who has limited energy and who shuns physical hardship. To be successful, he must enjoy working with wildlife.

A wildlife manager should be a good plant and animal ecologist. He should understand the management of the resources the land produces other than wildlife. The most efficient habitat management often can be effected through a well-coordinated land-use program. This requires that he also be proficient in public relations.

He should be a good photographer, as his work is likely to require the taking of pictures under extremely unfavorable conditions. He must be, above all, a man of great patience and of keen insight and understanding. He must be prepared to study animals both as active creatures under natural conditions and as laboratory animals under semiconfinement, and he must be prepared to perform autopsies to determine parasitism, disease, development of embryos, and food habits. For all these reasons the job of wildlife manager represents a true profession, one requiring intimate study and lifelong scholarship for success.

Men can gain both inspiration and appreciation of the subject from the biographies of the great biologists who have contributed much to our understanding of wild creatures. Such men as Henri Fabre, J. H. Comstock, and W. M. Wheeler, though primarily entomologists, used methods of study similar to those employed by all biologists. Charles Darwin, David Starr Jordan, C. Hart Merriam, Vernon Bailey, William L. McAtee, and Aldo Leopold have all made unique contributions.

Range Management

Range management is the protection and use of grasslands and other lands furnishing forage for the production of livestock, usable water, and other valuable resources.

Range management is a major concern of men charged with the responsibility for regulating grazing on western public lands, including forests. It is a concern of foresters who work in the southern states, for here, also, considerable numbers of domestic animals, such as cattle, swine, and horses, feed on forest land. Since the southern range differs radically from the western range, it presents its own peculiar problems.

Importance of Range Management. Grazing occurs on some 1,112,-000,000 acres of land in the continental United States.[10] This includes farm pasture, cropland grazed after harvest, and forested and wooded range, as well as native grassland and semiarid lands.

The grazing lands of the West cover some 728 million acres, or nearly 40 per cent of the total land area of the continental United States. A line running from about the center of North Dakota down to the mouth of the Rio Grande roughly separates the range territory from the eastern states, where little open range is available. Livestock growing is one of the major enterprises in these western states, and the livestock industry is closely integrated with other farming activities. It does not, however, represent the greatest dollar production from the land, being surpassed by timber production and by crops grown on both irrigated and dry-land farms. By 1900 the industry had reached a peak of some 21 million animal units, and it attained the same peak in 1920. One animal unit is defined as one beef animal or one horse. The number in 1936 was 17 million animal units. Beef cattle from the western range are commonly marketed in the fall of the year. Some go directly to slaughter, but many more are sent to feeding lots in Iowa, Illinois, and Kansas, where they are fattened for market. The use of the western range, therefore, influences agriculture in the West and in the Middle West and affects food prices throughout the country.[15]

The Condition of the Western Range. Grazing on public lands was carried out for decades with no general control other than that which ranchers themselves enforced. In 1905 the Forest Service began to regulate grazing on national forests, and in 1934 the Grazing Service began to administer the grazing districts.

Serious overuse existed before controls were attempted, and this situation could not immediately be corrected. As a result, range deterioration became widespread. It accounts in large part for the decline in livestock numbers noted above. Lack of precise appraisal of early conditions and of extensive recent surveys makes it impossible to give a true picture of range depletion resulting from domestic animals. The material in this section is based chiefly on the Forest Service report "The Western Range," which was prepared in 1935 when the western states were in the grip of a dry cycle and at a time when the livestock industry was off balance from the general economic depression.

Regardless of the type of ownership, climate, and topography, the Forest Service estimated the range to be 52 per cent depleted from its virgin condition. Depletion goes through the following cycle: First, overuse of the most palatable species leads to their decline in vigor. Gradually these plants die out and weeds or worthless shrubby species take their place. As the more palatable species of grass are killed out, sheet erosion begins and leads oftentimes to rill erosion and gullying.

The most productive land is the valley bottoms, which are often parklike lands surrounded by forests. Once the grass is badly overgrazed, gullying begins, lowering the water table; this, in turn, hastens further decline in vigor of vegetation.

One of the most disheartening results of overgrazing is the fate that overtakes mountain meadows. These moist, lush grasslands serve as reservoirs holding back water from snowmelt and winter rains and feeding it crystal clear to mountain brooks. They are a delight to the eye and a symbol of plenty to man and beast alike. Mountain meadows are particularly vulnerable to overgrazing, which cuts up the turf, packs the soil, and accelerates runoff and erosion. This leads to deep gullies that

FIG. 48 Water hole, Ouray Grazing District, Colorado. (*Bureau of Land Management photo.*)

drain away the moisture, thus exposing the grass to drought (Fig. 48). Eventually these rich meadows may lose their character entirely and be invaded by trees or woody scrub growth.

Natural meadow restoration is possible where grazing is excluded, as in national parks. Willows, aspen, and alders invade the eroded meadow; these, in turn, provide food for beaver that dam the gullies. Gradually the flooded land fills in and, after the beaver colony moves out to find other feed, the grasses may take over. This natural process sometimes moves with gratifying rapidity, though, more commonly, centuries rather than decades are required.

Estimates indicate no less than 589 million acres of rangeland to be more or less seriously eroded. As a consequence, soil productivity has been reduced and watershed services impaired. Tremendous quantities of silt have clogged major western streams. Reservoirs and irrigation systems are slowly being choked in many states.

The types and conditions of the major range divisions are shown in Table 7.[13-15] It should be kept in mind that rainfall must be higher in

TABLE 7. TYPES AND CONDITIONS OF RANGELANDS

Range type	Area, acres	Average rainfall, inches	Area required per animal unit of grazing capacity per month, acres	Per- centage depletion
Tall grass..............	18,513,000	20–40	¾–1½	21
Short grass.............	198,092,000	13	2½–10	49
Pacific bunch grass......	42,534,000	10–20	4–6	51
Semidesert grass.........	89,274,000	15–18	6–7	55
Sagebrush grass.........	96,528,000	10–20	9–15	67
Southern-desert shrub....	26,986,000	5–10		62
Salt-desert shrub........	40,858,000	5–10	18–20	71
Piñon-juniper...........	75,728,000	6–15	8–10	60
Woodland-chaparral......	13,406,000	10–20	2–3	50
Open forest............	126,367,000	15–30+	6–10	33

the South than in the North to produce the same degree of vegetative thrift.

Range Ownership and Use. Ownership of western rangeland in 1935 was estimated to be as follows: [15]

Area, million acres

National forests............	88
Grazing districts............	128
Indian lands..............	48
Other federal lands........	23
State and county...........	66
Private...................	375
Total...................	728

Private lands make up 52 per cent of the total; federal lands, 39 per cent; and state and county lands, 9 per cent. These several ownerships, aside from Indian lands, are highly interspersed. But even more significant, operation of a high proportion of ranch units requires use of both public and private land. A fairly typical operator might have a home ranch with irrigated hay lands and range for late fall and winter use. In spring and fall his animals might graze on public lands administered by the Bureau of Land Management and in midsummer on national forests. Successful operation is thus contingent on integrated use of public and private land. Although such use patterns have existed for decades, still the individual rancher may have no long-term leases or other rights that assure him use of public land. It is only natural for him to defend his use of public land, which he comes to consider his right. If he is deprived of such use, his ranch may prove to be submarginal.

Officers charged with administering public land have a responsibility to the ranchers. They also have other resources to protect. On the grazing districts, forage is the chief resource. To produce this in abundance, overuse must be avoided and, above all, the soil must be protected from erosion. The national forests occupy high lands that receive most of the snow and rainfall and are, therefore, the source of water for irrigation and municipal use. Also they produce timber and game animals and afford much recreation. All these uses as well as the soil must be protected.

With such conflicts in use it was inevitable that controversy should arise.[2]

What livestock interests have sought to establish is vested rights in the public rangelands that can be transferred when their ranches are sold. Without this their livelihood remains subject to control by public

Fig. 49   Recovery of grass in creek bottom on badly eroded land near Casper, Wyoming. (*Bureau of Land Management photo.*)

Fɪɢ. 50   Range reseeding operation near Glens Ferry, Idaho. The truck-mounted grain drill reseeds a swath 50 feet wide. (*Bureau of Land Management photo.*)

officers. Ranches that can be sold with grazing privileges on either national forests or public grazing districts have brought a higher price as a result of the privilege, even though no guarantee of its continuation is extended.

Stockmen claim that privately owned rangelands are better managed than public lands. Cases can be cited to support the claim. However, ranch owners with limited personal resources cannot be expected to make the investment in fencing, water development, reseeding, and other measures needed for regionwide range restoration. Large owners, on the other hand, can—and many do—install improvement measures.

Range productivity and use can be improved substantially by brush control, reseeding, fencing, water developments, application of fertilizer, and other measures that both increase yield of forage and distribute the animals over the range so that better use is made of the forage that is produced (Fig. 48). Applying fertilizers is a relatively new practice of promise. Reseeding has been given a rather thorough trial. In some areas it is possible to prepare the ground adequately by means of cultivation. When water supplies have been adequate, splendid results have been obtained. But reseeding in drought years has been disappointing, and attempts to reseed rocky soils or rough topography are expensive in proportion to the response obtained. Reseeding is more successful in the northern plains and the Northwest than in the arid sections of the West in general (Figs. 49 and 50).[5]

It would be unfair to attribute all western-range depletion to the livestock industry. Deer, elk, antelope, and even mountain sheep, when overabundant locally, deplete their range. The result, where hunting pressure is light, is herd starvation during critical months.

Out of the controversy over range control and use have grown better understanding and improved practices. These, together with more generous rainfall during the period 1940 to 1958, have had their impress on range condition. The Bureau of Land Management presents the data below on the reversal in trends since the inauguration of the Taylor Grazing Act in 1934.[17]

	Per cent
Trend 1930–1935:	
Improving................	1
Little or no change..........	6
Declining.................	93
Trend 1954–1958:	
Improving................	25
Little or no change..........	56
Declining.................	19

During the years from 1957 to 1961 droughts have again been widespread in western states. We may be entering a new dry cycle. If so, even greater effort will be required of range managers and range users to continue the gains that have been made. The fact that rangelands can be improved by proper management and that this pays the range user has now been generally accepted and applied.[4,17]

RANCH MANAGEMENT. Much of the controversy that has arisen between the western stockmen and the Forest Service is traceable to the latter's being concerned with the condition of the range rather than with the condition of the rancher. Range management cannot be divorced from ranch management.

Certain ranches in the West, like many farms in the eastern states, are too low in productivity for the owner to compete successfully in modern agricultural enterprise. A great deal of ranch consolidation has gone on, as Clawson points out.[4] Progress is slow because of many difficulties, especially the necessity for adjusting the ranch for a balanced operation. Balance is needed among spring, summer, fall, and winter range and winter feed from hay land.

Ranches also must be adjusted in size to the labor supply. The smallest ranch is one that can be operated successfully by one man, except for extra help for such seasonal jobs as haying. Where winter feeding is necessary, this means about 200 cattle; where year-round grazing is available, 400.

This leads to a third difficulty: the capital required to operate a ranch. Investments in cattle ranches averaged about $65,000 for the intermountain region in 1947 and nearly $150,000 for the Southwest in 1950. Ranches in the northern plains averaged about $85,000. Sheep ranches ran as high as $200,000 in the Southwest and $75,000 in the northern plains during the early 1950s.[5] By 1961 the average value for farms in the western mountain states, where livestock ranching is the major type, was $87,000.[16]

Fluctuating prices of livestock are a serious difficulty, especially when coupled with weather cycles. Beef-cattle prices at the farm have shown the following fluctuations: [4, 16]

Year	Price per pound	Year	Price per pound
1910	$0.05	1945	$0.12
1917	0.10	1950	0.23
1922	0.06	1951	0.29
1929	0.10	1953	0.16
1933	0.04	1960	0.20
1937	0.07		

Weather cycles are of greatest importance. Good years tend to come together and to be followed by a series of bad years. Throughout the northern range region, rainfall varies over cycles of about 16 years in duration; in the central region, cycles are of about 8 to 12 years in duration; and in the southern region, 5 years.[4] This tendency for wet years to be grouped together causes great temptation for ranchers to expand operations during good years. Clawson [4] points out that if ranchers kept their herds adjusted constantly to the forage available during the driest years, such as the 1930s, production of livestock in many sections of the range area would have been less than half what it actually was by allowing herds to build up in good years. Income of ranchers accordingly benefited, because the high prices of the 1940s coincided with heavy rainfall on the range. Had ranchers not expanded operations during this period, they would have missed a lifetime opportunity to accumulate savings, and meat supply during wartime would have been scarce indeed. The difficulty with accepting this pattern of range management lies in the impossibility at present of predicting with assurance the wet and dry cycles and in the slowness of ranchers in curtailing operations until nature or prices force them to do so.

Other difficulties that confront the rancher seeking to maintain a profitable operation are fluctuations in meat consumption, variations between relative profitability of sheep and cattle, transportation costs, poisonous and injurious plants, diseases of range animals, severe winters, irregular supply of credit, isolated living, and lack of outside employment opportunities during slack periods on the ranch.[4, 9]

Intelligent action is being taken by many ranchers to improve the breed of livestock; to improve breeding stock on individual ranches; and to develop the range by establishing watering tanks, reseeding, fencing, and other measures and by adopting ranch-management practices that provide efficient operations.

Public agencies are lending a helping hand through research, demonstration, and education and through improved management practices on public lands. The approach to range improvement through better ranch management offers real promise of long-term gains. A control system that rewards the man who improves his range and that penalizes the one who does not would hasten improvement of the public range.[4, 5]

RANGE USE IN OTHER LANDS. Danish farmers are among the world's best land managers. Their pasturelands are lush because of cool summers and abundant rainfall. Cows are staked out on the grassland with a sufficiently long tether to provide just the amount of forage needed for a day's supply. Systematically they are moved so that they harvest the grass uniformly as they go, thereby avoiding unnecessary trampling and loss. The English and Scottish moorlands afford medium-quality open range for sheep, cattle, and horses. In the main, the number of animals is adjusted to the productivity of the range. The damp, cool weather, as well as the carefully bred stock, is conducive to splendid wool production. Practices vary widely with local laws and customs. In some places the moor is broken up by heavy plows, cultivated, fertilized, and sown to good pasture grasses, thereby greatly increasing the carrying capacity.

In the Mediterranean region a relatively dry climate and limited natural resources have led to heavy overuse of the grazing lands. Even on protected game lands, the abundance of rabbits and other small mammals depletes the grass resource. Over much of the Mediterranean region grazing by sheep and goats has broken down land terraces built by ancient people and has led to serious erosion. Strenuous efforts are currently being undertaken to rehabilitate the entire region. Spain has taken the lead in the West and Israel in the East. The programs include torrent control, irrigation, restoration of rangeland, forest planting, and improved agricultural practice. Astounding transformations are being effected where concentrated effort has been expended.

The Valley of Kashmir is one of the loveliest regions of the world. Walled in by the high Himalayas, this 5,000-foot-high valley has a delightful summer climate and a deep loess soil unmatched in fertility. Its fame has been known for ages. Dotted with lakes and well supplied with streams of clear mountain water, it should be a paradise for mankind. But it no longer is. The nearby hills are grazed barren by sheep and goats. The mountain lands are overgrazed by cattle. The unprotected soil washes into the stream channels that cut deep gullies in the rich loess soils. Erosion has proceeded so far that many channels have been clogged with boulders. Gradually such streams build up boulder plains a mile or more in width. Unleashed natural forces tear away the rich soil. Meanwhile hungry mouths multiply as modern science checks early mortality. Elsewhere in India the same problem of overgrazing and soil erosion persists, in part, because little effort is made to control cattle population, the animals being considered sacred.

Seeking to improve the management of the world's grazing land is one of mankind's most urgent tasks. It will not easily be accomplished, because man must be supported while the improvement is taking place. Here is a real challenge to use agricultural surpluses of one nation to help another during a land-rehabilitation effort. Great potential for progress exists, as protected areas amply demonstrate. But education, capital loans, and modern technology must be applied for success.

THE RANGE MANAGER'S JOB. The successful range manager must understand the ranching business. He must be in a position to work out adjustments in public-land use with a minimum of hardship and with maximum benefits. The absence of long-term commitments to range users and particularly the tendency, which was widespread in earlier years, to reduce the grazing permits of large ranch operators to favor the medium- and small-sized operators simply added to the difficulty and increased the pressure on the range.

Range managers perform a wide variety of tasks. Each spring they travel over the range to examine the forage and its stage in development, correlate this with other phenological information, and so decide upon the opening dates for admission of grazing animals.

The range manager determines whether the range is in good, fair, or poor condition and whether the range is improving or deteriorating from year to year. To perform these tasks, he must be able to recognize the various species of forage plants at all stages in their development. He must know their relative palatability, their requirements for moisture and light, and their nutritional values in various stages. Above all, he must know how to recognize the signs of range deterioration in its incipient as well as its advanced stages.

Once the condition of the range is thoroughly appraised, it is usually possible to decide upon measures needed to maintain it in good condition or to improve it if in poor condition. Reseeding is one of these measures. This is most effective if the soil can first be cultivated. Badly deteriorated ranges grown up with sagebrush and various other shrubs

Fig. 51   Poor range supports poor livestock. Overgrazed cheatgrass range near Kinghill, Idaho. (*U.S. Forest Service photo.*)

and weeds, including poisonous plants, must often be given a drastic treatment before they can be rehabilitated. Mountain meadows require special measures.

Proper distribution of livestock is very important in good range management (Fig. 51). Distribution can be effected in part by distributing watering holes, by distributing salt widely over the range, and by riding to drive the animals from overgrazed to underused areas. Herding of sheep has proved very effective as a means of getting uniform use of large grazing areas. As a consequence, sheep range in many sections of the West is in better condition than cattle range, even though the sheep, if improperly herded, are far more destructive than cattle.

Rotation grazing is another technique that is sometimes used to rehabilitate the range. This may be done both seasonally and from year to year. If the range has been only moderately overgrazed, deferred grazing, rotation grazing, and reduction of the stocking are often the only steps that are required to start the range on the mend. Where areas have been intensively overgrazed for a long period of time, mere exclusion of animals will not result in prompt range restoration. Soil rebuilding, reseeding, and other measures are required in these cases.[14]

Outlook. The outlook for both wildlife and range management seems bright both in the United States and in the world. Wildlife management, being primarily important to man's use of leisure time, is likely to be favored or neglected according to the amount of leisure time available to the average man and the use he elects to make of it. Evidence exists of the growing popularity of family vacations which cut into the time the head of the household has for hunting and fishing. The growing scarcity of areas open to public hunting also limits the satisfaction to be derived from it. On the other hand, changed farming and forestry practices on the whole appear to favor an abundant wildlife population that will be available for use. It seems likely that there will also be plenty of people who will enjoy the sport of harvesting it. In any case, there will continue to be the problem of balance in land use in which wildlife will be a factor of major importance.

The future for range management seems secure. The output of animals from rangelands plays an important role in the nation's food supply, the demand for which increases with the population. Improved range-management practices have already led to improvement of forage, lessened erosion, increased weight gains of animals, and increased income to ranchers. In 1961 we seemed to be but in the first stages of range-improvement practices. As these become more widely adopted, research results will point to additional opportunities for increasing the output from rangelands. The rangelands, therefore, seem destined to continue to play an important role in meeting the nation's food requirements.

The opportunities for range improvement in other lands are even greater than those in the United States. The question remains as to whether these opportunities will be realized in the near future. Experts of the United States have much to contribute to other nations ready for range-improvement programs.

LITERATURE CITED

1. Allen, Durward L. 1954. "Our Wildlife Legacy," Funk & Wagnalls Company, New York. 422 pp.
2. Barrett Committee Report. 1948. "Report of Hearings before the Committee on Public Lands and the Subcommittee on Public Lands of the Committee on Public Lands, House of Representatives, on Forest Service Policy and Public Lands Policy," 80th Cong., 2d Sess., H. Rept. 2456. 15 pp.
3. Chapman, Oscar L. 1950. "Annual Report of the Secretary of the Interior" (fiscal year ended June 30, 1950), U.S. Government Printing Office. 411 pp.
4. Clawson, Marion. 1950. "The Western Range Livestock Industry," McGraw-Hill Book Company, Inc., New York. 401 pp.
5. Clawson, Marion, R. Bernell Held, and Charles H. Stoddard. 1960. "Land for the Future," The Johns Hopkins Press, Baltimore. 570 pp.

6. Day, Albert M. 1948. "Fish and Wildlife Service," Annual Report of the Secretary of the Interior (fiscal year ended June 30, 1948), pp. 285–315, U.S. Government Printing Office.

7. Kauffman, Erle, ed. 1958. "The Conservation Yearbook 1957–1958." Published by Conservation Yearbook, Washington, D.C. 272 pp.

8. Leopold, Aldo. 1933. "Game Management," Charles Scribner's Sons, New York. 481 pp.

9. Sampson, Arthur W. 1951. "Range Management Principles and Practices," John Wiley & Sons, New York. 570 pp.

10. Stoddart, Laurence A., and Arthur D. Smith. 1943. "Range Management," McGraw-Hill Book Company, Inc., New York. 547 pp.

11. Taylor, Walter P. 1954. "The Deer of North America," The Stackpole Company, Harrisburg, Pa. 668 pp.

12. Trippensee, Reuben Edwin. 1948. "Wildlife Management," McGraw-Hill Book Company, Inc., New York. 479 pp.

13. U.S. Department of Agriculture. 1941. *Climate and Man,* The Yearbook of Agriculture, Washington. 1,248 pp.

14. U.S. Department of Agriculture. 1948. *Grass,* The Yearbook of Agriculture, Washington. 892 pp.

15. U.S. Department of Agriculture, Forest Service. 1936. "The Western Range," 74th Cong., 2d Sess., S. Doc. 199. 620 pp.

16. U.S. Bureau of the Census. 1961. "Statistical Abstract of the United States," Washington. 1,037 pp.

17. U.S. Department of the Interior. 1959. "Annual Report of the Secretary," Washington. 459 pp.

CHAPTER 13. *Forests and Recreation*

RECREATION HAS BECOME one of the largest industries in America. It embraces motion pictures, radio and television, books and magazines, clubs, resorts, the theater and music, touring, museums, various indoor sports and games, and a host of activities carried on out of doors, from little league baseball to skiing, from fishing to mountaineering, and from picnicking to wilderness safaris. Outdoor recreation is leading the van both in growth of public participation and in changing popularity of activities. Annual expenditures by federal, state, and local governments to support outdoor recreation totaled about $1 billion in 1961. The expenditures of recreationists generated a $20 billion business.[2] It is important to national well-being that these expenditures yield a high return to the people in terms of physical and mental health, appreciation of our land and man's relation to it, and buoyancy of spirit that makes possible high achievement in a democratically governed nation. If, in addition, it can help provide a feeling of kinship by bringing together in friendly participation the executive and the skilled workman, the farmer and the tradesman, the professional man and the laborer, it may tend to develop mutual respect among occupational classes that promotes national unity. Experiences that promote a feeling of mutual respect are not to be neglected in a society becoming daily more complex and daily more interdependent, especially when it is strongly challenged by outside and inside forces.

The growing popularity of outdoor recreation is the result of many factors. One is the importance of relieving pent-up energy that finds little outlet in modern urban life. If this can be expended in climbing a challenging mountain, skiing a difficult slope, or pursuing game with gun and dog, it lends a certain purposefulness to an outing aside from the feeling of well-being that mild physical tiredness brings.

Leisure time from the eight-hour day and five-day week makes possible more time for outdoor experience. The personal motorcar has, perhaps, been the most important factor of all, for with its use many attractive outdoor recreation areas are within reach of almost every family.

About 90 per cent of United States adults participated in outdoor recreation in 1960.[2]

With need for physical exertion, leisure time, and the motorcar has come a demand for all kinds of facilities to accommodate the public, from the roadside eating stand to campgrounds, motels, and resorts. Lightweight, windproof clothing has opened winter as well as summer to outdoor recreationists. This has added a whole new element of challenge and satisfaction to the recreationist. Skiing and, above all, winter mountaineering are sports to test the skill and stamina of the most hardy. Thereby these sports evoke a feeling of kinship with pioneers as they breast the blizzards and prepare their shelters against the worst that nature opposes to man.

Outdoor recreation takes a variety of forms. At one extreme are the wilderness seekers who represent purists of a highly disciplined kind. From their jumping-off place they scorn motor-powered and other elaborate equipment. Backpacking, pack train, or canoe carries their gear into roadless areas. They seek wilderness conditions as near the pristine as possible. And they seek solitude, if not for the individual, at least for the group of which he is a part. It is their purpose, to which they are zealously devoted, to preserve as many truly wilderness areas in our nation as possible for the enjoyment and edification of man for generations to come. They demand no elaborate campgrounds, picnic areas, bathing beaches, or other costly facilities, but they do demand untrammeled space and lots of it.

At the other extreme are those wedded to the sound and smell of the internal-combustion engine who seek to have it propel them wherever they go. They want good roads leading directly to the picnic table or campsite. They want a firm ramp for launching their boat from its trailer. They clamp on an outboard motor to speed the boat over the water, towing one or more water skiers. In the winter they seek the "developed" ski area with motor-driven rope tows or chair lifts to take them up the slope. They prefer to use slopes packed by snow tractors. Ebullient in spirit, they seek a maximum of fun for the physical energy expended.

In between are a host of others who reap rewarding experience from more restrained forms of outdoor activities—the bird watchers; mineral collectors; amateur botanists, zoologists, and astronomers; and seekers of Indian relics are but a few. Each, however, seeks places where he is free to indulge in his sport or hobby, each tends to develop an interest in the out-of-doors beyond that of the pleasure of exercise, and each shares his experience and knowledge with his fellow devotees.

From this general survey a few hypotheses may be ventured:

1. Outdoor recreation should offer as much freedom of choice as possible to the individual and should involve a minimum of restraints.

2. Outdoor recreation should present individual challenges that lead to development of skills and knowledge.

3. Widely different forms of outdoor recreation have achieved popularity. Some, such as bird-watching and botanizing, may go hand in hand. Others, such as water skiing and fishing, do not.

4. Great opportunity exists for improving personal enjoyment of outdoor recreation by providing proper facilities and appropriate areas for different activities and for stimulating the curiosity and interest of recreationists in making their outdoor holiday one of increasing understanding as well as of escape from the daily routine.

5. Pleasing landscapes, scenic beauty, wild creatures, and native vegetative forms all tend to induce a degree of tranquillity and composure that is restful. But in the last analysis, what a recreationist really seeks is a state of mind. To a Bob Marshall or John Muir, nothing less than the great wildernesses of the West and Alaska sufficed. Aldo Leopold made his most thoughtful contribution to outdoor philosophy on a Sand County, Wisconsin, farm. Goethe won strength, composure, and philosophic insight from strolling in his garden. Henri Fabre could uncover a fascinating wilderness by exploring the activities of creatures in a dunghill. The real task is to arouse curiosity and perceptiveness, to evoke painstaking observation and sustained interest, to awaken wonder and a desire to understand, and to develop appreciation and a desire to share it.

Let us now focus our attention on the magnitude and scope of recreational demand and use, on the facilities available and needed—and their design and care—on the programs provided and their conflicts, and finally on the outlook for future developments. Our treatment will be restricted chiefly to outdoor recreation in or associated with forests or other wild-land areas.

The Public Park and Forest System

With the discovery in our country of great natural wonders, including hot springs, waterfalls, geyser basins, big trees, and rugged mountain scenery, came the demand for national parks. The thought of such areas falling into the hands of commercial exploiters was distasteful to high-minded citizens, who desired that this wonderland heritage be preserved for public enjoyment. Areas of historical or lesser scenic value were set aside for national monuments and state parks. Still later has come the demand for public fishing and shooting grounds. Parks and recreation areas are administered by schools, villages, counties, cities, states, and the federal government.

Forests, because they occupy large areas of land, offer a degree of seclusion, and shelter many interesting wild creatures, are especially popular with recreationists. Unless excluded, the public will naturally use both public and private forest land for hiking, picnicking, hunting, and collecting. Public foresters recognize this use and encourage it.

The national park system embraces national parks, national monuments, national historical and military areas, parkways, and miscellaneous areas. The number of areas, their total size, and the number of visits as of 1956 are set forth in Table 8. Similar information is given for national

TABLE 8. OUTDOOR RECREATIONAL AREAS AND THEIR USE, 1956 *

Type of area	Number	Size of area, thousand acres	Number of visits, thousands
National parks..............	29	13,131	20,055
National monuments.........	83	8,957	8,769
National historical and military areas...................	60	137	9,243
National parkways...........	3	85	7,438
National recreation areas......	5	2,050	5,119
National forests.............	149	180,354	52,556
Wildlife refuges.............	258	17,225	7,555
State parks.................	2,100	5,077	200,705
Total..................	2,687	227,016	311,440

* Clawson, Marion. 1958. "Statistics on Outdoor Recreation," Resources for the Future, Inc., Washington, D.C. 165 pp.

forests, wildlife refuges, and state parks. The system together embraces 227 million acres and attracts annually 311 million visitors. Of the areas listed, all except the national forests have recreational use as the primary purpose.[1]

The number of areas, their size, and the number of visits have increased sharply over the years. Between 1900 and 1956 the number of national parks increased from 7 to 29, the area from 3,286,000 to 13,131,-000 acres, and the visits from 121,000 (1904) to 20,055,000.[1,2] Corresponding data for national forests are: number, 38 to 149; area, 46,515,000 to 180,354,000 acres; visits (1924), 4,660 to 52,556. The Secretary of the Interior reported 75.8 million visits to the national parks during the fiscal year 1961, an increase of 6 per cent over the preceding year.[3] National forests in 1961 had 102 million recreational visits. The total visits had almost doubled since 1956. About one-third of all visitors to national forests and national parks camp and picnic.[2]

The public agencies having custody of these lands have provided, directly or through leases to concessionaires, camping and picnic grounds, swimming facilities, winter sports developments, organization camps, resorts, summer homes, roads, trails, scenic overlooks, and other developments for public use.

In recent years many companies engaged in lumber and paper manufacturing have opened their lands for public use and provided picnic areas and other facilities for visitors. Pressure for more space for recreational use is increasing rapidly. Recreationists are eyeing private as well as public forest lands. The forester thereby becomes in some degree a park manager. He must be guided by the same principles that guide park managers if he is to perform his services to recreationists cheaply and effectively. Gradually there has arisen a profession of park management that embraces planning, design, construction, operation, and maintenance of parks. It draws on the fields of regional planning, landscape designing, civil engineering, forestry, human behavior, and public administration.

Park management may be divided into planning and administration. The first has to do with developing land for use; the second is concerned with operation and maintenance. Actually, these two divisions merge, as it is necessary for the planner to consider operation, program, and maintenance if he is to plan well. The man concerned with administration is interested to see that development is such that it will enable him to administer the area in the best possible manner.

Planning Park Systems

The park planner must be well informed and imaginative to handle the many factors involved in planning a park system for a densely populated region. A basic job is making a survey of recreation needs. This requires determining the population, its density, growth rate, occupation groups, ethnic makeup, average financial income, and the time available for recreation (Fig. 52).

Public recreational facilities are not needed nearly so badly by people dispersed in rural areas or small villages as by those crowded in cities. Office workers have different requirements from factory workers.

Metropolitan areas that have marked racial or national groups have a special problem. Friendly commingling on spacious playgrounds can promote mutual understanding and respect. But people from other lands enjoy also the opportunity to hold folk dances and songfests and to play games they learned in their homeland. Such artistic expressions often

Fig. 52   Planning for park development may require the drafting of several preliminary layouts of facilities before adopting one for development on the ground.

provide entertaining spectacles to native Americans as well as satisfaction to participants. Our own culture is enriched thereby. Imaginative design can provide for the needs of all groups in such a way that the fullest possible satisfaction results.

Financial income of the various groups in the population makes a great difference in their demands for recreation and the types that they can enjoy. People of modest income will enjoy swimming, fishing, hunting, hiking, picnicking, and boating. Those of higher income may wish golf courses, bridle paths, and even public yacht harbors for sailing, motorboating, and cabin cruising. Nicety of judgment is required in balancing the needs of the family with lowest income against those of the family with a larger income.

The time available has an important influence on the need for recreational facilities and the type that should be provided. During the summertime, long evenings are available for recreation. Facilities close to the cities need to be provided for constructive use of this leisure time.

Avoiding Conflicting Uses. Age distribution of a population is also important. Older people enjoy the more passive types of recreation. Picnicking, pleasant views or vistas, floral displays, and an effectively landscaped park please them. They may also wish to sit in the sun, to watch the play of younger people, their sailing, swimming, horseback riding, and other more active recreational outlets. Small children enjoy wading pools in summer; larger children want playgrounds; and young adults want opportunities for such strenuous sports as baseball, football, soccer, ice hockey, swimming, skiing, and skating. Old and young alike enjoy the solitude of the forest. They thrill with pleasure at the sight of whole hillsides carpeted with spring flowers where only a few weeks before the land was brown. They enjoy hearing and seeing wild birds and observing the animals that live in forests. They seek to identify the many species of trees, shrubs, and herbs that lend variety and interest to our woodlands.

The skillful park planner will try, insofar as he is able, to provide facilities for mass recreation, such as picnic areas, swimming areas, and boating areas, and, at the same time, will try to reserve a portion of his park in as near a natural condition as possible. Here the bird lovers and the seekers for wild flowers can wander off on the little-frequented trails, gaining a certain satisfaction of adventure and exploration as well as an opportunity to become acquainted with the natural forest environment where it has been little disturbed by man. The truest test of successful park planning is to provide for both active and passive recreation, for group activities, for family activities, and for the pleasures of solitude (Fig. 53).

The seasonal needs of the population must also be considered. More and more our people are seeking year-round outdoor activities. Skiing, snowshoeing, and hiking across the snow-covered land bring as much enjoyment as can be had from an equal period spent out of doors during summer.

Promoting Understanding. Park planners have an opportunity to educate as well as to entertain people through the proper development of recreational resources. Historic locations are often made the site of county and state parks and national monuments. Restored battlefields, old forts, and other historic places may enable the imaginative citizen to relive in his mind the events of history. Here the utmost scholarship and subtlety are required if such an educational program is to be effective. The public will be educated only insofar as the displays provide them the imaginative thrill that comes from projecting themselves into historic situations.

The national parks offer conducted tours and nature talks which add greatly to the enjoyment and understanding of park visitors. A properly planned park system for a metropolitan area will normally include parks and historic sites having educational value. It may also include special

Fɪɢ. 53   Trail along St. Mary's Lake, Glacier National Park, Montana. (*National Park Service photo.*)

nature trails with appropriate signs, changed at regular intervals, to teach the people the names of the various wild flowers, trees, and plants; to show them the locations of birds' nests; and to point out other interesting features that might otherwise be passed by unnoticed.

Having sized up the population and the recreational needs of the various subgroups within it, the park planner must next survey existing facilities. In appraising these, he will want to give consideration to their present use, the effectiveness with which they serve the people who now frequent them, and whether or not improvements might be made that would enable them to serve a greater number of people or to serve the present number more effectively. Many parks are overused. Only by decreasing use can these be restored to a standard that will bring to the users the degree of satisfaction desired from outdoor recreation.

Projecting a Park System

A park planner must think of the population anticipated 15 years in the future. He must study the surrounding territory with an eye toward possible park locations. It is far better to acquire areas well in advance of their need than to wait until private development has increased property values and destroyed many of the recreational features of an area. The park planner will wish to consider a number of locations and a variety of types of parks which, taken together with existing facilities, will provide a park system tailored to meet the needs of the metropolitan region concerned. He will then establish priorities for acquisition and development, estimate the overall cost for each unit, and present his findings to the public park boards for their consideration and action.

Detailed Planning of Individual Parks

Every improvement in a public park area needs to be carefully designed and located. First, consideration must be given to overall planning so that traffic in the park flows with a minimum of congestion and interruption. The major recreational features of the park are first located. Road system, parking area, and trail system must be provided so that the people may move readily into the park from their motorcars to the major points of interest. The trails should radiate from the necessary centers of congestion, such as parking areas, bathing houses, historic museums, and other features. Appropriate signs must be erected to

Fig. 54 Rehabilitated rangeland offers an object lesson in land management to interested vacationists. (*U.S. Forest Service photo.*)

guide park users to the various facilities. These may be simple lettered signs or pictorial signs; but, in any case, they must carry their message clearly so that the visitor is not confused or misdirected. Parking areas, picnicking areas, picnic tables and benches, drinking water, fireplaces, shelters, bathhouses, toilets, refuse pits—all the essentials for the comfort and enjoyment of the people must be properly located, attractively designed, and integrated with other features (Fig. 54).

Any park area that is to be used by large numbers of people is naturally subject to wear, and many of the attractive features may even be destroyed. To minimize public misuse of parks, the park planner uses simple signs, along with proper location of trails and facilities, and informs the public where and how it can satisfy its needs. A properly planned park will require a minimum of policing. When it is made easy for the public to do the right thing, they are less inclined to do the wrong thing.

Building the Park

Park construction requires engineering skill in the laying out of roads, trails, facilities, and buildings and in their construction. Roadways and trails should be naturalized insofar as possible. Concrete and asphalt are to be avoided, and gravel and grass walkways and trails should be used wherever these will stand up under the traffic to which they will be subjected. Buildings and facilities must be serviceable, simple yet rugged in design, and easy to service and keep in order. Above all, they must be adequate for their purpose.

Maintaining the Park

Park maintenance may involve simple custodianship of the facilities and protection of the park area against fire and misuse. Use of any park area by the public introduces a major disturbing factor that tends to destroy many of the features most desired in a park. Constant trampling wears out grass, compacts soil, leads to erosion, tends to kill trees and other vegetation, oftentimes invites attack of trees by insects and fungi, and consequently requires constant vigilance on the part of the park custodian to direct public use so as to minimize such damage. All parks require a certain minimum maintenance. In rare cases this may be provided by the users themselves if they are well disciplined and truly appreciate the facilities placed at their command. More often a park custodian is employed to keep the park in a neat and orderly condition and to supervise the use of the park by the public.

In addition to simple custodianship, there is regulation of traffic, assignment of facilities, and the appointment of guards to direct the public in the use of the park area. Where swimming and boating facilities are provided, lifeguards are needed. The park manager will have the guards wear uniforms or carry an appropriate badge so that the public will know that they are in charge of the park and will cooperate with them. Where fees are charged, the collecting of such fees provides an opportunity to point out special features or attractions and to build an understanding between the park authority and the using public.

The most intensive type of park management is that which involves recreational and educational programs, guided tours, museums, nature trails, and other special educational or recreational activities. These are oftentimes found in the national parks and in some of the state, county, and city parks.

Park Administration

Strictly speaking, a forester is perhaps concerned only with large natural park areas, such as national and state parks; yet in these as well as in large city and county parks, such as those of Westchester County, New York, or the city of Denver's mountain parks, the activities of the park planner and park superintendent merge with those of a city-park manager and the national-park superintendent. All have many activities in common and all require the same basic philosophy in planning and maintaining park facilities.

A park organization like the National Park Service or many of the state park services is large in size, spends considerable sums of money, and serves the needs of millions of people. For this reason park administration becomes an important activity, requiring the same type of managerial skills demanded of forest administrators and even business administrators. The superintendent of the national park has many functions. He must plan the acquisition of land, the development of road and trail systems, the organization of a fire-protection system, the erection of campgrounds and picnic grounds, and the division of the park into ranger districts. He assigns duties and inspects the performance of the rangers and naturalists. He must maintain good relations with the public, both the people that visit the park and those that live in the surrounding territory. He must perform all other duties that are necessary to maintain the park in good condition and provide for economic expenditure of public funds dedicated to this purpose.

The National Park Service

The National Park System dates back to 1832, when Congress put aside four sections of land comprising the Hot Springs Reservation in Arkansas for permanent public use. In 1872 Congress set off the lands of the Yellowstone for a public park for the benefit and enjoyment of our people. This law of 1872 set forth the major policies to be followed in the management of Yellowstone Park, and these principles have been adopted for subsequent parks as well. It is mandatory upon the Park Service to preserve from injury and exploitation all timber, mineral deposits, and natural curiosities or wonders within the park, to retain the park in its natural condition, and to protect wildlife from wanton killing or commercial exploitation. Fishing is allowed on most areas under National Park Service regulations.

The National Park Service is a bureau of the U.S. Department of the Interior. The field service is administered through five regions, each of which has a regional director. Service to the individual regions and parks is provided through six divisions in Washington:

1. Administration
2. Operations
3. Design and Construction
4. Interpretation
5. Recreation Resource Planning
6. Audits

Technical Jobs in Park Management and Their Requirements

The jobs of the modern park planner and administrator call for a variety of technical skills. Among the professional people employed by the Park Service are engineers, architects, landscape architects, historians, naturalists, archaeologists, and biologists. The Service also employs many foresters for land acquisition, appraisal, and management. Planners and administrators may be selected from these professionals or from specialists in these fields. The strictly professional requirements of park planners and administrators have been recognized by special committees of three nationwide park organizations: the National Conference on State Parks, the American Institute of Park Executives, and the National Park Service. The committees pointed out the need for studying the basic sciences such as botany, chemistry, geology, entomology, and zoology. In addition, they urged the inclusion of specific subjects related to forest areas such as wood technology, wildlife management, pathology, forest entomology, and silviculture. But, most important of all, they stressed the need for a background in landscape design, an appreciation of architecture, a knowledge of engineering and construction methods, and familiarity with plant materials other than forest trees.

Landscape architecture has been defined as "the fitting of land for human use and enjoyment." Such a definition is especially applicable to the planning of lands for recreational use. Training that fits men for national, state, county, and municipal park work also fits them to think properly about the development of private land as well. The city planner receives his basic training in landscape architecture, as do the men who become camp planners, recreational planners, and park planners.

Drawing is to the landscape designer what writing is to most people, a means of expression. Since landscape planning deals with the presentation of ideas visually, drawing is the best means to the end. Park planners need to use drawings to show others what they plan to do and how they plan to do it. Those called upon to study a drawing are inclined to judge the skill and knowledge of the planner by the ability he has to express himself in the drawing.

The park manager also must have the ability to understand the wide range of purposes and ideals which will be found among his clients. He will need to express himself well in writing and speaking as well as in the graphic arts. His success will depend largely on how well he can "sell" himself and his ideas to his superiors. Skill in dealing with people is an essential trait for the person interested in park management.

Park management therefore is a special professional field closely related to forestry but with its own specialties in landscape design, land-use planning, and recreational planning.

Outlook for Forest Recreation

A comprehensive study of future outdoor recreational needs for America was completed by the President's Outdoor Recreation Resources Review Commission in January, 1962.[2] The Commission's report indicated that the population of the United States was expected to increase to about 350 million people by the year 2000 and their demand for outdoor recreation to increase at least threefold over that of 1961. This increased recreational demand is expected to arise as a result of increased leisure, along with increased income that will enable people to enjoy their leisure. The Commission found that simple forms of outdoor recreation such as motoring for pleasure, walking for pleasure, playing outdoor games and sports, swimming, sightseeing, bicycling, and fishing are by far the most popular. Other forms that get considerable attention, such as water skiing, canoeing, sailing, mountain climbing, and snow skiing, are indulged in by a relatively limited proportion of the total population. The survey also revealed that as family income and years of education increase, the participation in outdoor recreation also increases. It also found that people participate more in outdoor recreation when facilities are available within reasonable distance for their use. The increased mobility of people, however, has evoked a great increase in demand for resource-oriented outdoor recreation such as unique natural areas and primitive areas. Forest areas, both public and private, play a key role in public outdoor recreation.

A particularly significant finding of the Commission was that there is plenty of land for outdoor recreation, but the problem is to make it available and fitted for the type of recreation which the people need. As they expressed it, "The need is not for a series of crash programs. Large-scale acquisition and development programs are needed; so is money—lots of it. The essential ingredient, however, is imagination. The effectiveness of land, not sheer quantity, is the key." The Commission stressed especially the need for planning suburban development so that outdoor recreation becomes a part of it. They ask such significant questions as "Do the children have to be driven to school—or can they walk or cycle to it safely over wooded paths?" It is in the development of our suburban communities and their environs that the greatest opportunity lies for meeting the day-to-day outdoor recreation needs of our expanding population.

Outside the rural areas much can be done to take the concentrated use away from a few specific areas by developing and publicizing historic sites, interesting land-use developments, demonstration forests, nature trails, geologic features, and other natural phenomena of note that can intrigue the recreationist. The Commission recommended a comprehensive approach to future outdoor recreation. Provision should be made for high-density recreation areas; general recreation areas; use of natural environment such as forests; use of unique natural areas that contain spectacular waterfalls, peaks, or other features; primitive areas; and historic sites.

It recommended that a Bureau of Outdoor Recreation be established in the Department of the Interior that would have the responsibility of giving overall consideration to federal recreational resource management, including federal aid to states and federal support of education and research in recreation. It did not recommend that all recreational areas be transferred to the proposed bureau on recreation, but rather that each area continue to be administered by the agency that now administers it or by the one that is best suited to administer it. Stress also was placed upon the importance of private recreation developments that the public might use for modest fees.[2]

The Commission's report attracted widespread public interest and commendation. A Bureau of Outdoor Recreation was promptly established in the Department of the Interior to coordinate and review programs. The Secretary of Agriculture saw in surplus agricultural land an asset for possible conversion to recreational use. The U.S. Forest Service and other agencies set about expanding their facilities for use by recreationists. New York and Wisconsin began vigorous programs of recreational-land acquisition and development. Other states were expected to follow their lead.

One of the characteristics of forest recreation is the challenge it poses to man's physical resources. May it always do so. But it requires, in addition to sheer physical vigor, some knowledge on the part of the participants. Probably devotees of forest recreation in the decades ahead will give increasing consideration to developing such skills as winter mountaineering, rock climbing, and finding one's way through trackless forest.

It may be hoped also that forest recreation as well as other types will bring to the participant something in addition to mere fun. Complete devotion to self-amusement ultimately becomes boring in itself unless it adds to the skills and knowledge of the participant as well as diverts him.

LITERATURE CITED

1. National Park Service. 1949. "Areas Administered by the National Park Service," U.S. Department of the Interior, Washington. 43 pp.
2. Outdoor Recreation Resources Review Commission. 1962. "Outdoor Recreation for America," Washington, D.C. 245 pp.
3. Udall, Stewart. 1961. "Resources for Tomorrow," Annual Report of the Secretary of the Interior for the fiscal year ending June 30, 1961, U.S. Government Printing Office. 471 pp.

CHAPTER 14. *Protecting Soil and Watersheds*

NEW YEAR'S EVE in 1933 was a time of destruction, sorrow, and death for people who dwelt in La Canada Valley near Los Angeles. Heavy rains fell for 2½ days on the steep San Gabriel Mountains, and a flood rushed out of the mountains, carrying silt, sand, and boulders weighing as much as 60 tons. The water with its heavy burden spread over the valley floor, wrecking homes and gardens and blocking highways. As floods go, it was not large nor was the total damage impressive. What was significant about this flood was a contributing cause of it. A few months earlier a fire had swept over the chaparral-covered mountains, laying bare 7½ square miles. Rain fell equally on both burned and unburned slopes, but studies made after the flood revealed that, acre for acre, burned land contributed 50 times as much water to the flood flow as unburned land.[4] The area damaged by flood, 3 square miles, was almost half that burned by the fire.

An even more widespread cause of floods is overgrazing and cultivation of steep mountain slopes. In the Philippines entire villages have been wiped out by flood waters descending from cultivated mountains. The deep-soiled lands at the base of the Himalayas in Kashmir and India are carved up by mile-wide boulder-strewn stream channels that show but a trickle of water during dry seasons. Floods are particularly damaging to soils in dry regions such as the Mediterranean countries, much of Africa and South America, and our own western states. Here the sparse vegetation provides but scanty protection at best. When lands have been heavily grazed or destroyed by cultivation, floods almost inevitably follow each heavy storm.

Importance of Protecting Soil and Watersheds

Floods in the United States during the period 1924 to 1943 are estimated to have destroyed $2.2 billion worth of property. Total direct and indirect flood damage, based on 1947 prices, has averaged $465 million annually in recent years.[4]

Providing ample pure water for municipalities is becoming an increasingly costly process. Philadelphia alone spends $40 million each year to

236

improve the taste and odor of its water. Water in North Carolina from piedmont farmlands costs three times as much for desilting and chlorination as that from forested Appalachian watersheds. The United States Corps of Engineers estimates expenditures needed for water projects for the next 50 years to be $48.1 billion, based on 1947 prices.[4] This amount includes expenditures needed for flood control, navigation, hydroelectric power, irrigation, drainage of wet lands, and abatement of pollution. Water control is expensive.

How Forests Protect Soil and Water

Erosion is a geologic process that goes on continuously wherever air or water moves over land. Neither man nor vegetation can stop erosion completely. Even well-forested slopes may have streams that become turbid after heavy rains. What vegetation can do is to slow down the process so that soil is formed through mechanical and chemical breakdown of rock more rapidly than it is carried away by erosion. Erosion is then unnoticeable and unimportant from the human viewpoint.

When rain falls on bare soil, individual raindrops strike with considerable force, splashing soil on nearby objects to a height of over 12 inches above the ground and a distance twice as great. The surface soil is quickly puddled; that is, the pores leading to lower depths are sealed. Even light rainfall may cause surface runoff. Suspended silt in the water gives it a murky color as well as abrasive action. Sheet erosion begins where surface runoff starts. The water soon collects into rills that cut small trenches and run together, adding volume to the flow and power to its erosive action. Gully cutting begins. If allowed to proceed unchecked, accelerated erosion will eventually convert unprotected soil into deeply gullied badlands.[2]

Vegetative cover stops the process all along the line. Any form of continuous vegetative cover provides good protection for soil. Natural vegetation is usually better than cultivated crops, because it covers the soil more completely and because the litter and humus help maintain porosity. Forests, because they have heavy crowns and deeply penetrating roots, provide maximum protection against erosion of soil and against rapid surface runoff.

Trees intercept rainfall and break the force of the falling drops. At the same time they retain on their leaves and branches a considerable amount of moisture, especially from showers of short duration, much of which is reevaporated into the air without ever reaching the ground surface. This phenomenon is of benefit in eliminating water that might cause floods but represents a loss of water to feed streams for irrigation and for municipal use. Experiments have shown that tree crowns may intercept as much as 30 to 50 per cent of the total precipitation when this occurs in small showers of short duration separated by periods of clear weather. For long rainfall the percentage interception may still be 10 to 40 per cent, depending on species and density of forest.[5]

After the rain or snow penetrates the tree canopy, it falls, not on bare ground, but on a litter-strewn forest floor. Here leaves, remnants of leaves, twigs, and sometimes a cover of herbaceous plants again intercept the raindrop and prevent soil movement. The resilient, litter-covered forest floor absorbs all the force of the falling drops and allows the clear water to filter slowly through the organic debris and to enter the soil gently without sealing the natural pores. Surface runoff, therefore, is almost totally lacking from a forest-covered area until after the soil mantle becomes saturated with water.

Experiments have shown that forest litter and humus have especially effective action in slowing down the rate at which water enters the mineral soil. This action seems to be largely a matter of obstructing the flow of water and holding it back through absorption by the many small particles of litter and humus material. These fine particles tend to swell as they become wetted, and in this manner they absorb two or three times their weight of water. It has been found that a layer of rich forest humus 6 inches in thickness may detain as much as 4 inches of rainfall. Within a period of four or five days more than half this water seeps downward to the underlying soil. The litter is then again ready to accept and hold an appreciable amount of rainfall.

The soil mantle, if relatively dry and deep, can absorb and detain vast amounts of rainfall. Each foot of soil can absorb from 1 to 5 inches of water. Since this water is retained against the force of gravity, it is available for the growing of plants. This water does not reach underground water-storage reservoirs. The soil acts like a self-emptying reservoir in holding back much floodwater.

The roots serve as a great binding force in holding the soil together and preventing it from moving down the steep slopes. Of particular importance is the binding of the upper 6 to 8 inches of soil. If this is held firmly in place, the underlying layers are less likely to slip. As tree roots are concentrated largely in the upper 6 inches of soil, oftentimes completely permeating it, they add greatly to soil cohesion. For municipal watersheds trees have an especially valuable function in preventing the washing of contaminating materials into the reservoirs. The abundance of small plant and animal life that inhabits the forest floor makes it a great sanitizing agent by breaking down dead material. Toxic and infectious plant and animal remains are broken down completely to harmless chemical compounds by the organisms of the soil. Consequently, contaminating materials seldom are carried by water or other means more than a few inches from where they fall in the forest.

Forest fires destroy the litter and may even convert the humus into bare, reddened mineral soil. Such burned land is highly vulnerable to erosion. Where grazing is heavy, domestic animals compact the soil, cut up the litter so that it quickly decomposes, and make bare paths, down which water runs with erosive force. Studies on pasturelands in Pennsylvania show that runoff from simulated rainfall applied at the rate of 1.4 inches for a one-hour period may vary from none to 80 per cent, depending on the intensity of grazing. Compaction of soil was the primary cause of excessive runoff on heavily grazed pastures. The combined effect of compaction and high runoff greatly reduced pasture productivity.[1]

Timber cutting in itself does not directly change the soil, but absence of an overhead canopy causes soil heating and rapid depletion of humus. Lack of tree cover precludes the annual leaf fall that would renew the litter. Skidding of logs makes pathways for erosive water. A cycle is thereby set in motion that impairs watershed protection until a new cover grows and the humus layer is restored.

Use of Water by Forests

Trees require large amounts of water to maintain their life processes. Water is a medium for the transport of minerals needed by the plants. A small amount actually enters into the plant substance in the form of cellulose and lignin through the photosynthetic process. Most of the water absorbed by the trees is transpired into the atmosphere. It has been estimated that a medium-sized elm tree will transpire as much as 15,000 pounds of water on a single hot, dry, clear day. Transpiration is particularly heavy from trees that grow along watercourses, where they have access to an abundant supply. Trees, like men, are prodigal in the use of water when plenty is available and use water sparingly only when it becomes scarce. In the southern Appalachian regions losses of water through evaporation and transpiration from well-drained forested slopes may amount to 15 inches or more per year (Fig. 55).[3]

Types of Damage Reduced by Forests

Snowslides. In steep, mountainous country snowslides are often caused by the heavy fall of new snow on top of an old crust. Where slopes are very steep, the new snow may slide; and in areas that are subject to frequent snowslides, forests are prevented from growing. Such areas often occur at the heads of very steep valleys and along small side valleys. Protection can be achieved to a limited extent by encouraging tree growth and installing other protective measures on the sidewalls. The valley heads can be held only by engineering construction, which may or may not be justified.[5]

Landslides. These are often frightening affairs. They occur when a

Fɪɢ. 55 Contrary to popular belief, removing a forest cover may result in a substantial increase in water yield from a watershed, especially during the summer and fall months. Clear-cut watershed, Coweeta Hydrologic Laboratory, North Carolina. (*U.S. Forest Service photo.*)

great mass of soil lying on a steep slope becomes saturated with moisture and slides over the underlying rock surface. A single severe storm that occurred along the Lehigh River in 1943 gave rise to over 50 small avalanches in a 20-mile reach. These descended onto the railway tracks and, together with bank cutting by the river, caused damage of some $500,000. The valley walls in this case were rocky and covered with tree and shrubby growth, but frequent fires had thinned out the tree cover, thereby reducing its protective influence. It was observed that very few of the avalanches occurred on areas that had a good cover of trees. Avalanches may occur frequently in high mountains where tree cover is lacking or stunted.[5]

Gullies. Where heavy surface runoff rushes across unprotected soil having no permanent stream channels, gullies occur. Those that are actively eroding cannot be stopped by the simple expedient of planting trees. The water which causes the cutting must first be diverted or impeded in its course and the soil stabilized to some extent by other measures. Once this has been achieved, tree growth is possible and permanent stabilization of the gully may be effected.

Silting. The silting and drifting of hardwood leaves into municipal reservoirs can be minimized by planting the borders to conifers. Some cities even control the entire watershed and maintain a forest cover on it. In the western section of the United States water is precious, more precious than land. Water caught in the high mountains makes possible the irrigation of fertile valley lands that yield rich agricultural harvests. The yield of water for irrigation is the all-important factor in the economic development of much of the West. Forests play a dual role in western water supply. They are necessary to protect soils and ensure infiltration of water, which is fed into the streams gradually throughout the summer, supplying irrigation water when it is most needed. At the same time, the forests intercept rain and snow and use water for their own needs, thereby restricting the water supply for the valley. The proper balance between these two actions is the objective of the watershed manager.

Flood Damage. Minimizing flood damage is perhaps the most spectacular of all the roles of forests. More than $100 million worth of damage is caused annually along the Mississippi River system alone. The more the land is cleared of forests and the more clean-tilled cropland that exists on the watershed, the more frequent and serious floods become. The more we build up our cities on the great flood plains of the rivers, the greater the property destruction when floods do occur.

Erosion by Wind. Forests protect soils against erosion by wind. The great program of shelterbelt planting in the prairie-plains section of the United States has helped to reduce wind erosion and has ameliorated living conditions in this vast area.[7]

Forests stabilize sand dunes along the seacoasts and along the shores of our Great Lakes. Dunes, once started moving, can destroy large areas of valuable agricultural, recreational, and even residential land unless they are stabilized. A spectacular demonstration of dune control is under way along the west coast of Taiwan. Here the coastal water is quite shallow. This, together with strong winds, favors dune formation. Foresters, by using lath fencing and dune grass, stabilize the dune surface so that Australian pine (*Casuarina*) may be planted. Within three to four years this forms a closed canopy affording complete protection. Meanwhile, the dune builds up in height so that a new strip of land may be reclaimed from the sea. In a period of 10 years' time 20,000 acres of new land was thus reclaimed from the sea at modest cost. Machine-gun bunkers established by the Japanese to defeat landing parties now look out over $\frac{1}{4}$ mile of forest plantation instead of the open surf.

Watersheds for Irrigation and Municipal Supplies

Parks, municipal watersheds, and strategic flood-source areas are managed with soil protection in mind. The task is by no means simple and varies from one region to another. The job of the protection forest manager in much of the western mountain region is primarily to obtain the maximum water yield from the land. He must, of course, also make certain that this water yield is in usable form and occurs at the proper season of year. This means that he must learn to cultivate those types of forest that intercept and transpire a minimum of water. The forests and other cover must be such that they hold the soil in place and allow the water to flow through the soil rather than over the surface. Special examination of such watersheds must be made frequently to determine the capacity of the vegetation covering the soil to hold it in place and yet not use too much of the precious water. Grazing and timber use should be permitted to the extent possible without impairing watershed protection.

In the eastern states, water supply is rapidly becoming of major concern to industries, municipalities, and agriculture. Many manufacturing processes use enormous quantities of water. To make a ton of steel requires 31,842 gallons of water; a barrel of refined petroleum products, 480.3 gallons of water; and a ton of paper, 10,000 to 90,000 gallons of water. The growing use of air conditioners in theaters, hotels, stores, offices, and dwellings has placed a greatly increased demand on municipal supplies. The abundance and character of the water supply in the eastern states will be a major factor in determining location of industries and municipal growth. Agriculture in the East is learning that irrigation is a profitable practice for many farm crops. Both quantity and quality of yield can be improved. Irrigation is especially helpful in improving the yield of vegetable crops. The practice seems surely to increase wherever it is feasible to bring water to these crops.

Although the eastern states generally enjoy generous rainfall, the day seems rapidly approaching when water supply will be a major consideration for communities too far removed to tap Great Lakes water. This will mean that water yield as well as timber yield will be a responsibility of the eastern forest land manager. For those managing municipal watersheds it will, of course, be the major responsibility.

River-basin Planning

In 1950, the federal government offered a program of aid to states for comprehensive planning for river-basin development. Such planning is to encompass measures for control of floods. But it is to go further to include water for municipal use and irrigation, power developments, erosion control, pollution abatement, improvement of streams for fishing and recreation, and general development of forest and other renewable resources. The Tennessee Valley Authority program is perhaps the nearest we now have to action of the type proposed. All federal agencies active in a river-basin area are being drawn into the planning groups, and representatives of the several state governments have been invited to participate. As of 1961, legislation was still pending in the federal Congress to provide for federal, state, and local participation in comprehensive river-basin development.

Many states are taking steps on their own initiative to improve their water resources. Interstate compacts are also being drawn up to develop resources of river basins. The Delaware River is a case in point where New York, New Jersey, Delaware, and Pennsylvania have, together with the federal government, planned for the future use and development of this basin's water resources. Perhaps of more significance in the long run are the plans being made by individual communities and groups of communities in cooperation with state and federal authorities. Their plans to develop their own water supplies and resources are intimately associated with expanded urban, suburban, industrial, and agricultural development.

Shelterbelt Planting

The story is told that when President Franklin Roosevelt was caught in a severe dust storm in Oklahoma, he penciled a note asking the Chief of the Forest Service why he could not plant a mile-wide belt of trees from Canada to the Gulf to stop such storms. The Chief was at a loss to answer until one of his advisers pointed out that while one belt of trees would not stop dust blowing, hundreds of them properly placed would go far toward doing so. Thus the Prairie Plains Shelterbelt Program came into being.

The soils, natural vegetation, and results of past tree planting were surveyed throughout the region. Hardy trees and shrubs suited to the various conditions to be encountered from north to south were selected and propagated. Planting designs were made, consisting of shrubs, low trees, and high trees. Contracts with farmers to fence, plant, and cultivate the trees were drawn up. Between 1935 and 1949, 26,873 miles of tree belts were planted and additional plantings were made to protect farm homes and gardens.[7] Shelterbelt planting has also been active outside the prairie states. Wisconsin farmers have planted 5,942 miles; California fruit-tree growers, 2,000 miles; and Indiana muckland farmers, 100 miles.

Shelterbelts trap snow, thereby building up soil moisture in a region of deficient precipitation. They prevent soil from blowing on newly seeded fields. They protect crops from hot, dry winds of summer, and they shelter barns, livestock, and the farmers' homes against driving winter storms. Farmers of Nebraska and South Dakota estimate the cash value of shelterbelts in crop protection to be $43 to $60 a year per farm. Cotton yields in Oklahoma and Texas are reported to have increased from 8 to 17 per cent, depending on nearness to the protecting belt. The total protected area extends a distance to leeward of 20 times the height of the trees.

Forests and Climate

Climate has a great influence on forests. Where annual rainfall is less than 15 to 20 inches in temperate regions or 35 to 40 inches in the tropics, forests, as such, disappear, although trees may still persist in sheltered valleys, along stream courses, and as scattered scrubby individuals. Because many regions that supported trees in the past have become arid wastelands following forest removal by man, the question arises: Do forests influence climate? The answer to this is that locally they have marked influence on climate but that this influence diminishes so as to be indistinguishable within a short distance outside the forest boundary.[8]

Tree canopies may absorb and reflect 70 to 90 per cent of sunlight, thereby reducing light to support undergrowth and heat to warm the soil. By intercepting substantial quantities of rain and snow, they allow it to evaporate without reaching the ground. They may reduce wind movement to 20 per cent of that occurring outside the forest. Evaporation is decreased and relative humidity increased. Temperature extremes are moderated. Coniferous trees impede snow melting in spring. All these effects are easily measurable.

Forests also evaporate large quantities of moisture, which may equal throughout the year 50 to 70 per cent of all rain that falls. Where forests are extensive, this amount adds appreciably to atmospheric moisture that must be reprecipitated somewhere. Forests may be as effective as free water surfaces or more so in adding to atmospheric moisture. During summer, because of the cold temperature of the water, Lake Superior dries rather than humidifies air that passes over it. Because air masses travel great distances, it is impossible to assign any quantitative effect of forests on world-wide climate. Their influence is believed to be of minor significance compared with that of oceans.

Induced Rainfall

Man has achieved some success in inducing rainfall by seeding clouds with dry ice or silver iodide smoke.[6] Whether cloud seeding resulted in more rainfall than would have occurred naturally is still a controversial question. It has been used in western states as a means of discharging electrically charged cumulus clouds likely to set forest fires. The future usefulness of cloud seeding as a means of augmenting natural precipitation remains in doubt.

Pollution Abatement

Pollution of streams with industrial and municipal waste has rendered many natural supplies unfit for use or useful only after costly treatment. Pollution arises from local sources; hence, its correction has been considered a local and state responsibility. It is of concern to forestry for two reasons: the pollution caused by forest operations and wood-processing industries and the possible use of forest lands as a clarifying agent. Some damage to water supply may be caused by logging operations and logging roads, but by judicious management this can be minimized. The pulp and paper industry is by far the major forest industry causing water pollution. Changes in pulping practices and proper treatment of white water from the paper machine are necessary to reduce this pollution.

Forests have been used on a limited scale to clarify waste water in New Jersey. Here large quantities of water are used to wash vegetables in preparation for canning. The wash water carries a large amount of vegetable waste in portions unsuited for canning. This water has been sprayed on forest lands having sandy soil at the rate of up to 8 inches of water per day. The tree cover breaks the fall of the heavily charged water. Soil organisms have multiplied greatly, consuming the vegetable matter and keeping the soil channels open for water penetration. The possibility of further use of such a system awaits study of the effectiveness of the soil organisms as a sanitizing agency.

Conversion of Sea Water

Few studies of future water resources are considered complete without reviewing the possibilities of obtaining fresh water directly from the sea. Several processes are under investigation. In arid regions, of which Kuwait is an example, extensive water reclamation is under way. The prospects of cheaper power sources in the future hold forth the promise of much more extensive operations. Costs nevertheless seem likely to be high in terms of water that is brought to moist regions naturally by solar energy. A plant opened at Freeport, Texas, in 1961 was converting sea water at five times the cost of natural water.

LITERATURE CITED

1. Alderfer, R. B., and R. R. Robinson. 1947. "Runoff from Pastures in Relation to Grazing Intensity and Soil Compaction," *Journal of the American Society of Agronomy*, 39:948–958.

2. Bennett, Hugh Hammond. 1939. "Soil Conservation," McGraw-Hill Book Company, Inc., New York. 968 pp.
3. Craddock, George W., and Charles R. Hursh. 1949. "Watersheds and How to Care for Them," *Trees,* The Yearbook of Agriculture, pp. 603–609, U.S. Department of Agriculture, Washington.
4. Frank, Bernard, and Anthony Netboy. 1950. "Water, Land, and People," Alfred A. Knopf, Inc., New York. 331 pp.
5. Kittredge, Joseph. 1948. "Forest Influences," McGraw-Hill Book Company, Inc., New York. 394 pp.
6. Langmuir, Irving. 1950. "Control of Precipitation from Cumulus Clouds by Various Seeding Techniques," *Science,* 112:35–41.
7. Stoeckeler, Joseph H., and Ross A. Williams. 1949. "Windbreaks and Shelterbelts," *Trees,* The Yearbook of Agriculture, pp. 191–199, U.S. Department of Agriculture, Washington.
8. Zon, Raphael. 1941. "Climate and the Nation's Forests," *Climate and Man,* The Yearbook of Agriculture, pp. 477–498, U.S. Department of Agriculture, Washington.

CHAPTER 15. *The Business of Forestry*

A FOREST MANAGER is employed to operate a property in accordance with the wishes of the owner. If the owner is the public, these wishes may encompass many things: watershed protection, public hunting grounds, grazing, recreation, and timber production. If the owner operates a wood-using plant, he will need to meet all or a part of his timber requirements. Private individuals or corporations dependent on the forest as a primary source of income will want the land managed so as to produce a profit, and they will want this profit to be produced as regularly as possible. Return on investment is the major concern of such owners, but profit may be a minor concern to owners primarily interested in recreation or hunting or to wood-using industries whose main source of income is from processing rather than growing timber.

The manager of a retail store can obtain from departments of commerce and other sources information on capital, floor space, inventory, and turnover for a given business volume. How the budget should be distributed among such costs as rents, advertising, labor, store supplies, and miscellaneous expenses may also be learned. The Agricultural Extension Services can advise a prospective dairy farmer on size of herd, land area and quality, and the crops he should grow. He is furnished feeding schedules for dry stock and milkers. Equipment needs and over-all capital expenditures can be estimated. Suggested work schedules to budget his time most effectively and appropriate accounting records to determine the financial success of his farming venture are also offered. These serve to minimize business risks.

A man desiring to enter the business of timber growing finds few such comprehensive services to aid him. Public foresters will advise timber owners on tree planting, on silviculture, and even on how to sell timber, but they have little tested business advice to offer. The owner must rely mostly upon his own judgment and upon the opportunities that come his way. A recent study by Webster [13] points out the tremendous variation in response that may be expected from investment in various forestry measures. Thinning young hardwood pole stands turned out to yield highest returns in terms of investment costs. To achieve the same returns from planting scrub oak lands would require an expenditure 75 times as large. This very fact, that returns in relation to cost vary so greatly and that few reliable analyses of such variability in response have been made, points up the high risk involved in forestry investment. It also suggests that potentially high returns may be expected by those who can judge astutely the basic business factors involved and are willing to venture into a new field of investment.

Basic Factors in Timber Growing

A producing timber property has certain basic features analogous to those to be found in a manufacturing enterprise. Climate, topography, and soil are the timber grower's basic physical factors governing the supply and availability of his raw materials. As such, they are analogous to the location and building that houses an industrial plant. The soil supplies two raw materials: water and mineral elements essential for tree growth. These may be available in ample amounts or in limited amounts that restrict rapidity of growth. The third raw material, carbon dioxide of the air, is so widely distributed that it never need give concern to a forest manager. Sunlight supplies the energy for manufacturing woody substance from minerals, water, and carbon dioxide. Temperature and the efficiency of chloroplasts determine how fast these raw materials can be converted into wood products by the trees. The forest manager, once his location has been set, has no feasible way to modify climate, topography, or the physical character of the soil. All he can do is to adjust his operations so as to take the best possible advantage of these basic factors.

The Producing Machinery. The producing machinery of a forest is the growing stock, that is, the trees of all sizes and ages that occupy the soil. If this growing stock is well distributed over the land, if it is likewise well distributed as to age, and if it is made up of valuable species and well-formed units, it will produce regular crops of high-value products. If the growing stock is sparse or scattered, if it is composed of a high percentage of low-value species or poor-quality units, it will produce a low volume and low-value products. Such a forest is analogous to a factory using improperly arranged, worn out, and obsolete machinery. A fire may just as effectively destroy the producing machinery of the forest as might a fire in an industrial plant.

One striking difference exists between the forest and the industrial plant. The trees that grow the wood are both the producing machines and the end product. This fact has confused many people unfamiliar with forest management. An industrial owner would scarcely expect his factory to be productive if he sold off his machinery, allowed fire to gut his factory, and invested no new capital to replace it. But that is exactly what some people seem to expect of forests. They expect land from which the producing machines—the growing trees—have been stripped off and on which the young trees have been killed by fire to produce valuable timber crops with little or no investment of capital.

Forest Valuation. A forest property may be evaluated as an industrial plant on two bases: its liquidation value and its value as a productive plant. Its liquidation value is the value of the standing trees for immediate harvest, or harvest as early as feasible, plus the value of the land and improvements. Young unmerchantable timber is considered as valueless in such an appraisal. Because the economics of growing timber have been little appreciated by most buyers and owners, this is the basis on which most forest properties have been bought and sold. The value of a forest as a productive property is based on how much it can yield continuously above expenses. Growth rate is here the all-important factor. This growth, when converted to dollar value and after deducting expenses, is then capitalized at an appropriate rate of interest to reflect business risks. A property yielding a net revenue of $10,000 annually would have a value of $200,000, assuming a 5 per cent return for capital and risk. The liquidating value of such a property might be considerably less or more than this amount.[4,5]

Bare forest land that must be planted and tended for 40 years or more before products can be harvested has very low value. In fact, it may have only a negative value for the private investor because the costs and risks involved may exceed prospective return. Such lands, if extensive, can be restored to forest only by the slow process of nature or at public expense. In the latter case, subsidiary values inherent in productive forest land would be expected to offset the short-time deficit in return.

Selecting Land for a Forestry Investment. The individual or corporation seeking to obtain a profit from managing forest land must first give the utmost care to selecting an area of land. Basic factors to consider are available markets now and in the future; climate; topography; soil productivity; present stocking of timber trees, the species, size, quality of stems, and distribution of age-classes; the local taxes; the accessibility to public roads and the ease of road construction; the prevalence of destructive insects and diseases and the measures available for their control; the prospects of supplemental income from leasing hunting rights, from mineral or gravel deposits, or from leases for recreational purposes; the attitude of local people toward forestry; and the willingness of timber operators to use cutting practices that will lead to building up the value of the growing stock rather than depleting it. As timber growing of necessity is a long-term investment from which, despite the relatively heavy risks involved, only modest returns are to be anticipated, special care must be taken to ensure that land titles are clear of claims that might lead to loss of the land and all investments made on it. The judgment of an experienced forester is required to evaluate such factors.

Tending the Forest-producing Machine. The job of operating the forest factory so as to produce efficiently high volume and quality of timber products is the job of the silviculturist. It is through silviculture that we select those producing machines that are most efficient and eliminate those that produce a poor-quality product. Silviculture means making sure that the land owned is well stocked with growing trees. It involves eliminating the ineffective timber producers, by thinning, improvement cuttings, release cuttings, and other operations, so as to concentrate the growth on those trees that will develop the highest quality of timber.

Organization of the Timber Factory. An industrial plant may have the best of raw materials and the best of modern machinery and may be suited to turning out the finest products in the field; yet unless this factory and its working force are organized so that the various operations of production proceed in an orderly and efficient manner, the enterprise will be doomed to financial failure. The production manager's job in an industrial plant is to organize machinery, labor, and flow of materials so that high-quality products can be turned out with the minimum total cost in manpower, machine power, and factory rent.

The forest manager's job is to organize the forest for efficient use of soil, growing stock, labor, and equipment. He decides what roads, trails, skidways, and other improvements are needed. He locates his protection equipment so that the producing plant can be readily protected against fires and trespass. He decides on an orderly arrangement of forest compartments so that the road and skidway systems will be used to best advantage, thereby minimizing his costs of operation (Fig. 56). He attempts to adjust his growing stock so as to provide a regular yield of products, year by year.[10] He will time his timber-cutting operations so as to take advantage of good markets and will curtail selling when markets are low. He knows that he can store his inventory on the stump and have it progressively increase in value through growth, and he also knows that there is a limitation as to how long he can allow his inventory to accumulate without having it congest his factory so that total production slows down. Generally, he will seek to manage his land intensively for high-value products, thereby reducing the relative importance of those fixed costs, such as roads, boundary maintenance, prevention of trespass and land taxes, that increase directly with size of ownership. He will, however, give concern to investing first in those forestry measures that bring the highest return on costs. He is almost certain to find that some of his lands—steep, rocky slopes and thin or swampy soils—cannot return a yield on a forestry investment. He will either eliminate such lands from

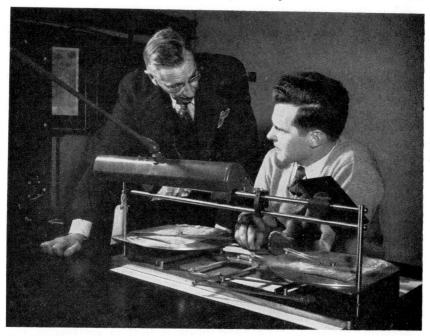

Fig. 56 Foresters are able to reduce the time required in field work by preparing preliminary maps of forest types and condition classes from aerial photos. A stereoplotter is being used in the photo. (*Photo by C. Wesley Brewster, Syracuse, New York.*)

his holdings or recognize that they must be carried but in doing so spend as little as possible on them.

The forest manager also decides on what equipment he requires to manage his forest most effectively. This includes personal transportation, protection equipment, logging equipment, road-building and maintenance equipment, and record-keeping equipment. He should give special consideration to what equipment he should own and what he should lease or contract for. As he will want his woods work done as efficiently as possible, he will be alert to new equipment developments and may well find it expedient to pioneer in new equipment use. He will find only limited published information or local advice to guide his decisions.

Forest Labor. The industrial manager employs labor to tend his machines that perform various manufacturing operations. The forest manager employs forest labor to protect his forest and to keep it in good growing condition. He also requires labor to prepare his products for shipment, that is, to fell, limb, buck, skid, and haul his logs and other forest products. As his producing plant may cover several thousand acres, he, like many industrial managers, may need to consider housing his workers. He must decide how many workers he can employ permanently and the extent to which he can depend on temporary labor to speed up his operations during times of good markets. This may mean providing housing for permanent workers and camps for temporary workers. He must decide also on what jobs he will perform with his permanent labor force and what jobs will be contracted to timber operators.

Markets. One of the major tasks of the forest manager is to find good markets for all the different types of products his factory produces. The forest factory produces a large amount of medium- and low-grade products and a relatively small amount of high-grade products. Some forests, in fact, produce almost no high-grade timber, and even the best of forests, having all age classes represented, will produce a large volume of small-sized timber that is difficult to market. This fact immediately confronts the forest manager with the necessity of deciding how far he should enter into the timber-processing field in order to provide a market for his products. He may decide to operate a small portable sawmill to convert to rough lumber the low-quality logs that will not pay transportation costs to a permanent mill.[2]

It is in the marketing field that forest managers encounter their most serious difficulties. It is here that the greatest financial headaches arise. Nationally, the markets for forest products tend to get progressively better decade by decade, but this may not be true locally. Local markets depend on the presence and economic prosperity of local wood-using industries. Timber is so costly to transport that a good market for fuel wood in New York City means nothing to the Adirondack timberland owner.

The forest manager must always balance carefully the cost of owning wood-processing equipment against that of hiring the use of such equipment. The same applies to logging trucks and tractors. If the forest manager has full-time use for such equipment, he can well afford to own it. If he has only part-time use for it, he might better rent or contract for its use.

Decisions on direct operation as opposed to contract operations will be determined in large degree on the size of operation and the wisdom of incurring costs for machinery, a permanent labor force, and the clerical and supervisory aid needed to manage efficiently a dispersed operation. Generally, the further the landowner is able to go in timber processing, the better market he is able to provide for his products. But his marketing task becomes increasingly more complex and the capital tied up in inventory burgeons as the variety of products to be sold multiplies.

Record Keeping. The forest manager obviously cannot know whether his operations are financially successful unless he keeps accurate records, including an inventory of his land, growing stock, improvements, and equipment. He must know whether his land is increasing or decreasing in value and whether his timber inventory is getting smaller or larger in volume, lower or higher in quality. He must keep separately his costs for taxes, protection, general management, logging, sale of products, and timber processing. Costs of unit operations reveal which of his various operations are making money and which ones are losing money and form the basis for intelligent action to produce profits.

Credit for Forestry Business

As forestry is necessarily a long-term operation, credit becomes both a pressing need and a risky investment. It must, therefore, be sought and extended only with great circumspection. Credit can safely be extended only with assurance by both borrower and lender that it will be productively used—that the forest operation to be undertaken will yield ample returns to repay the loan within the time period of the loan. The forest manager will be wise to invest first in those forest stands and forestry operations that promise to yield the highest return on his investment. If the yield to be expected is but little more than sufficient to cover his interest costs, he should be cautious about making the expenditure. Once his business is well established he may use credit extensively, provided its use leads to a marginal interest return above the rate he must pay.

The long-term growth rates of forest stands are not high—from 3 to 5 per cent for northern hardwoods and up to 10 per cent for southern pines. At certain stages in the life of a tree or stand, however, the value increase is very rapid. For example, a 60-year-old hard maple tree growing in diameter at a constant rate might be 12 inches in diameter. It would contain about 50 board feet and would be worth but 50 cents if, indeed, merchantable at all. At 90 years, it would grow to 18 inches in diameter, contain 200 board feet, and be worth about $6. This is a twelvefold increase in value in 30 years. Likewise, a 60-year-old northern hardwood stand might bring per acre but $10 if sold for pulpwood; but if held 30 years more, it could have 5,500 board feet worth $110. It is such knowledge of growth potential from which the forest investor will seek to benefit and that justifies his use of credit.

Forest financing also involves forest insurance and insurance required of those who employ labor. Adequate insurance of forest properties against fire is difficult to obtain at reasonable rates. Large forest property owners require no insurance against the small fire but do require insurance against large fires that might destroy the major portion of their forest.

Insurance against severe damage by windstorm, ice, snow, insects, tree diseases, and animals is even less obtainable. All these are potential sources of crippling losses, especially to young growth. The owner's best insurance is intensive management that will provide for prompt salvage of whatever losses occur. A hurricane, such as swept over New England in 1938, or a huge fire, such as burned over 220,000 acres in Maine in 1947, can destroy a forest business for the lifetime of any individual owner.

The timberland owner, particularly if he engages in logging or any other timber operations, must carry workmen's compensation insurance and social security for his workmen. He must, in fact, be well informed on all requirements affecting his financial and business operations. Basic knowledge of business law and contracts is essential.

Business Acumen

The overall success of the forest manager will depend, in the last analysis, upon his business acumen. This means the skill with which he is able to manipulate his forest, his growing stock, his forest labor, his marketing and sales, and his use of credit and insurance so as to maximize financial returns from operating the property. Business acumen in forestry is made up of sound basic knowledge of silviculture, logging, personnel management, mechanical equipment, accounting, budgeting, marketing, and business law. Energy and drive must also be put into managing operations and seeking profitable markets for products. The forest manager must keep an adequate reserve of working capital so that his operations may be flexible. Forced liquidation of valuable growing stock when markets are badly depressed can be disastrous. A man may be skilled in most phases of forest management, but if he neglects any one essential element, the entire operation may fail. The wise manager gives attention to all phases of his operation.

The greatest financial hazards to the business of timber growing are market fluctuations caused by business and building cycles (Figs. 36 and 37). Timber markets may virtually vanish for two or more years at a time. This may cause no hardship to the casual forest owner who depends on other income for his livelihood; but for an owner who receives all his income from timber, and who has annual fixed charges for labor, interest, and taxes, a prolonged business depression can be ruinous.

Business cycles cannot be predicted nor their turning point identified, except in retrospect. It seems unlikely that economists in government and in business will have sufficient understanding of the forces that influence business cycles to control them completely in the near future.

How Business Cycles Affect Building Cycles. It is during periods of expanding business activity that manufacturers expand their plants and that workmen have sufficient money to build or purchase homes of their own. Consequently, building activities expand very rapidly during the ascending phase of the business cycle. Building cycles show higher peaks and lower troughs than industrial production. The index of building activity in 1918 at the close of the war was approximately 25; by the year 1925 it had risen more than tenfold to 260. During the same period business activity as measured by industrial production increased only from 60 to 90. By 1932 building had dropped from index 260 back to 20, and industrial production, which reached its peak in 1929, dropped from 115 down to about 55.[14]

Lumber production in 1918 was 29.4 billion board feet. It rose to 34.8 in 1919, fell to 29.9 in 1920, reached a high of 38.3 in 1925, and dropped to 10.2 in 1932. Between 1945 and 1954 lumber production fluctuated between 32 and 38 billion board feet.[8] Lumber production appears to fluctuate less violently than the building cycle but more violently than the business cycle.

When lumber production fluctuates violently, it obviously influences logging operations, prices of stumpage, and, consequently, the entire forest economy of the country, both public and private. A forest manager should be prepared to make relatively heavy timber harvests during periods of high lumber demand and to restrain operations during periods of low demand. During such periods he might appropriately engage in planting and other activities that build up the value of the forest but do not put products on the market. To do this requires both sound business judgment and ample working capital.

Long-term Trends in Prices. Long-term trends in American business enterprise have been marked by an increase in abundance and quality of output and a decrease in labor requirement. This has frequently meant a decline in price or at least a decline in man-hours of labor required to purchase the products. This, in turn, has been possible by increasing greatly the productivity of labor through modern production techniques, standardized design, power machinery, and applied research. Living standards have risen thereby. This trend has characterized the manufacture of such products as chemicals, steel, motorcars, household appliances, and power equipment.

This has been somewhat less true of the lumber industry (Figs. 35 and 57). During the period 1798 to 1836 wholesale prices of lumber increased but 33 per cent.[8] From 1836 to 1862 the increase was an additional 33 per cent, but most of it occurred in one year, 1837. From 1862 to 1866, during the Civil War, lumber prices almost doubled, but they declined thereafter so that by 1898 they stood at but 21 per cent above the 1862 level. From 1900 to 1956 lumber prices increased 9.7-fold, all commodities but 3.1-fold. As a result the competitive position of lumber in the building and other industries has become weaker (Fig. 35). One of the major causes of increase in lumber price has been the increase in the cost of labor in logging and sawmill operations without a corresponding increase in output per workman. Where trees are scattered and small in size and the lumber sawed is knotty, it has been impossible to maintain quality of product at the same price as in former years. When good trees are cut and poor ones left, quality declines. As the pressure

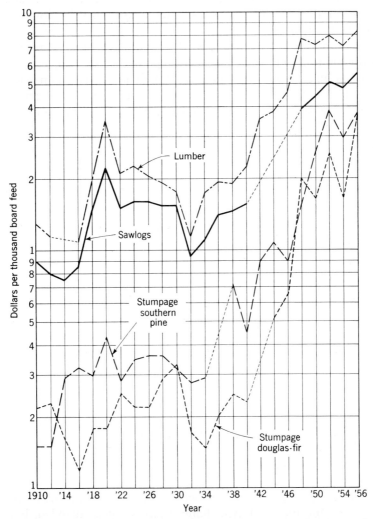

FIG. 57 Trends in prices (in dollars per thousand board feet) of Douglas-fir stumpage, sawlogs, and lumber and of Southern pine stumpage from 1910 to 1956. (*U.S. Department of Agriculture, Forest Service.* 1958. *"Historical Forestry Statistics of the United States," Statistical Bulletin 228. Compiled by Dwight Hair. Washington. 36 pp.*)

for cutting extends down to smaller-sized trees, output per worker continues to decline and cost of product to increase. To arrest this trend will require fairly intensive forest management, and certainly much business and financial skill (Fig. 57).

It will be seen from Fig. 57 that during the period 1910 to 1956 prices of Douglas-fir lumber increased 6.3-fold; of sawlogs, 6.1-fold; and of stumpage, 17.0-fold. This might seem to suggest that the forest landowner has profited greatly at the expense of the lumber buyer. Actually this has not been the case. Stumpage prices have not yet in the United States borne any relation to the cost of growing the timber. The situation is gradually being corrected, however, as stumpage price trends since 1940 indicate (Fig. 57). The price of stumpage in 1956 represented 46 per cent of the wholesale price of lumber. In European countries in which timber-growing costs must be covered, stumpage cost represents 50 to 60 per cent of the wholesale lumber price.

Sources of Information on Forestry Business

The foregoing may have given the impression that anyone who launches a forestry business does so completely in the dark. This is far from the case. Certain phases of forestry are well advanced, and a businessman can accept knowledge in these fields with little reservation. Foresters can advise timberland buyers on quality of soil, value of species, and the rate at which they may be expected to produce timber. Books on forest finance present methods that are used in financing forest operations, along with a discussion of the relative merits of each. The prospective timberland buyer can determine how forests are evaluated and thus be in a position to judge for himself the desirability of a particular forest property for investment purposes. Estimating timber is possible with a high degree of precision. Hence, no one need buy a forest property without knowing what it contains and what growth rate he may expect.

Books on logging give information on how the timber crop can most easily be harvested. Data on distribution of costs among stumpage, logging, and lumber manufacture are available for average operations.[1–4, 6, 7, 10–12] Information is also obtainable on how to organize a forest property for efficient management.[9]

It is, after all, in the planning of the timber operations that much of the success or failure of property operation is determined. The plans for operating a forest property may consist of a master plan together with special plans for managing recreation, timber resource, wildlife, grazing, fire control, the road system, tree planting, and other specific operations. In elaborate cases the timber-management working plan will include a discussion of the soils, timber types, growth rates, expected yield, cutting cycles, rotations, markets for timber products, availability of labor, and requirements of local industries. Such elaborate plans are ordinarily prepared only for public forests, but the items contained therein need to be given some consideration by private forest land managers as well. Even more detailed consideration must be given to business and financial planning so that operations are conducted with a minimum use of capital and labor and a maximum long-term financial return.

A great deal of information does exist on various phases of the business of forestry. What is mainly lacking is the integration of all this information into management manuals that can be effectively used by the forest owner. The difficulty is that few properties have been managed on a long-term basis. Hence little information on the financial results of management is available, particularly on the management of properties on which a variety of products are harvested. Operations where all types of products grown by the forest are processed in the mills of the company are still few, and detailed financial information on these is not available. It is this overall task of bringing together all the information from a wide variety of sources that must be successfully performed by the forest manager who wishes to make a financial profit from timber growing.

Unfavorable and Favorable Factors

Unfavorable factors in the business of forestry include the following:

1. The scarcity of concrete examples of successful long-time forestry business.

2. Hazards caused by fire, insects, disease, windstorm, animals, snow-break, and other factors and the limited availability of insurance against the risk of damage from such factors.

3. A high degree of fluctuation in the national and local markets for forest products in accordance with business and building cycles and shifting consumer preferences.

4. The relatively low rate of timber growth, 3 to 5 per cent annually in the North.

5. The lack of appreciation by the public generally of the services the private forest landowner furnishes free to the public, that is, soil protection, watershed protection, some protection against floods, useful wildlife, and public recreation. The public is also careless in respecting the rights of the owner.

6. The present depleted condition of much of the cutover forest lands and the long period that will be required to build these forests up to a high producing level.

7. Limited government support for owners attempting to improve the productivity of their forest land.

8. Local taxes unrelated to timber yields.

9. The general lack of integrated markets to absorb all the products the forest property produces.

10. The lack of a tradition of long-term forest management and a labor force that appreciates it.

Favorable factors are:

1. An abundance of forest land and good forest-producing soils throughout much of the United States.

2. A wealth of forest species that produce woods of high technical quality.

3. The general abundance of natural regeneration of valuable trees.

4. Depletion of accessible standing timber with corresponding increase in stumpage values.

5. A rapid increase in forest research that is making possible new uses for wood and more valuable products, justifying a high stumpage price.

6. A high level of knowledge of soils, species, silviculture, and general management practices.

7. A satisfactory level of fire control, largely publicly supported, covering most forest lands in the country.

8. A growing interest in forests on the part of the public, the timber processors, and forest landowners.

9. Favorable consideration by the federal income tax law. Growth on forest land is taxed as long-term capital gain; hence the maximum tax is 25 per cent.

10. Widespread public aids in the form of research, statistical information, advice, and service.

Miscellaneous Revenue

The foregoing discussion has omitted consideration of income that may be derived from sale of hunting and trapping rights, water, recreation privileges, grazing rights, use for berry picking, and other subsidiary uses. Where income from such sources can be realized, it may stabilize and augment earnings from timber use, but such resources frequently yield insignificant income. Hunting and even grazing rights which have been allowed the general public without charge may not always be sold for restricted use without creating local resentment. Goodwill of local residents can mean much in fair taxation, care with fire, and reduction of trespass. The owner looking to timber for his main income will be slow to take steps that might alienate the goodwill of his neighbors.

All forest land supports game. All serves as a protective cover for watersheds. All protects the soil. Almost all serves to some extent as a source of aesthetic pleasure and perhaps for active recreation for people other than the owners. The management of every property directly and indirectly affects the livelihood of the people who harvest the timber and process it. The forest land manager, therefore, is much more than a custodian of timberland and purveyor of stumpage. He is, so to speak, the ruler of a small empire. It therefore behooves him to acquire the dignity, restraint, and wisdom of a ruler because the decisions he makes are bound to affect others besides himself. If his decisions are wise, he can gain the admiration and support of his neighbors, his workmen, and his customers. Unless, therefore, a man is willing to assume responsibility for his acts and unless he has or can develop skill in dealing fairly with his fellow men whose interests his actions are certain to affect, he cannot be in the long run a successful forest manager.

The business of forestry is still a pioneering and exciting venture. It calls for a wide variety of skills coupled with energy and determination. Opportunities for amassing wealth are limited, but once the many difficulties are understood and overcome, the business of forestry may prove to be one of the most desirable and stable in our country. Forestry in many European countries is considered both sound and stable. The greatest speculative hazards in forestry are those due to fluctuating timber values caused by uncertain markets, business cycles, and the natural hazards of fire, windstorms, ice damage, insect outbreaks, and disease. Ultimately, insurance may be needed against these major hazards. It is appropriate to consider whether government, which has a major responsibility for protecting forests against fire, insects, and diseases, should not help underwrite such insurance. Government has already considered the desirability of extending long-term credit to timberland owners to enable them to avoid liquidation of their growing stock because of financial stringency.

The general outlook ahead for the business of forestry is bright. Opportunities are perhaps greater now, when hazards are high, than they will be after hazards to private forest management have been minimized. Forestry, therefore, presents an opportunity and a challenge to those who have the capital, interest, and daring to make it a business.

LITERATURE CITED

1. Brown, Nelson C. 1949. "Logging: The Principles and Methods of Harvesting Timber in the United States and Canada," John Wiley & Sons, Inc., New York. 418 pp.
2. Brown, Nelson C. 1947. "Lumber: Manufacture, Conditioning, Grading, Distribution, and Use," John Wiley & Sons, Inc., New York. 344 pp.
3. Brown, Nelson C., and James Samuel Bethel. 1958. "Lumber," 2d ed., John Wiley & Sons, Inc., New York. 379 pp.

4. Buttrick, P. L. 1943. "Forest Economics and Finance," John Wiley & Sons, Inc., New York. 484 pp.

5. Chapman, Herman H., and Walter H. Meyer. 1947. "Forest Valuation," McGraw-Hill Book Company, Inc., New York. 490 pp.

6. Davis, Kenneth P. 1954. "American Forest Management," McGraw-Hill Book Company, Inc., New York. 482 pp.

7. Duerr, William A. 1960. "Fundamentals of Forestry Economics," McGraw-Hill Book Company, Inc., New York. 579 pp.

8. Hair, Dwight. 1958. "Historical Forestry Statistics of the United States," U.S. Department of Agriculture, Forest Service, Statistical Bulletin 228, Washington. 36 pp.

9. Matthews, Donald M. 1935. "Management of American Forests," McGraw-Hill Book Company, Inc., New York. 495 pp.

10. Matthews, Donald M. 1942. "Cost Control in the Logging Industry," McGraw-Hill Book Company, Inc., New York. 374 pp.

11. Simmons, Fred C. 1951. "Northeastern Loggers' Handbook," U.S. Department of Agriculture, Agriculture Handbook 6, Washington. 160 pp.

12. Wackerman, A. E. 1949. "Harvesting Timber Crops," McGraw-Hill Book Company, Inc., New York. 437 pp.

13. Webster, Henry. 1960. "Timber Management Opportunities in Pennsylvania," U.S. Department of Agriculture, Forest Service, Northeastern Forest Experiment Station, Station Paper No. 137, Upper Darby, Pa. 37 pp.

14. Zivnuska, John A. 1949. "Commercial Forestry in an Unstable Economy," *Journal of Forestry*, 47:4–13.

CHAPTER 16. *Social Benefits of Forestry*

MAN HAS ADOPTED a number of methods for gaining a livelihood from the forest. The simpler forms, hunting and trapping, if not overdone have little effect on the forest itself. This is followed by clearing and planting food crops. In its simplest form this is done by girdling trees, broadcast burning, planting on the newly cleared surface, and harvesting one, two, or at most five or six crops, by which time the minerals available in the ash leach out and the soil no longer will support a crude agriculture. A move is then made to a new area and the process is repeated. This practice, known as shifting agriculture, has occurred in many lands and is still common in the tropics today. A cycle of some 10 to 12 years from forest to cropland and back to forest has not been uncommon. Alternating between food crops and fuel-wood crops is, in fact, a crude way of renewing a depleted soil, but it never results in lifting the level of the people practicing such primitive agriculture to a standard of living appropriate to civilized man. At best, it provides only subsistence. Where the land is not too steep, where the soils are of reasonably good quality and not susceptible to erosion, and where trees of valuable species readily seed up the land as abandoned, little permanent damage is caused. The more usual case, however, is clearing off steep slopes, severe soil erosion, failure of valuable species to reseed the area, and invasion by coarse grasses or shrubs that hold the land for decades against species valuable either for forage or for timber.

Shifting agriculture has its parallel in the shifting or migratory nature of the lumber industry. Starting in Maine, it moved south to New England, New York, Pennsylvania, the Lake States, and the South, and to the Pacific Coast. These moves often meant complete abandonment of such improvements as forest roads or railroads, sawmills, and often of sawmill towns and the farms that grew up near the sawmill to supply food for workers and teams. Few industries in the Northeast have undergone any more serious censure than the lumber industry, primarily because of the cut-out and get-out practices of the past.

Such practices contrast sharply with the intensive sustained-yield forestry that many progressive lumber and pulp and paper companies were practicing in 1962. But examples of poor forest-management practices with their accompanying impoverishment of forest and people still persisted in many forested regions. White pine lands in New York and New England were cut heavily for lumber and boxboards during the Second World War. Only trees too small to place on a saw carriage were left after logging. Later these, too, were removed for pulpwood, letting the land grow to brush and low-value hardwoods. Some land was abandoned for taxes. The logger was obliged to shift his operation from sawtimber to pulpwood. As many operators were bidding for the market, prices paid for wood dropped to barely enough to cover wages. Individual loggers, themselves landowners, cut their own land often two or three times in an interval of less than 10 years, harvesting each time progressively smaller trees and lower volumes per acre. Thereby the base of thrifty young timber that in time could have supported wood industries has been removed for decades from the land. The result has been an impoverished forest and an impoverishment of the populace dependent on the forest.

It is the mission of the forestry profession to prevent human impoverishment through misuse of forest land. In 1927, a property of 2,200 acres was acquired by a college as a demonstration forest. The property at the time of purchase included 11 farms, of which only three were occupied. The owners of these were dependent on outside work for income. Most of the timber had been cut off. The college employed a forester to plant the open lands, thin the young stands, and convert the cut trees into lumber, which was sold locally. Cutting was concentrated on the poorer-quality trees and the white pines infected with blister rust fungus, and it was kept in line with growth of the old trees. After 20 years of forest management the property was providing full-time work for 11 men, a level it has since maintained for a decade. The timber volume, instead of decreasing, was increasing. Land that had been a social liability became a social asset through application of the forester's skill.[5]

The Nature of Social Benefits

Social benefits of forestry include protection of soil and water, amelioration of floods, the fostering of useful wildlife, public recreation, the aesthetic value of forests as opposed to barren wasteland, favorable modification of local climate, supply of raw materials for industry, maintenance of reserve timber for national emergencies, and a source of useful work for human employment. It is the sum of these social benefits that justifies public action to support forestry programs. All except the last two have been dealt with in earlier chapters (Fig. 58).

Fɪɢ. 58 An integrated hardwood sawmill, Connor Lumber and Land Company, Laona, Wisconsin. The Company operates a sawmill, dry kilns, flooring mill, dimension mill, furniture factory, and wood-flour plant. Operations are supported by 45,000 acres of industrial forest land. (*AFPI photo.*)

Use of Forests and Forest Products in National Defense. The people of the United States have always used natural resources with great prodigality when at war, and their use of wood has been no exception. Yet when it is recalled how much labor must go into the harvesting, processing, and use of wood for any purpose, we can realize how vital wood is. Lumber for cantonments and for packaging material to ship abroad made heavy inroads on reserve stocks in 1942. Requirements of the British and other Allies used much high-grade spruce, Douglas-fir, and veneer-grade birch. Spruce lumber and birch, basswood, and yellow-poplar veneer were used in the construction of aircraft, particularly training planes. Oak and ash went into truck bodies. Two-inch lumber was used in very large quantities in the construction of bases, warehouses, and docks. Lumber to repair bomb damage was also an urgent need. Piling for wharves was in heavy demand. The lumber required to package war material for overseas shipment in 1944 exceeded 16 billion board feet, half the total lumber produced that year.

In the fighting areas lumber was needed in generous amounts for bridges, road repair, supply dumps, hospitals, and temporary shelters. The abundance of wood available to build up advance bases greatly facilitated the rapid movement of American troops once the offensives got under way.

Paper was scarce during the war, and extra effort had to be exercised to keep the pulpwood supply flowing to the mills so that enough paper and paperboard could be manufactured to supply the industries producing munitions and essential civilian supplies.

New wood products—Compreg, Impreg, Stapack, and molded plywood—found special uses during the war period. Laminated keels and skegs were developed for use in patrol torpedo boats, mine layers, and other wooden craft used during the war.

New water-resistant fiberboards were designed especially for packaging food and other materials.

Such expanded uses are possible in wartime only if our nation has at all times an adequate reserve of standing timber, including ample high-quality trees of useful species. The timber should be readily accessible to transportation and processing plants to avoid undue use of scarce manpower in times of national emergency, for lumber and most other wood products are too bulky to stockpile for war use. The most efficient method is to maintain adequate reserves of high-quality standing timber in managed forest properties.

The initial stage of a war using nuclear weapons would be one of vast destruction. Thereafter the nations that survived would be obliged to occupy the enemy land and to reconstruct devasted areas wherever they occurred. This would place ever greater demands on timber resources than occurred during the first two world wars.

Employment for People. During the great depression of the 1930s any resource that could provide useful work for people was looked upon with high favor. Public leaders found in our undeveloped forests an almost inexhaustible supply of useful work that would add to the future value of the resource. Building needed roads and telephone lines, planting trees, and improving cutover lands figuratively soaked up man-days of labor. Needed work on public forests alone had by no means been exhausted when the programs terminated after a total of nine years of operation.

Of far greater importance than emergency programs has been the year in, year out employment in protecting forests and in harvesting and processing products (Figs. 58 and 59).

Forestry as a Form of Land Use

The social values that stem from forestry are not easy to grasp in abstract terms. Understanding of the national and world-wide significance of applied forestry can be furthered by examining the situation in a specific county and region. The older sections of our country that have gone through a high stage of industrial development well illustrate the trends. It is here that wealth is abundant, markets for labor and products highly developed, and evolution in land use well advanced. It is in some of these states also that progressive steps have been taken to change the use of land to fit modern economic conditions. Such a case is Broome County, New York.

Forests of Broome County, New York. Broome County, New York, is one of the more prosperous counties of the Empire State. The valley in which the Triple Cities—Endicott, Johnson City, and Binghamton—are located, has been called the Valley of Opportunity. It has been the valley of opportunity for many people; for in these three cities are lo-

Fig. 59 Ponderosa pine logs moving up the jack ladder to the sawmill. Graegle Lumber Company, Graegle, California. (*U.S. Forest Service photo.*)

cated some of the most prosperous and rapidly growing industries of the United States.

Outside the cities, opportunities are far more circumscribed. Originally, most of the county was farmed. The rural picture is similar to that in many rural counties of New England, the Middle Atlantic states, and the Lake States.

During the past 23 years there has been a substantial increase in forest land and a decline in agricultural land in Broome County.

The changes in land classes that occurred over a 12-year period are shown in the following table.[7]

Class and description	Area, acres	
	1938	1950
Unsuited to agriculture, mostly idle or forested.............	120,636	146,165
Submarginal for permanent agriculture.....................	104,237	136,647
Will support commercial agriculture in normal times.........	181,674	105,622
Will provide a satisfactory living if well managed...........	17,723	13,908
Will provide a good living if well managed.................		976
Residential..	30,130	39,526
Publicly owned...		11,556
Total..	454,400	454,400

The two surveys reveal a limited amount of good land and a substantial decrease during the 12-year period in land suited to farming. The questions naturally arise: Why was this land cleared for agriculture in the first place, and what has been happening over the years to drive the farmers off the land?

The early settlers who came to New York found the uplands much the easiest to clear for cultivation; the land was high, away from the "miasma" and mosquitoes that infested the lowlands, and natural drainage existed. Consequently, the hill farms were the best farms in the early days. But erosion washed away much of the fertile topsoil and, gradually, the initial fertility disappeared. The advent of machine tillage and other advances in scientific farming added to production of hill lands, but it added the same percentage increase to fertile, easily tilled valley farms. The income spread between the good and the poor farms expanded enormously, and hill farmers were forced out of competition. What once seemed a logical land-use pattern had been completely reversed.

A study of the land that remained in forest revealed that the area supporting sawtimber of medium and high volume was only 13,000 acres.

Light sawtimber and high-volume pole timber occupied 60,000 acres; low-value pole stands, seedlings, and saplings occupied 82,000 acres; forest plantations occupied only 3,900 acres.[3]

Timber volume was concentrated in trees less than 14 inches in diameter. The low-value species, beech, elm, and red maple, exceeded in volume, by far, the high-value species of hard maple, white ash, basswood, and white pine. The unsatisfactory stocking and species distribution and the low volume in large tree sizes were the direct result of cutting the most valuable trees in the past and allowing the less desirable to remain standing.

Optimism might be expressed over the fact that the annual growth of sawtimber, 14 million board feet, was found to be almost twice that removed by cutting, 8 million board feet. When it was realized, however, that most of the timber harvested came from the 44,000 acres in sawtimber stands and that relatively little came from the remaining 114,000 acres, the picture was not bright. The growth per acre annually was about 84 board feet. If the land had been properly stocked, it could have easily been twice this amount.

Were Broome County heavily dependent upon its forests as the major economic base, this situation would be tragic. As it is, the county pays out in freight on lumber shipped in from other states an annual bill of over $750,000, an amount exceeding the current income from all the forest lands in the county. It uses 37 million board feet of lumber, of which only 5.5 million feet is grown within the county.

Broome County presents an opportunity in forestry, but to convert the idle land to timber will require a heavy capital investment.

The Forest Lands of the Lake States

The three states of Michigan, Wisconsin, and Minnesota loomed large in timber production at the turn of the century and in the two following decades. Immense stands of white pine and red pine covered almost one-third the forest area. Valuable hardwoods were plentiful in Wisconsin and the upper peninsula of Michigan. These lands, for the most part, were cut with no thought for future productivity of the land. Fires burned through the slashings. What had been superb forests were converted into brush fields, into grassland, or into stands of aspen, jack pine, and paper birch that had negligible commercial value. When first covered by the forest survey during the period 1932 to 1940, there were some 50 million acres of forest land of which 34 million acres supported timber below commercial size.[1] The land was reappraised as of January 1, 1953. By this time, there had been a reduction in the poorly stocked and deforested areas and in the seedling and sapling areas, and an increase in the amount of pole timber.[2] The distribution for the two periods was as shown below:

	Area, million acres	
	1938	1953
Sawtimber.....................	5.9	6.5
Pole timber....................	9.6	16.0
Seedlings and saplings.............	22.0	20.4
Poorly stocked and deforested.......	12.5	10.4
Total....................	50.0	53.3

Even in 1953, 51 per cent of the sawtimber and pole-timber stands were judged to be poorly stocked, along with 23 per cent of the seedling and sapling stands.

The two surveys brought out the fact that there had been a substantial increase in the volume of growing stock of standing trees. Sawtimber trees had increased from 6.4 to 10.7 billion cubic feet; pole timber, from 13.0 billion to 14.5. The region is slowly coming back as a result of greatly improved protection against fire, of forest planting programs of the federal and state governments, and of the natural process of young timber growing up into merchantable sizes.

One of the states, Michigan, was resurveyed in 1955. The results showed still further improvement over the appraised situation in 1953.[4] The net annual growth per acre had increased from 53 to 59 board feet.

The social dislocations that follow unrestricted cutting of timber have harassed hundreds of Lake States communities. Lumber operations in their heyday bring a feverish prosperity. Sawmills are erected, followed by homes, schools, churches, stores, and civic buildings. Nearby farms share in the prosperity by providing food for men and horses. When the timber is finally cut out, the mill closes and itinerant workers leave; but the home owners, storekeepers, and service workers find themselves stranded. Community decay sets in unless new industries arise. Many communities disappear completely. Others may maintain a vicarious existence by processing the remnants of the forest or by other means.

The village of Cass Lake, Minnesota, went through such a boom during the logging of the Chippewa National Forest from 1902 to 1925. Huge timber sales were made. By 1925 the mills had cut the timber and closed, and the village of Cass Lake began a period of rapid decline.

Houses were no longer painted or kept in repair. Stores and hotels closed. Churches were barely able to keep open. The village relied heavily on the limited payrolls of the national forest headquarters and a local Indian office. During the depression years of the thirties the Civilian Conservation Corps and other relief activities were the main source of income.

Meanwhile, the forest administration began seeking markets for the despised aspen and jack pine and for small-sized red and white pines. Production of piling, poles, mine timbers, box lumber, and fence posts was added to the sale of sawtimber and pulpwood. Applied research greatly increased the effectiveness of forestry measures. A cooperative of timber operators provided finances for men with little or no capital. As a result of all these measures, employment spread, stumpage prices increased, and prosperity gradually returned. As local people gained confidence in the stability of their livelihood, civic pride grew. The community changed from a debilitated lumber camp to an orderly, growing village of confident, loyal citizens.

The Pacific Slope

Cutting without regard to the future productivity of the forest has been the common practice in countries where forest resources were abundant. One might even ask whether it is politically possible to establish sustained-yield forestry in a country until the importance of permanent forests has been clearly demonstrated through their scarcity.

Guthrie and Armstrong studied the forest industry of the region comprised of the 11 western states of Arizona, California, Colorado, Idaho, Montana, Nevada, New Mexico, Oregon, Utah, Washington, and Wyoming, the Province of British Columbia, and the new state of Alaska.[6]

The population of this region was 27 million in 1958. The forest-products industries accounted for 13 per cent of the value of industrial production in this region and for 17 per cent of the total employment. The region contained in 1957 more than 3 trillion board feet of sawtimber, over half the sawtimber volume in North America.

These authors sought to determine whether this region could expect to maintain its relative position in lumber, pulp and paper, and veneer and plywood production in the years ahead looked at from two viewpoints: (1) could these industries maintain their competitive position in the eastern and world market; and (2) would the forest resources of the region be sufficient to permit this continued high rate of use without serious depletion of the timber supply? Their conclusions were positive on both questions. They felt that because of high quality and rapid growth of its timber and, particularly, because of the reserve old-growth timber available and the efficiency of logging, sawmill operations, pulp and paper plants, and veneer and plywood manufacturing, their products could remain competitive in the eastern market. They recognized, however, that certain changes were inevitable. There would have to be a substantial shift in the species of timber used for the three products with an expansion in the use of the true firs, spruces, and lodgepole pine. This would necessitate a certain shifting of location by individual industries that would not have sufficient resources near their present mill sites. Also it would be necessary to use lower-quality logs for veneer. Continued timber cutting would result in some reduction in the reserve supply of old-growth timber. They recognized further that the success of the industry in adjusting to these changes would depend to some extent upon the policies that the industries themselves adopted and the policies which the governments adopted in managing public forest lands. For the region as a whole, 83 per cent of the commercial forest land and about 81 per cent of the total timber volume were under the jurisdiction of forestry agencies of the United States government and the Provincial Government of British Columbia. These agencies practice sustained-yield management, interpreting this to mean production at the highest practical rate that the land can indefinitely support. The authors point out that it may be necessary to adopt a certain degree of flexibility in the interpretation of the principle if industry dislocations are to be kept at a minimum in the future. They do expect, however, that such adjustments will be minor in nature.

World-wide Examples of Good and Poor Land Use. The thrifty Dutch push back the Zuider Zee, leach out the salt from the soil, and cultivate the land to produce hay, vegetables, flowers, and the many other plant and animal products that give the Dutch the well-earned reputation of being the world's best farmers. The Danes have converted the heath on Jutland into good farms and forests. Through use of forest plantations, shelterbelts, proper farming practices, patience, and hard work, they have built up prosperous communities, supporting as many as 25,000 people, in a region that once supported only scattered villages and a few nomadic shepherds. The Swedes have been particularly successful in building up a high standard of living through proper care of their forests, fields, pasturelands, and mineral resources.

Norwegians inhabit a most inhospitable land. The western coast is outstanding for its beauty and ruggedness, but for this very reason it has a minimum of level land on which agriculture and forestry can be practiced. Through fishing and through diligent cultivation of forests and crops on the small patches of moderately sloping land along the fiords, however, the people maintain a good standard of living, educate their children, and live in harmony with their environment. Switzerland has Europe's most rugged topography, but the Swiss practice intensive dairying, farming, and forestry.

Italy, Greece, Albania, much of North Africa, and the Asia Minor region stand in sharp contrast to the good land-use practices just described. Mountain slopes have been denuded of timber, erosion is severe, and human poverty and misery have become widespread throughout a region that once was the garden spot of the world. Yet here, too, the last decade has seen a turn for the better. The Italians are making important conifer plantations in the Apennines, depending meanwhile on rapidly growing hybrid poplars and *Eucalyptus* planted on agricultural soil to tide them over. Spain, France, Greece, Turkey, Israel, and the countries of North Africa are engaged in a vast Mediterranean land rehabilitation program involving forest planting, pastureland improvement, and irrigated cropland.

On the Island of Formosa, Chinese and the native Taiwanese have planted more than 500,000 acres of steep eroding land to forests.[8] Thereby they are helping to tame their flashy streams that wash out rice paddies or leave them strewn with boulders. Hard, dogged work has been required. Every acre that can be held in agriculture is being saved and supported by tree planting on the steep surrounding slopes. Land is precious on this densely populated island, and the hardworking people are striving heroically to save and expand it.[8]

The Philippine Islands have some of the best tropical hardwood forests to be found anywhere in the world. Huge stands running 80 per cent or more to red and white lauan, the Philippine mahogany of commerce, cover extensive areas in Mindanao and other southern islands. These trees may rise to a height of 80 feet or more clear of limbs, with diameters up to 50 or 60 inches. The quality of the timber is generally sound. Following partial cutting, the stands can grow at a rate of 1,000 board feet per acre annually; and under favorable circumstances, twice this fast. The Philippine government owns most of the forest land. Under its Bureau of Forestry standing timber is being sold to various operating companies. The Bureau requires that all timber operators harvest on a partial-cutting basis, leaving smaller-sized trees for future cut. Heavy West Coast logging equipment is required (Fig. 30). As of 1960, about 60 per cent of all the timber harvested was shipped to Japan in log form for processing. The remainder was manufactured on the Islands into lumber, veneer, and plywood. Timber export was assuming major importance as an earner of foreign exchange, accounting for some 15 to 20 per cent in 1961. Export of forest products, therefore, has been a major item in supporting local economy. Newly emergent tropical nations have looked upon the success of the Philippines in exploiting their timber resources and are planning to do likewise.

This is on the bright side, but there is a dismal side as well. When loggers open up roads into the forest, they are followed by kaingineros and squatters, men with little capital other than a machete, a hoe, an axe, and enough seeds to plant a crop. By use of fire and girdling, they convert the partially cut timber stands into rude clearings. On each clearing they erect a rustic hut, sow their seeds, and harvest one or two crops. The rains wash away the soil nutrients and much of the topsoil that produced the fine stand of lauan timber. After two years, the soil is so depleted that it will not justify sowing a third crop. The kainginero then moves on to repeat his operation on a new tract, abandoning his land to cogongrass. Cogongrass grows so thickly that it prevents tree seedlings from starting. Though it does slow down erosion, it is unfit for use by cattle or man. In two short years, the kainginero has converted the land on which he operates from a forest capable of producing timber at a high rate and of high value to land that can support neither man nor beast.

From the forester–timber operator's viewpoint the kainginero poses a gigantic police problem. From the government's viewpoint it is a sociologic and economic problem that must be met by finding a better source of livelihood for the kainginero. Unless it is solved soon, the rich forest patrimony of the Philippine people will be completely squandered and future Filipinos will be obliged to wrest a livelihood by scratching over the bare hillsides while watching the remaining soil flow down the streams to the sea (Fig. 60).

Forest Land Use

The world is replete with examples of destructive exploitation of forests and of soil. The most striking examples are to be found on lands that are marginal between forest and agricultural land, or between grazing and agricultural land. Some of the most pressing examples of accelerated soil erosion are to be found in such semiarid regions as Kashmir and the Himalayan front in India, the Mediterranean region, (particularly Sicily and Greece), in our own western rangelands, in South Africa, in China and Korea, and in those densely settled tropical regions where cultivation is being pushed up the mountainsides, as in Central America. A few countries, especially those with a stable and responsible government and with large land-owning corporations or individual land holdings, have adopted progressive forest land use with a view toward meeting national timber supplies. The progress in our own West Coast area is a valuable case in point. It should be recognized,

Fig. 60 Kaingin shelter hut, Manobo tribe. Nasipit Lumber Company Concession, Mindanao. Mother, father, and daughter dressed up for the photo. (*Photo by Martin Hurwitz, Peace Corps volunteer.*)

however, that here public ownership of some 80 per cent of the forest and timber has been a stabilizing influence that has served as an example to the private timber holders.

As we look at the social benefits of forestry, we recognize that it is not only a national but a world-wide problem and one in which future American foresters will inevitably be enmeshed. Newly emergent nations in Africa, Asia, and the rapidly developing populations and economy in Latin America highlight the need for an extensive world-wide forestry movement. The Forestry and Forest Products Division of the Food and Agriculture Organization of the United Nations sees this as a major challenge. This organization, in looking to the year 1975, foresees the need for some 300,000 foresters, four times the number currently active in the world.

LITERATURE CITED

1. Cunningham, R. N., and Forest Survey Staff. 1950. "Forest Resources of the Lake States Region," Forest Resource Report 1, U.S. Department of Agriculture, Washington. 57 pp.

2. Cunningham, R. N., and Forest Survey Staff. 1956. "Lake States Timber Resources," U.S. Department of Agriculture, Lake States Forest Experiment Station Paper 37, St. Paul, Minn. 31 pp. mim.

3. Davis, James E., Miles J. Ferree, and Neil J. Stout. 1953. "Broome County Forest Data," State University College of Forestry at Syracuse University, Bulletin No. 27. 63 pp.

4. Findell, V. E., R. E. Pfeifer, A. G. Horn, and C. H. Tubbs. 1960. "Michigan's Forest Resources," U.S. Department of Agriculture, Lake States Forest Experiment Station Paper 82, St. Paul, Minn. 46 pp.

5. Foster, Clifford H., and Burt P. Kirkland. 1949. "Results of Twenty Years of Intensive Forest Management," The Charles Lathrop Pack Forestry Foundation, Washington, D.C. 36 pp.

6. Guthrie, John A., and George R. Armstrong. 1961. "Western Forest Industry: An Economic Outlook," The Johns Hopkins Press, Baltimore. 324 pp.

7. Pasto, Jerome K., and Howard E. Conklin, 1949. "An Economic Classification of Rural Land, Broome County, N.Y.," Cornell Economic Land Classification Leaflet 1, Cornell University Press, Ithaca, N.Y.

8. Tao, Yu Tien. 1960. "Forestry of Taiwan," Taiwan Forestry Bureau, Forestry Information Bulletin No. 21, Taiwan, China. 47 pp.

CHAPTER 17. *Forest Resources in National and World Economy*

EGON GLESINGER, Director of the Forestry and Forest Products Division of the Food and Agriculture Organization of the United Nations, in a talk before the Fifth World Forestry Congress, sketched boldly the present world forestry situation. He pointed out that the forests of the world produced in 1960 almost 60 billion cubic feet of wood. In weight this amounted to 1,350 million tons and exceeded considerably the 800 million tons of cereals and 290 million tons of steel produced. The value of this wood approached $35 billion, which is in the same order of size as the national income of countries such as France, Germany, and Great Britain. The world's forests and forest industries furnished employment for 17 to 18 million people.[6] Throughout history, forest lands have been taken up for agriculture, grazing, and other purposes, and this is still going on throughout much of the world. As countries raise their standard of living, wood consumption inevitably increases. During the decade 1950–1960, the wood use in cubic feet per capita increased in Europe from 13.6 to 17.5; in South America, from 5.2 to 8.4; in Africa, from 1.4 to 1.7; in Asia, from 1.7 to 3.2; and in Oceania, from 32.5 to 40.8. Glesinger forecast double the 1960 level of wood use by the year 2000 and warned that this may occur as early as the decade 1980–1990.

World wood needs in the future will depend upon world population. A review of the outlook for population growth is first in order.

Population and Resources

The population of the world grew slowly from the dawn of history up to A.D. 1000. It then began accelerated growth that has continued to the

276

present. Estimates of world population since 1650 are as follows: [12]

Year	Population, millions	Year	Population, millions
1650	545	1900	1,608
1750	728	1950	2,406
1800	906	1960 [15]	2,842
1850	1,171		

United States population [8] growth has been even more rapid.

Two factors have been operative: a decline in death rates due to public health measures and better medical attention, and greatly increased production of food and manufactured products due to industrialization.

In nations such as Japan, India, and China, where population presses heavily upon resources, there exists a strong national drive for industrialization in hopes of easing the burden of poverty. Demographers recognize that the immediate effect of such measures is to increase birth rates and reduce death rates, thereby intensifying the demand on resources.[17]

Eventually, birth rates as well as death rates tend to decline in industrialized nations.

India is facing her population problem realistically, seeking both to reduce the birth rate and to increase productivity. Communist China began a vigorous education program directed toward limited size of families, but relaxed it.[2] She is making desperate efforts to industrialize and increase production.

While population has been expanding at a rapid rate, good agricultural land has been shrinking in area. Erosion by both water and wind has taken a heavy toll of fertile topsoil throughout most of the densely populated regions, thereby reducing cropland. Except in a few countries, forests have been cut with little or no provision for their reestablishment. Sewage disposal in modern nations tends to hasten flow of essential plant mineral elements to the sea. The base for supporting a growing population is diminishing. To be sure, scientific agriculture has vastly increased output from the land, yet the potentialities appear by no means to be inexhaustible. Demographers feel that at best science can but provide temporary alleviation of subsistence living while population takes a new surge forward.

Many predict a dire future for mankind unless world population is rapidly stabilized and a drastic change is made in the way in which farms, forests, and other land resources are used.[1, 11–13, 20]

In the study of these resources region by region, it should be kept in mind that the press of people on the land is the dominant factor determining use. It may lead either to destructive use or to highly intensive and intelligent use, depending upon the wisdom and self-discipline of the people.

World Forest Resources

The total forest area of the world was estimated in 1960 at some 10.9 billion acres.[19] This is roughly 34 per cent of the land area of the earth. Agricultural land made up about 7.6 billion acres or 24 per cent; arid land and wasteland, some 13.4 billion acres or 42 per cent of the world's 32 billion acres of land. Of the total forest land, 62 per cent was considered to be accessible and about 33 per cent was in use for timber production. The actual area under systematic forest management was given as 1.35 billion acres. The remainder was cut with little thought for future productivity or was virtually without timber use.

Industrial use requires about 85 per cent conifers, but only 37 per cent of the productive forest land supports conifer timber. Temperate hardwoods occupy about one-ninth of the forest area and tropical hardwoods five-ninths. One of the major opportunities in world forestry has been to find commercial uses for tropical hardwoods so that more dependence may be placed upon this relatively abundant resource. Of the conifer forest area, the Soviet Union has some 2,210 million acres; North America, 1,225 million acres; and Europe, 215 million acres. Together these three areas have 91 per cent of all conifer forests (Table 9).

Tropical forests furnish us with many rare and useful woods such as mahogany, Spanish cedar, rosewood, satinwood, teak, balsa wood, ebony, lignum vitae, and others. But in the natural tropical forests these valuable species are sparsely distributed throughout dense forests of trees having woods that are hard or cross-grained, that check badly when seasoned, or that are nondurable. A density of one tree of mahogany per acre has been considered a good average logging chance. Logging, therefore, has been extremely expensive. Attempts to cut over the tropical forests, removing only the highly valuable cabinet woods, have yielded relatively little in return for the effort. Until uses are found for the majority of woods as they occur in the forest, no intensive forest management is possible. Such development, though urgently needed, has been slow to materialize. The outstanding need is for greatly increased local use of native woods.

Nations seem to go through a broad pattern in use of forest products. In primitive societies wood is used mostly for fuel and in small sizes to construct huts. With the coming of sawmills lumber use grows. It soon becomes the chief material for construction. With further increase in living standards, masonry and other products tend to replace lumber, but use of plywood, fiberboard, and particle board expands. Paper consumption is very low in primitive societies, but with education use expands greatly. As modern merchandising develops, use of paperboard for packaging becomes a major item in wood consumption. Western

TABLE 9. WORLD FOREST AREA BY REGIONS IN RELATION TO POPULATION *

Region	Popula-tion,† millions, 1957	Total forest area		Forest land in use		
		Million acres	Per capita acres	Conifers, million acres	Hard-wood, million acres	Total, million acres
United States.............	174	784	4.5	263	266	529
Europe ‡..................	414	348	0.8	198	136	334
North America ¶...........	191	1,810	9.5	622	366	988
Soviet Union..............	200	2,790	14.0	893	240	1,133
Central and South America...	190	2,510	13.2	31	193	224
Africa....................	225	1,865	8.3	5	304	309
Asia.....................	1,556	1,285	0.8	109	474	583
Australia and Pacific area...	15	237	14.8	10	39	49
Total..................	2,791	10,845	3.8	1,868	1,752	3,620

* United Nations, Food and Agriculture Organization Staff. 1960. "The World's Forest Resources," *Unasylva*, 14:137.
† Golenpaul, Dan, ed. 1959. "Information Please Almanac—1960," McGraw-Hill Book Company, Inc., New York.
‡ Excluding U.S.S.R.
¶ Excluding Latin America.

Europe and the United States have passed their peak in per capita use of lumber, but per capita use of paper and paper products is still expanding.

Forest Conditions and Practices in Various Sections of the World

Europe (FAO). Forestry is practiced more intensively in Europe than elsewhere. Even there overcutting was common before the Second World War, and some overcutting occurred during the war. Since Europe, outside of Russia, has insufficient land to supply total needs, imports have been required. Wood is one of the mainstays of the economy of the Scandinavian countries, which are important exporters of wood to central and southern Europe. International trade in forest products was predominantly inter-European trade before the Second World War.

Consumption of softwood lumber in Europe increased from 16.7 billion board feet in 1913 to 21.6 billion board feet in 1955. Per capita consumption during this period decreased about 13 per cent. Hardwood lumber consumption was much less—4.7 billion board feet in 1955.

Hardwood consumption has increased more rapidly than softwood since 1937. An even more rapid increase has occurred in consumption of plywood, fiberboard, and particle board. Production of paper and paperboard was 5.5 million tons in 1913 and 16.1 million tons in 1955.[16] The total consumption of industrial wood in 1957 was 6.9 billion cubic feet. The total timber cut averaged 10.62 billion cubic feet per year for the period 1955 to 1957. Use had probably increased to the same level.

Forestry in Europe has experienced notable progress since 1945, and especially since 1953. During the five-year period 1953 to 1958, the forest area managed with working plans increased from 42 to 50 per cent of the forest area; average growing stock increased from 1,070 to 1,140 cubic feet per acre. Average growth in 1958 was 35.8 cubic feet per acre and annual cut was about 9 per cent less than growth.[19] Perhaps of even greater significance were the steps being taken to improve timber growth and use in Europe. Germany, Scandinavia, Italy, and Spain were expanding research in forestry and forest products. International cooperation in forestry has developed on an elaborate scale. Special international commissions have been created on poplar, chestnut, and Mediterranean forestry. The International Union of Forest Research Institutes has been especially strong in Europe. Working groups of this and of FAO dealt with afforestation and reforestation, protection against torrents and avalanches, ecology of the Mediterranean region, *Eucalyptus,* wood properties and structure, forest work and working conditions including mechanization and safety, pulp and paper, and forest and forest-products statistics. Frequent international study trips are made to discuss various problems of silviculture, management, products, and policy. In Germany and other countries special efforts are being made to help small woodland owners, through land exchanges, to consolidate small holdings and to build up productivity through various aid programs. Abandoned agricultural land is being forested. Broad economic and land-use studies are being sponsored by high government officers. The European Forestry Commission and the Commission on Agriculture have joined forces to study land-use questions. Forestry receives special consideration in the European Economic Community, as forest products form a major industrial commodity.[9]

All these activities point toward continued improvement of forestry and the forest-products industries throughout Western and Southern Europe.

For most countries outside of Europe and North America, statistics on forest resources are fragmentary and of unknown accuracy.

Union of Soviet Socialist Republics. The Soviet Union is well endowed with forest lands. They stretch from the Baltic Sea to the Pacific. The total area included in the State Forest Reserves in 1960 was 2,790 million acres, about half the land area of the U.S.S.R. Of the land in reserves, 1,780 million acres were covered with forests.[18] Coniferous species occupy about 78 per cent of the forests, and hardwoods occupy 22 per cent. The major species and percentage of area they occupy are as follows:

Species	*Per cent*
Larch	40.3
Pine	16.0
Birch	13.5
Spruce	10.6
Cedar	4.7
Fir	3.4
Other conifers	3.0
Aspen	2.0
Oak	1.4
Other hardwoods	5.1

The forests of the U.S.S.R. occupy two general zones. The northern zone, made up largely of conifers, gives way to the Arctic tundra on the north and to the vast steppe lands on the south. Much of the northern forest is underlain by permafrost. Also, about one-third of the northern forest is swampy, requiring drainage for good growth. Some 1.46 million acres had been drained by 1960. The southern forest occurs as a narrow belt of oaks and other hardwoods south of the steppe land along the highlands and mountains in the south.

Annual growth rate varies widely from about 16 cubic feet per acre in Siberia to almost three times this amount in the Ukraine. The annual average has been about 18 cubic feet per acre, or a total growth of 30 billion cubic feet. Timber cutting has increased rapidly in recent decades from 5.9 billion cubic feet in 1929 to 13.8 billion cubic feet in 1958. Almost two-thirds of the forests were of commercial timber size in 1960. Forests under management were reported to total 775 million acres in 1959. Current cutting practice is clean-cutting except in intensively managed zones, greenbelts around cities, and mountain lands, where selective cutting is used. The northern forest usually reproduces well naturally but may take up to 20 years to do so. Seeding and planting have, therefore, been widely practiced on cutover lands. In 1959, 1.4 million acres were seeded or planted and 1.7 million acres were treated to aid natural reproduction.

A major obstacle to intensive forest management in the U.S.S.R. has been lack of transportation. Swamps make highway and railway construction costly. The major rivers flow north to the Arctic. These thaw at the source while the mouths are still icebound, restricting floating to about two months during the year. The difficulties in exploitation probably exceed those found in the interior of Alaska. Both the U.S.S.R.

and the United States will find it more profitable to concentrate major forestry efforts on the accessible and highly productive lands rather than on their remote northern forests.

The total standing timber was given in 1960 as 2,650 billion cubic feet, or over four times that of the United States.

Against the background of the shortage of rail, highway, and water transportation, and undeveloped lands, the Soviet Union has nonetheless made progress. Electric and gasoline chain saws have been introduced for felling, limbing, and bucking. Special skidding tractors with wide treads have been developed that operate as a combined tractor and logging arch. Logging camps and villages have been established. Special tractor sleigh roads have been built for bringing out logs in winter on sleds. Sawmills have been modernized and wood processing has been improved by mechanization and automation. Huge plows that can make meter-deep furrows have been built to drain swamps and make fire lines. It is stated that the Soviet Union has spent some $2 billion on research to mechanize forestry operations.

The regional forest research institutes, the forestry schools, and the Academy of Sciences Forest Institute have been concerned with sound forest land management. The resources for research at their disposal, though, were still meager compared with those available to the timber industries.

The question naturally arises, will the U.S.S.R. become a major agency in the international timber trade in the near future? That she has the timber-resource potential to do so is obvious. If she were to bend her strength in this direction, her timber-exporting neighbors—Finland, Sweden, and Austria—might suffer. Effort in 1960 was concentrated on increasing timber harvest for national needs, rather than for export. The U.S.S.R. operated 11 forestry schools and 12 departments of forestry graduating 1,500 engineers annually in 1958. This is evidence of her interest to strengthen greatly her forestry and forest-products industries.[18]

Middle East and North Africa. This region, the seat of powerful empires before Greek and Roman times, has presented since modern times an outstanding example of forest destruction and land abuse. The crying need of this area has been for reforestation and long-range forest programs, but these measures were handicapped by political instability and by the general poverty of the countries.

The forests that originally clothed the mountains have been largely cleared off and the land has been given over to grazing. Erosion has taken off much of the soil. As the land became poorer, the people were obliged to use it the harder to gain a livelihood. The result has been widespread impoverishment of both land and people.

Fortunately, a beginning has been made at forest restoration. In Spain,

Italy, Greece, and Turkey substantial reforestation programs have been started. Potted plants are sometimes used to provide soil for initial establishment, and artificial shade may be needed. The results achieved are not impressive in area but are significant in terms of the difficulties that have been overcome. In Cypress, an active reforestation program was under way, matched by a program of pasture improvement. Spain, Italy, and France were cooperating actively with the Food and Agriculture Organization Mediterranean Development Project to encourage integrated planning and development of agriculture, livestock farming, forestry, and water supplies.[14] These have high promise for the future. So has the work in Israel, where an intelligent, determined people are restoring to productivity a badly depleted land.

Prospects for substantial timber production in the future may develop in Iran, Ethiopia, and Afghanistan. Plantations of poplars, *Eucalyptus,* and *Casuarina* support modest wood-using industries in these areas. The region seemed destined to remain for many years a net importer of forest products. If living standards and industrialization progress as rapidly as these nations hope, substantially increased wood imports will be required.

Central and South America. The nations of Latin America have together 2,510 million acres of forest land.[10] They are surpassed in forest area only by the U.S.S.R. and in potential timber production by no region of the world. Yet these countries collectively, as of 1957, cut only 6.7 billion cubic feet of timber, most of which was used for fuel. They produced only about 1 billion feet of industrial wood, less than that produced by Sweden. Production of sawn wood was about 29 million cubic feet, less than 3 per cent of world production. Pulp and paper production was expanding and in 1958 totaled 395,000 tons of pulp and 1.5 million tons of paper. In 1958 the area as a whole imported 64 per cent of its chemical pulp, 84 per cent of its newsprint, and 29 per cent of its paperboard.

Great opportunity for future development exists in Latin America (Fig. 61).

Much of the timber is of modest or negative value throughout Latin America; hence, it is not surprising that forestry lags. Moreover, difficulties are enormous. Only one-third of the forests were considered accessible in 1958 and only one-twelfth were in actual use.[10]

Among the countries of Central and South America, only Mexico and Brazil have important areas of softwood timber.[1, 5, 10] Mexican softwoods occupy mountain areas in relatively dry regions. The Paraná pine region of Brazil, though small, is a very important timber-producing area. It has a total timber stand estimated to exceed 60 billion cubic feet. Undeveloped forest lands remote from existing transportation occur in most of the South American countries. The development of such areas must await improvement of transportation and studies of wood technology to determine the value of the several woods.

Brazil is estimated to have more standing timber than any other country in the world, but most of the forests are unexplored and unexploited. Shifting agriculture has already made heavy inroads on the forests outside the rain-forest zone. Argentina has limited forest areas, of which the 3 million acres of Paraná pine are perhaps the most valuable. Fires have caused severe damage, particularly in the areas bordering the Andes. Although the Chaco region contains extensive forests, it was largely unexplored as of 1960.

Fig. 61 Experimental plantation of teak and other tropical hardwoods in Honduras. The tree shown is 24 years of age and about 30 inches in diameter. United Fruit Company lands near Lancetilla, Honduras.

Half of Peru is forested; yet before the Second World War Peru imported 50 per cent of the lumber she consumed. Western Peru is practically treeless. The eastern slope of the Andes, particularly the Upper Amazon Basin, is heavily forested. An east-west railway has been projected to open these forests to use.

Colombian forests were explored and mapped in 1959. Potentially, they form a very important resource for the country—particularly for the production of rubber, oils, gums, and nuts. Eventually, they may also produce substantial amounts of timber.

Chile has approximately 40 million acres of forest land, but much of it lies in the southern portion in rugged terrain where logging will be difficult. *Eucalyptus* and other plantations have proved highly productive and supply timber for local use. A development program was begun in 1951.

Increased use of the forests of Latin America was taking place in 1960. Modern pulp mills were being erected, experiments on pulping tropical hardwoods were being conducted, and advanced-design sawmills and plywood mills were being constructed. Schools for education of foresters and forest technicians had been developed in Mexico, Brazil, Argentina, Venezuela, Chile, Colombia, Costa Rica, and other countries. Regional centers for research and education were operating in Puerto Rico; at Turrialba, Costa Rica; and at Mérida, Venezuela.

Africa. Africa with 1,865 million acres of forest land ranks third in forest area of the major world regions. About one-sixth of the forest land was in use in 1960. Tremendous diversity exists in climate, soil, vegetation, culture, and economic conditions throughout the continent. In much of Africa, particularly the dry sections, the wood is so small, crooked, and poor in quality as to be useful only for fuel. By contrast, the west coast area produces a few woods of such decorative value as to be shipped to Europe and the United States. Cost of producing such timber is high. Locally produced lumber is often more expensive than that shipped from Europe.

Plantations of *Eucalyptus*, *Radiata* pine, teak, and wattle, especially in South Africa, have produced high yields of timber and high returns to plantation owners. The average natural stand may produce only 280 to 420 cubic feet per acre of commercial timber.[21] This is often in trees of huge bulk. Lack of transportation and mechanical equipment makes extraction very costly. As a result, Africa produced only about 1 per cent of the world's industrial wood in 1960. Planting and timber-stand improvement, with and without intercropping of food plants during the period of establishment, seem to offer substantial opportunity for greatly increased forest values in the future.

The extent to which improvement of forests and even care of existing forests will be carried out must depend upon new governments. Much of Africa is emerging from colonialism. Important efforts were made by colonial administrators to use African forests, but the results were disappointing. The new governments face social and economic problems that press far more heavily on local administrators than long-range forestry development. Still, the enthusiasm generated by freedom, if skillfully channeled, could lead to increased community responsibility and through this to improved land and forest practice. As local needs seem likely to increase almost as rapidly as exploitation develops, it appears that a long time will elapse before Africa contributes substantially to the world's timber supply.

South and East Asia. In no region of the world is there greater need for increasing the contribution of forests to human needs than in South and East Asia. The total forest area is large—1,285 million acres; but the population is also large—1,556 million people, more than half the total in the world. Industrialization for the most part is weakly developed and subsistence livelihood the rule for the bulk of the people. Moreover, population is increasing about as rapidly as production is increasing. Many governments are new and still have the task of developing sufficient national unity and public discipline to support long-range forestry programs. East Asia is a wood-importing area and seems destined to remain so. South Asia may in time become a modest exporter of wood. For the region as a whole, net imports seem likely to be required for some time to come.

Forestry is highly developed in Japan, and substantial development has also occurred in the Philippines. Much of the progress made under outside administration in the Philippines and to a lesser extent in Burma was threatened by inadequate administration by the newly independent governments. Waste of national resources has characterized the action of many peoples in their early stages of democratic government. The United States did not escape it.

Fortunately, India and Pakistan have avoided unrestrained forest destruction. Both countries face a difficult task in flood control and soil stabilization in mountain areas. Grazing of forest lands by cattle, sheep, and goats augments the difficulty. The pact negotiated between India and Pakistan for development and use of the waters of the Indus River is a favorable development that can lead to greatly increased development of the forests as well as agricultural land.

Governments generally seem to be taking increased interest in forestry. Notable progress in tree planting has been made in Japan, India, Korea, and Taiwan. Forest-products industries are expanding rapidly. During the four-year period 1954 to 1958 plywood production doubled in Japan and India and more than doubled in Taiwan and the Philippines; fiberboard production in Japan increased almost fourfold, and wood-pulp production increased by 42 per cent.[4] Forest surveys using aerial photos had been completed or were under way in 1960 and 1961 in Burma, Thailand, Pakistan, Ceylon, Malaya, Cambodia, North Borneo, Korea, and the Philippines. Interest was growing in forest genetics. Steps were being taken in Vietnam, Malaya, Cambodia, Borneo, and India to control shifting cultivation through resettlement and other measures. New research institutes were being established or expanded in the Philippines, Burma, Thailand, Pakistan, and Korea. Modern equipment for log extraction was also coming into use. Export markets were being developed for some little-used species. All this was evidence of progress.

The difficulties are great. Not the least has been lack of capital. FAO and bilateral aid plans have helped to augment technical competence and have brought in some capital. Gradually aversion to use of foreign private capital has seemed to be abating, but the confidence of foreign investors must be restored before substantial funds become available. The heavy timber needs of the densely populated countries, especially Japan, China, and India, are more than sufficient to use all forest products the region can produce. Major tasks are to establish more protection forests in China, India, and Pakistan and to improve forest practices generally (Table 9).

Pacific Area. The Pacific area includes Australia, New Zealand, Indonesia, and other island areas. Together these lands have a total of 237 million acres of forest land, of which slightly less than one-fourth is in use. Population pressure is heavy in Japan, the Philippines, and Java, but light in Sumatra, Borneo, Australia, and New Zealand. Aside from Japan and the Philippines, which were grouped with Asia in the above discussion, the most intensive forestry is in Australia. This country is and seems likely to remain a wood-importing nation. Its splendid *Eucalyptus* forests occur in a narrow belt along the East Coast. Plantations of *Radiata* pine have done well. Forest research, particularly wood-products research, is on a high level, as is the education of foresters.

New Zealand forests contain some magnificent trees and stands. Forests cover about one-fourth of the land area. Plantations of exotics approach 1 million acres. Timber is exported in substantial volumes to Australia and in small amounts to other countries. On the other hand, New Zealand imports Douglas-fir, redwood, and Australian hardwoods (Table 9).

The forests of Java, Sumatra, and Borneo support a wealth of tree species, some of which are reported as still unknown to science as well as to trade. Much of the land is rugged, transportation is poorly developed, and consequently the forests are still unused. The potential of much of these forests for production of commercial timber is still to be determined.

Canada. The forests of Canada cover about 1,000 million acres and hence are about one-third larger than those of the United States. Much of Canada's forest land lies in northern latitudes, where growth is meager compared with that of forest land farther south. Unlike those of the United States, 90 per cent of Canada's forests are publicly owned crown lands administered by 10 provincial forest authorities. The practice is to grant leases on lands, called limits, to private corporations. These may extend for varying periods up to 20 years. Even longer periods up to 100 years are being considered so that companies may benefit from forestry measures they apply. Cutting practices were similar to those in the United States in 1961. Private forest ownership totaled about 63 million acres. About one-quarter of the drain from Canadian forests is for sawtimber and almost an additional one-quarter for pulpwood. It was estimated that almost one-third the drain of Canadian forests in 1960 was due to fire, insects, disease, and windstorm. Forest management was on an extensive basis.

As in the United States, progress in forestry has been very rapid since 1945. During the period 1955 to 1960 management plans were extended from 119 million acres to 223 million acres.[7] Forest surveys have been completed which revealed a total of 83 million acres of productive forest above previous estimates. Canada had a vigorous program of forest insect and disease control in 1960, one of the best of any country. Destructive insects were attacked on a large scale and with a high degree of success. Research in tree physiology, insect and disease control, genetics, silviculture, wood properties, and pulp and paper technology was vigorously carried out by the Dominion government and the four forestry schools. Enrollment in forestry schools totaled 686 in 1959. Canada also had four ranger schools and one technical institute training about 200 rangers annually.

Good practice on farm woodlands was encouraged by extension foresters and the Canadian Forestry Association and through the Tree Farm Program. Canada has been an important exporter of forest products and should continue so for many years to come.

Forests of the United States

When Europeans first settled in America, they found a virgin land, abounding in rich resources. The forests were the most valuable and the most extensive that had been discovered. The original forest area was approximately 822 million acres, almost equally distributed between hardwoods and softwoods.* In addition, there were some 93 million acres

---

* To permit valid comparisons of changes in time, the forests of the states of Alaska and Hawaii are covered in a separate section. The data in the following sections relate to the 48 contiguous states.

of woodlands interspersed among prairies, plains, and deserts. The virgin country that the Indian knew was made up of the vegetative types shown in Table 10.

TABLE 10. ORIGINAL VEGETATIVE TYPES OF THE
UNITED STATES AND AREAS THEY COVERED *

Vegetative types	Area, million acres	Per cent of total
Hardwood forest................	403	21
Coniferous forest..............	419	22
Total forest.................	822	43
Woodland....................	93	5
Total forest and woodland....	915	48
Desert shrub..................	267	14
Tall-grass prairie..............	304	16
Short-grass prairie............	267	14
Other grassland................	152	8
Total nonforest..............	990	52
Total land area.............	1,905	100

* Shantz and Zon. 1924. "Atlas of American Agriculture," U.S. Department of Agriculture, Washington.

Land Use in the United States. Occupation of the land and clearing for agriculture have profoundly modified our country's native vegetation. Forests have been cleared for farmland; prairie lands have been plowed and cultivated. Roads, railways, canals, reservoirs, airports, cities, and villages occupy substantial areas. Virgin lands have mostly been exploited. The uses of land as they have developed since 1933 are shown in Table 11.

During more than three centuries of occupation and use the total forest land of the United States has declined from 822 to 648 million acres. This is not an overwhelming change when it is realized that much of the cropland and pastureland and a high proportion of land now in urban use were originally forested. Actually the trends since about 1910 have been toward an increase in forest land at the expense of pasturelands, though the latter is masked somewhat by the conversion of open range to farm range. A temporary increase in cropland at the expense of range occurred during the Second World War when demands for grain were heavy and moisture supply in the plains area proved adequate to mature the crops.

TABLE 11. LAND AREAS OF THE UNITED STATES BY USE PATTERNS, 1933–1953

Land-use practice	Area distribution by years *				
	1933 †	1938 ‡	1945 ¶	1953 §	1953, per cent of total
	Millions of acres				
Cropland in farms...............	413	415	525	411	21.6
Pasture and range lands in farms...	379	⎫	301	470	24.7
Open range and desert...........	317	858	306	222	11.7
Farmsteads, roads, urban, etc......	179	⎭	147	152	8.0
Total nonforest land...........	1,288	1,273	1,279	1,255	66.0
Commercial forest land..........	495	462	461	484	25.4
Withdrawn for parks and preserves	11	⎫ 168	13	15	0.8
Noncommercial forest...........	109	⎭	150	149	7.8
Total forest land..............	615	630	624	648	34.0
Total land area..............	1,903	1,903	1,903	1,903	100.0

* It should be borne in mind that the area estimates for the different years reflect not only actual changes in areas but also changes in standards of what constitutes forest land.

† "A National Plan for American Forestry." 73d Cong., S. Doc. 12, 1933, p. 121.

‡ U.S. Department of Agriculture, Forest Service. 1939. "A National Forest Economy— One Means to Social and Economic Rehabilitation," processed p. 257.

¶ U.S. Department of Agriculture, Forest Service. 1946. "Gaging the Timber Resource of the United States," Report 1, from "A Reappraisal of the Forest Situation," Washington.

§ U.S. Department of Agriculture, Forest Service. 1958. "Timber Resources for America's Future," Forest Resource Report 14, p. 503, Washington.

It is an interesting fact that the regions in which abandonment of agricultural land occurred earliest and has proceeded the farthest are those thickly populated eastern states where markets for agricultural products are best and where agriculture has already reached a high stage of development.

Future withdrawals of land from forests will be made largely for suburban and industrial use; for roads, parkways, and airports; and for recreational use as parks, natural areas, and wilderness areas. A limited amount may be converted to cropland.

Early statistics on forest resources in the United States have been weak. Attempts to gather them date back to the 1880s, but the first comprehensive study was made by the Bureau of Corporations, U.S. Department of Commerce and Labor, in 1909. In 1930, the U.S. Forest Service began a nationwide survey of forest resources, forest growth, drain, and present and potential requirements. Estimates based on survey data and other information were made in 1933, 1938, 1945, and 1953. The 1945 estimate by the U.S. Forest Service was paralleled by an independent estimate prepared by the American Forestry Association, with the two in substantial agreement. The 1953 study was the most thorough and is believed to be more accurate than the earlier ones. In this the states and private industries pooled their information with that from the nationwide forest survey. Data on forest resources and their interpretation were submitted by the U.S. Forest Service to a number of forestry agencies, and the final report published in 1958 was issued only after consideration of the comments submitted.

Regional Distribution of Forests. The forest areas by condition classes are shown for three broad regions in Table 12.

TABLE 12. DISTRIBUTION OF COMMERCIAL FOREST LANDS
BY REGIONS AND CONDITION CLASSES *

(In millions of acres)

Region	Saw-timber	Pole timber	Seedling and sapling	Non-stocked and other	Total forest
North.....	48	65	44	17	174
South.....	60	78	39	16	193
West.....	70	26	12	9	117
Total...	178	169	95	42	484

* U.S. Department of Agriculture, Forest Service. 1958. "Timber Resources for America's Future," Forest Resource Report 14, p. 505, Washington.

Timber Volume. Although forest area in the United States has declined by only one-third since white settlement, timber volume during the same period has declined by more than two-thirds (Table 13). This decline in volume has been accompanied by declines in accessibility, size, and quality of timber, and in softwoods in relation to hardwoods.

It is significant that most of the timber-growing land lies east of the Great Plains—367 million acres as opposed to 117 million west of the Plains. The western states contained 68 per cent of the sawtimber volume and only 24 per cent of the forest land area in 1958. The eastern states contained the lowest proportion of sawtimber area to total forest area.

This, of course, was merely an expression of the long-continued heavy demand for forest products in this section of the country.

Soon after the white man began clearing forests for agriculture and harvesting timber for construction, a decline in standing-timber volume began. By 1909 but 40 per cent of the original volume remained (Table 13). Further decline continued until 1945 (Table 13), when the produc-

TABLE 13. ESTIMATES OF TIMBER VOLUME
IN THE UNITED STATES

Year	Timber volume, billion bd. ft.	Year	Timber volume, billion bd. ft.
1492	5,200	1938	1,764
1909	2,290	1945	1,601
1933	1,668	1953	1,968

tivity of second-growth stands together with lower standards of utilization effected an apparent balance. Eastern hardwoods appear to have increased in sawtimber volume by about 17 per cent between 1945 and 1953, whereas western softwoods showed a 5 per cent decline. The net change, a gain of 2 per cent, was too small to be significant in view of sampling errors.

Though timber volume, particularly total cubic volume, seemed no longer to be declining in 1960, the same could not be said for timber quality. The bulk of the sawtimber cut was still coming from old-growth timber stands of the West Coast, while the bulk of timber growth was on second-growth stands still mostly too young to produce timber of high quality. Actual change in quality of standing timber has not been estimated in the field, so opinions cannot be balanced by facts. On intensively managed properties foresters have been seeking to improve quality, but this is a long-term task on which only a beginning has been made.

A comparison of growth and cut since 1920 shows a substantial gain in growth, while timber cut has declined slightly, as shown in Table 14. This table does not take into account losses due to fire, insects, disease, and windstorm, estimated to be about 9 billion board feet in excess of that salvaged.

By expressing volume only in terms of board feet, the actual situation is obscured somewhat. Only trees and stands of sawtimber size can be cut for lumber manufacture, but smaller-sized trees may be used for poles, posts, pulpwood, and fuel. They also grow into trees of sawtimber size in time. Only 178 million acres bore trees of sawtimber size in 1954, but pole timber covered 169 million acres; seedlings and saplings, 95 million. The timber volume for sawtimber trees was 360 billion cubic

TABLE 14. SAWTIMBER CUT AND GROWTH BY YEARS *

(In billion board feet)

Year	Annual cut	Annual growth
1920	56.1	9.7
1930	54.6	11.7
1938	42.4	32.0
1944	49.7	35.3
1952	48.8	47.3

* U.S. Department of Agriculture, Forest Service. 1958. "Timber Resources for America's Future," Forest Resource Report 14, pp. 149, 161, Washington.

feet; for pole-timber trees, 138 billion cubic feet. Softwood volume was 355 million cubic feet; hardwood, 162 million cubic feet.

Timber Growth and Requirements. The really significant issue to be faced is: Will timber growth for the next 40 years match the requirements our people will place upon the forests? The growth rate of timber was probably higher in 1962 than at any other time in the history of our country, and the unsalvaged losses due to destructive agents were probably lower than at any other time. Total growth in 1962 was 33 per cent in excess of cut. Denuded lands were restocking naturally or being planted. All this encouraged an optimistic outlook for timber supply. Other factors lent support to such an outlook (Fig. 62). Manufacture of paper pulp from hardwoods by semichemical and other processes was reducing the cutting pressure that would otherwise be placed on young softwood stands. The declining use of fuel wood and the use of chips and edgings for paper pulp were helping also. The rapid growth in plywood, fiberboard, and particle board was reducing the demands for lumber. Salvage of waste in wood-processing plants was increasing. Timber preservatives were prolonging the life of wood in service. Perhaps most promising of all was the great increase in numbers of foresters employed by industries and government. The fruit of their combined efforts was reducing losses to standing timber and was effecting rapid restocking of cutover lands. Some people, in fact, expressed the opinion that supply would exceed demand, resulting in depressed timber prices. This might be true for low-grade products and less favored species, both of which seemed to be increasing at the expense of quality products. Moreover, the decline in market for fuel wood and chemical wood limited the outlet for such timber. A major factor in declining use for low-grade timber was its small value in terms of its harvesting, transportation, and processing

F<small>IG</small>. 62 Salvage logging operations have kept two contract loggers busy for almost a decade on Kogap Manufacturing Company lands near Medford, Oregon. (*AFPI photo.*)

cost. The demand for high-quality lumber, veneer, plywood, and other quality products remained high, and the prices reflected this.

Attempts to forecast future demand are always open to challenge. This does not relieve the U.S. Forest Service as the government's technical agency in forestry and forest products from the responsibility of attempting such a forecast. Projections made for the years 1975 and 2000 involved the following: population, labor force, gross national product, disposable income, raw-material demands, and timber products in the national economy. Certain basic assumptions were made—that peace with military preparedness would prevail and that high level of employment would continue. The nation's demand for lumber for housing, nonresidential construction, crossties, furniture and other manufacturing, pallets, and dunnage was projected on the basis of stable and of increasing price trends. The same was done for pulpwood, veneer logs, piling, fuel wood, and minor products.

The Forest Service made three separate projections. The medium projection was based on a population of 215 million by 1975 and 275 million by the year 2000, as well as on the assumption that timber prices would maintain their 1954 relation to prices of competing products. The gross national product was projected to be $630 billion by 1975 and $1,200 billion by the year 2000. The upper projection was based on a higher population, 360 million by 2000, and a gross national product of $1,450 billion. The lower projection used the same population and gross national product as the medium projection but assumed that timber products would rise in price substantially faster than competing products. The projections are shown in Table 15.

As of 1960 it appeared that population by 1975 would be 224 million

TABLE 15. CURRENT AND PROJECTED TIMBER CONSUMPTION *†

(In billion board feet)

Year	Level of projection	Saw- timber	Total all timber products
1952	Actual cut	36.6	48.8
1959	Actual cut	36.9	
1975	Lower	40.7	56.0
	Medium	47.9	65.4
2000	Lower	47.3	69.0
	Medium	69.5	95.1
	Upper	79.5	111.0

* U.S. Department of Agriculture, Forest Service. 1958. "Timber Resources for America's Future," Forest Resource Report 14, p. 470, Washington.

† A more recent projection of consumption demand for lumber for the year 2000 was presented by Resources for the Future in the book by Hans H. Landsberg, Leonard L. Fischman, and Joseph L. Fisher, 1963, "Resources in America's Future," The Johns Hopkins Press, Baltimore, 1017 pp. These authors' projections for the year 2000 of demand for lumber, plywood, and pulp are the following:

	Low	Medium	High
Lumber (billion board feet)............	31.5	97.6	213.5
Plywood and veneer (billion square feet):			
Softwood.........................	25.8	62.7	137.4
Hardwood........................	29.8	70.2	147.4
Pulp (million short tons).............	76.4	110.1	169.6

These projections are considerably higher than those of the U.S. Forest Service presented in Table 15.

instead of 215 million and that gross national product would be $770 billion instead of $630 billion.

Of the three projections the upper level to the year 2000 seemed least probable of attainment, as it would require that growing stock be built up to provide an annual cut of 111 billion board feet while the cut itself was being expanded. This would require an average growth rate of 227 board feet per acre per year on the total 484 million acres of commercial forest land. Even the medium projection will tax the productive capacity of the land and the skill of foresters to attain such a level. The projection, therefore, pointed to the need for increasing intensity of use of forest land and more efficient wood-processing techniques.

Another important factor to be considered is the ability of the lumber industry to log and mill lumber at prices that will encourage continued high use. Craig [3] has stated that lumber prices were too high in the decade 1950–1960 to encourage maximum use. In a period of rising house construction, use of lumber declined and use of substitute material increased. Profits of the lumber industry, that were plagued by rising costs without corresponding increases in output, suffered. Craig's outlook for the industry may have been unduly pessimistic. Studies by Zaremba [22–24] indicated that at least some trends away from wood use in housing have proved to be temporary, such as using a concrete slab as foundation. Use of masonry instead of wood siding appeared to be a more permanent trend. He pointed out, however, that consumer preference as well as price determined use; also that housing space occupied and wood used in housing increased with family income. Family income was expected to double between 1954 and 1975 to 1980. On the basis of current use, the wood requirements per single family dwelling, instead of declining or remaining constant for the period, would increase by 60 per cent.

The outcome will depend largely on three major factors:

1. The success of foresters in growing an abundant timber supply
2. The success of research workers and technologists in improving the product and keeping the price in line with other materials
3. The success of the lumber industry in maintaining consumer preference for the product

Fortunately action has been intensified in all three directions. The outlook should, therefore, be considered as favorable but one that will nevertheless challenge the ingenuity of foresters, lumber manufacturers, and lumber salesmen.

Forests of Alaska, Hawaii, and Puerto Rico

The above discussion omitted reference to the forests of Alaska, Hawaii, and Puerto Rico. Alaskan forests are made up of two types. The coastal forests cover 16.5 million acres, of which 4.3 million acres support good stands of Sitka spruce, western hemlock, Port-Orford-cedar, and western redcedar. These forests extend inland some 5 to 6 miles. They were being exploited for sawtimber and pulpwood in 1960. The 4.3 million acres they occupy may be added to the commercial forest land of the United States. The interior forests cover a vast land area, some 120 million acres, of which one-third is considered to be commercial. The commercial forests are made up of paper birch, white spruce, aspen, and black spruce that have stands of 4,500 board feet per acre or more. They tend to follow the major river valleys. Most of the land area has been burned over, and extensive fires are a major source of loss. Permanently frozen ground may occur at a depth of 1 foot or more, resulting in poor drainage, weak root anchorage, and slow growth. The commercial forest land was estimated to support 180 billion board feet of sawtimber with a net growth of some 3.9 billion board feet in 1960. Most of the timber was harvested by natural agents—fire, insects, and disease. These forests have made little contribution to the economy of Alaska, nor is it likely that other than local use will be significant for a number of years to come.

The forests of Hawaii, Puerto Rico, and the Virgin Islands are made up mostly of tropical hardwoods. The total forest area is small, less than 2 million acres of commercial timberland. The products are mainly for local use; only a few items of furniture and novelties enter into trade with the mainland.

World Outlook

The forest resources of the United States and of the world seemed ample in 1960, but the long-term outlook was only moderately favorable. It was true that 67 per cent of the forests remained to be brought into regular use. Extending use to remote areas and enriching the impoverished forests of many lands and the naturally poor stands in many tropical countries are bound to be slow and costly processes. The world demands of 1980 to 2000 will have to be met largely through intensifying efforts on developed forest land as well as opening up those most accessible new lands that support timber of commercial value. Success in meeting future world needs will require efforts along many diversified channels. Wide difference exists today in the growth rate of forests in different countries. The highest growth rate on the average is found in Denmark: 104 cubic feet per acre annually. One of the best-managed forests of Denmark has stands growing as much as 300 cubic feet per acre annually. This contrasts with an average of 29 cubic feet in Finland and Sweden and virtually no net growth on the large areas of devastated and untouched forest land. Moreover, even in countries with fairly intensive forestry, such as Finland and Sweden, foresters estimate that current

FIG. 63   The National Research Center for forestry and forest products near Rome, Italy. The program includes breeding experiments on poplars and *Eucalyptus*, tree physiology, entomology, pathology, wood technology, and wood chemistry.

yield could be almost doubled by adopting the best-known silvicultural practices. The opportunities of still further augmenting the timber supply through use of better genetic strains were being explored through vigorous research programs (Fig. 63).

From the world's 10.9 billion acres of forest land, mankind harvested annually 58 billion cubic feet, or the equivalent of less than 6 cubic feet per acre, in 1960. Since this cut actually came from only one-third of the world's timberland, the yield from land that was cut over was about 16 cubic feet per acre per year. If forest productivity throughout the world could be built up to the standard attained in Finland and Sweden on lands being operated for timber, the average use could be doubled. The long-term potential for world forest production was great, perhaps two to six times the 1960 use. The obstacles to achieving such use were also great; the most obstructive were of human and political rather than physical or biologic origin. But much cause for hope existed in the international collaboration being carried out and in the enthusiasm with which new nations were seeking to build up their resources.

The review of forest resources of the United States in terms of potential future demands makes it clear that our nation cannot look forward to maintaining a substantial export trade in timber. Specialty products such as veneer logs, plywood, and some paper products may continue to be exported. These will be largely matched by imports from Canada and other countries. The outlook for continued imports from Canada and South America seems good, though these can scarcely be expected to become a major factor in national supply. Main reliance must be placed on supplies from within the nation. This is true not only because of the relatively generous timber resources within the country but also because of the generally high technical quality of the native timber species.

The Responsibility of the United States in World Forestry

The United States has an interest in the supply of forest products that can be imported from other countries and in the market for forest products that can be exported from our own country. The United States is also interested in helping to improve the forest economy throughout the world. It is making available to the nations of the world the techniques in forestry and utilization of forest products that have been developed in the United States. It feels a particular obligation to those countries which have relatively undeveloped forest lands. In these tasks it can expect the aid of other nations having advanced forestry programs.

The United States had in 1960 forestry missions operative under the Agency for International Development in many lands. Primitive forestry organizations have been built up and made highly effective. Missions were active in a number of countries to improve forestry schools, research institutes, and public forestry agencies. The United States also was furnishing a major source of support to the Food and Agriculture Organization, which had technical forestry missions in many lands. Several United States foresters were serving on such missions. Probably up to 100 American foresters and forest-products specialists were serving abroad in some technical capacity in 1960. The objective of both AID and FAO missions was to build up schools and services in cooperating countries so that each nation could become technically self-sufficient or nearly so.

World Forestry Organizations

World forestry organizations in 1961 were chiefly associated with the Forestry Division of the Food and Agriculture Organization of the United Nations, which is known internationally by its initials, FAO.

The FAO grew out of the Hot Springs Conference held in 1943 and became the first international agency of the United Nations group. Forestry was early conceived to be an important function of FAO. An interim-commission report published April 25, 1945, contains a good summary of early attempts at international cooperation in forestry.

The Forestry Division was formed early in 1946 with Marcel Leloup as Director; S. B. Show, Chief of the Division of Forest Management; and Egon Glesinger, Chief of the Division of Forest Products. One of its first tasks was to publish a report entitled "Forestry and Forest Products —World Situation, 1937–1946," Stockholm, 1946. This organization, which has received modest support from the United Nations, has performed many valuable functions in helping nations to appraise their forest situation. It has sponsored several international meetings concerned with forestry. It publishes, bimonthly, *Unasylva,* in which forest conditions in various parts of the world are described and world summaries of forest conditions are set forth. It also issues other technical reports.

FAO has established seven regional forestry commissions with appropriate branch headquarters that include all member countries. These commissions hold regional meetings and stimulate regional studies on forest resources and forestry problems.

The International Union of Forest Research Organizations, founded in 1893, has been concerned primarily with technical problems in forestry. These include the preparation of an international forest bibliography, standardization of permanent sample plot technique, international studies of tree races and tree seed, and an international timber-testing program. Its most comprehensive project in 1961 was the standardization of concepts and terminology in forestry and the preparation of a multilingual dictionary of forestry terms. It also sponsors important collaboration in research in many branches of forestry.

Other international organizations in forestry functioning in 1961 on a regional basis include the Commonwealth Forestry Institute (United Kingdom); the Pan-American Union, Division of Agriculture and Conservation; Northern Forestry Union (Denmark, Sweden, Norway, and Finland); Pacific Science Association, Forestry Committee; Institute for International Collaboration in Agriculture and Forestry (Russia, Czechoslovakia, Poland, Yugoslavia, Bulgaria); Caribbean Research Council, Committee on Forestry.

A major force in international forestry is the world forestry congresses. The first met in Rome in 1926, the second in Budapest in 1936, the third in Helsinki in 1949, the fourth in Dehra Dun, India, in 1954, and the fifth in Seattle in 1960. The congresses furnish a forum for expression of technical opinion. They deal with both technologic and policy issues, and they promote interchange of information, personnel, and techniques among the several nations. They also set certain standards of practice and goals for collaboration and improvement.

One of the features of the world forestry congresses is a report on the current progress in forestry in the several regions of the world. The growing interest in these congresses and scope of material included in the programs are evidence of the enlarging sphere of forestry activities. The first congress, at Rome, met in a single section. Two sections were organized at Budapest, three at Helsinki, five at Dehra Dun, and ten at Seattle. The sections meeting at Seattle were:

>Silviculture and Management
>Genetics and Forest Tree Improvement
>Forest Protection
>Forest Economics and Policy
>Education in Forestry
>Forest Products and Utilization
>Forest and Range Watersheds
>Forest Recreation and Wildlife
>Logging and Forest Operations
>Tropical Forestry

The total attendance was about 1,900, making this congress the largest of any forestry gathering held prior to 1960. Members from outside the United States numbered in excess of 800. The two preceding congresses, the third and fourth, had less than 500 members each. A total of 71 nations were represented and 65 sent official delegations. The spirit was high throughout the congress because of the high quality of the discussions and the fact that almost all nations had important progress to report. One cannot participate in such congresses without becoming imbued with the enthusiasm they generate for international cooperation and the faith they exude in the growing contribution forests can make to human welfare.

LITERATURE CITED

1. Baker, Richard St. Barbe. 1959. "Green Glory," A. A. Wyn, Inc., New York. 253 pp.
2. Chandraseknar, S. 1959. "China's Population Problems," *Population Review*, 3(2):3–28.
3. Craig, George A. 1960. "Forestry's Space Age Future—Flying or Falling—" *Journal of Forestry*, 58:93–98.
4. Din, U Aung. 1962. "Forestry Progress in the Far East," *Proceedings, Fifth World Forestry Congress*, Seattle, 1960, Vol. I, published by the Executive Committee of the Congress, Washington, pp. 223–228.
5. Gill, Tom. 1951. "Land Hunger in Mexico," The Charles Lathrop Pack Forestry Foundation, Washington, D.C. 86 pp.
6. Glesinger, Egon. 1962. "The Role of Forestry in World Economic Development," *Proceedings, Fifth World Forestry Congress*, Seattle, 1960,

Vol. I, published by the Executive Committee of the Congress, Washington, pp. 191–195.

7. Harrison, J. D. B. 1962. "Progress in Forestry in North America," *Proceedings, Fifth World Forestry Congress,* Seattle, 1960, Vol. I, published by the Executive Committee of the Congress, Washington, pp. 233–239.
8. Golenpaul, Dan, ed. 1959. "Information Please Almanac—1960," McGraw-Hill Book Company, Inc., New York.
9. Jungo, Josef. 1962. "Evolution de la Foresterie en Europe occidentale et meridionale depuis 1954," *Proceedings, Fifth World Forestry Congress,* Seattle, 1960, Vol. I, published by the Executive Committee of the Congress, Washington, pp. 205–210.
10. Kalkkinen, Eero. 1962. "Forestry Progress in Latin America," *Proceedings, Fifth World Forestry Congress,* Seattle, 1960, Vol. I, published by the Executive Committee of the Congress, Washington, pp. 229–232.
11. Osborn, Fairfield. 1958. "Our Plundered Planet," Little, Brown and Company, Boston. 217 pp.
12. Sax, Karl. 1955. "Standing Room Only," Beacon Press, Boston. 206 pp.
13. Sears, Paul B. 1935. "Deserts on the March," University of Oklahoma Press, Norman, Okla. 231 pp.
14. Shawki, M. K. 1962. "Forestry Progress in the Near East," *Proceedings, Fifth World Forestry Congress,* Seattle, 1960, Vol. I, published by the Executive Committee of the Congress, Washington, pp. 216–219.
15. Singhania, Sir Pandampat. 1957. "Population Growth and Indian Economy: A Projected Prospective," *Population Review,* 1(2):17–20.
16. Streyffert, Thorsten. 1958. "World Timber—Trends and Prospects," Almquist & Wiksells, Stockholm, Sweden. 246 pp.
17. Thompson, Warren S. 1958. "Plenty of People," The Ronald Press Company, New York. 281 pp.
18. Tseplyayev, V. P. 1962. "Forestry Development in the U.S.S.R.," *Proceedings, Fifth World Forestry Congress,* Seattle, 1960, Vol. I, published by the Executive Committee of the Congress, Washington, pp. 210–215.
19. United Nations, Food and Agriculture Organization Staff. 1960. "The World's Forest Resources," *Unasylva,* 14:131–150.
20. Vogt, William. 1958. "Road to Survival," William Sloane Associates, New York. 335 pp.
21. Watterson, G. G. 1962. "Forestry Progress in Africa," *Proceedings, Fifth World Forestry Congress,* Seattle, 1960, Vol. I, published by the Executive Committee of the Congress, Washington, pp. 219–223.
22. Zaremba, Joseph. 1961. "Family Income and Wood Consumption," *Journal of Forestry,* 59(6):443–445, 448.
23. Zaremba, Joseph. 1961. "Softwood Lumber Markets and Southern Forestry," *Journal of Forestry,* 59(5):360–362.
24. Zaremba, Joseph. 1960. "The Vanishing Lumber Market for House Exteriors," *Forest Products Journal,* 10(12):642–643.

CHAPTER 18. *Current Programs*

FORESTRY OPERATIONS were being conducted in 1961 by federal agencies, state agencies, county and local government agencies, quasi-public bodies, corporations, and individuals.

Federal Programs

Federal agencies engage in forest land management, research, and cooperative effort with states and industries to protect forests and improve the use of forest land and products.

National Forests. The largest single forest program in the United States is that on the national forests. In 1960 these totaled 151 separate forests. The total area was approximately 181 million acres. National forests were found in 39 states, and two other states had national-forest purchase units.

Idaho, Alaska, and California had from 20 to 22.5 million acres each in national forests. Others with large areas in national forests were: Montana, 17 million acres; Oregon, 15 million; Colorado, 14 million. Minnesota and Michigan led eastern states with 2.8 and 2.6 million, respectively.[18] Of the total national forest area only 84.8 million acres are classed as commercial timberland.[16] National forests were reported to contain 765 billion board feet of timber as of 1953, over one-third of the total live volume in trees of sawtimber size.

National forests are managed on the principle of multiple use under the general directive set forth by Secretary of Agriculture Wilson in 1905[7] (see Chap. 3). In 1960 the Multiple Use–Sustained Yield Law was enacted by Congress. This provides in Section 2:

The Secretary of Agriculture is authorized and directed to develop and administer the renewable surface resources of the national forests for multiple use and sustained yield of the several products and services obtained therefrom. In the administration of the national forests due consideration shall be given to the relative values of the various resources in particular areas. The establishment and maintenance of areas of wilderness are consistent with the purposes and provisions of this Act.

303

The Service maintains high standards of fire control on the national forests.[15] The area burned annually has averaged about 0.1 per cent of the total area protected. Control is also exercised over insect pests and disease.

The national forests are important sources of water for irrigating arid regions of the West. Attention is given to managing forests for both water yield and flood protection. The national forests provide range for some 1.14 million cattle and horses and 2.0 million sheep. Cooperation between livestock permittees and the U.S. Forest Service has gone a long way toward restoring depleted ranges and bringing use in line with long-term productivity.

The same cannot yet be said of national forest recreation areas that were sorely taxed by some 102 million recreational visits in 1961. "Operation Outdoors" was launched in 1957 as a special five-year program to expand and improve national forest recreation areas. The Service has been giving increased study to how it can best handle the rapidly growing recreational use of national forests.[18] To help meet recreational demands the Forest Service has issued 58,000 permits covering use of 3.5 million acres. Permits covered 500 resorts, 154 winter sports areas, and 19,000 summer homes in 1960.[18] Some 14.7 million acres in 83 separate areas have been designated as primitive areas to preserve wilderness conditions.

The national forests are estimated to support about one-third of the country's big-game animals and one-fourth of its wild turkeys. Other game species also occur. It is estimated that the national forests received 7.6 million visits by hunters and 14.5 million visits by fishermen in 1960.[18] The hunter take in 1960 included 659,000 big-game animals and 10,000 turkeys.

Most important from the economic viewpoint is the timber harvested from the national forests. In 1905 this was only 68.5 million board feet. By 1945 this had increased to 3.4 billion board feet; by 1955, to 6.3 billion; and by 1960, to 9.4 billion.[18] The revenue from timber sales had increased even more rapidly and in 1960 was $140 million. The amount of timber to be removed is regulated so as not to exceed the sustained-annual-yield capacity, the 1960 cut being an average of 110 board feet per acre for the commercial forest area. The sustainable annual cut is gradually being increased by applying intensive silviculture, planting up nonproductive lands, and increasing accessibility through extension of roads.[2] Total receipts from all national forest resources have closely paralleled receipts from timber, the largest item. In 1960 receipts from timber were $139.9 million; from grazing, $3.7 million; and from all other sources, $2.8 million. All receipts are deposited in the United States Treasury. The law provides that 25 per cent of these receipts be turned over to the states in which the national forests are located. The state apportions this to the counties on the basis of their national forest area, and the money is used for county purposes. The law also requires the Forest Service to expend an additional 10 per cent of receipts on roads and trails on national forests located within the state from which receipts came.

The U.S. Forest Service in 1959 developed the "Program for the National Forests." [17] This included both short- and long-range development plans for protection and use of the forest resource. This program included increased research along with steps needed to effect full development of timber, water, forage, wildlife, and recreational resources.

Department of the Interior. The early concept of government custodianship of the public domain was to convert it into revenue for government support. This task was assigned to the "General Land Office" that was made a part of the Department of the Interior when the latter was organized. After most of the agricultural land had been disposed of under the homestead and related laws and the forest reserves had been transferred to the Department of Agriculture and renamed national forests, the Department of the Interior still had jurisdiction over some 622 million acres, mostly in the western states and Alaska. This included large areas of grazing and timberlands. In 1946 these lands were placed under the jurisdiction of the newly created Bureau of Land Management, which took over the functions of the Grazing Service and General Land Office. [2]

BUREAU OF LAND MANAGEMENT. The major forest lands administered by the Bureau of Land Management are the O & C lands and the interior forests of Alaska. The Oregon grants (O & C lands) are lands that reverted to the government when the Oregon and California Railroad and the Coos Bay Wagon Road grants were revested in the federal government through failure of the respective companies to fulfill their contracts. These lands, administered by the Bureau of Land Management, include approximately 2.1 million acres and contain 50 billion board feet of merchantable timber. Because of the policy of granting alternate sections of land to railroads, many of the O & C lands are intermingled with national forest lands and private timber holdings.

Congress in 1937 enacted legislation providing for administration of the O & C lands. The 1937 law provided for cooperation between government and private landowners to operate their combined lands on a sustained-yield basis. This principle was restated and extended in the Sustained Yield Units Act of 1944.

The allowable sustained-yield cut from these lands is 874 million board feet. In the fiscal year 1960, sufficient dead timber and thinnings were harvested to bring the total cut up to 1 billion board feet that brought a gross income of $34.3 million.

The O & C law requires that 50 per cent of gross receipts be paid to counties in lieu of taxes and an additional 25 per cent be set aside to reimburse the counties for taxes accumulated before the O & C law was enacted. The checkerboard pattern of O & C, national forest, and private lands greatly complicates administration. Despite these complications public officers on the ground have sought to divide responsibilities so as to minimize overlapping jurisdiction.

ALASKAN TIMBERLANDS. The Bureau of Land Management is responsible for managing some 125 million acres of forest land in Alaska. About 40 million acres have timber comparable in size and quality to commercial timber in other parts of the United States.[12] The interior forests contain white spruce, Alaska white birch, cottonwood, willow, and tamarack. These forests are drawn upon by the local population for fuel, lumber, poles, and other products. In the past, fires set to drive mosquitoes from camp, or for other reasons, burned unchecked. Even in 1947 the area burned was estimated to exceed 1 million acres.[9] Organized protection was begun in 1939. Sales of timber, largely for local use, in 1949 totaled 9.7 million board feet, valued at $27,099. In 1960 sales were 14.7 million board feet, valued at $61,447.

The Alaska Statehood Act permits the state to select 103 million acres from the unreserved public-domain lands. It is expected that the state will include the better timberlands in its selection.

INDIAN FORESTS. The Department of the Interior serves as federal trustee officer over Indian lands. This authority is exercised through various treaties and executive orders. It was expected that these trusteeships would be terminated as the Indians developed the capacity to take care of their interests in a private-enterprise economy. Logging operations under the Bureau of Indian Affairs began about 1890 and have continued since that time. The Indian Reorganization Act of 1934 laid the foundation for Indian participation in the management of reservation timber. It also provided that cutting on federally controlled Indian lands be conducted on the principle of sustained yield. Indians have been encouraged to develop self-sustaining communities and industries. Tribal-owned sawmills have been established and operated by the Menominee, Red Lake, and Navajo tribes.[2]

Reservations having large stumpage holdings include Klamath and Colville with 4 billion board feet each; Warm Springs and Yakima, 3.5 billion each; and Tahola, 2.9 billion. In 1960 the total cut from Indian lands was 595 million board feet, bringing in cash revenues of $12.25 million.[12]

The Klamath Termination Act of 1954 and as amended in 1958 and 1959 provides for the sale of the Klamath Indian Reservation and termination of Bureau of Indian Affairs' responsibilities over this land. One sustained-yield timber unit of 91.5 thousand acres was sold in 1960. Ten other units were transferred in 1961 to the Department of Agriculture but not sold. Further efforts are being made to dispose of the land. Federal supervision of the affairs of the Menominee Indian terminated in 1961. Similar terminal proceedings were under way in 1960 for the Colville, Catawba, and Choctaw reservations.[12]

NATIONAL PARKS. The national parks, totaling some 24 million acres, have 8 million acres of forest and woodland. These include heavy timber stands, which, however, are permanently protected as examples of unmodified natural areas. Timber cutting and grazing of domestic livestock are excluded except from lands acquired with this right reserved for the owner's life.

WILDLIFE REFUGES. The Fish and Wildlife Service has jurisdiction over 261 wildlife refuges, aggregating some 17 million acres.[10] These include migratory-waterfowl refuges, colonial nongame bird refuges, big-game refuges, general refuges, and refuges for special research. Game is protected on the refuges. Controlled public hunting and trapping is being introduced on some refuges as a part of the management program. Refuges include some 2 million acres of forest land, which is managed in the interest of the wildlife. Returns to counties in lieu of taxes are 25 per cent of gross receipts from sale of surplus products.

The Tennessee Valley Authority. The Tennessee Valley Authority has a Division of Forestry Relations. Since more than 54 per cent of the Tennessee watershed is wooded, forestry plays an important role in the overall program of the Authority. Consequently, the utilization of timber, control of forest fires, reforestation, and forest land management are encouraged by the TVA. The agency itself has a considerable area of forest land around the reservoirs, for which the Forestry Division is directly responsible. It operates two forest nurseries and carries on research in forestry and forest utilization. Special effort is made, through cooperation with existing extension agencies and farm foresters, to promote forestry among all landowners of the Tennessee Valley.

Other federal agencies own and may manage forest land incidental to their main task. Those holding and managing large areas include the Department of the Army, 1,350,000 acres; the Department of the Navy and Marine Corps, 250,000 acres; and the Atomic Energy Commission, 75,000 acres. The total contribution to the nation's timber supply from forest operations on these lands is modest, but locally they do improve the forest land and the economy.[2]

Federal Cooperative Programs. Federal cooperative and other research programs will be dealt with in Chap. 22. Federal cooperative programs with the states will be dealt with under state programs.

The U.S. Forest Service has a Division of State and Private Forestry authorized to cooperate with private timberland owners in promoting

better forestry. The major portion of the work of this division is channeled through the state foresters. Upon request the Forest Service does
render expert service to large forest landowners. This usually takes the
form of advice on location of plants; special suggestions on management
programs and policies; help on special forest-survey tasks; and distribution of new information on mechanized logging, sawmill operation, lumber seasoning, waste use, and other problems in which specialists in the
Forest Service can render unique help to industry. The Service prepares
various informational bulletins.

The federal government has supplied direct aid to farmers through
a variety of programs aimed at reducing surplus agricultural production
and conserving soil, water, wildlife, and forests. In 1961 substantial payments could be had by farmers through placing a portion of their lands
under the Conservation Reserve (Soil Bank) program, the latest of such
programs up to 1961. This program by 1960 had encouraged tree planting
on some 2 million acres of farmlands, with payments in some cases sufficient to cover direct outlays by the farmer. The following agencies of
the U.S. Department of Agriculture were participating in farm forest
programs in 1961: The Soil Conservation Service, the Agricultural Conservation program, the Farm Home Administration, the Federal-State
Cooperative Extension Service program, and the state and private cooperative forestry programs handled through the U.S. Forest Service and
the state foresters. The Fish and Wildlife Service of the Department of
the Interior has sponsored financially the planting of game food and cover
plants by farmers.

State Forestry Programs

State foresters or comparable officials were employed by 49 of the
50 states in 1961. Arizona, the one state without a state forester, had
most of its forest land in federal ownership and management.

The Association of State Foresters made a survey in 1961 of the current programs in state forestry.[8] Forty-nine of the fifty states had at least
some forestry programs. The total of all expenditures was $111 million,
of which $60 million was spent for fire control. The states administered
33 million acres of public forest land and received income of $26 million
from sale of seedlings, stumpage, and miscellaneous products. The states
employed a total of 11,819 people, of whom 1,817 were graduate foresters.
The formal merit system had been established by statute in 28 states,
and 43 had retirement programs. The states made total appropriations
of $65,734,000 for forestry purposes and received from county and private
owners $13 million and from federal agencies an additional $13 million.

States leading in forestry activities in 1961 are listed in Table 16.
Twenty-eight of the states had expenditures of over a million dollars.

TABLE 16. STATES LEADING IN FORESTRY ACTIVITIES IN 1961

State	Total expenditures, dollars	Forest land administered, acres	Graduate foresters employed
California.......	24,780,000	30,000	95
Oregon..........	7,804,000	769,000	120
Pennsylvania....	6,450,000	1,878,000	110
Wisconsin.......	6,065,000	2,568,000	118
Washington.....	5,942,000	2,000,000	157
New York.......	5,382,000	3,100,000	79
Florida.........	5,041,000	300,000	72
Georgia.........	4,843,000	36,000	71
Michigan.......	3,200,000	3,700,000	62
Minnesota.......	2,463,000	4,890,000	40
Texas..........	1,760,000	4,200,000	26

The states leading all others in public land administered were: Minnesota, 4,890,000 acres; Texas, 4,200,000 acres; and Michigan, 3,700,000 acres.

State forestry organizations manage state-owned forest lands; provide fire control on forest lands throughout the state (except on national forests and parks); administer timber management, marketing, and processing programs under the Cooperative Forest Management Act; conduct forest research; operate a forest-land purchasing program; operate nurseries; provide planting stock for state lands and for private forest landowners; conduct important control operations against destructive forest insects and tree diseases; carry on educational programs to stimulate interest by the public in better forestry, particularly in the prevention of forest fires; and in a number of states regulate timber-cutting practices on private lands.

Under the Clarke-McNary Act the states receive federal aid in fire control, distribution of planting stock, and extension forestry. They receive help in farm forestry and other programs under the Cooperative Forest Management Act (Fig. 64). The cooperative programs are under the general guidance of the U.S. Forest Service, but states have wide latitude in administration.

The four major state forestry activities are fire control, management of state forests, service to timberland owners and wood processors, and regulation of forest practice on private lands.

The most costly task was fire prevention, detection, and control, which required $60 million in 1961. The area provided protection in 1945 was

Fig. 64   A Maine farmer uses his field tractor to skid white pine logs to a landing. Farmer logging was little practiced by commercial farm operators in 1962. (*U.S. Forest Service photo.*)

303 million acres; in 1950, 360 million; in 1955, 387 million; and in 1960, 403 million. In 1960 approximately 97 per cent of all forest land was covered by organized protection. The effectiveness of the program can be measured in part by the decline in area of land burned each year. Total area burned by years was: 1945, 17.2 million acres; 1950, 15.1 million; 1955, 7.4 million; and 1960, 3.9 million.[18]

State foresters administered a total of 32,664,000 acres of land in 1961.[8] These lands were managed for timber production, recreation, public hunting grounds, and watershed protection.

Income from state-managed forest lands for the fiscal year 1960 was substantial in some states—Michigan, $1,448,000; Montana, $398,000; Idaho for two years, $4,295,000. Timber sales accounted for about 80 per cent of the forestry income for Montana and Idaho.*

Activities under the Cooperative Forest Management Act may be appreciated by examination of the program of New Jersey [11] (Fig. 65). Owners desiring help to sell timber sign a contract with a state forest

* See reports of the respective state conservation departments for the year 1960.

F<small>IG</small>. 65 A farm forester instructing a Wisconsin farmer's son in proper log bucking with a chain saw. (*U.S. Forest Service photo.*)

officer in which they agree to carry out a forestry program. The state estimates the timber, marks the trees to be cut, and refers the owner to timber agents. The timber agent, for a fee equal to 10 per cent of the stumpage value, makes a sale contract with a timber operator, supervises the sale, collects the money, and reports to the owner, accounting for each tree cut. If the owner violates the timber agreement by cutting unmarked trees within one year of the date of agreement, he is obliged to pay the state $3 per thousand board feet for all trees marked. The cooperative program began in 1938. In 1961 about one-third of the timber cut in the state was handled under the program.*

By 1955 seventeen states had undertaken to regulate cutting practices on private lands. Maryland has forestry boards to regulate cutting practices and to license timber operators. These boards also set up minimum forest-practice standards for their counties. Washington and Oregon have minimum cutting practices specified by law. Owners must obtain the

* Personal communication from George R. Moorhead, Chief, Forest Management Section, Department of Conservation and Economic Development, State of New Jersey, 1962.

state forester's approval of cutting practices that depart from these standard minima. Oregon may require a performance bond of owners not following approved practice to ensure that the owner will reforest his land either naturally or by planting. Maryland and Washington laws have been tested and upheld in the courts. California has a law similar to Maryland's with two important exceptions: Forest practices are determined by committees and approved by vote of owners holding two-thirds of the land. The state forester is empowered to require compliance with these rules. Diameter-limit cuttings have been established in Idaho, Minnesota, and Nevada. Seed trees must be left in Louisiana, Minnesota, Mississippi, and Virginia. Massachusetts requires that owners notify the state of their intent to cut timber; and the state forester then makes a plan for cutting, which the owner is encouraged, but not obliged, to follow. New York provides technical advice and assistance in marketing timber to forest owners who agree to follow the standards set by forest-practice boards. Cooperators under the Forest Practice Act are also provided at modest cost trees for planting open lands (Fig. 66). No penalties other than withdrawal of future state aid are attached to the New York State law. Missouri lowers taxes for those who follow approved cutting practices. Colorado has a board authorized to regulate cutting practices.

It has long been recognized that an annual ad valorem assessment of

Fig. 66 An abandoned farm on Class II land in New York. This farm has neither been incorporated in adjoining farms nor planted to trees. Class II land is unsuited for full-time commercial farming.

taxes against a forest crop that can be sold only at intervals of decades tends to be confiscatory. To avoid this, 30 states had by 1960 enacted special forest tax laws. About half these laws provide for a special yield tax at time of harvest.[2] Many require of the owner certain minimum forest practices to be eligible for special tax treatment.

Colleges of Forestry

Colleges of forestry and universities with forestry departments manage college properties for research, demonstration, and education in forestry. They carry out important research in all phases of forestry and forest products. Many, either directly or through the state agricultural extension service, engage in spreading forestry knowledge among landowners, school children, and the general public. Extension forestry will be covered in Chap. 21.

County and Community Forests in the United States

Community forests have been established in 40 states. Those leading in numbers and total areas are:

State	No. of forests	Total area, acres
Wisconsin.............	359	2,212,000
Minnesota.............	87	869,000
New York.............	725	180,000
Michigan.............	883	173,000
Thirty-six other states....	1,577	992,000
Total United States....	3,631	4,426,000

Of the total area, counties and townships owned 3,414,000 acres; municipalities, 795,000 acres; schools, 163,000 acres; and organizations, 44,000 acres.[10]

Almost a third of the municipal forests are held for watersheds. These generally are restricted in the use the public can make of them, since recreational use is usually deemed to be inconsistent with maintaining a sanitary water supply. Watershed forests may be cut for timber production, if care is taken to avoid creating conditions conducive to erosion and pollution.

School forests provide recreation for school children. More important, they serve as a center for instruction in biology and in manual arts. Imaginative teachers have even used school forests as an aid in instructing the students in music and in mathematics. In some cases school forests have brought the schools revenue that has been used for special projects. They may stimulate in pupils a practical interest in forestry and conservation.

Organizations, with Boy Scouts perhaps leading, have a total of some 96 forests. Some of these yield substantial revenue from timber operations and provide campgrounds and places for other scouting activities.

Most communities permit free public recreational use of their forests, but charges may be made for special services. On some forests special recreational buildings may be rented at nominal fees by organizations desiring exclusive use for picnics. Fees for fuel wood, parking, and other use of the county property are sometimes levied, providing money that helps to offset operating expenses.

County forests in Wisconsin and Minnesota are much more than recreational areas. These were established by the counties as a means of rehabilitating abandoned cutover land that was tax-delinquent. Under the Wisconsin laws the state was willing to pay to the counties in lieu of taxes 10 cents per acre annually to help support local government. The state provided an additional 10 cents per acre annually to cover expenses of improving and developing the forest. When the forests are harvested, the state recaptures at least a part of its investment through a 50 per cent severance tax. The annual return from Wisconsin's county forests was $150,000 in 1948. Because of the heavy demand for pulpwood in this region, it is to be expected that the revenue will increase very rapidly within the next few years.

Foresters are employed by many counties and communities. They are especially needed by communities with municipal forested watersheds of large areas and by cities, such as Chicago, that operate extensive forest preserves.[4, 5]

Industry and Other Private Forest Programs

The Group Programs. The American Forest Products Industries (AFPI) [1, 5, 6, 14] sponsors the voluntary tree-farm program. It cooperates with the several states to publicize and certify tree farms. A tree farm is an area of forest land which the owner pledges to operate for permanent timber crops. Standards of fire control, protection from grazing, and forest practice are required. Both standards and inspection for compliance vary from state to state. Independent appraisal finds results good. The movement began in 1941 and by 1962 embraced over 59 million acres of forest land in 47 states.

Certain forest industries in the East, South, Central, and Lake States have encouraged owners to join "Tree Farm Families." The industry provides technical service in return for first bid on any timber to be sold. The owner benefits from both the technical service and a priority market when he wishes to make a sale.

Linked with the tree farm movement, the "Busy Acres" program seeks to educate owners in the beginning steps of forest management.

The AFPI has a widespread educational program for public schools and other agencies. It sponsors the Keep America Green movement channeled through state Keep Green committees. The AFPI also sponsors the More Trees programs. The AFPI is supported by lumber, plywood, pulp, and paper companies and by timberland owners.

The West Coast Lumbermen's Association and the Northwest Logging Congress have long actively promoted industrial forestry. The American Turpentine Farmers Association has had an active program of forest conservation since 1936. It has been particularly effective in stimulating research and in spreading good turpentining practices among its membership and others engaged in naval-stores operations.

Various other private associations are engaged in stimulating good forest practice on forest lands throughout the country. The Southern Pulpwood Conservation Association carries on a campaign to promote good forest practices by member mills and by owners who sell pulpwood to these mills. The Western Pine Association has long aided in fire-control programs and conducted research in forest products. It also has taken leadership in insect control and forest management.

A group of pulp and paper companies in Wisconsin sponsors the Trees for Tomorrow program. They hold conservation camps for school children, distribute tree-planting stock, encourage good forest practice on farm woodlands, and in other ways try to improve the care of woodlands in the state.

Other important groups and associations sponsoring forest programs include the American Forestry Association, American Bankers Association, Chamber of Commerce of the United States, Junior Chamber of Commerce of the United States, Friends of the Land, Izaak Walton League of America, American Paper and Pulp Association, state forestry associations, and a number of other regional and national associations. As of 1949 it was estimated that well over 1,000 organizations were interested in our forests. These include 200 trade associations of the wood-products industries, a large number of sportsmen's organizations, farmer associations, park associations, outdoor-recreation groups, fire-protective associations, bird clubs, Boy Scouts of America, 4-H Clubs and Future Farmers of America, American Legion posts, labor unions, garden clubs, and many others. These have done effective work in forwarding forest conservation.[6]

Individual Industry Programs. The activities of individual companies are equally impressive. Some 20 or more railway companies employ foresters to encourage good forestry in the regions they serve, realizing that what adds wealth to their territory will bring traffic to their road.

The programs of the Illinois Central and Seaboard Air Line railroads have been particularly impressive. The latter features a conservation train and includes movies, talks, demonstrations, field days, and other promotional activities.[3]

Power companies and many of the pulp and paper companies have similar programs. Of special note is the policy followed by several pulp and paper companies of supplying technical forestry service to farmers and other owners of small forest properties.

Industrial forestry has made enormous progress since 1945. Before this time industrial programs were the exception rather than the rule among large corporations. By 1962 large pulp and paper and land-owning lumber companies were conspicuous if they did not have a forestry program. In fact, by 1962 one looked to the industrial forest holdings for examples of the most advanced practice. Specific accomplishments included the operation of 34 forest nurseries producing 259 million seedlings annually; the planting of a total of 3.5 million acres during the decade 1951–1960; and the direct seeding of 80,000 acres in the year 1960.[1] Companies, both individually and through organizations, were also actively promoting forest research in such fields as genetics and forest tree improvement, tree physiology, forest soils and tree nutrition, insect and disease control, wood structure and properties, wood preservation, use of low-quality wood and of sawmill residues, pulping techniques, and paper manufacture. In southern states companies were paying up to $40 per acre for lands to be planted to trees. Many company lands that had grown up to brush and low-quality hardwoods were being cleared by heavy machinery in preparation for planting.

Pulp and paper companies were also practicing integrated utilization, by selecting good sawlogs and veneer logs for sale, and, in turn, were purchasing chips made at sawmills from slabs and edgings. Of particular significance has been the advance in hardwood pulping that has resulted from research on the semichemical and related processes. This has made possible use of materials heretofore of little value and has greatly increased the reserve of pulpwood timber available to supply the mills.

As of 1961 research and advanced practice in lumber manufacture and wood processing had failed seriously to keep pace with that in pulp and paper technology. However, the veneer and plywood industry was sponsoring research, and lumber companies on the West Coast were seeking uses for wood infected with white pocket rot and were performing other research on lumber use. One company engaged in secondary manufacture has made enormous strides in improving its machining processes as to both precision and efficiency. These steps point the way for others in the field. A variety of new products and newly designed old products of wood are appearing on the market. In the field of wood processing and design, however, only a bare beginning has been made compared with the potential that could be realized through creative research and imaginative application of technology to design of furniture and other consumer products.

By 1962 almost half the foresters, wood technologists, and wood chemists were employed by private industry, and the need for additional men continued. Excellent cooperation existed between timber operators and state forest marketing services such as prevail under the cooperative forest-management and other programs. Industry as well as government can justly view its forestry programs with pride in tangible accomplishment.

Practice in the Forest

The foregoing discussion has dwelt mainly on current programs as viewed in the front offices of federal, state, and corporate forestry agencies. It is equally important to examine forest practice on the land (Fig. 67). The discussion which follows is based largely on the facts and opinions presented in the U.S. Forest Service publication of 1958,

FIG. 67   A farm forester inspects with the owner a thinning operation in a northern hardwood farm woodland in New York. (*U.S. Forest Service photo.*)

"Timber Resources for America's Future," and on the author's interpretation of these facts and judgment of the opinions.

In Chap. 17 it was brought out that the area of commercial forest land has shown relative stability since 1933; that the decline in gross timber volume that had gone on for over three centuries seemed to be arrested if not in fact reversed; that quality of timber was still declining though foresters were seeking also to reverse this trend; and that the decline in use of lumber seemed also to have reached a low point in the 1930s and to have been reversed. The Forest Service report contains an abundance of additional facts necessary for a current appraisal, some of which give little cause for satisfaction.

Distribution of commercial forest land and standing timber shows a pronounced imbalance (Table 17). One-fourth of the commercial forest

TABLE 17. DISTRIBUTION OF FOREST LAND AND TIMBER VOLUMES BY
MAJOR FOREST REGIONS

Region of the United States	Commercial forest land		Sawtimber volume	
	Million acres	Per cent of total	Billion bd. ft.	Per cent of total
North..........................	174	36	266	13
South..........................	193	39	357	17
West...........................	121	25	1,434	70
Total United States.............	488	100	2,057	100

land supports 70 per cent of the sawtimber volume. Understocking of forest land is serious in the East, and nationwide 26 per cent of the commercial forest land is less than 40 per cent stocked. Only 46 per cent is 70 per cent stocked or better.

A similar imbalance occurs with respect to timber cut and timber growth. Western forests provide 46 per cent of the annual cut but only 24 per cent of the growth. The South is responsible for almost half the timber growth.

Timber growth is increasing and exceeds cut, but the excess is in eastern and southern hardwoods. Low-grade and cull trees make up 74 per cent of the eastern and southern hardwood timber. This means that nationwide timber quality is declining, as cut comes mainly from old-growth western softwoods of high quality, and growth surplus is mostly on eastern hardwoods of low quality.

Timber use is concentrated on a few groups of species while others remain underutilized. Douglas-fir provides 24 per cent of the cut but only 9 per cent of the growth. Oaks provide 10 per cent of the cut and 15 per cent of the growth.

Recent cutting practices on farm and nonindustrial private forests that make up 60 per cent of total commercial forests have left less than half the cutover lands in the upper productivity class, whereas almost 80 per cent of recently cut lands of public and industrial owners is in the upper productivity class. This focuses attention on the small forest landowners as those whose practice is most in need of improvement (Table 18).

TABLE 18. OWNERSHIP OF COMMERCIAL FOREST LAND AND PRODUCTIVITY OF RECENTLY CUT AREAS

Owner class	Areas owned		Volume owned		Proportion in upper productivity class, per cent
	Million acres	Per cent of total	Billion bd. ft.	Per cent of total	
Farm................	165	34	308	15	41
Other private........	131	26	772	37	52
Forest industries.....	62	13			77
National forest......	85	17	766	37	
Other federal	18	6	135	7	80
State and local......	27	4	76	4	
All ownerships.....	488	100	2,057	100	65

Losses of timber from various causes are high. One-fourth of the timber cut becomes logging and plant residues that are unutilized. Chipping of slabs and edgings for pulp manufacture is helping to reduce these residues, but much further progress would appear to be both possible and feasible.

Insects, diseases, fire, weather, and other destructive agents cause an annual mortality of 12.7 billion board feet of timber. Even more serious is their impact on growth through death or injury to seedlings and saplings. This is estimated to be the equivalent of 31.1 billion board feet annually. The two losses together almost equal the net annual growth. Disease is the chief agent causing impact on growth. Insects are responsible for the heaviest mortality.

Sixty per cent of the commercial forest land is held by farmers and nonindustrial private owners who, as a class, are less able financially, economically, and technically to manage their lands well than are industries and government.

Small size in itself is a severe handicap in making sales, in organizing forest protection and timber-stand improvement, and in obtaining professional service. Stoddard [13] has classed forest holdings of less than 100 acres as distinctly submarginal economic units. Half the forest land owned by farmers is in holdings of 100 acres or less, and one-third of the other private nonindustry holdings are of this size.

Stoddard considers economic opportunities fair on forest holdings of 100 to 500 acres. Farmers hold 59 million and "other private" hold 37 million acres in this size group. Economic opportunities are considered to be moderate on the holding of 500 to 5,000 acres and good on holdings of over 5,000 acres. Approximately 90 million acres fall into this economically good ownership class. It is this last-named size group that offers the best opportunities for acquisition by industries or by those well-financed individuals and corporations who wish to enter timber growing on a commercial basis.

The growth that would be realized if all commercial forest lands in each region were managed as well as the better-managed properties is estimated to be 100 billion board feet, or more than double the current growth.

Summary of Forest Situation in 1961

At the close of the year 1961 the nationwide forestry picture was one of sharp contrasts. The highlights were the intensive management and research programs of a few outstanding industries and industry groups; the generally high-level practice on most forests managed by government and industry; and the leadership taken by the pulp and paper industry in financing research in company laboratories, at the Institute of Paper Chemistry, at schools of paper technology, and in government laboratories. This research has opened up markets for hardwood for pulp manufacture, has greatly increased the variety and serviceability of paper, and has led to a host of new paper products. The industry has also generously financed scholarships to attract able young men to its industry. There is strong evidence that this effort is succeeding.

Pulp and paper companies, because of their size, financial strength, and need for long-term timber supplies, have been leaders among wood-using industries in forest practice on the land. They have also encouraged lumber companies to chip their residues for pulp manufacture.

Perhaps of even greater long-term significance have been the programs of governments in control of fire, insect damage, and disease losses in management of public holdings, in aid to private owners, and especially in education and research. States were supporting 40 of the nation's 43 forestry schools. States and the federal government together were financing practically all the research in wildlife management, range management, watershed management, and recreational use of forests; almost all of that devoted to forest-management research; and a substantial part of that spent on research on wood properties and wood processing, including chemistry of wood and pulp and paper technology.

There were other bright spots in the picture. The increased use of logging and mill residues was bringing more of the timber harvested to the consumer. Logging machinery, particularly that for use in western timber, had been greatly improved in size and function. Research on range management had led to range restoration practices that checked erosion and increased food value for animals. Sportsmen were cooperating with public conservation agencies in research on wildlife and management of game. And nationwide, the people had become concerned over water resources, watershed management and research, pollution abatement, and planning for future supplies.

A new effort that brightened the general picture was the program of the lumber industry to promote better understanding of wood and its use in construction and industry. Opportunities for new design of wood for interior and exterior use seemed unlimited. Certainly exploiting modern technology of wood and its processing by imaginative engineering and by functional and artistic design was still a largely undeveloped possibility.

The shadows in the picture, and some were very deep, were also prominent. The imbalance in distribution between forest land and timber volume and between species growth and growth surplus, as well as the declining quality of growing stock, pointed to painful adjustments in the years ahead. More than that, it seemed evident that the forest-products industries would see even more of their potential market captured by other industries.

The darkest shadow fell on the small forest holdings. Many obstacles confront such owners. Financial stringency is a widespread difficulty. This impels men to cut the forest whenever merchantable products can be removed, even though that may be the very time when trees are growing most rapidly. Where no regular market exists, owners are obliged to sell when operators are in their territory or to defer sales indefinitely. Small properties frequently have so little timber that the operator feels he must cut all an owner has to be justified in negotiating a contract. Individual owners are very much at a disadvantage in bargaining with a timber operator and often must accept his cutting methods or forego a sale. The scattered nature of small ownerships, absentee ownership, failure of owners to pool their holdings into units of manageable size, depletion as a result of past cutting, and high preponderance of cull trees and low-grade species are further difficulties that impede forestry on small holdings. These are also reasons why large companies find such properties uneconomical to acquire.

Such lands for the most part seem destined to remain in small ownership. Furthermore, is it wise to allow most of the forest acreage to drift into the hands of government or large private landholders, thereby eliminating the small owner from the forestry scene? Americans have cherished deeply the thought that our country is a land of opportunity, where the energetic individual can by his own efforts build up an independent enterprise. The opportunities to build up such an enterprise in forestry appear to be relatively good for men with patience and fortitude, proper technical background, practical experience in logging and sale of timber products, and a reasonable amount of backing for capital expenditures.

Some investors, among them professional foresters, have, in fact, been acquiring forest land for long-term timber management. A survey in 1950 indicated that 691 members of the Society of American Foresters owned some 206,000 acres outright and had part ownership of some 2,748,000 acres. Ownership by foresters and their clients has probably increased considerably since then.

Opportunities for expanding such ownership are still good, provided the foresters can procure sufficient capital and are willing to be patient long enough to build up the growing stock on the land they acquire. The difficulty that now confronts such individuals is in finding forest properties that can be operated immediately. Most are so understocked with timber that 15 to 30 years must elapse before any appreciable income can be had from the land.

Looked at in another light the shadows in the picture may be thought of as opportunities for individuals, corporations, and government. If our timber growth is but 50 per cent of what might be expected by applying, generally, practices now in use, here is, indeed, a huge opportunity highlighted by the expectation that our population will increase to need the wood as rapidly as it can be grown.

The Department of Agriculture in January, 1962, announced a new program that, though geared primarily to farmland, also covered the need for meeting the nation's future timber supply. This looked forward to much more intensive management of the national forests so that they might meet in perpetuity at least one-fifth the total timber demands of the nation. This was expected to be achieved with little change in current national forest ownership. The program looked forward to substantial increase in state and private forest cooperation in forestry research and to increased productivity of farm and other small woodlands. Among the proposals under consideration were direct aid to landowners, leasing arrangements, and in some cases purchase for resale in order to build up economic-sized units.

LITERATURE CITED

1. American Forest Products Industries. 1961. "Progress in Private Forestry in the United States," Washington, D.C. 49 pp.
2. Clepper, Henry, and Arthur B. Meyer. 1960. "American Forestry—Six Decades of Growth," Society of American Foresters, Washington, D.C. 319 pp.
3. Craig, James B. 1950. "A Railroad Crusades for Forestry," *American Forests*, 56(2):6–9, 38–39.
4. Duthie, George A. 1949. "Community Forests," *Trees*, The Yearbook of Agriculture, pp. 394–398, U.S. Department of Agriculture, Washington.
5. Gill, Tom, and Ellen C. Dowling, compilers. 1949. "The Forestry Directory," The American Tree Association, Washington, D.C. 420 pp.
6. Gillett, Charles A. 1950. "Citizen and Trade Associations Dealing with Forestry," in Winters, Robert K., ed., "Fifty Years of Forestry in the U.S.A.," pp. 285–298, Society of American Foresters, Washington, D.C.
7. Granger, C. M. 1949. "The People's Property," *Trees*, The Yearbook of Agriculture, pp. 299–304, U.S. Department of Agriculture, Washington.
8. Guernsey, Roger L. 1961. "State Forestry in the United States, 1961," Memorandum to Ralph Wible, President, Association of State Foresters. 5 pp. mim.
9. Heintzleman, B. Frank. 1949. "Forests of Alaska," *Trees*, The Yearbook of Agriculture, pp. 361–372, U.S. Department of Agriculture, Washington.
10. Kauffman, Erle, ed. 1958. "The Conservation Yearbook 1957–1958." Published by Conservation Yearbook, Washington, D.C. 272 pp.
11. Moore, E. B., and A. N. Lentz. 1951. "The Cooperative Forest Management Program in New Jersey," *Journal of Forestry*, 49:31–34.
12. Secretary of the Interior. Annual Reports, 1960 and 1961, Washington. 390 and 471 pp.
13. Stoddard, Charles H. 1958. "The Small Private Forest in the United States," Resources for the Future, Inc., Washington, D.C. 171 pp.
14. Timber Engineering Company. 1944. "The Forest Industries Blaze New Trails," Washington, D.C. 32 pp.
15. U.S. Department of Agriculture, Forest Service. 1946. "The Management Status of Forest Lands in the United States," Report 3, from "A Reappraisal of the Forest Situation," Washington. 29 pp.
16. U.S. Department of Agriculture, Forest Service. 1958. "Timber Resources for America's Future," Forest Resource Report 14, Washington. 713 pp.
17. U.S. Department of Agriculture, Forest Service. 1959. "Program for the National Forests," Washington. 26 pp.
18. U.S. Department of Agriculture, Forest Service. 1961. "Report of the Chief of the Forest Service 1960," Washington. 49 pp.

CHAPTER 19. *Forest Policy*

THE POLICIES GOVERNING use of any major raw material, such as forest products, affect everyone dependent upon the national economy. The nation as a whole needs timber for national defense and to house our growing population. The forest landowner needs a forest program that will stabilize markets for the products from his woodland. Labor is concerned because some 3.3 million workers are directly or indirectly dependent upon the forest industries for their source of employment and forest industries need a dependable wood supply.

The forest policy of a farmer in earlier days might have been quite simple—to use his woodlot for his fuel supply, as a source of fence posts and poles needed about the farm, and as an occasional source of cash income from sale of sawlogs, fuel wood, maple sugar, or other products. The policy of early lumber companies was equally forthright—to harvest logs, saw them into lumber, and sell the lumber.

The policies of the federal government are far more complex. They involve both immediate and long-term timber supply, protection of soil, water, wildlife, forage and recreation resources, and management that will tend to promote stable prosperity to industry, community, and nation.

Announced policies of various groups change with changes in time and economic conditions. The initial establishment of forest reserves caused little controversy, but when the U.S. Forest Service began to control the use of these reserves by stockmen, controversy was bitter. This battle was won by the government but had to be refought in later years to bring grazing use into balance with forage capacity. In the 1930s the depressed condition of the timber market caused the spokesmen for private forest industries to urge withholding public timber from sale so that private owners might have what market there was. Many also were selling their lands to the federal government because taxes and interest made these a heavy financial burden. Some 12 years later industry spokesmen were urging the exact opposite—greatly increased sale of national forest timber because the market was good and stumpage becoming scarce, and halting further expansion of national forest holdings as the industries were expanding their holdings of forest land.

In the 1930s and 1940s the Forest Service was advocating public regulation of private forest practice. In the late 1950s this advocacy was curtailed because large holdings were, on the whole, being well managed, and regulation of the many small holdings of farmers and others posed almost overwhelming administrative difficulties.

Forest Policy Is Controversial

From the foregoing it is evident that public forest policy is controversial. Moreover, this controversy involves our basic concept of human rights to hold and manage property. It also involves resources that must be managed so as to protect the long-term supply for such basic needs as water, shelter, clothing, and food. Opinions on government responsibility for natural resources vary widely. Some maintain that natural resources originally belonged to all the people and that they should be used for the benefit of all, not the profit of a few. At the opposite extreme are those who hold that natural resources should be managed by private individuals and companies with a minimum of government interference. They declare that self-interest will lead the individual owners to develop the resources for the benefit of all citizens and that private management is cheaper and more desirable than public ownership and development. The first theory carried to extremes would lead to nationalization of natural resources; the second to a complete laissez-faire policy. All shades of opinion lie between these two extremes.

Few foresters can escape such controversy. However, the area of agreement among those informed on the forest situation exceeds that of disagreement. All recognize that a far greater forestry effort is needed than is now being exerted. A few hold that existing programs, given ample time for development, will meet our country's forestry needs. Others believe firmly that additional measures must be adopted.

Unattained Forestry Goals

The need for additional effort on existing programs and for new public and private forestry measures can be appreciated by first reviewing goals still to be achieved. These include the following:

To place fire control on a satisfactory basis. Large losses still occur.

To reduce losses from insects and diseases that now, through direct mortality and reduction in growth, account for as much timber as does the annual harvest.

To restrict clear-cutting of immature timber where this is wasteful of wood and of growing space.

Fɪɢ. 68   Badly depleted private rangeland in need of improved management. Many such overgrazed lands await rehabilitation effort. (*U.S. Forest Service photo.*)

To provide rehabilitation for some 52 million acres of poorly stocked and denuded forest land.

To reduce the accident rate in logging and lumber manufacture to levels comparable to those in other leading industries.

To increase the output per worker in lumber manufacturing as rapidly as other industries have improved their labor output.

To provide stable year-long employment to forest workers.

To prevent the growth of rural slums in many forest regions.

To keep lumber prices in line with prices of other manufactured commodities, and to promote better appreciation and use of wood.

To provide optimum control of erosion and stream flow on forest and range watersheds (Fig. 68).

To recognize and compensate properly the private landowner for the public services his forest provides in soil stabilization, watershed protection, wildlife food and cover, public recreation, and scenic beauty and to provide suitable discouragements to those who practice measures that lead to soil erosion, flashy water flows, poor conditions for wildlife, restricted public use, and unsightliness such as erecting billboards and operating auto junkyards along public highways.

To provide a reasonably stable market for standing timber so that forest ownership becomes attractive to the private investor.

To classify forests and forest practices by economic potential so that effort may be concentrated on forest areas and forestry measures that will yield the highest returns.

To develop a comprehensive program for owners of small woodland holdings that will make possible better management of such lands and encourage their consolidation, through land transfer or cooperative effort, into units of economic size.

To develop a pattern whereby the full recreational potential of public and private forest lands can be developed for the mutual benefit of recreationists and the landowner.

To provide increased research on the physical, biologic, and economic potential of forest lands and forest products so that policies and practices may be directed toward full use of forest resources.

To introduce modern technology and design into uses and products of wood so that consumer satisfaction is built up and wood maintains its place in the modern economy.

Programs Generally Supported

Representatives of the majority of agencies interested in forestry agree in supporting certain basic programs. These include the following:

Adequate federal, state, and private expenditures to provide effective protection of all forests and watershed lands from fire.

Protection against insects and disease under the Forest Pest Control Act of 1948 and other federal and state laws developed under a plan providing for joint federal, state, and private effort. Early detection and control before serious outbreaks occur is the objective.

Education of the public to the importance of forests, the need for care in use of forests, and the reasons for expending public moneys to support forestry measures. This is a never-ending job (Fig. 65).

Encouragement of private owners to hold forest lands that can be profitably managed for continuous production of timber crops.

Adjustment of taxes on forest land so that they are neither confiscatory nor so light that they exempt the forest owners from contributing their fair share to the support of government.

Support of state forestry organizations in all states on a basis that will ensure competence in the management of state forests, in the protection of all forests from fire, and in carrying out state programs that deal with private forests and forest products.

Encouragement of research as the basis for increasing the productivity of forest lands in both products and services and for expanding the utility of forest products.

Provision, at reasonable cost, of insurance for forest owners against the natural hazards of timber growing. These include damages due to fire, insects, disease, heavy windstorm, ice, and snow.

Offer of public and private inducements to landowners to plant barren and poorly stocked forest land.

Expansion of efforts to realize more fully the social benefits of forestry: recreation; wildlife, water, and soil protection; stable employment at good wages; and prosperous, permanent forest communities.

Permanent year-long employment at good wages with stable and moderate prices for forest products is a general goal of industry, labor, and government. Labor has emphasized safety in its programs.[2] The high accident rate in logging and lumber manufacture is ample cause for doing so. All these goals are interrelated. Measures that can increase output per worker and extend working days throughout the year will tend to stabilize communities, employment, and wages. By attracting high-class workmen, these measures will also tend to reduce accidents. Better worker training then becomes possible as well as rapid mechanization.

Size of operating unit is an important factor. Small operators often work intermittently, can afford only modest or secondhand equipment, have limited resources for training workers, and must cut corners to survive. These should profit from industry-wide training programs and services such as the American Pulpwood Association provides.

Issues on Which Disagreement Exists

Not all forest owners are in a position to undertake sustained-yield operations. Not all forest communities can be made permanent. The remaining resource may be too meager to permit this. Despite the best intentions not every timber-operating company is financially in a position to diversify its output so as to maintain current employment in the face of diminishing raw material. How far government should go in forcing sustained-yield management is questionable.

Aids to Private Owners and Timber Operators. Representatives of the forest-products industries would go slowly in extending public credit and services to private forest owners. They feel that public funds and credit should not be used to support private timber holdings that are uneconomical, either because of size or because of management practices of the owner. They favor limited use of benefit payments to farmers for forest practices.[4]

The U.S. Forest Service occupies an intermediate position, favoring public credit for timberland holdings where owners meet acceptable management standards. The Service has not vigorously promoted the extension of direct financial assistance to forest owners of the type extended to farmers.

Organized labor has advocated liberal use of public subsidies for all timber owners and operators. These would cover road building,

FIG. 69 As timberline is approached, forest trees show the result of buffeting by snow and high winds. Bristlecone pine on the Arapaho National Forest, Colorado. (*U.S. Forest Service photo.*)

forest improvement measures, safety measures, and timber cutting and operating. Organized labor also has proposed liberal loans to owners, including loans based on work done by the owner himself to improve his own woodlands.[2]

Public Ownership of Forests. Lands too low in productivity to pay costs of protection and management, or of such strategic importance for soil and watershed protection or screening of defense installations that timber harvesting must be seriously restricted, should be publicly owned and managed (Fig. 69). This is what the U.S. Forest Service advocates. The forest-products industries agree with this principle. They favor exchange of land between public and private owners that would lead to consolidation of management units on both public and private lands, with both groups giving up and receiving lands. The Forest Service has gone slowly in exchanging public land for private land but often exchanges stumpage from national forests for private land.

Actually, a wide gap exists between the forest-products industries[4] and the U.S. Forest Service[10] on public forest ownership. Because of the growing scarcity of high-quality private timber holdings, the industries would welcome control over some of the better-quality national forest lands. Where national forest lands are checkerboarded with private lands that owners are managing on a sustained-yield basis, a plausible case can be made for such a transfer.

The Forest Service has held national forests for over half a century with only limited opportunities to demonstrate high-standard, sustained-yield management. Now that private operators are ready to undertake national-forest logging on a large scale, the Service wishes to demonstrate good forestry over these vast areas. Furthermore, the Forest Service would like to block up its holdings within national forests and to establish new national forests on low-quality forest land unlikely soon to be reforested in private hands. The Service feels that it has an especial obligation to grow the large-sized high-quality timber that the nation will need but that would be too costly and long delayed for private effort. The industry prefers that additional public forests be mainly state-owned. State foresters generally support this position. Middle ground is represented by the American Forestry Association, which has advocated for each state a permanent planning committee to determine an appropriate distribution among private, state, and federal holdings.[1]

Regulation of Private Forest Practice. Public regulation of private forest practice was a hotly debated issue between 1935 and 1953. It received little attention between 1955 and 1961 because of greatly improved practice on private lands. Such regulation is commonplace in European countries, where it finds some of its strongest advocates among the forest-products industries that need a permanent wood supply and feel they must avoid the depressed prices that liquidation cutting would bring about.[3,8] The issue is likely to arise again in America if demand for timber products presses on available supplies. It may be well, therefore, to review briefly the status of the debate at the time it was dropped in the 1950s.

The industries favored independent state action on regulation of private forest practice without any federal interference or intervention.[4] The forest industries supported enactment of the regulation laws in Washington and Oregon. They also supported the voluntary laws in California, Massachusetts, and New York. They vigorously opposed bills in the Congress that would give the federal government control over private forest practice.

The American Forestry Association[1] favored state laws to avoid unnecessary destruction of young timber and to establish practices that would maintain continuous forest production. The Forestry Association, the Society of American Foresters, and the state foresters felt that such regulation should be state rather than federal.

The U.S. Forest Service favored a federal-state cooperative regulation plan that would prohibit premature and wasteful cutting and extensive clear-cutting, protect the forest, and reserve sufficient desirable growing stock to keep the lands reasonably productive.[9,10] The Forest Service favored such action by states but believed that the federal government should have authority to regulate private forest practice within a state that failed to act effectively within a reasonable time.

Organized labor and others [2,5] have advocated nationwide federal control over private forest practice.

Various bills to empower the federal government to regulate private forest practice have been introduced from time to time since 1920. None passed either house of Congress.

Proposals have been advanced, from time to time, that would lead to federal control over forest practice through various leasing and lending activities.[9] These have been vigorously opposed by the forest industries.

Wilderness Areas

The most hotly debated forestry issue in 1962 was legislation to establish a national wilderness program. This issue stems from the national park legislation and, in New York State, the constitutional provisions for maintaining the State Forest Preserve as wild forest land. Wilderness advocates find their strength in the Wilderness Society, the various societies for protection of the Adirondacks, the Boone and Crockett Club, the Sierra Club, the Quetico-Superior Council, the Audubon Society, and similar organizations that advocate preservation of large areas of land uninfluenced by man. Although wilderness enthusiasts have been denounced as a handful of selfish fanatics interested in preserving at public expense large areas of forest land containing much high-quality timber for their own exclusive use, they nevertheless have on many occasions mustered considerable political following. In New York State they have in effect dictated exactly what could and what could not be done with the $2\frac{1}{2}$-million-acre Forest Preserve. Every public campground that has been developed, every major highway relocation, every ski development and damsite proposed that involved Forest Preserve land has been authorized or defeated according to the position they took.

The present system of roadless, natural, and wild areas has been established largely on the national forests, though national parklands, too, are involved. The legislation proposed would set up national standards for management of such areas and maintain their integrity by congressional legislation. At present such areas are established by administrative order of the Secretary of Agriculture or the Secretary of the Interior.

Fig. 70   Recreationists on the trail to a high Sierra Camp in the Yosemite. (*National Park Service photo by R. H. Anderson.*)

Little objection has been raised to wilderness areas where these involved mainly high peak lands having little or no commercial timber (Fig. 70). The wilderness advocates have been insisting of late that wilderness areas be expanded to include substantial areas of highest-quality commercial timber. As regulations prohibit timber operations in wilderness areas, both the U.S. Forest Service and the forest industries have opposed such extensions. Wilderness forces have countered by seeking a substantial expansion of the national park system to include wilderness.

The wilderness lovers have their greatest opponents not in the U.S. Forest Service or the forest industries, but in the recreationists themselves who swarm over the land. Aided by outboard motors, jeeps, "doodlebugs," and small aircraft, people are penetrating wherever motor-powered vehicles can carry them. The aims of the wilderness seeker and his motor-operating opposite are the same, to penetrate where others do not or cannot go. They differ little in objective, only in their method of getting to it. The wilderness seeker sanctions the horse but would ban the motor. The modernist feels that the gasoline motor is today as much a companion of man as the horse of yesterday. He may work just as hard with winch and cable to drag his jeep up an abandoned wagon road as the hiker works carrying his gear on his back.

The real objective is to preserve some areas that are vast enough to evoke a feeling of solitude and that display only minimum evidence of our mechanized way of life. Difficulty of access is the main reliance for protecting such areas. Other means of restricting access may need to be employed. If this is done, many extensively managed forest areas may afford to all except the most venturesome the experience of vastness and natural forces that is the chief attraction of wilderness. For wilderness enjoyment is after all a response of the mind.

New Legislation Required

Most of the proposals for future forest programs actually involve the strengthening of existing public and private programs rather than new legislation. The many proposals included in the comprehensive study of forest policy by a joint committee of the Society of American Foresters and the National Research Council that reported in 1947 also involve primarily more liberal financing of existing programs.[7]

New legislation will be needed if the public is to sponsor insurance of forests against natural hazards and to extend credit to forest owners. Although the property tax may be administered fairly on forest land, it is not always so administered. The yield-tax laws of some states appear satisfactory to owners but result in irregular income for local governments unless cushioned by state payments to counties on an annual basis.

Aids to small private forest owners that will enable them to rehabilitate barren forest land and to develop understocked forest properties for high yield are not adequately provided by existing legislation. At present only owners who have an income from other sources can engage in such activities. Public financial aid for planting, drainage, and other improvements of the type provided in Norway, Sweden, and Finland are still to be worked out in America. These may be the best answer to getting forest production reestablished on scattered small holdings.

After an extensive review of the various difficulties confronting the owners of small forest properties, Clawson, Held, and Stoddard came to the conclusion that a considerable change in the present organizational structure seems to be needed before small holdings of forest lands not a part of farms will be effectively managed. Such changes might take the form of consolidation into larger holdings, cooperative management, or special land-management services to be provided by consulting foresters. These authors hold out little hope that direct public aids in themselves will result in bringing these small private holdings into high-level timber production without other measures that will lead to consolidation of ownership or at least of management over economic-sized areas.[6]

Some form of regulation of private-forest cutting practices was provided in 17 states in 1961. Changes in some existing laws and enactment of legislation by additional states are needed. The role that the federal government is to play in this field is still to be determined.

Legislation could be helpful in improving working conditions and output of forest, sawmill, and wood-processing workers. Forest work studies in Scandinavia cover measures for encouraging young people to engage in forest work, improving living and community life of woods workers, training in handling tools and equipment, insurance, and social security. Such programs are sponsored jointly by industry and government.

Legislators might well give consideration to providing landowners who permit public recreation and hunting on their lands some aids or tax concessions. The same applies to owners of strategic watersheds. Authority for extending special aids to owners of watersheds that need improvement for public benefits may be needed. Regulations governing forest practice on such watersheds might well precede nationwide regulation of private forests.

Legislation is also needed in most states to develop a satisfactory system for taxing forest lands. In few states are property taxes assessed against forest lands related to either existing or potential productivity of the forest or value of products harvested.

Forestry Programs in European Democracies

Perspective can be had on the proposed programs for the United States by reviewing practices that have developed in European democracies up to and after the Second World War.

Switzerland passed a basic law in 1902 prohibiting clear-felling, except by permission, restricting grazing and other harmful practices in mountain forests, grouping private protection forests for management, and requiring reforestation within three years of forests destroyed by fire, avalanches, or windstorm.[3] *Belgium* and *Holland* have less strict laws but endeavor to encourage private forestry by tax concessions.[3]

France had mild regulation of private forestry until the country was occupied by Germany in the Second World War. The Vichy Government established strict regulation adopted from the German pattern. Some relaxation occurred with reestablishment of the republic in 1944. In 1946 France passed legislation directed toward making the nation self-sufficient in forest products. This provides public help to landowners but requires definite standards of practice.[3]

Since 1945 *Great Britain* has made strenuous efforts to build up her forests. Her objective is to increase the total forest area of the country to 5 million acres. The program includes government acquisition of land for forests, general planning of land use throughout the nation, and an intensive program of private forestry. Private forest owners are urged to dedicate their forest lands to permanent forest management. The government will reimburse the owner for 25 per cent of his excess of expenditures over receipts for any one year or will provide a direct payment for forest planting. The planting subsidy in 1960 averaged £20 per acre. Additional grants were available for maintaining the plantations after they were set out.

Disputes between the owner and the Forestry Commission over forest practice can be referred to a special investigating committee.[8] As of 1960, the number of properties dedicated was 1,704 having an aggregate area of 621,957 acres.

Denmark, a country fervently devoted to democracy and with a high sense of individual freedom and initiative, requires owners to follow good forestry practices. All Danish forests are reserved. Owners are obliged to manage them as high forest, using approved silvicultural principles. Hardwoods may not be diminished in area. State forest officers inspect private forests and advise owners on management. Small owners who do not employ a forester look to the state inspectors to mark trees for cutting. Owners may join a cooperative, subsidized by the state, and hire a forester to manage their lands. Owners of less than 10 years' tenure may not cut timber for sale without state approval but may cut for domestic use. Approval for sale may be given for one to three years. This precludes speculation in woodlands. Despite the authority lodged in the Danish forest officers, they act with discretion, and little friction arises between the forest owners and the public foresters.

Finland and *Sweden* have good forest practice on private lands and have a wholly democratic system of regulating cutting practices. This is exercised through local forestry boards that employ county foresters. These boards get financial support from the central government for carrying out their forestry program. They determine cutting-practice standards, and they supervise the payment of state subsidies for forest draining, tree planting, forest improvements, and other purposes.

The Swedish law of 1948 differentiates between vigorous and nonvigorous forest stands. Vigorous stands may not be cut, other than by thinning, without the consent of the Forestry Conservation Bureau. Forest stands that fail to reproduce after cutting must be brought into a satisfactory condition within reasonable time.

The landowners are free to cut their timber provided they stay within the minimum practice standards.

These procedures have been effective in getting good practice on the forest lands of Sweden and Finland. The Finnish and Swedish programs have the merit of being nationwide in application with a maximum of flexibility on a county-by-county basis and with completely democratic formulation and administration of regulations. Familiarity with the functioning of Finnish, Swedish, and Norwegian public regulation practices should prove helpful to those in other countries interested in activating public forest programs.

Preserving Natural Beauty

Switzerland has developed public controls over rural land use that should be of growing interest to Americans. Since their country is Europe's favorite vacation land, the Swiss wish to maintain its attractions to outside visitors. Aside from providing hotels, cable cars, and ski lifts to bring people to their superb Alpine playgrounds, they have an alert citizenry that seeks to protect natural beauty. This private organization has the aid of the government in printing a nature-protection and anti-littering message on candy wrappers, from which a small tax is collected. With this and private contributions a campaign is conducted to educate the general populace. Nature protection has become a national virtue. As a result, specialists advise on highway location, on national parks, and on land development in suburban areas so that the natural beauty of the landscape is disturbed as little as possible. New residential construction is confined to villages in certain valleys, and fields are kept free of signboards and unsightly structures. Lakes on which weekend camps had been erected have been cleared and zoned for public use. Special encouragement and protection are provided for birds and wildlife. The movement has the active support and participation of the nation's leading foresters. European countrysides generally have a tidy appearance free from auto junkyards and other eyesores.

Similar programs are found in other lands. The open ski slopes in the Austrian Tyrol that are private land in summer become free for public use when snow-covered; Great Britain has its Nature Conservancy, Germany its *Naturschutz* and its *"Hilf durch Grüne,"* Holland its seacoast reserves and its bird sanctuaries. France keeps her historic Loire Valley neat and tidy, and Sweden runs excursions on its scenic Göteborg Canal. Norway offers superb scenic attractions and has taken steps to keep her lands attractive for both her own people and foreign visitors. These countries have not hesitated to mobilize public opinion and invoke public controls to protect scenic areas.

The Role of Foresters and Citizens

Men with forestry training are expected to inform themselves on the forestry situation in the United States and the measures that need to be taken to place it on a sound basis. They are not expected to be unanimous in supporting any specific methods for achieving this objective. Obviously, the opinions of foresters may be expected to differ, just as do the opinions of other men. It must be emphasized, however, that public programs of forestry on a nationwide scale do not come into being without a great deal of effort on the part of many people. As foresters justify their existence on the basis of their ability to provide adequately for the nation's timber supplies and other forest resources and services, it is up to foresters to take the lead in advocating public measures that will attain these ends. The nation's economic resources, of which the forests are one, must be protected; and in protecting these resources we should strengthen rather than weaken democratic processes. The experience of such nations as Sweden, Denmark, and Switzerland presents ample evidence that such an objective can be achieved if we have the patience and determination to strive for it.

LITERATURE CITED

1. American Forestry Association. 1946. "A Program for American Forestry," *American Forests,* 52(8):352–356, 387.
2. American Forestry Association. 1947. *Proceedings, American Forest Congress,* Oct. 9, 10, 11, 1946, pp. 86–102, Washington, D.C.
3. Anderson, M. L. 1950. "State Control of Private Forestry under European Democracies," Oxford University Press, Fair Lawn, N.J. 112 pp.
4. Black, S. R. 1947. "Program of Forest Industries Council," *Proceedings, American Forest Congress,* Oct. 9, 10, 11, 1946, pp. 37–45, American Forestry Association, Washington, D.C.
5. Clapp, Earle H. 1949. "Public Forest Regulation," *Journal of Forestry,* 47:527–530.
6. Clawson, Marion, R. Bernell Held, and Charles H. Stoddard. 1960. "Land for the Future," The Johns Hopkins Press, Baltimore. 570 pp.
7. Graves, Henry S. 1947. "Problems and Progress of Forestry in the United States," Society of American Foresters, Washington, D.C. 112 pp.
8. Moore, Barrington. 1950. "Trends in British Forestry," *Yale Forest School News,* 38:69–71.
9. Raushenbush, Stephen. 1949. "Our Conservation Job," The Public Affairs Institute, Report 4, Washington, D.C. 64 pp.
10. Watts, Lyle F. 1949. "A National Program for Forestry," *Trees,* The Yearbook of Agriculture, pp. 757–760, U.S. Department of Agriculture, Washington.

CHAPTER 20. *Administration in Forestry*

MOST FORESTERS sooner or later find themselves engaged in administrative work at some level. In response to a questionnaire 41 per cent of the graduates of one college of forestry, including those out of college only one year, indicated that they were engaged chiefly in supervisory or administrative work. Supervisory and administrative skills, therefore, weigh heavily in determining promotions, salary, and ultimate position. No forester can begin too early to cultivate those attitudes and traits that fit him for administrative responsibility.

A forester becomes an administrative officer as soon as his duties include the supervision of at least one assistant. As his responsibilities grow to include many assistants, and more than one class of work, administration increases in the amount of time it requires and the complexity of its demands (Fig. 71). Administrative or executive work involves planning and decision making governing the work to be done by others. Skillful administration, however, involves much more than the conventional boss and employee relationship.

The responsibility of administrators is to attain policy goals, utilizing the personnel and the physical resources placed at their disposal. Administrators leave their impress on an organization by determining to a large extent its objectives, ethics, and the amount, kind, and standards of work performed. The degree to which the forestry profession satisfies its future obligation will depend largely upon the intelligence, foresight, judgment, and ability of the administrators who are responsible for directing the work. To the extent that wood becomes scarce or too high-priced, that wild lands produce floods, that natural resources are needlessly destroyed, forestry fails to attain its goal. Such failure is the failure of forest administrators to accomplish their task, although it may not be the direct fault of any one or any group of administrators.

Every type of work that is organized requires administrators. Large organizations are usually headed by skilled administrators. Small organizations may tolerate certain administrative weaknesses, provided they are not sufficiently outstanding to wreck the organization. The techniques

338

Fig. 71 A national forest ranger station in a western state. (*U.S. Forest Service photo.*)

of administration employed by governmental and private organizations are much the same, but working conditions may differ markedly. The man in governmental service must always strive to put the public interest before that of any individual or special-interest group. If he fails to do this, he fails to fulfill his responsibility as a public servant. What he does must be well considered and capable of withstanding detailed public scrutiny. Administrators in private enterprise are answerable only to the head of the organization or to a board of directors. The private administrator is primarily concerned with advancing the welfare of his organization and weighs his actions in that light. Men in private enterprise are, of course, conscious of the public interest, but they make their decisions without undue fear of being rebuked by individuals outside their organization.

The Nature of Administrative Work

People have a tendency to think that leaders are "born not made." There is, of course, truth in such a statement. Good health, abundant energy, and a good intellect are strongly influenced by heredity. A friendly nature, consideration for others, an inquiring mind, and a desire to excel in accomplishment are all influenced by early training and environment. So also are the desire for perquisites that high administrative work carries such as prestige, good income, authority, respect, and a certain freedom of decision and action. But these alone do not qualify a man to head a large organization. Leadership qualities must be demonstrated through hard work, loyalty, thoughtfulness, technical competence, acceptance of responsibility, and outstanding performance.

The popular picture of the "big wheel" as a playboy, an aloof aristocrat, a hard-to-please boss, or a rapid-fire decision maker is a gross simplification.

Aloofness, austerity, disregard for opinions and viewpoints of associates and subordinates, and off-the-cuff decision making can be indulged in only at the risk of ill-considered action. The successful executive is more likely to be a friendly, considerate, inquiring individual who makes important decisions after careful study of the factors involved and review of staff work if appropriate. As many decisions as possible are delegated to those near the scene of action.

The Functions of Administrators

An administrator is a person who is responsible for the efforts of others, both as to policy and as to practice, and exercises authority in seeing that decisions are carried out.

The man in an administrative post is not primarily engaged in doing the detailed work of his organization, although he functions prominently in developing overall plans and in setting up general policies. The administrator is chiefly concerned with providing leadership and with doing the specialized work associated with maintaining the organization in operation.

Luther Gulick [3] defines the duties of an administrator as including these functions:

1. Planning the work to be done and how to do it.

2. Recruiting personnel, training them, and establishing favorable working conditions.

3. Organizing the functions and defining the responsibilities of various subdivisions and the channels through which their activities are to be reported and coordinated.

4. Budgeting funds for the several divisions and activities and maintaining fiscal control.

5. Coordinating the various activities and divisions for smooth and effective operation.

6. Reporting to those to whom he is responsible on the work of the entire organization and maintaining free two-way communication between himself and his subordinates through suggestions, records, inspec-

tion, and research. He also interprets his organization to his employees and the general public.

7. Directing the work by making decisions and transmitting these through directives and instructions. Serving as leader of the organization.

The extent to which an administrator performs each of the major duties depends upon the size and complexity of his organization. In small enterprises the owner usually performs the bulk, if not all, of the administrative functions himself. In large enterprises the above functions are organized in separate departments.

Perhaps a clearer picture may be gained by describing the functions of an administrative officer (a supervisor of a national forest) and those of a foreman in industry.

Functions of a National Forest Supervisor. A national forest supervisor is likely to have responsibility for the management of the resources on a national forest of some $1\frac{1}{2}$ million acres. This will be divided up into four or more ranger districts and will involve a year-round staff of between 75 and 100 people of which approximately one-half will be professionally trained men. The national forest may be supplying stumpage for sawmills, veneer and plywood mills, pulp and paper mills, grazing for livestock, water for irrigation or power, and recreation for many people. It is likely to be the chief source of livelihood for approximately 50 per cent of the people who live within its boundaries or nearby. The duties of the supervisor will be discussed under the seven headings above.

planning. The supervisor has the responsibility, within the overall legal and administrative framework of the national forest system, for planning all the activities to be carried out on the national forest. He must think, first, of the mission his particular national forest must meet. This involves specifically the industries dependent upon the forest for stumpage, forage, or water; the recreational visitors; and others who depend on use of the resource. He must give first thought to protecting the forest and the resources it contains. This means planning for detection and suppression of fires, of outbreaks of destructive insects or diseases, and of damage to soil or forest cover from animals (wild or domestic); and for protection against trespass. His second responsibility is to plan for the orderly development and use of the resources the forest affords. The timber-management plan is likely to be the most complex of these. The supervisor will establish the broad framework for timber management. This will cover production goals, rotations, cutting cycles, and division of the forest into appropriate working circles. He will prepare similar broad plans for recreational development, watershed management, range management, and wildlife management. He will also give consideration to preparing a system of roads and trails adequate for the forest. It is his responsibility to review the annual work plans of each of the rangers and staff specialists to make suggested changes where these are needed. They, in turn, will assist in the preparation of his plans. Specialists may include an engineer, timber-management specialist, fire-control specialist, range specialist, wildlife specialist, and various others, depending on the relative importance of the particular resources on his national forest.

RECRUITING PERSONNEL. The recruitment of personnel for the national forests is, in part, a responsibility of the forest supervisor, but in this he is aided by the regional personnel officer. It is, however, the forest supervisor's final decision on which men he will employ, what training programs he will develop for his new recruits, and what working conditions he will maintain on the ranger districts and in the national forest headquarters. It is usual practice to have one or more special schools for the new recruits to get them indoctrinated into the policy of the Forest Service and the overall management objectives on the particular national forest. He will also want them to become familiar with the resources and personnel of the national forest and will seek to make them feel a part of the overall organization.

ORGANIZING. The forest supervisor has the responsibility for organizing the national forest into ranger districts or for changing the boundaries of existing ranger districts, or combining them or dividing them as in his judgment may be necessary for most effective operation. He also has the responsibility for organizing the team of specialists who assist him in the supervisor's office and for maintaining clear lines of responsibility between himself and his staff specialists, on the one hand, and between himself and the rangers, on the other.

BUDGETING. The forest supervisor will prepare each year his budget requests for the following fiscal year. Usually he must begin this task at least 14 months before the fiscal year opens and he must plan up to the end of the fiscal year, which means planning expenditures for a period at least 26 months in advance. He will obtain from his forest rangers and staff specialists estimates of needs for equipment, for fire control, for general administration, for planting or timber-stand improvement, and for any special projects that the ranger feels are necessary in his district. These will involve such things as the construction of new roads; the building of office and headquarters buildings, garages, and warehouses; the erection of fire-lookout towers and their repair; and similar improvements. If the national forest has a nursery, and many do, the supervisor will call upon the nurseryman to make up his estimates of needs for capital improvement, repairs, and operation. And finally, the supervisor must budget the needs of his own central office for space, equipment, personnel, and supplies. He will have the services of an administrative assistant in preparing his budget estimates. His budget is forwarded to the regional forester's office, where he may be called in for conference on specific items, particularly those that require a substantial increase in expenditures over those of the preceding fiscal year. Special projects such as forest highways, campground developments, headquarters buildings, and new major programs will require particular consideration. The supervisor will want to explain these to prominent local citizens and their Congressman, who like to know what is planned for their district.

Once a new budget is passed by the Congress and allocated by the Chief and regional forester to the various national forests, the supervisor has the responsibility of allocating this budget among the several ranger districts and the several major activities planned for his national forest. In doing this, he must keep within the general framework of the budget as presented to him from the regional office. During the course of the year he may reallocate funds subject to approval of the regional forester.

COORDINATING. Coordinating the work on the several ranger districts and between the central technical staff and the ranger districts is a major responsibility of a forest supervisor. This is carried out in part by various instructions and directives which the supervisor himself will issue, in part by conferences of the technical staff alone, and in part by inspections which the technical staff and the supervisor himself will make. It is the practice of most supervisors to visit each ranger district several times each year. This may be done in connection with the inspection of some particular project or in escorting important visitors. The supervisor will normally make a thorough inspection of each ranger district at least once annually, often in company with a high-ranking officer from the regional forester's office.

REPORTING. The forest supervisor must prepare reports on current activities and annual reports to the regional forester. These will cover all major activities, with special reports on personnel. The preparation of the budget in itself is one means of reporting projected plans and activities. The supervisor also has responsibility for reporting to the general public. This reporting will include major plans and developments for which the forest has received budget allocations, reporting on new personnel and transfers of personnel, reporting on the use of the national forest, advertising timber sales, and giving out special warnings in cases of extreme fire danger or special hazards to motorists and others using the national forest. The supervisor will seek to keep his local public well informed on policies and program, and to encourage their support for the work on his national forest (Fig. 72).

DIRECTING. The forest supervisor will expect his individual rangers to be responsible for most of the day-to-day operating decisions that have to be made. The supervisor will review and approve plans and projects

FIG. 72 Explaining to timber contractors and others national forest timber sales policy and administration. (*U.S. Forest Service photo.*)

initiated by the ranger and developed by the help of staff specialists. The supervisor must act on appointments, promotions, and transfers of personnel, the closing of the forest in case of extreme fire danger, the decision on new lines of work or new projects including decisions on where timber sales are to be made, how large such sales are to be, and what marking rules or other practices are to be invoked. The supervisor will decide the terms of the timber sale contract, subject to review by the regional office. He will approve yearly work plans of the rangers and staff officers, decide when and where conferences are to be held, what topics are to be discussed, and what changes may be needed in the major overall plan for the national forest. He will inspect the quality of the work performed. Where the work does not meet appropriate standards, he must inform the responsible individual of the fact and take the necessary steps to ensure that improvements will be forthcoming. In his directing of the overall work, the supervisor has the responsibility for maintaining high morale of the workers on his national forest, close understanding between himself and his rangers, and good relations between the Service and the local citizens.

He directs through well-understood objectives, by maintaining a free flow of ideas up and down the administrative channels, and by delegating responsibility for decision and action as fully as possible to the man in the field.

The Chief Forester, assistant chief, regional forester, national forest supervisor, and ranger are all concerned with administration, that is, with carrying out the seven functions described. Important objectives of administration are to get trees grown and harvested, fires prevented and extinguished, range protected and utilized, and roads built and maintained. The last men in the administrative hierarchy are the assistant ranger and foreman.

Duties of a Foreman in Industry. Riegel generalizes the duties of a typical foreman in industry as follows: [5]

I. To administer his own department
1. To plan and schedule operations in his department in cooperation with any central planning unit
2. To execute plans
   a. To organize operations in terms of personnel, materials, and machines
   b. To direct operations to attain standards of quality, quantity, economy, and safety
   c. To keep department clean, orderly, and safe
3. To develop subordinates
4. To improve the efficiency of operations by the development of methods and processes
5. To develop and maintain desirable personnel relations
II. To cooperate with superiors, associates, and other departments in furthering general aims of the enterprise
III. To represent his management to his employees and his employees to his management
IV. To increase his fitness to meet present and new situations by improving his abilities and personality traits

An excellent discussion of supervising work in forestry is given by McCulloch.[4]

The beginner in supervision can get many useful hints from various books that have been written on the subject. An especially suggestive one for the man starting his first supervisory job has been prepared by the American Management Association.[1]

Decision Making

No one function of the top-level administrator is more important than decision making. He makes a decision when he decides on a long-range goal for his organization; when he selects his immediate subordinates; when he negotiates a labor contract; when he employs an advertising firm; when he accepts or declines an invitation to make an important address; when he prepares or comments on legislation; and when he decides that he will require additional information before reaching a specific decision. One of the marks of good administration is, in fact, the extent to which decision making is made at the place where the greatest degree of competence can be brought to bear on it. Simon [6] (1957) recognizes two elements in decision making, "factual" and "value." Factual elements can be determined by appropriate technology or expertness. They are correct or incorrect. Value elements have to do with value judgments, or ethics. They depend on determinations of the relative desirability of the alternatives. Decisions on factual questions can best be made where the facts are determined. Decisions on value or ethical questions must be made at the top of the organization. However, value decisions can and should be delegated to the extent that appropriate standards for decision are established in general policies of the organization.

Many decisions have both factual and value elements. Even the factual elements may be too complex for the human mind to rationalize. The real qualities that enable a man to hold many very complex physical and human interrelationships in mind and out of these arrive at a workable or useful decision are imperfectly understood even by those most skillful in making good decisions.

The advent of the electronic computer, which has amazing capacity to process very quickly enormous quantities of complex data and interrelationships, has led progressive administrators to look to this valuable tool for aid in bringing the final decision making into a compass with which the human brain can cope successfully. Foresters have already used electronic computers for this purpose. The advantage of the computer is that it can quickly work out the effects of a number of possible decisions on such elements as costs, value of products, or benefits to clientele. The use of electronic computers in the decision-making process is still in the beginning stages. Use of machines further brings out the need for detailed study and research to select key factors and to learn how one affects another. The more precisely such relationships can be worked out, the better the computer may be used to arrive at the optimum solution to managerial questions.[7]

Aptitudes for Success in Administration

In "The Art of Leadership" Ordway Tead [9] has listed the most important qualities demanded of the administrator as (1) abundant physical and nervous energy, (2) a sense of purpose and direction, (3) enthusiasm, (4) friendliness and affection, (5) integrity, (6) technical mastery, (7) decisiveness, (8) intelligence, (9) teaching skill, and (10) faith. Howard Smith in his book "Developing Your Executive Ability" [8] states that the dominant urges of the good executive must be (1) to deal with his fellow men on the basis of concern for their welfare as well as his own and (2) to climb to leadership on the basis of demonstrated worth and with the approval and respect of his fellows. The necessary administrative qualities are consequently those of character, personality, and ability.

Mason,[2] in an attempt to single out traits of good administrators, compared successful executives with successful salesmen, production men, and technical men. Unclassified college students were used as a control group. No significant differences were found among the five groups in these abilities: (1) reasoning in arithmetic, (2) judgment in estimating, (3) symbolic relationships, and (4) word comparisons, though all these abilities must be exercised by administration.

Mason next selected 33 executive traits grouped into four categories: (1) health and drive, (2) judgment of fact, (3) reaction to human qualities, and (4) leadership. The scores on this test are shown below:

	College students	Sales group	Executive group	Technical group
Health and drive...................	0	−4	+16	+2
Judgment of fact...................	0	−3	+10	+4
Reaction to human qualities..........	0	+6	+10	−2
Leadership.......................	0	+1	+14	−6

The administrative group received markedly higher scores in each category than any of the other groups. Obviously, many traits and abilities are important for success (Fig. 73). A successful administrator must draw the best from the personnel in his organization. He must at the same time give each person a sense of personal accomplishment. He must have the ability to make the teamwork of the group far more effective than the separate accomplishments of the individual workmen.

It would be unwise to conclude from the above that administrators are not human; they are. They are sensitive to personal affront, they enjoy being esteemed by others, they may have one or more shortcomings that disqualify them from meeting ideal standards. They must, however, have some compensating traits that enable them to discharge their responsibilities effectively. Also, administrators may make mistakes, and they must certainly expect that subordinates to whom they delegate

Fig. 73 Richard E. McArdle, former Chief of the U.S. Forest Service, delivering the keynote address at the Fifth World Forestry Congress, Seattle, Washington, 1960. (*Gene Weber and U.S. Forest Service photo.*)

responsibility likewise will make mistakes. They must, however, be quick to learn from their mistakes and must have the capacity to overcome quickly those that are damaging, lest the entire organization fail. As long as administration remains an art, and it seems likely that it will so remain for decades to come, there will be room for the virtuosity of an artist in guiding the destinies of large human organizations.

Not All Men Should Aspire to Become Administrators. Many men will find their greatest usefulness, and therein their greatest satisfaction, by serving in staff positions with responsibility for the development of certain technical phases of forestry. Those whose energy is limited or who dislike working under pressure and assuming heavy responsibility under trying conditions will find administration highly irksome.

Even men who aspire to leadership should realize that administrative posts are few and competition keen. Many fortuitous circumstances may stop their career short of their life's ambition. In both public and private careers, men in advanced administrative positions may be called upon at times to take a courageous position which may disqualify them for advancement. Such occurrences are most frequent in the field of politics, but they occur in private business and public administration as well.

Training Required

The student who wishes to prepare himself for forest administration may select the curriculum which includes the field of his primary interest. Attention should be paid to the obvious fact that graduates from certain curricula find employment with larger organizations than do others. As the number of men doing the same kind of work within an organization increases, the need for administrative direction increases.

The election of courses in history, public administration, business administration, economics, and psychology is desirable in preparation for administrative work. Also, participation in campus or other extracurricular activities may be helpful. The contacts formed are valuable in developing poise and self-confidence. Moreover, they offer an opportunity to listen to varying points of view, to weigh evidence, to suggest logical conclusions, and to carry out activities that build up the qualities of leadership.

It is characteristic of American institutions that activities are directed with little use of disciplinary measures. The skillful administrator anticipates weaknesses and corrects them long before disciplinary measures need to be taken.

Graduate study is of increasing importance in providing specialized training for men who have demonstrated their aptitude for administrative work. In the past, struggles for administrative leadership have brought forth many talented administrators, but in the process young men have wasted considerable time learning skills that could have been acquired more rapidly through systematic study. Personality traits can be evaluated, intelligence recognized, and, to some extent, talent for leadership predicted. When men selected for these basic qualities are given graduate training in administrative functions and activities, they normally advance rapidly toward important executive posts.

A number of colleges are now giving short courses in administration. On-the-job training is frequently provided by special assignments or by transfers. Young men who show promise as administrators should be given opportunity to develop as rapidly as possible. They should be assigned to positions of increasing responsibility as soon as they demonstrate that they are ready for them. To the man impatient to get ahead, such training programs may seem onerous, but shortcuts have their pitfalls. Political preferment, nepotism, favoritism because of fraternal affiliations, common alma mater, personal liking, and other reasons exist to a limited extent perhaps in all types of organizations and particularly in small ones.

All forms of favoritism lower employee morale. Men will not do their best work unless assured of fair treatment and opportunity to advance. The administrator who holds his position as a result of favoritism, therefore, has a doubly difficult task in maintaining satisfactory performance of his organization. His tenure is likely to be short.

Career Ladders

Within each organization there is a theoretical career ladder, that is, steps through which a man is expected to pass as he advances from one level of administrative responsibility to another.

Simplified career ladders are shown in Figs. 74 and 75 for a private and a public forestry organization. Men may follow separate career ladders until they reach a certain plateau where both are performing primarily high administrative functions. At this level they may interchange posts with a minimum of difficulty. It is not uncommon for men who

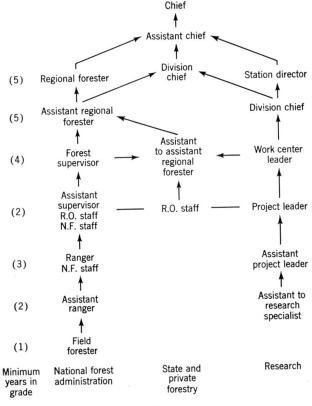

Fig. 74 Career ladders in the U.S. Forest Service (simplified).

have attained high administrative leadership in the U.S. Forest Service to transfer to similar posts of high authority in business, in association work, and in other government agencies.

Opportunities for advancement in administrative work are greater in organizations that are growing rapidly, in organizations that handle a wide variety of tasks rather than routine work, and in those that are concerned primarily with action programs rather than with research. A man may develop his administrative skill by shifting from one employer to another among small organizations.

Young men desiring to advance in administrative work should follow recognized rules of effective conduct. Loyalty to the organization and to superiors and subordinates is indispensable to advancement. Friendly consideration for coworkers and readiness to accept responsibility and to discharge it fully will gain a reputation with superiors. Participation in nonofficial tasks, if important, helps to develop leadership.

Helpful Rules for Administrative and Supervisory Work

Have clear-cut objectives to which all workers can wholeheartedly subscribe.
Interpret these objectives in terms of the job of every man in the organization.
Have clear-cut lines of responsibility and delegate authority commensurate
    with responsibility.
Except in emergencies, never act without facts.

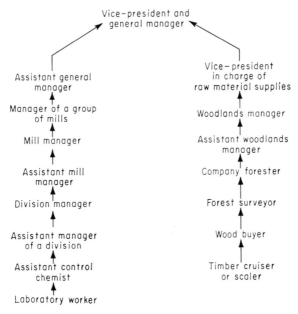

Fig. 75 Career ladder in a pulp and paper company (simplified).

Anticipate contingencies by keeping constantly alert to needs and morale of organization.

Dispel unfounded rumors by tracing them to their source.

Be accessible to everyone in the organization who feels that he must see you personally, but do not encourage men to bring things directly to the top that should go through channels.

Be clear and explicit in instructions and patient to answer questions.

When criticism or correction is needed, do it promptly and privately.

Most men want to please their superiors. Rare is the individual who deliberately causes mischief. The latter should be promptly taught to mend his ways or be discharged.

Constant carping, criticism, and faultfinding will have one of two effects: break the employee's self-confidence and morale; cause him to become indifferent because nothing he does pleases.

Be genuinely concerned about the personal welfare of the workers and show it.

Through conferences and otherwise, encourage free discussion of future plans and policies; but once these are decided, pursue them with vigor.

Keep physically and mentally alert.

Have systematic measures for checking performance and for keeping informed on the performance of your entire organization. Use staff conferences to build teamwork and to encourage reliable staff work.

Have confidence and faith in yourself, your staff, and organization.

Appoint some competent assistant to act for you when you are away; check his work upon return, praising where deserved, suggesting better courses of action where he made mistakes.

Frankly and promptly admit your own mistakes. This will encourage others to do likewise.

Have a definite training program for each new employee and for each man eligible for promotion.

Make it a practice at least once a year to review each man's performance and to discuss with him his future career in the organization. Do not try to hold a man in your organization if brighter opportunities exist elsewhere. He will be discontented.

Avoid gossip. Hold in strict confidence such of the essentials concerning the organization and its employees as deserve to be kept confidential. Neither seek nor repel the personal confidences of associates and employees; but when they are offered, hold them inviolate.

Become a clear writer and an effective speaker.

Give careful thought and effort to building up and maintaining favorable public relations and public attitude toward your organization. Appropriate news releases and speeches are far more effective than advertising. Convince the public of the sincerity of your desire to serve them.

Place service to the objectives of your organization ahead of profits or salary, but recognize that operations must be fiscally sound and compensation fair and, if possible, generous.

Always be generous in giving credit to others.

Organize the work so that a minimum of routine or detailed matters come to the top for decision. Plan constantly for improving the organization and its performance.

Men who cannot or will not accept and carry heavy responsibilities are unfitted for forest administration. However, for those who are willing to devote themselves to the objectives for which their organization is working and who are temperamentally fitted to lead and to carry the load, it is the field of endeavor which offers largest monetary compensation and rich opportunity for worthwhile service.

LITERATURE CITED

1. American Management Association. 1957. "Leadership on the Job: Guides to Good Supervision," New York. 303 pp.
2. Cleeton, Glenn W., and Charles W. Mason. 1946. "Executive Ability: Its Discovery and Development," The Antioch Press, Yellow Springs, Ohio. 540 pp.
3. Gulick, Luther. 1937. Notes on the Theory of Organization, "Papers on the Science of Administration," Institute of Public Administration, Columbia University, New York. 195 pp.
4. McCulloch, Walter F. 1950. "The Forester on the Job," Oregon State College Cooperative Association, Corvallis, Ore. 105 pp.
5. Riegel, John W. 1941. "The Selection and Development of Prospective Foremen," Bureau of Industrial Relations, Bulletin 11, University of Michigan, Ann Arbor, Mich. 69 pp.
6. Simon, Herbert A. 1957. "Administrative Behavior," The Macmillan Company, New York. 259 pp.
7. Simon, Herbert A. 1960. "The New Science of Management Decision," Harper & Brothers. 50 pp.
8. Smith, Howard. 1946. "Developing Your Executive Ability," McGraw-Hill Book Company, Inc., New York. 225 pp.
9. Tead, Ordway. 1935. "The Art of Leadership," McGraw-Hill Book Company, Inc., New York. 308 pp.

CHAPTER 21. *Education in Forestry*

FORMAL AND INFORMAL courses in forestry were offered as early as 1870.[4] Professors of agriculture, botany, or horticulture at Michigan, Michigan State College, Minnesota, Nebraska, Iowa State College, Cornell, and Yale were among the first to begin collegiate-grade instruction in forestry. Education at the professional level began in 1898 with the establishment of the New York State College of Forestry at Cornell University and the Biltmore Forest School at Biltmore, North Carolina. Both were short-lived, closing in 1903 and 1913, respectively. A successor to the former, The New York State College of Forestry at Syracuse University, was opened in 1911. The Yale School of Forestry, established in 1900, is the oldest operating college of forestry in the United States. The first two schools were headed by European foresters, the third by an American who took his training in Europe. To begin with, all three schools and the others that were established during the 15 years immediately following the turn of the century were obliged to depend heavily upon European forest technique for subject matter and teaching methods. It was not until after some 15 years of forest practice in our own country and after many forest investigators had studied American forests that a truly American forestry began to emerge. Teachers now rely heavily upon the results of practice and research that have proved their worth in American forests.

Between 1903 and 1914, 21 additional schools of forestry were established, most of which are still functioning.[4] The number of schools has continued to grow. As of 1962, 43 colleges and universities were offering four-year training in forestry. The rapid increase in colleges of forestry during the past 64 years has been paralleled by the greatly enlarged scope of the profession. The original concept of forestry embraced mainly protecting forest lands, regulating the timber harvest, and starting new timber crops on their way. Today forestry includes all phases of forest land management, the harvesting of timber and other forest crops, and the processing of forest products for human use. In other words, foresters serve where trees serve and where wood serves.

Requirements for Forestry

The technical requirements and working conditions in forestry impose certain standards that men who desire to enter the profession must meet. The education offered in colleges of forestry demands high intellectual capacity and serious devotion to study.

Leadership in forestry requires men of high mental competence and mature judgment, for their jobs are very important to our national economy. Forestry also has jobs in which men of good intelligence, high character, and devotion to duty can expect to achieve a satisfying life of service. Colleges of forestry admit and graduate only men who the faculties believe have the capacity to perform useful service in forestry.

A forester's work must be done largely on his own initiative and through his own ingenuity and sometimes in opposition to pressures from special interests. Foresters should, therefore, possess high standards of character, responsibility, and personality. They must be able to endure isolation without losing intellectual alertness. They must often persist in the face of discouragement. Emotional stability, facility in meeting and dealing with people, self-denial necessary to place the requirements of the job above physical comfort and, frequently, even above the wishes of friends, are tests of character successful foresters must meet.

The Training of a Forester

A forester requires a broad education in the natural and social sciences as well as intensive training in his own special field. A successful forester must be able to express himself clearly and forcefully in written and spoken English, in simple mathematical language, and by means of sketches and drawings. Failure to acquire facility in expression is almost certain to handicap his future. Written reports inform his superior of the work accomplished and supply the information upon which future plans can be based.

Oral expression is indispensable to clear understanding and smooth relationships among people. Mathematical formulas are in almost constant use by foresters in their day-to-day jobs. Maps, graphs, pictorial charts, sketches of simple layouts for headquarters sites, recreation areas, and roads, plans for buildings, and designs for new equipment all require some facility in graphic expression (Fig. 76).

A forester needs to understand fundamental biologic laws. Forests are far more than land covered by trees. They involve the complete biologic, hydrologic, and edaphic complex that occupies the land. To manage this

Fig. 76 Students in landscape architecture are examining with professors their plans for a highway interchange development in a mountain recreation area.

complex so as to harvest from it products useful to man with a minimum expenditure of money and human effort requires understanding of the interrelationships between the various plants and animals that make up the forest community.

A forester needs basic knowledge of chemistry, physics, geology, and engineering. This helps him to understand this biologic community and to survey land, lay out and build roads, and erect buildings and fire-lookout towers. It also helps him to understand the principles of telephones, radios, internal-combustion engines, and the many types of equipment that are used in developing the forest and harvesting and processing the products the forest yields.

An understanding of fundamental economics and business methods, government, and simple business law is the basis for operating a forest property economically. The major purpose of forestry is to provide for human needs. This must be guided by basic economic and business principles. The management of land, the harvesting of timber, and the conversion of forest products into useful commodities involve operations affecting the economic welfare of communities as well as of individuals and companies. The forester will seek to conduct his operations so as to strengthen his community and enlist the goodwill of citizens and government officials. By setting objectives acceptable to all men of good will and making these understood by all, he can help strengthen human cooperation in productive enterprise and free government.

Finally, a forester must understand how to live and work with people. Forestry is to a large extent a public activity, and almost every forester must deal with timberland owners, timber operators, employees, customers, and citizens. He should be aware of civic responsibilities and learn to live a happy and useful life.

The foregoing may be summed up by saying that a forester should have a good general education in the broad meaning of this term. It is especially important that he understand and deal effectively with himself, his fellowmen, the society of which he is a part, and the physical universe in which he lives. Thereby he is prepared to live a productive life in harmony with his associates and environment.

Curricula in Forestry. Colleges of forestry have sought to establish curricula that would prepare men for service throughout the United States. They also seek to offer specialized training by fields of forestry and by regions. A standardized curriculum for all colleges has few advocates. Feeling is widespread, however, that all curricula in forestry should include certain basic subjects. Subjects that Dana suggests as indispensable for a general forestry curriculum are dendrology, forest ecology, silviculture, forest protection, forest measurements, forest management, forest economics, forest policy, and forest administration.[1]

Major curricula offered by colleges of forestry in 1960 covered the following subject-matter fields:

General forestry with or without options in science, social science, management, and industrial forestry
Range management
Wood utilization with options in chemical technology and engineering
Wildlife management
Wood technology
Recreation management
Landscape architecture
Park management
Lumber merchandising and light construction
Furniture industry
Logging engineering
Conservation of natural resources
Pulp and paper technology

Wood chemistry and plastics
Packaging technology

Additional curricula have been urged upon the schools by various industries.

Debate is vigorous between those who would limit the title "forester" to men who have been trained to manage land for production of timber crops and those who would broaden the title to include men with forestry background who specialize in wildlife, range, watershed, and park management; in wood technology; and in forest utilization.

As forestry grows in complexity, specialization becomes inescapable. The question remains as to where the line between foresters and non-foresters should be drawn and whether academic training is a sound basis for making the distinction (Fig. 77).

A study of the tasks performed by foresters graduated from the State University College of Forestry at Syracuse University reveals some interesting facts. Supervision and administration occupy 41 per cent of their time, research 13 per cent, sales and promotion 11 per cent, and technical

FIG. 77   Scale models help students to visualize construction details which can only be indicated in blueprints. (*Photo by C. Wesley Brewster, Syracuse, New York.*)

forestry work only 8 per cent. Of course, forestry knowledge is used in many of their supervisory, administrative, and other duties. Still it may appropriately be questioned whether training to perform the tasks of these advanced jobs should not be considered as desirable as technical knowledge.

Detailed descriptions of various curricula in forestry may be found in catalogs of the several colleges of forestry. Almost all colleges are studying their curricula with thought toward improvement, and changes are introduced yearly. Critical analyses of curricula and other features of colleges of forestry are given by Graves and Guise.[2]

Crowded curricula are characteristic of almost all colleges of forestry. To encompass the subjects desirable in the training of a forester, some colleges have required a fifth year. Others require 150 or more semester hours of work for graduation, thereby requiring the equivalent of five years' work at normal undergraduate loads. A few are seeking to condense subject matter so that an undergraduate professional curriculum can be completed in four years without being overloaded with courses.

Graduate Study in Forestry. Two colleges of forestry, Yale and Duke, offer only graduate degrees in forestry. Graduate training has a twofold purpose: to increase breadth of understanding and to permit concentrated effort in a special field. Independent scholarship and research are usually required. The master's degree is awarded for 30 or more semester hours of work beyond the bachelor's, and the doctor's degree for 90 or more semester hours of work beyond the bachelor's. A thesis based on independent research may be a part of the master's program and is always a requirement for the doctorate.

Men studying at the graduate level may specialize in any one of the several subject-matter fields of forestry or in basic sciences underlying forestry. Undergraduate students who have definite plans for graduate study would usually be wise to use elective hours to broaden their knowledge of the basic sciences and to study one or more languages. They will then be in a strong position to pursue work at the graduate level. Men graduating in the upper half of their class are generally considered capable of profiting from graduate study (Fig. 78).

A graduate degree is considered a requisite for most college-teaching and research positions. Men planning to enter these fields should look forward to studying for the doctor's degree.

Colleges of Forestry. For 1961 the Society of American Foresters reported by name 28 accredited schools and 16 nonaccredited schools.[5] Enrollment in the 28 accredited schools was 7,903, of which 6,856 were baccalaureate candidates, 696 master's candidates, and 351 doctoral candidates.

Graduate students accounted for 11 per cent of total enrollment in

1961. The 16 nonaccredited schools enrolled 1,848 students, mostly candidates for the bachelor's degree. For the two groups of schools, enrollment by undergraduate classes was: freshmen, 2,806; sophomores, 2,046; juniors, 1,918; and seniors, 1,934. Total enrollment was 9,751. In addition, several schools were giving introductory or special courses, and four ranger schools were operating.

Scarcely an annual meeting of the Society of American Foresters passes without some debate on how many men should be trained in forestry. Opinion reflects the speaker's conception of the breadth of forestry. Those advocating a broad interpretation foresaw no surplus of trained men even at the peak rate that prevailed in 1948.[3] Those with the narrower

Fig. 78   The electron microscope is used for studies of the structure of cell walls of woody fibers.

concept have stated many times in the past that too many foresters were being trained. Yet the profession has absorbed most of these.

Employment in Forestry Education

In a study of employment of foresters conducted by the Society of American Foresters in 1961 and 1962 it was estimated that 1,150 men were employed in education in forestry.* This includes instructors in secondary schools teaching conservation, extension foresters, and teachers in ranger schools and professional forestry schools. To maintain this number the annual replacement will be approximately 40 men.

College Teaching. Working conditions for teachers in colleges of forestry are among the best the profession affords. Academic life provides many delightful amenities. Association with students, alumni, and faculty presents constant and stimulating challenges.

Colleges and universities recruit their faculty with great care. Records are scrutinized and personal interviews often precede appointment.

Training for teaching in forestry is of two types: academic and practical. Schools prefer men who hold the master's and Ph.D. degrees, and who have practiced their profession in the field.

A man planning to enter college teaching should select as his specialty one of the major fields of forestry. Opportunities appear to be brightest for men trained to teach forestry economics and forest utilization.

Lucid writing and speech are requisites of good teaching. So also is skill in the art of teaching. The latter may be acquired best by training under a good teacher who knows how to grip students' attention and awaken a zest for learning.

College teachers are chosen primarily for their knowledge of the subject matter, personality, and scholarly ability.

ATTRIBUTES OF A GOOD TEACHER. The successful teacher should be patient and should understand youth.

To keep abreast of latest developments in the profession and related fields, teachers must be lifelong scholars. They must have the background and critical ability to evaluate new developments and to give them proper perspective in the overall training program.

The teacher usually is expected to carry on research. Students, especially graduate students, select their college on the basis of scholarly eminence of faculties.

Education has a very important role to play if world peace and democracy are to live. Skimpy training in such broad fields as citizenship and the art of successful living has been often charged against technical colleges. No course or group of courses will likely be found to provide

* Eyre, Francis H. 1962. "How Many Foresters," manuscript. 4 pp.

the specialist with a complete general education. Instead, it will be up to the teachers of professional subjects to inculcate in their students' minds their obligations to society as a whole and to set before them desirable standards of successful living.

Forestry curricula fortunately provide a great deal of general education.

WORKING CONDITIONS. Salaries for college teachers are likely to be below the best in private industry. Teachers may have limited opportunities to augment their regular salaries by gainful vacation employment, part-time consulting work, lecturing, and writing.

Vacations for college teachers are ordinarily generous—usually a month and sometimes as much as three months. When faculty members are free of academic duties, they are expected to travel and do other work for professional advancement. Sabbatical leave is available in many institutions for professional improvement, serious writing, and research.

College teachers have wide opportunity for self-expression. They are expected not only to teach but also to develop their subject matter, carry on research, and engage in technical writing and professional activities. They are encouraged to serve their profession through membership on committees and through holding offices in the professional societies.

College teachers have wide latitude in hours of employment. They themselves, in the last analysis, are the only judges of their own working hours and standards.

For men of imagination, energy, devotion to professional achievement, interest in research, and, above all, real understanding and sympathy with the problems of students, teaching offers satisfactions rarely found in any other type of employment (Fig. 79).

Other Teaching Opportunities. RANGER SCHOOLS. Teachers in ranger and other subprofessional schools require somewhat different preparation from college teachers. The curriculum is short, must be highly practical, and is ordinarily concentrated in presentation. Their work is vocational in nature. The ranger-school teachers, if outstanding in their fields, may have opportunities for advancement equal to those of college teachers.

One weakness of the forest industry in America is lack of subprofessional training. The jobs of harvesting timber, manufacturing lumber, processing wood, and handling the various other technical jobs that lie between the forest and the consumer of wood products yearly become more technical and difficult. The amount and types of power equipment used in woods operations have grown rapidly. Efficient use of mechanical loaders, special skidding devices, road-building equipment, and timber harvesters places new demands on workmen. Specifications for particular products, such as handle, shoe last, and bowling-pin stock, aircraft veneer logs, and blanks for ball bats, require a degree of knowledge for

Fig. 79 Instructing Georgia State students in forest wildlife. Chattahoochee National Forest. (*U.S. Forest Service photo.*)

the selection of material that hitherto was not required of the timber operator and sawmill worker. Operating headsaws, supervising lumber piling, operating dry kilns, and grading lumber are jobs that require training and devotion to detail.

Safety alone in logging operations is of sufficient moment to justify special training for woods foremen and others who supervise logging and sawmill operation. Accident rates are high and compensation insurance is expensive. As a result, evasion of responsibility by financially weak operators is a constant source of annoyance to state administrators.

JUNIOR COLLEGES. Men with forestry training have found satisfactory employment as teachers in community and junior colleges. Such institutions are growing rapidly, and some are introducing preforestry training.

SECONDARY SCHOOLS. High schools, secondary schools, and trade schools also offer opportunities for teachers with the background in science required of foresters. Teachers in such institutions must generally be trained in education as well.

Extension Forestry. Forestry extension is administered by the Federal Extension Service in cooperation with the state agricultural extension services and thus constitutes a part of the overall agricultural extension program of the land-grant colleges. The major objective of the farm-forestry extension program is to maintain a system of management for farm woodlands which will enable these areas to contribute fully and regularly to farm income and a more satisfying farm life. Chief responsibility for the accomplishment of this objective rests upon the extension foresters, who work through some 7,000 county extension agents, local farm leaders, and numerous county and community committees representative of the farm people. The work of extension foresters includes a certain amount of assistance to individual owners of farm woodlands. The bulk of their activity, however, is directed toward reaching large numbers of people and thus involves the use of such media as public talks, film strips, movies, radio scripts, news releases, bulletins, circulars, and method demonstrations.

In 1962, 44 states and the Commonwealth of Puerto Rico were cooperating with the Department of Agriculture in farm-forestry extension work. The number of extension foresters employed on the staffs of the state extension services totaled 93.* In addition, two extension foresters were employed by the Federal Extension Service to serve in a liaison capacity between the Department of Agriculture and the state extension services.

Farm Forestry. The work of farm foresters is authorized under the Cooperative Forest Management Act of 1950. While this program is similar in many respects to farm-forestry extension work, it is considerably more intensive in its approach. It concentrates upon providing in-the-woods technical advice and assistance to individual owners of small woodland areas. In most states the farm foresters are employed by state foresters, with the U.S. Forest Service cooperating in supervising and financing the program. The total number employed in 1962 was 661.* The foresters are organized on a project basis within the state, the territory covered by each averaging from three to four counties. The farm forester will prepare a simple management plan for a woodland, covering such operations as timber cutting, planting, thinning, and protection from fire, insects, disease, and grazing. When the farm forester finds the owner has timber ready for harvest, he recommends a method of cutting. He marks trees for cutting, estimates volume, and suggests timber buyers. Farm foresters under the cooperative forest-management program do not serve as agents for the farmers in making sales.

Cooperative forest-management projects in 1962 were active in 47 states and in Puerto Rico.† The Forest Service annual report indicates that 82,188 landowners holding 4,116,000 acres were assisted in 1960.[6] The timber harvested under this program had a gross sale value of $14

---

* Personal communication, U.S. Forest Service.

† Both extension and farm forestry programs were expanding in 1963.

million. Administrative costs shared between the states and the federal government totaled $3,854,000.

Public-relations Foresters. Railway companies, power companies, chambers of commerce, and pulp and paper and lumber companies employ foresters to promote forestry in the territory they serve and to explain the policy of the companies to landowners and others. Programs of forest-fire control, planting, and forest management have been sponsored by various railways in the South. Other railways in the Lake States and elsewhere have promoted tree planting, care with fire, and conservative methods of timber harvesting that will promote future timber growth. The major objective of all these companies is to build up the forest resources of the territory they serve. These jobs require special training and aptitude for meeting the public and convincing individuals that conservation is their business as well as that of timber companies.

Public-relations foresters are employed by the American Forest Products Industries and by various regional associations. Federal land banks oftentimes employ foresters to promote good forestry among their clients. All public forestry agencies such as the U.S. Forest Service and the Soil Conservation Service must get their messages across to the public if they are to be effective. The need for developing specialists becomes progressively more acute.

Special training in public-relations work is now offered at more than one college of forestry. Success in this field requires training in the techniques of radio, motion pictures, television, news writing, and other means of mass education. But success also depends upon the public-relations forester's having a good background of field experience upon which he can draw to get his message to his public.

Trade-association and Conservation-association Foresters. Many of the national and regional trade associations of lumbermen, pulp and paper producers, and other forest-industry groups employ technical foresters, who serve as staff advisors, liaison men to instruct and assist association members, and promotional personnel. The American Pulpwood Association is an outstanding example. It has undertaken to help test new mechanical equipment developed to facilitate pulpwood cutting and to disseminate the results to its members. It also has a program for training woods workers, promoting safety in woods operations, and preparing films and other instructional material to bring its message home to timber workers. The need for this type of service is growing constantly.

Conservation associations, sportsmen's organizations, and organizations such as the Boy Scouts of America, mountain clubs, and other organizations dealing with the out-of-doors employ some executive officers. Men with forestry training may find in these desirable employment. Opportunities and employment conditions vary widely from one organization to another. Such jobs provide opportunities for wide contacts and satisfying service.

LITERATURE CITED

1. Dana, Samuel T., and Evert W. Johnson. 1963. "Forestry Education in America Today and Tomorrow," Society of American Foresters, Washington, D.C. 402 pp.
2. Graves, Henry S., and Cedric H. Guise. 1932. "Forest Education," Yale University Press, New Haven, Conn. 421 pp.
3. Herbert, Paul A. 1949. "Are We Set Up to Train Too Many Professional Foresters?" *Proceedings, Society of American Foresters' Meeting*, 1948, pp. 21–25, Washington, D.C.
4. Hosmer, Ralph S. 1950. "Education in Professional Forestry," in Winters, Robert K., ed., "Fifty Years of Forestry in the U.S.A.," pp. 299–315, Society of American Foresters, Washington, D.C.
5. Markworth, Gordon D. 1962. "Statistics from Schools of Forestry for 1961: Degrees Granted and Enrollments," *Journal of Forestry*, 60(3):171–177.
6. U.S. Department of Agriculture, Forest Service. 1961. "Report of the Chief of the Forest Service," Washington.

CHAPTER 22. *Research in Forestry*

RESEARCH, APPLIED TECHNOLOGY, and human ingenuity have contributed to the American way of life fully as much as an abundant supply of natural resources. The American tradition implies high wages, short working weeks, and low prices of manufactured goods. These, in turn, require high output per worker and mass production and distribution. America has seen tremendous progress in agriculture. For example, between 1940 and 1960 in New York State, farm population decreased from 704,000 to 378,000 and the number of dairy cows from 1,362,000 to 1,173,000, but milk production rose from 7,591,000 to 9,915,000 pounds. In colonial times 80 per cent of our workers were engaged in agriculture. By 1962 the proportion so engaged was in the neighborhood of 10 per cent, yet never in our history had the people had greater variety, quality, and quantity of food nor at a lower price in relation to income. Applied research and technology were largely responsible for this increased efficiency.

During the period 1900 to 1932 output per worker in the lumber industry remained essentially stationary, but that of steelworkers increased 24 per cent; stone, clay, and glass workers, 58 per cent; workers in paper and printing, 62 per cent; workers in nonferrous metals, 120 per cent; and workers in motorcars, 1,000 per cent. The increase in output per worker has been almost directly related to the amount of research carried on by these several industries.

A study of research by industry made in 1952 revealed that of 31 industry groups the lumber and wood-products industry ranked at the bottom in the percentage of firms having research organizations. The paper and allied products ranked fifteenth among the 31. It seems clear that the lumber and wood-products industries generally have a long way to go in building up their research to a level that will enable them to compete effectively in new developments with the other major industries of our country.[6]

Development of Research

Research in forestry began long before extensive practice of forestry by either public or private agencies. Early investigations were concerned mainly with descriptions of species and general descriptions of forest types. John Bartram in colonial times and his son William in post-Revolutionary days made extensive studies in Georgia, Florida, and other states. Johann David Schoepf, a German surgeon with forestry training, made critical observations on the forests of Pennsylvania, Maryland, and Virginia during the days of the Confederacy. In 1819, "The Sylva of North America," a translation of an earlier edition in French by François-André Michaux, provided the first authoritative book in English on American trees. Nuttall, Emerson, Hough, and Sargent brought the study of American trees to a high level. The Arnold Arboretum founded in 1872 has been the outstanding center for study of the classification of woody plants.[4]

The first federal recognition of forestry was the authorization in 1876 for the Department of Agriculture to investigate forest production, consumption, and influences.[5] Research was the chief activity of the first three federal forest officers, Hough, Egleston, and Fernow. Before the year 1900 substantial knowledge of forest trees, timber resources, and the behavior of timber types was ready for use by the first practicing foresters.

In 1908, research was formally organized in the U.S. Forest Service according to a plan prepared by Raphael Zon. Stations were established on the national forests where long-term experiments could be carried out. At the beginning, the value of these stations as training centers and demonstration forests was envisioned. The Forest Products Laboratory at Madison, Wisconsin, was established in 1910. In 1921, research was extended to eastern forests. The McSweeney-McNary Act of 1928 provided organic legislation for nationwide coverage by forest experiment stations, for the survey of timber resources, and for enlarged research appropriations.[5] This followed an extensive study of research needs by Clapp.[2]

Agricultural colleges and experiment stations and universities began forest research before the year 1900. This work has now largely been centered in the colleges of forestry. Many of these have substantial programs of research in forest land management, game management, and use of forest products.[4, 6, 8]

State conservation departments have carried on research since 1900. Maine has been outstanding for its investigations on forest insects. Pennsylvania, New Hampshire, New Jersey, Ohio, New York, Texas, Michigan, and California have done important research in forestry.

Fig. 80 Exterior view of Simpson Timber Company's new research center shows folded plates and diamond box beams used in roof construction. (*AFPI photo.*)

Research in forestry by industries is estimated to exceed in cost that by all other agencies. Much of it is directed toward improving forest products or processing techniques (Fig. 80). The pulp and paper industry exceeds all others in wood-products research. Altogether, some 900 manufacturers, processors, and consumers of forest products and their associations participate to some extent in forest-products research.[4] A few private research institutes have carried on projects of importance to forestry.

Studies of research in forestry were made in 1926, 1929, 1937, and 1953.[1, 2, 6, 8] Expenditures for forest research in 1926 were estimated to total $4.4 million; in 1937, $14 million; in 1953, $45 million; and in 1961, $92 million. Kaufert projected an estimate for the year 1978 at $200 million. This projection is based, in part, on the trend of the past, but more upon the needs of forest landowners and the forest-products industries for increased technical knowledge of forest land and forest products and services.[6] Kaufert brings out that the expenditures for research have risen rapidly in total dollars and in percentage of gross-product value. For 1953 the national average spent for research was 1.1 per cent of gross-product value. The same year the forest-products industries spent but 0.25 per cent, a rate corresponding to the national average of 1930. In projecting a fourfold increase in forest research by 1978 Kaufert was merely expecting it to achieve the national average for all research as of 1953. A more recent estimate by the U.S. Forest Service is that expenditures will approximate $180 million by the year 1972.

Objectives of Forest Research. The broad objective sought through forest research is to increase human benefits from forest land by discovering and applying scientific knowledge to forests and forest products. Timber growing needs to be made a more certain and profitable enterprise. Output and safety of workers in timber harvesting and processing need to be increased. Properties of wood must be well understood in order that timber stands, various kinds of wood, logs, and boards may be put to their highest uses. If we are to maintain our forests and perpetuate their products and services, we must understand how forests retard erosion, promote water penetration into soil, and shelter wildlife; how forests can best be protected against destructive insects, diseases, fire, animals, and windstorm; and how timber can be economically harvested (Fig. 80). Fundamental as well as applied research is needed.

Organization of Forest Research

Much forest research involves experiments that are continued for several years or resources beyond the means of the individual worker. He must have the backing of an organization such as a forestry school, a forest experiment station, or a large industrial corporation if the long-term work he starts is to be carried to logical completion. This means that careful working plans must be prepared and instructions issued so that anyone properly trained can carry on an experiment once it is started. Organized long-term research is expensive. Much forest research by its very nature requires fairly large-sized operations. Cutting methods must be tested on plots of 40 acres or larger. New pulping techniques must undergo pilot-plant tests. Properties of wood vary with the growth rate of the tree, with the territory from which it comes, and with other factors. Consequently, wood from many trees and different locations must be tested before valid data representative of the species in question are obtained.

Federal Research. Federal research in forestry is centered in the U.S. Forest Service. In 1961, this was organized under an assistant chief in charge of research supervising the following divisions: Forest Management, Range Management and Wildlife Habitat, Watershed Management, Forest Fire Research, Forest Insects, Forest Diseases, Forest Products and Engineering, and Forest Economics and Marketing. In the field, the work is carried out through the Forest and Range Experiment

Stations and the Forest Products Laboratory. The Forest and Range Experiment Stations are located at Columbus, Ohio; Ogden, Utah; St. Paul, Minnesota; Upper Darby, Pennsylvania; Portland, Oregon; Berkeley, California; Fort Collins, Colorado; Asheville, North Carolina; and New Orleans, Louisiana. The Forest Products Laboratory is located at Madison, Wisconsin. In addition, the Forest Service operated the Alaska Forest Research Center at Juneau and the Tropical Forest Research Institute at Río Piedras, Puerto Rico. Other federal agencies cooperating with the U.S. Forest Service in forest research included the Soil Conservation Service, the Bureau of Animal Industry, the Bureau of Sport Fisheries and Wildlife, the Weather Bureau, Bureau of the Census, the Tennessee Valley Authority, and the Bureau of Foreign and Domestic Commerce.

The station directors are responsible for all research of the Forest Service in their respective territories. Station division chiefs in the above-named fields report to the director. Individual research projects are the responsibility of project leaders. The project leader prepares a problem analysis to determine the relative importance of problems, assigns priorities, and recommends a definite work program. A working plan is prepared, which sets forth in detail the types of individual studies to be conducted and outlines the methods by which they will be carried out and by which the data are to be summarized and analyzed. Individual studies may be assigned to assistants. The end result of a well-conducted project is one or a series of bulletins that set forth proper management techniques for the particular type.

In 1962 the Forest Service, under Public Law 480, had 47 research projects under way in 11 foreign countries and had 17 more grants under negotiation. This work is financed by funds received from the sale of surplus agricultural commodities where sizable credits in local currencies have been built up. Its objective is to promote basic research of benefit to American forestry, and it is carried out in foreign scientific institutions such as universities and nonprofit private laboratories. The subject-matter coverage in these projects is broad, including such topics as genetics, physiology, nutrition, soils, cytology, chemistry of lignin and cellulose, biological control of insects, susceptibility of North American tree species to foreign pathogens, forest survey techniques, combustion factors, and studies in ecology. Grants under this program are expected to reach the level of $3½ million or $4 million annually.

The Forest Products Laboratory at Madison, Wisconsin, has its own director and a series of division chiefs. The research divisions in 1961 were: Wood Chemistry, Packaging Research, Wood Preservation, Pulp and Paper, Timber Growth and Utilization Relations, Physics and Engineering, and Timber Processing.

FIG. 81   Coweeta Hydrologic Laboratory, Franklin, North Carolina. (*U.S. Forest Service photo.*)

Research in Forestry Schools and Agricultural Experiment Stations. Formerly, most research in forestry schools was organized on an individual basis. The work took the form of building up school forests, establishing permanent sample plots, and doing detailed work in dendrology, silviculture, wood technology, and other specific phases of forestry (Fig. 81).

Schools of forestry have also been entering into organized research. Outstanding examples are the wood-products laboratories operated by Oregon State College, the University of California, and State University College of Forestry at Syracuse University (Fig. 82). The research program of the last-mentioned is organized under a research director, who works with the several department heads in the college. Important research in forest products and forest management is being done at many other colleges of forestry.

Where forestry colleges are part of a land-grant college system, they normally participate in the research activities of the agricultural experiment station. This helps to finance projects and lends stability to long-term experiments. Agricultural experiment stations have made some important advances in research in silviculture, forest soils, forest entomology, forest pathology, and utilization of forest products.

The McIntire-Stennis Act of 1962 authorized the Secretary of Agriculture to augment support of forestry research at the land-grant colleges and forestry experiment stations and to include the state universities having colleges of forestry and offering graduate programs in sciences basic to forestry. Appropriations are to be distributed on a formula basis to the 50 states and Puerto Rico. Total appropriations in any year may not exceed one-half the amount expended by federal forest research agencies the preceding year. A new agency is to be established in the Department of Agriculture to administer the act.

Private Agencies in Forest Research. Private research organizations vary widely from company to company. Generally, they are headed by a director of research, who may have one to several project leaders and assistants reporting to him. Much of the research carried on in industrial

FIG. 82 Studying the rate of heat movement in wood by means of thermocouples.

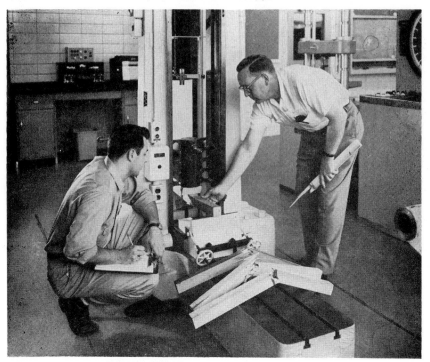

Fɪɢ. 83 Testing wood for resistance to impact. Such testing is continued until failure occurs.

laboratories is kept confidential, as it is expected to improve the company's processes and products and thereby enhance the competitive position of its sponsor.

Industrial corporations also sponsor research projects at institutes such as the Mellon Institute, and at various colleges and universities. Sometimes this may be merely sponsorship of an industrial fellowship, where wide latitude is left to the institution and fellow to select the problem and the methods of study. In other cases, special confidential studies are undertaken in which the industry may participate directly.

Industry research has been mostly in forest products where the company could expect to benefit directly and exclusively in the results. However, one large company has built up a special research program in forest biology and silviculture. The work projects include physiology, genetics, and basic ecology. The results are published freely for use of all concerned with forestry. Other industries have, through individual or joint action, supported research in silviculture, forest tree improvement, genetics, insect pests, and tree diseases. Results of jointly sponsored research also are made public (Fig. 83).

Cooperation in Research

Cooperation among research agencies in forestry is common practice. In 1949 the U.S. Forest Service had 644 cooperative research agreements.[7] No formal count has been kept of such agreements in recent years, but the total active in 1961 probably exceeded 1,000. About half of these were with colleges and research agencies and about half with industry. In 1960 about one-half million dollars was expended on 39 cooperative-aid projects at 23 institutions. Many others involved no transfer of funds. The Society of American Foresters, the Forest Products Research Society, and other scientific organizations serve to bring research workers together for exchange of ideas and coordination of effort. These many formal and informal exchanges facilitate overall efficiency without restricting freedom of action by workers.

Expenditures for Forest Research

Of the $45.4 million spent for research in 1953, $31 million was expended for forest products and utilization. Kaufert[6] assumed that research in economics, wildlife, and range management would increase less rapidly than the average for all forest research and that the greatest increase would occur in genetics, soils, watershed, and recreation, areas in which only modest expenditures were being made in 1953. Trends between 1953 and 1961 would bear this out. All agencies were expected to increase their research efforts, with the forestry schools increasing somewhat more rapidly than other agencies. This was primarily because strong graduate programs to prepare men for research could be carried on only in institutions where research work was active.

Expenditures by the U.S. Forest Service for research during the fiscal year 1940 were $2,100,000; for 1953, $5,400,000; and for 1960, $15,400,000. In the seven-year period from 1953 to 1960, therefore, the U.S. Forest Service had increased its expenditures 2.8-fold. The expenditures of forestry schools for research in 1953 were $1,700,000. The projected expenditure for 1978 was $15 million. The estimated expenditure for the fiscal year 1961–1962 was $7.5 million. The schools, therefore, within a seven-year period had increased their research more than fourfold and were at the halfway point for their goal of $15 million for the year 1978. Industry also had greatly expanded its research. In view of this progress, one is forced to the conclusion that the estimate of a total expenditure of $200 million by the year 1978 is probably conservative. Should present trends continue, this goal will probably be reached by the year 1973.

The estimated expenditures by agencies for fiscal years 1961 and 1962 were as follows: *

* Personal communication. (1962 incomplete except for federal expenditures.)

Agency	Expenditures, millions of dollars	
	Fiscal year 1961	Fiscal year 1962
Federal..................	17.3	22.5
Industry.................	62.0	62.0
Educational institutions....	6.5	7.5
States and other..........	0.4	0.5
Total.................	86.2	92.5

Achievements in Forest Research

Kaufert, in his study of 1953, asked whether the $45.4 million spent that year had resulted in accomplishments sufficient to warrant the expenditure and the increased expenditures estimated to be needed in the future. Opinions were sought from some 200 leaders of considerable stature in the industries and the public agencies. After discussion with the research investigator, these leaders invariably came to the conclusion that the products, practices, and processes with which they dealt had been greatly affected by research accomplishments. The pulping of southern pines and of hardwoods and the improvement of all pulping processes and most paper products have been the direct result of research. Harvesting equipment has been completely changed through industrial research. Forestry operations, from collecting seed through to the harvesting and final manufacture of wood products, have been modified greatly by research, most of which has been carried out within the past 25 years. Of more long-range importance than developing new or expanded uses for wood, new pulping processes, or new methods of manufacturing boxes, crates, cartons, and other products is the fundamental research that applies the basic principles of physics, chemistry, mathematics, biology, and social science to the growing of timber and the manufacturing of products from wood.

Specific accomplishments are legion. These vary from such prosaic work as designing and nailing crates for packaging material to extracting vanillin from lignin (Figs. 83 and 84). Modern timber connectors make possible the erection of huge unsupported spans; laminated timber and plywood avoid natural weaknesses; modern adhesives make possible better joining of wood. Impregnated wood is hard, fire-resistant, and dimensionally stable. "Compregnated" wood has extreme density, high strength, and resistance to abrasion and can be made with variable density.

Important also are the achievements in silviculture, forest surveys, and forest management. Little publicized but highly useful has been the research to determine proper methods of collecting, extracting, storing, germinating, and sowing forest tree seeds.[9]

Proper nutrition in nursery beds, weed control, protection against insects and damping off fungi, hardening stock to resist frost and drought, proper field planting techniques—all these problems were successfully attacked by forest-research workers.

Factors affecting forest-fire occurrence and behavior have been studied under various conditions of weather and fuels. Systematic classification and integration of these factors have greatly narrowed unknown elements in fire control. Good judgment thereby becomes the easier to apply to this highly dynamic forest enemy.

Fig. 84 Elaborate apparatus is required for studies in wood chemistry and plastics. (*Photo by C. Wesley Brewster, Syracuse, New York.*)

The classification of trees by rate of growth, value increment, and susceptibility to insect and fungal attack has simplified the process of selecting appropriate trees for harvesting. New hybrids have been developed through systematic tree breeding that display rapid growth and other desirable characteristics.

During the Second World War period forest-research workers discovered that output per worker in the naval-stores industry could be increased from 60 to 80 per cent through the use of a new method of bark chipping and the application of acid to the freshly cut streak. Output per worker in hardwood-pulp cutting could in certain timber stands be increased from 40 to 80 per cent through restricting cutting to trees 9 to 16 inches in diameter. Yield of spruce-fir lands in Maine could be almost doubled by reducing the cutting cycle from 60 to 20 years. Economic research in Pennsylvania has revealed that returns from various forestry operations vary widely. Thinning northern hardwood stands was found to be 80 times as remunerative as planting scrub oak lands. Such research enables the owners to reduce the speculative risk in forestry investments.

Special Aptitudes Required of Forest-research Workers

Forest research requires high scholarship, lively imagination, persistent endeavor, critical and objective thinking, self-discipline to work hard, patience to await results, and determination to acquire the necessary training and background through study and search of literature before embarking on a new undertaking. Forest research requires elaborate training.[1] Men entering research in the biological phases of forestry need to be well grounded in mathematics, physics, chemistry, and fundamental biological sciences, and to have a reading knowledge of one or more foreign languages. Those entering forest economics need to understand basic economics, political science, and business administration as well as forestry and the forest-products industries. They should be able to appraise the effect that proposed public measures are likely to have on forest practice throughout the country. They need to be well informed on the total forest resources, the potential growth rates, and the present condition of our forests.

Forest-products research requires comparable skills in all phases of wood technology, especially in timber physics and wood chemistry and their related engineering applications.

Employment and Outlook

With an annual expenditure of some $90 million in 1962 and with prospects of double this expenditure within a 10- to 15-year period the broad outlook for forest research is indeed bright. The actual number of men employed in 1962 in all phases of forestry and closely related research was probably in the neighborhood of 4,000, with about one-fourth that number in the U.S. Forest Service. Many were employed in pulp and paper companies, plywood companies, and cellulose companies where competence in chemistry, chemical engineering, mechanical engineering, and other backgrounds are needed rather than forestry.[3]

The long-term outlook remains good. The only means by which our country's needs for forest products can be continually met and expanded with a dwindling old-growth timber supply is through applied research.

Opportunities in Tropical Forest Research

The tropical forests of the Western Hemisphere represent the world's greatest virtually untapped forest resource. Intensive use of this resource depends upon detailed and extensive research into the properties of the various woods, tree-growth rates and ecology, methods of exploiting the forest, types of transportation, and methods of making the tropical lands healthful places in which workers can live and work. A number of tropical countries are interested in developing this great resource.

Very little research has been carried out in tropical forestry in the Americas. The Institute of Tropical Forestry is maintained by the U.S. Forest Service at Río Piedras in Puerto Rico. Other research in tropical forestry is being carried on at Turrialba, Costa Rica, and at forestry schools and government laboratories in several of the Latin American countries. Latin Americans understandably wish to maintain their own research institutes. Opportunities for research in India, Africa, and other tropical regions also seem likely to increase as new nations build up their forest economy.

LITERATURE CITED

1. Bailey, I. W., and H. A. Spoehr. 1929. "The Role of Research in the Development of Forestry in North America," The Macmillan Company, New York. 118 pp.
2. Clapp, Earle H. 1926. "A National Program of Forest Research," American Tree Association, Washington, D.C. 232 pp.
3. Eyre, Francis H. 1962. "How Many Foresters," manuscript. 4 pp.
4. Dana, Samuel T. 1950. "Forest Research," in Winters, Robert K., ed., "Fifty Years of Forestry in the U.S.A.," pp. 316–339, Society of American Foresters, Washington, D.C.
5. Graves, Henry S. 1947. "Problems and Progress of Forestry in the United States," Society of American Foresters, Washington, D.C. 112 pp.
6. Kaufert, Frank H., and William H. Cummings. 1955. "Forestry and Related Research in North America," Society of American Foresters, Washington, D.C. 280 pp.

7. U.S. Department of Agriculture. 1950. "Report of the Chief of the Forest Service," Washington. 69 pp.
8. U.S. Department of Agriculture, Lake States Forest Experiment Station. 1938. "Forest Research in the United States." St. Paul, Minn. 138 pp.
9. U.S. Department of Agriculture, Forest Service. 1948. "Woody-plant Seed Manual," Miscellaneous Publication 654, Washington. 416 pp.

CHAPTER 23

Employment in Forestry and Related Fields

FORESTRY HAS ITS specialists and its generalists. The specialists are experts of high competence in such areas as forest pathology, forest entomology, forest genetics, forest taxation, and logging engineering. Generalists are those who serve as land and plant managers and administrators. In a subject-matter area as broad as forestry, a man may more quickly establish himself as an expert in some special field than as an outstanding generalist. One might say that widest opportunities for the young man exist as a specialist and for the mature man as a generalist. A young man considering separate fields of forestry in which he might specialize would do well to consider not only the immediate prospects for employment in the field, but whether or not the field leads to broad opportunities later in life.

Forest lands produce timber, water, forage, wildlife, and recreation. We, therefore, find specialists in timber management, watershed management, range management, wildlife management, and recreation and park management. Increasingly, however, lands are being managed for multiple use. The national-forest supervisor must certainly consider all five of these resources as falling within his responsibilities. The same can generally be said of the manager of state forest lands. Increasingly the manager of industrial forest lands is giving attention to conserving soil and water, to maintaining a favorable habitat for wildlife, to providing forage for domestic livestock, and to opportunities for public recreation. For example, in 1960 a nationwide survey of recreational activities on industrially owned forest land indicated that some 6 million recreational visits were made to private lands, that 107 companies were operating parks and picnic areas, that 53 million acres were opened for public hunting, and that some 735,000 acres of lakes and 37,000 miles of fishing streams were open to public use. The man who is responsible for the management of a specific area of forest land, therefore, is increasingly given responsibility for the total resources present on this land.

Men have achieved a high level of responsibility in forestry by starting

381

their careers in a variety of ways. For example, chiefs, assistant chiefs, regional foresters, and directors of forest experiment stations in the U.S. Forest Service have risen to these high positions through beginning their careers in forestry both as administrators and as research men. Among them have been men who entered as geologists, chemists, botanists, economists, and engineers. The profession is still sufficiently small in size that a man who makes an outstanding record either in the management of a specific area of land or as a specialist in some branch of forestry soon attracts attention and is given opportunities for advancement and wider responsibilities.

Forest Protection

Protecting forests against fire, insects, bacteria, fungi, animals, and other destructive agents is primarily the task of the forest land manager. In this he may be assisted by specialists in the behavior of these forest enemies. The specialists find employment largely in federal and state forestry organizations.

Control of fire is a major task of state forestry departments, requiring the greatest allocation of funds and much attention to organization and equipment. This work will continue to provide employment for foresters and forest guards for the indefinite future. Between 1933 and 1960 the number of acres burned annually in the United States decreased from 44 million to 4.5 million acres. The costs of providing protection and the number of men employed have risen correspondingly. In 1960 almost half the forest area burned annually was unprotected.[4] Extending protection to this land, particularly increasing protection on the interior lands of Alaska, will require increased numbers of trained foresters.

In the last decade our nation has given much attention to reducing the annual losses from insects and diseases. The use of powerful pesticides including antibiotics is opening up entirely new possibilities for attaining quick results. Both forest entomology and forest pathology offer attractive employment opportunities for specialists in these subjects. Research and control men both are needed. Most of the employment opportunities exist with state and federal agencies, but industries also are employing pathologists and entomologists.

Forest Land Management

The broadest activities for foresters exist in land management. Good reasons exist for expecting both public and private forestry to increase in intensity in the years ahead. The responsibility for managing the woodlands of a large pulp and paper or lumber company is one of the most remunerative and in many ways satisfying positions in forestry. The top executives generally give their woodlands managers considerable freedom in carrying out their operations. As long as the mill quantities of wood at a reasonable cost and with the future assured, forest managers are likely to be given wide authority. The forestry work of a large industry may be more integrated, and this in itself gives to the forest manager a degree of control over his operations that the public forester or even the private timber landowner does not possess. For all the front-office talk, the woodlands manager, after all, has a clear-cut task. He knows that recreational use of the land and the management of wildlife are strictly secondary to his main task of growing timber for conversion into useful commodities. The task requires the capacity to integrate skills and functions for highest success. Management of public forests is also a challenging job requiring high technical and managerial skills. Timber management is but one of several responsibilities. Harmonizing multiple use of land to suit the demands of stockmen, sportsmen, water users, and recreationists while at the same time contributing in a substantial way to the nation's wood supply is a demanding and often frustrating job. But the manager on the ranger district or state forest has considerable latitude to develop his forest uses in response to overall demands, and many have done so with distinction. Few positions offer more varied experience in dealing with complex local issues or a better training to prepare for advanced-level administration. As public ownership of forest land is expanding but slowly, employment opportunities are mostly for replacements and intensification of work.

Administering public aids to private forest owners employs many foresters. Some men may find limited satisfaction in such work, for such foresters have little real authority. Their stock in trade is education and persuasion of landowners.

Despite substantial aids to small timberland owners, the practice generally in 1961 was below what was believed necessary to enable these timberlands to meet the growing needs of the nation for wood. Measures were being sought through both private and public means to increase the forestry effort on some 260 million acres of privately owned lands in small holdings.

Estimates have been made from time to time as to the number of men who would be needed to bring about good forest practices on all the commercial forest lands of the nation. If forest productivity is to increase to the level needed to meet estimated timber requirements to the year 2000, some 30,000 foresters may be needed in land-management activities. This is double the number who were employed in 1961. A preliminary estimate made of the total number of foresters needed on a world-wide basis by the year 1975 was 300,000; the estimated number employed in 1960 was 75,000. Such an estimate may, however, bear little relationship to the number who will actually be employed. The latter depends very much on economic circumstances and upon the resources which the nations are willing to devote to building up their forest lands.

Managing Forests to Conserve Soil and Water

Water for municipal and industrial use and for irrigation is becoming progressively more valuable year by year. It is also becoming scarcer. At the same time, floods tend to increase in frequency and in severity. They also increase with the growth of our major cities, most of which are located in river valleys where important sections are subject to inundation.

It seems inevitable that our people will continue to occupy and cultivate land subject to wind erosion in the prairie-plains region. A need for intensification of shelterbelt programs in this area will continue for many years.

Even though our nation needs to give increasing attention to its sources of water supply and to its lands subject to erosion by water and wind, the total number of foresters who are likely to be employed in these specific fields is somewhat limited. It is unquestioned that municipalities will be seeking additional watershed areas. Cities such as Boston, New York, and Seattle have substantial watershed areas that require the services of men informed in forest management as well as watershed management. It seems, however, that the major water supplies of the future are likely to come from lands managed for multiple uses. Specialists in watershed management will be needed, however, to determine, through research, standards for management of land for public water supplies and for minimizing flood runoff. Need appears to be developing for at least double the number of men who were so employed in 1961. Several forestry schools are offering programs in watershed management so that estimated needs are likely to be met.

Wildlife Management

Perhaps no field of forestry has had more appeal to young men than wildlife management. Though still a young profession, by 1949 thirty-two colleges and universities were offering training leading to a degree in this field. Two studies made at that time of the outlook for employment were not encouraging [1,3] in terms of the number of men preparing themselves in this field. This outlook, however, did not dim the enthusiasm of young men to enter the field nor of universities offering programs. In 1960, there were 16 schools of forestry offering degree programs at the bachelor's and master's level in wildlife management, with senior classes totaling 206 and graduate enrollment totaling 159. Some 12 other schools were offering four-year professional programs.

The employment record since 1950 has shown the above studies to be conservative. The number of men seeking outdoor through hunting and fishing has continued to increase. Ea/ makes a contribution, through the purchase of hunting and ฮรน..._ licenses, through tax on sporting arms and ammunition and other taxes, to the money available to employ game protectors and wildlife biologists. As a result, the number of positions and the quality of programs on the land have continued to increase (Fig. 85). Annual replacement alone is now sufficient to absorb many new professional men. The rate of increase in employment has, however, declined substantially since the early 1950s. Many state conservation departments, because of its popular appeal, focus far more of their effort on fish and game management than on forest management. There remains, however, a limitation as to how

Fig. 85 Posting a den tree from cutting on the Shawnee National Forest, Missouri. (*U.S. Forest Service photo.*)

far the wildlife manager can go in improving game habitats through his own efforts. Major responsibility falls on the land manager, whether he be a farmer, rural resident, or forester. It is for this reason that at least some men who have entered the field of wildlife management have sought to shift their work to the broader field of forest land management. The wildlife manager's job is becoming increasingly one of attempting to harmonize the desires of the landowner to enjoy the use of his property in peace and quiet and that of the increasing army of sportsmen to find land on which they may pursue wild game. He, therefore, has his task of composing human relations as well as trying to fit in the requirements of wildlife with the landowner's personal use of his land. There has been a constant increase in the posting of private lands. In part, this has been due to provocation by careless hunters who ignore landowners' rights. Whether public hunting on private land can be maintained in the indefinite future is an open question.

Foresters specializing in wildlife management find employment with the Fish and Wildlife Service, the land-management agencies in the Departments of the Interior and Agriculture, state conservation departments, schools, and a few private agencies.

A few wildlife managers have gone into business for themselves as trappers; fur dealers; leasers and managers of land for hunting, fishing, and wildlife production; and as operators of resorts and other facilities for sportsmen. The opportunities are quite varied, and success depends upon the initiative and imagination of the individual as well as upon obtaining a favorable setting for such private activities.

Range Management

Domestic animals graze on some 300 million acres of public range in the South and West and on substantial areas of private lands as well. Range management is a practical, down-to-earth task of the range technologist to support the livestock industry. During the past decade substantial improvement has been made in range conditions through new practices including destruction of brush and reseeding of palatable range plants. Other special actions have been taken to protect and restore lands injured by overgrazing, by drought, and by outbreaks of grasshoppers and other pests. The range manager operates generally over large areas on an extensive rather than intensive basis. In the last decade, however, intensive measures have proved increasingly economical and have been practiced by public land-managing agencies with the assistance of the range users.

Instruction in range management was given at seven forestry and 16 other schools in 1961. A total of 86 seniors and 38 graduate students were enrolled in range-management studies at forestry colleges. It is believed that the students enrolled are sufficient to meet the need for replacements and additional employment in this particular field. Specialists in range management find employment in the Bureau of Land Management, U.S. Forest Service, Bureau of Indian Affairs, state agricultural experiment stations and extension services, and with large ranch owners and livestock operators.

In 1962 the American Society of Range Management had a total membership of slightly over 3,700. Not all were professionally trained in range management, but a high proportion were.[*]

A few men have acquired their own ranch outfit and become independent operators. Opportunities of this sort are many throughout the West. Considerable capital is required in animals, hay lands, and ranch equipment.

Job prospects in range management appear to be rather good for the long run. The stockmen of the West are insisting on range improvement.

Men who are to engage in range management need a fundamental understanding of range livestock and of ranch and livestock economics. They need to understand range ecology and how to detect signs of range deterioration through the invasion of weeds and other plants. They particularly need to understand the soils, their susceptibility to compaction and to erosion, and how to manage the soil so as to obtain a high yield of forage with a minimum of soil destruction.

Management of Lands for Parks and Recreation

Outdoor recreation is one of the nation's most rapidly growing activities. It supports a host of service industries that supply equipment, housing, outdoor facilities and land, and special services for the camper, hunter, fisherman, skier, hiker, mountain climber, and sightseer. The outlook in terms of facilities needed is almost frightening (see Chap. 13). Outdoor recreation is creating the need for a large number of specialists to design facilities and manage land for such outdoor use. These facilities vary from intensively used areas such as campgrounds and picnic areas on national and state parks to wilderness areas that have a minimum of development.

The management of public playground areas needs the services of such general land managers as foresters together with the planning and designing skill of landscape architects. There seems to be increasing need also for those who can instruct the public in the enjoyment of the out-of-doors. This includes ski instructors and instructors in mountaineering as well as instructors in swimming, canoeing, overnight camping, wilderness trips, and recreational camp operation.

[*] Personal communication from John G. Clouston, Executive Secretary.

Near the top of the list is the landscape architect and planner. It is he who has the skill to design campgrounds, picnic areas, scenic highways, bathing areas, marinas, hiking trails, and the various other facilities that must be provided for intensive public use of outdoor recreational areas. The demand in 1962 for landscape architects by the U.S. Forest Service, state highway departments, the National Park Service, and the various conservation and park departments of states, counties, and municipalities was several times as great as the number of men available. This situation seems likely to prevail for at least a decade and perhaps longer. In fact, the demand for such services is so great that the profession may see men with other backgrounds entering into park planning and park administration. Young men preparing themselves in landscape architecture are almost certain to find good job opportunities awaiting them upon graduation for many years to come. Beyond this immediate need for recreational planning is the broader one of planning for use of rural lands throughout the nation. This would appear to have great potentialities for talented individuals. A rough estimate in 1962 indicated that by 1980 some 7,000 professional men might be needed in outdoor recreation work. To plan and administer recreational use on national forests may ultimately require in the neighborhood of 900 men.

Timber Operating

However tight employment opportunities for foresters in land management may be, plenty of openings in logging and sawmill operation are likely to exist for decades to come. It is the foresters who understand how to harvest and process timber efficiently who will occupy the key jobs in the profession in the future, just as such men are the key industrial foresters of today. Logging and milling are the two basic forest industries without which others cannot operate.

It is common practice among large timber-holding and operating companies to have all woods activities in charge of a woodlands manager (Fig. 86). The woodlands manager is responsible for purchasing wood from outside owners, for planning and carrying out all operations on company lands, and for supervising all activities of the forestry division. He may supervise divisions of accounting, supply, engineering, and the general staff offices. A woods manager in a large company will have district managers responsible for logging and forestry activities.

Work in logging must often be done in unfavorable weather. In the Douglas-fir region the rainy period may extend from October to June. Unless it is physically impossible, work continues during this period. Low temperatures and heavy snowfall in the winter may accentuate seasonal fluctuations of the industry in other regions.

Accident rates in logging are the highest among industries. Work in

FIG. 86 Planning logging operations on St. Regis Paper Company lands. Washington County, Maine. (*U.S. Forest Service photo.*)

the woods requires a person who is mentally alert. Eastern timber, being small, is less hazardous to log than the heavy timber of the West. However, because operations are small, widely scattered, and often inadequately supervised, occurrence of accidents per 1 million man-hours employed is higher in the East than in the West.

A prospective logger-forester will need to be basically well grounded in mathematics, surveying, and physics. As advancement is made in the industry, knowledge of forest pathology, mensuration, logging techniques, accounting, and business methods will assume importance. Ability to express oneself both in speaking and in written reports is also important.

The forester will rarely match the skill of the practically trained man of long experience, but the practical man often lacks the ability to conceive and execute planning and executive jobs.

Lumber Manufacture and Sale

Employment opportunities in sawmills parallel to some extent those in logging. Throughout the United States are some 40,000 to 60,000 mills.

Almost half the lumber is sawed by fewer than 1,000 mills. The many scattered small mills, like the small loggers, operate intermittently and have high rates of business failure.

The big mills cutting 100 million board feet or more per year are all in the West and South. Each one saws a few species into a limited number of products. They are usually located in small communities and are affected by the same general conditions that apply to logging. Work is highly mechanized.

Working conditions in a small sawmill in the North or South may be primitive. The small sawmill is typically located in an open, unheated shed and has a minimum of safety devices. Hazard in sawmill operations is high, second only to logging among American industries. The lumber industry as a whole fluctuates widely in activity, and in parts of the country operations are seasonal.

Unionized labor characterizes the large sawmills of the West and some of those in the Lake States. Living conditions in small sawmill towns may be far from ideal, though many western mill communities are attractive villages.[2]

The forestry college graduate has to make his own job in the mill. The jobs depend more upon experience than technical training, and positions at the top are normally beyond the ability of a young fellow lacking experience.

Fortunately, the picture is not discouraging. There will probably be increasing opportunity among the small mills where the top and bottom are not far apart. As the manufacturing processes go beyond the sawing of logs into lumber, the technical problems become greater and the need for technically trained men increases. Various phases of remanufacture, fabrication, and merchandising offer good opportunity to college men.

In many mills the job of dry-kiln operator offers an entering wedge several rungs above the bottom of the ladder. Scaling, tallying, and assisting in inspection are good ways to gain a quick knowledge of a mill's operation, and such jobs may be available to a man young in the profession. Time studies, cost analyses, production control, and quality control require abilities not ordinarily developed by even the above-average worker. Here the college man enjoys a distinct advantage. Some may enter the field by way of general office and accounting routine. College background along these lines enables the trained man to bypass much of the step-by-step advancement up the labor ladder. A college-trained man should be better able than others to appreciate the many problems of personnel and labor relations. The ability to read and make use of such material as is issued both by government agencies and by trade associations is something that is not learned by handling lumber.

The small sawmill also offers the forester with some experience an opportunity to go into business for himself. Capital requirements are modest, and financing can often be arranged through concentration-yard operators. Lack of large blocks of virgin timber makes the small sawmill the dominant harvesting machine in the East. A forester with business ability who applies good practices to his operation, maintains an adequate timber supply, uses efficient handling methods, and reduces waste to a minimum has a good chance to succeed.

One feature above all must not be neglected—marketing. The small mill owner who wishes to realize full value from his labor must learn to grade his lumber, season it, and hold it for truck or carload shipments. Otherwise he will spend his time working for concentration-yard operators. Time spent in finding profitable market outlets for his product is likely to be highly remunerative.

Lumber Selling and Construction

Forestry colleges number among their graduates several presidents of lumber companies and many successful wholesalers and retailers. Beginning jobs in lumber selling will be mostly of the apprentice type. Advanced jobs include price estimating and materials handling and expediting for the contractor. Planning and designing homes are important jobs which must be well done. This may lead to partnerships in the business, and it trains the worker for the establishment of an independent contracting business. Business ability and security for borrowing the necessary working capital are essential for independent contracting, but the capital outlay need not be large.

Although the typical American dwelling is a custom-built product, more and more houses are "built to sell" rather than built on the customer's order. In either case, a beginning contractor needs only sufficient capital to erect one home at a time. Usually he can borrow money on land and on a partially constructed building. Financial backing is not difficult to obtain when tangible security in land and buildings can be offered.

Few college men have entered the field. Hence, competition is largely from men who have had limited opportunities to learn the fine points of the business.

As in milling, lumber-sales jobs are many and widely dispersed. One estimate indicated the need for over 100,000 trained men in the light-construction field. Opportunities are plentiful for those desiring careers in house construction.

Wood Processing

The wood-processing industries are numbered in the thousands. Approximately 1,000 were operating in 1961 in New York State alone. Their products are legion, their basic processes limited. These include seasoning, machining, gluing, and finishing, in all of which technical knowledge is valuable.

A thorough understanding of basic physics and chemistry and some knowledge of economics and business administration are needed. Knowledge of wood technology, including wood structure and identification, timber physics, wood seasoning, wood machining, glues, and finishing, and sufficient advanced chemistry to understand the chemical treatments of wood so as to modify its properties will enable the forester to make a real contribution. Ingenuity is especially valuable in designing new tests to meet special requirements of industrial research in wood processing.

The forestry graduate will ordinarily have to find his own job. Frequently, he will be obliged to accept a job at labor wages to get a start. Patience, good practical sense, and willingness to undertake any task that needs to be done are attributes that should lead to success in the long run.

As factory conditions in America go, working conditions may be far from ideal. This is partly because many of the plants are small and the workers unorganized.

Gradually, trained men entering the wood-processing industries may be expected to work into managerial positions. Because the wood-using industries are characteristically small and because relatively few foresters or wood technologists have entered these industries, opportunities for advancement to high posts are good. Foresters, considering the number entering, have probably made a better record of achievement in these industries than have graduates in business administration or engineering.

The long-term employment outlook is favorable. The industries taken together bulk large and can absorb ultimately a large number of technical men. It is anticipated that, once well started, employment in the wood-processing industries will grow at a geometric rate. Leveling off should not be reached until such time as wood technologists are performing all functions they effectively can in the modern wood-processing industry. This will require men numbered in the thousands.

A man, after having accumulated some capital, may enter into the business as part or full owner of a small wood-processing plant. Opportunities are particularly bright for young men with a flair for design and artistic sense. There seems to be increasing appreciation in America of furniture and other woodwork that bear the mark of thoughtful design and careful workmanship.

Pulp, Paper, and Wood-chemical Industries

The pulp and paper industry is characterized by relatively large operations. A progressive, though fluctuating, increase in output has occurred over the years. Small mills have generally been at a disadvantage in competition with large ones unless they devoted their efforts primarily to specialty papers. During periods of business depression the pulp and paper industry has suffered along with the others. During periods of high business activity it has difficulty in keeping up with the demands. The long-term outlook for the industry is favorable. Production in 1961 was the highest on record. Year by year new uses are found for paper products and new skills are developed in manufacturing which make it possible to maintain a strong competitive position.

The pulp and paper industry is highly dependent upon its raw-material supply, of which it uses a large amount. The decline of many pulp and paper mills in the past has been due in part to shortage of local sources of suitable wood for manufacture of the pulp. The industry generally recognizes this shortcoming, and many companies have undertaken progressive steps to establish a dependable pulpwood supply. This is being brought about by purchase of land, planting of trees, and encouragement of good forest practice on the lands of private owners tributary to their mills. Even more significant has been the widespread pulping of hardwoods.

Other things being equal, an integrated pulp and paper mill with a substantial area of timberland from which to draw its material is a more stable company for the long pull than those that manufacture pulp only or paper only. During the period 1943 to 1949, a large number of pulp and paper mills were bought up by publishing concerns seeking to ensure a supply of paper to meet their needs. The industry on the whole, therefore, is becoming more and more characterized by a few large companies. Such control, however, does not mean that independents are frozen out. The more the large manufacturing plants are devoted to a few major products, the greater the opportunities for the small concerns with versatile equipment to produce a wide variety of specialty papers and thus maintain their position in the field.

Competition for well-trained pulp and paper technologists was very keen in the decade 1951–1961. This competition seems likely to continue for some years to come. The industry itself has sought to attract young men to the paper field by offering generous scholarships in the leading schools of pulp and paper technology. The demand for technologists has increased because of the increased technical demands of the manufacturing process on the one hand and because of the relatively vigorous research programs that the industry sponsors. This has led to attractive positions at good salaries for men entering the paper industry and allied fields and for rapid advancement once they are established.

Entering positions in the paper industry are as control chemists, assistant research chemists, assistant foremen, or assistants to the superintendent. Some of the larger companies have special training programs by which new men are moved from department to department until they are finally placed in positions in the manufacturing or sales department. Starting salaries in 1961 were around $6,000 a year. After 10 years' experience many men have become assistant superintendents, superintendents, assistant chief chemists, or chief chemists with salaries ranging upward from $10,000 a year. Further advancement leads to positions in management with salaries going considerably above this level.

Entering positions in the chemical manufacturing companies are generally as research chemists in the technical sales department. Starting salaries are about the same as those in the paper industry. After 10 years' experience men are generally employed as salesmen, special technical representatives, or head chemists.

Students trained in pulp and paper manufacture or in special courses based on pulping, with instruction in high polymers added, are equipped for technical positions in the cellulose-plastics field. Working conditions and salaries are similar to those in the pulp and paper industry. Employment may be in large or small companies that manufacture consumers' goods.

Because of the large investment required for pulping and manufacturing paper, little opportunity exists for a man without large financial resources to become an independent manufacturer; however, he may become a consultant or broker.

Industries engaged in extracting and refining naval stores, tanning materials, essential oils, and other wood-chemical products also offer employment opportunities. Forestry schools offer only limited training in these specialties. Most of the technique must be learned on the job. Men with a good background in pulp and paper technology might, however, seek out these fields should employment in paper mills become slack.

LITERATURE CITED

1. Graham, E. H., C. R. Gutermuth, Lloyd W. Swift, Clarence M. Tarzwell, and R. M. Rutherford. 1950. "It's Time to Take Stock," *Journal of Wildlife Management*, 14:237–242.
2. Moir, Stuart, DeWitt Nelson, Michael Bigley, William H. Price, and W. D. Hagenstein. 1949. "What is Private Forestry Doing in the West?" *Proceedings, Society of American Foresters' Meeting*, Boston, 1948, pp. 169–181, Washington, D.C.
3. Turner, David B. 1948. "Professional Opportunities in the Wildlife Field," Wildlife Management Institute, Washington, D.C. 208 pp.
4. U.S. Department of Agriculture, Forest Service. 1960. "Report of the Chief of the Forest Service," Washington. 49 pp.

CHAPTER 24. *Employers and Regions*

EVERY YOUNG MAN entering a profession has certain potentialities and latent powers. Whether these powers are gradually developed as his years of service increase or atrophy because of frustration or complacency depends to a large extent upon the opportunities presented to him by the agency for which he works.

The graduate should seek employment with agencies that have objectives he can freely accept and that provide opportunities for professional development. Preferably he should seek an organization that is growing.

Large agencies usually offer better long-run opportunities for promotion and for wide experience than do small agencies. However, some small agencies, such as a highly respected firm of consulting foresters, may cover a wide variety of fields and thus bring the worker into contact with many opportunities. The broader the field of service that a given agency encompasses, the wider, in general, the opportunities for advancement and for self-development. Finally, a forester would do well to consider the past performance of a prospective employer in terms of the number of professional men he has employed and the opportunities he has placed before them.

The Society of American Foresters made estimates in 1951 and in 1961 of where foresters were employed and by what type of agency. The results are shown in Table 19.

Table 19 excludes 41 United States foresters working overseas in AID programs and 12 working on FAO assignments.

The study, made in cooperation with forestry schools, revealed that 4,450 graduates were out of forestry or had retired from active work, and 1,160 were deceased. The report revealed that 3,400 were out of touch with their school and their whereabouts unknown. Only 62 were reported to be unemployed.

The survey revealed a substantial increase in the number of foresters employed by the several agency groups, with the largest increases in federal agencies, industries, and education. Little change was reported in state employment or association employment. The increase in employ-

TABLE 19. ESTIMATED EMPLOYMENT OF FORESTERS IN THE UNITED STATES
FOR THE YEARS 1951 AND 1961

Agency	Number employed		Per cent of 1961 total
	1951	1961	
Federal................	3,550	6,750	35
Industry..............	4,400	6,050	31
State.................	2,500	2,650	14
Education.............	600	1,150	6
Self-employed.........	450	950	5
Association...........	200	200	1
Local government......	100	200	1
Other.................	450	1,400	7
Total...............	12,250	19,350	100

SOURCE: Data furnished by the Society of American Foresters: Eyre, Francis H. 1962. "How Many Foresters," manuscript. 4 pp.

ment in education reflected increases in student enrollments and increased research activities at the schools. To some extent it may be taken as an index of future employment because foresters must be educated before they can be employed. Table 19 reveals therefore a rapidly growing profession and one that seems destined to continue its expansion for several years ahead. Annual replacements alone will require some 645 men, as deaths, retirements, and those who leave active work for other reasons limit the average service period of individuals to about 30 years. The annual requirements for replacement totaled about 36 per cent of the 1961 graduating class.

Federal Employment

Foresters in all federal agencies other than government corporations such as the Tennessee Valley Authority are subject to civil service rules. This protects the employee from political discrimination and it also sets certain other rules as to leave, hours of duty, salary increments and advancement, and retirement into which each employee must fit. Entrance is through a civil service examination, of either the assembled or the unassembled type. The assembled examination requires an aptitude test and proof of professional training. The unassembled examination requires a detailed statement of training, experience, and accomplishment. Once a man has entered the federal civil service system, he may be advanced without further examination, though his name on a higher register may facilitate his promotion.

Initial appointments are for a probationary period during which the performance of the appointee is carefully observed. In large federal agencies new appointees may be sent to a formal in-service training school. This gives young men an opportunity to demonstrate their fitness and to get acquainted with upper-echelon personnel in the organization. On-the-job training is likely to continue throughout a man's career, taking the form of special assignments, periodic transfers, conferences, and task-force assignments.

Federal supervisors are obliged to report on the performance of each of their subordinates once annually. In many cases, it is the practice of the supervisor to discuss a performance rating with the individual and to suggest to him personal shortcomings, areas for study that would improve his competence, and outside activities which might enhance his value to the organization as a whole.

Most men enter at grade GS 5. Students who graduate in the upper one-fourth of their class, those who hold a master's degree, and those who have had appropriate experience may be employed at grade GS 7. Men with satisfactory efficiency ratings receive periodic salary increases up to the top of their salary bracket (see below). Several positions including ranger, supervisor, and regional forester may cover two salary grades. The highest classified grade is GS 18 at $18,500, for which men of unusual talent who can assume heavy responsibility are eligible.

The federal salary scale for various positions in the U.S. Forest Service, effective 1964, is given below:

Position	Grade	Salary range, dollars
Entering forester.............	GS 5	4,690–6,130
Assistant ranger..............	GS 7	5,795–7,550
District ranger...............	GS 9–11	7,030–10,650
Assistant supervisor..........	GS 11	8,410–10,650
Forest supervisor.............	GS 13	11,725–14,805
Assistant regional forester......	GS 14	13,615–17,215
Regional forester.............	GS 15	15,665–19,270
Assistant chief...............	GS 17–18	18,000–20,000
Chief......................	....	20,000

Employees are entitled to up to 26 days of annual leave with full pay and up to 13 days of sick leave with full pay, depending on their length of service. Sick leave may be accumulated from year to year without limit. Annual leave is cumulative up to 30 days.

Employees accepting temporary positions in government service have no stability of tenure. They are usually employed for a specific length of time and at the termination of the work are discharged.

The key jobs in federal organizations such as the U.S. Forest Service, particularly ranger and supervisory jobs, have a high degree of stability and are unlikely to be affected by ordinary cuts in appropriations.

Opportunities for Self-expression and Self-development. Even in beginning jobs encouragement is given the individual to study his job critically and to make suggestions for improvements. Advanced jobs in almost all fields of federal service offer foresters wide latitude for self-development and self-expression. Much responsibility and authority are delegated to the field men. They must, to be sure, conform to overall policy, laws, and regulations governing the handling of federal property and funds and the management of civil service personnel.

Retirement. Permanent federal employees are obliged to deposit 6½ per cent of their salaries in a retirement fund. Retirement is optional at ages 55 and 60 if the employee has 30 years of service, but with a reduced annuity if under age 60; and at age 62 retirement is optional with five years of service. Retirement is compulsory at age 70, provided the employee has 15 years of service. Annuities cannot exceed 80 per cent of an employee's highest five-year average salary. The present retirement law provides survivor benefits for widows and children of employees who die in service. The law also provides disability retirement benefits for employees who have five or more years of service and are not able to perform the duties of their positions. Retirement rates for employees with 35 years' service, since June 31, 1956, provided for 66.25 per cent of average highest salary over five consecutive years.

Federal employment is not ideal. The civil service organization is cumbersome in operation. Most technical jobs have some unique requirements, and administrators have little discretionary power in adjusting salaries. During periods of inflation, salaries of public employees traditionally lag behind those for private employment.

Progress has been made slowly in improving public employment. Reforms advocated would greatly improve federal employment and would give work agencies far greater authority in handling personnel.[1, 3] Overtime work is no longer allowed as a day-to-day requirement without appropriate compensation. Organization of employees is permitted, but they may not strike.[8]

Future expansion in federal forestry work will probably be less rapid than it has been in the past. Federal management of forest land seems unlikely to extend to substantially greater areas than it now covers.

National forests, national parks, national monuments, and game refuges are rapidly approaching a mature stage.

The U.S. Forest Service

In 1961 the U.S. Forest Service employed a total of some 6,312 professionally trained men, about 4,491 of them foresters. This, the largest agency employing foresters in the United States, is a highly decentralized organization. The 10 regional forest offices have under their jurisdiction the national forests, each with its independent headquarters. These also supervise federal grants-in-aid to states for fire control and cooperative forest management. The eight forest and range experiment stations have branch work centers.

The U.S. Forest Service has been outstandingly successful in bringing about close coordination of its widely scattered units. The overall policies and programs are carried through with a high degree of conformance to the intent of the organization.[7] Luther Gulick made an intensive study of this question in his book "American Forest Policy." He found that employees soon develop a loyalty to the Service and a tendency to identify their own interest with the advancement of the public interest in forestry.[5]

Working conditions on the national forests are attractive for those who like to work on the land (Fig. 87). Employees are expected to adopt a professional attitude toward their work, which means that they take personal responsibility for getting the necessary jobs done and done on time, even though this may mean some overtime work and some sacrifice in personal convenience. They learn to accept fire duty and other strenuous or even distasteful tasks as a part of the overall job.

Employment conditions in research may parallel those in administration, or men may be stationed in university communities where they enjoy some or all academic privileges and the intellectual stimulus the university atmosphere provides. A reasonable amount of travel is expected. Transfers are necessary for broadening experience and sometimes for the education of children.

Future development planned for Forest Service functions, if activated fully, will require 550 additional foresters annually over the next several years.*

Many leaders in federal, state, and private forestry have been selected from among men who spent their early years in the U.S. Forest Service. The organization has a long tradition of devotion to the public good, high standards of achievement, *esprit de corps*, and friendliness. Loyalty and devotion are expected; initiative, imagination, and skill in adminis-

---

* Personal communication.

Fig. 87 Though fast going out of use, pack trains were still employed to service a few forest operations in 1960. The sign designates the route followed by Lewis and Clark in 1805. Lolo National Forest. (*U.S. Forest Service photo.*)

tration are needed. To the men who can unstintingly provide such qualities of service and leadership, the Forest Service offers high satisfaction and substantial rewards beyond those of salary alone.

The Bureau of Land Management. The Bureau of Land Management is responsible for managing the 142 million acres of federal range, the 144 million acres of interior forests of Alaska, the Oregon and California Railroad and Coos Bay Wagon Road revested grants, and for miscellaneous other land-management functions. The Bureau manages the forage, timber, and wildlife resources of these lands on a sustained-yield basis. It employs foresters, range managers, wildlife experts, and other technologists to carry out its functions.

The National Park Service. A national park superintendent has duties paralleling those of the supervisor of the national forest. He must protect the public interest in concessions that are made to private companies operating transportation or hotels within the boundaries of the national parks. He is responsible for collecting fees and administering park regulations. As national parks are federal territory, any offense committed within a national park is a federal offense; consequently, the park superintendent, park rangers, and other park officers are, in fact, law-enforcement officers within the boundaries of the national park.

The Planning and Construction Division of the Service supervises architectural and landscape design and construction. It is responsible for approving all major improvement on national park areas. The Recreational Planning Division supervises nationwide planning for recreation in cooperation with other federal and state agencies. It investigates proposals for new developments. Through publications, conferences, and other devices it promotes recreational developments by others.

Men with training in landscape architecture are especially needed in the planning divisions. Extended travel is often required of men in these divisions. They must have the capacity to appraise areas for historic and scenic merit and must understand how to develop such areas for public use without jeopardizing the major feature which gives them outstanding merit. Foresters may be employed as park rangers and may rise to park superintendent and higher positions.

The Fish and Wildlife Service. The Fish and Wildlife Service is responsible for research, control, and management activities involving game birds, other birds, mammals valuable for game and fur or for other reasons, commercial and sport fishing, fur seals, whales, and other marine mammals, shrimp, lobster, shellfish, reptiles, and amphibians. The Service employs both foresters and forest biologists. Foresters are employed as refuge managers and for directing forestry operations on 800,000 acres of timberlands under intensive management for wildlife.

Through the Pittman-Robertson and Dingle-Johnson laws the Fish and Wildlife Service administers public funds collected from special excise taxes on sporting goods amounting to several million dollars annually. This money is distributed to the states for research on game and fish management and the establishment and maintenance of conditions conducive to an abundant wildlife population on public and private lands and refuges.

The conditions of employment in the Park Service and Fish and Wildlife Service parallel those in the U.S. Forest Service. Extensive field work is often required. This may involve travel for considerable distances and long periods of field observation uninterrupted by return to headquarters. This is especially necessary for men assigned to studying bird migrations, nesting habits, or conditions for winter survival. Because of its wide contact with state organizations, the Fish and Wildlife Service can prepare men for high posts in state work.

Other Federal Agencies

Other agencies scattered through several of the major federal departments also employ foresters. The Bureau of Indian Affairs, having responsibility for some 50 million acres of lands on Indian reservations, has need of foresters, range managers, and other land managers. The Bureau makes it a practice to employ Indians whenever qualified men can be found.

The Tennessee Valley Authority seeks to promote good forestry and watershed management in the valley region. A limited amount of research in forestry and forest products is carried on. The Authority has its own recruitment service and standards for employment. Foresters are employed by the Soil Conservation Service and various other agencies in the Department of Agriculture which have been set up from time to time to enhance the income of farmers.

A limited number of foresters of mature experience are employed in the Division of the Budget, the Bureau of Internal Revenue, the Department of Commerce, the Bureau of the Census, the Bureau of Foreign and Domestic Commerce, the Department of Labor, the Department of Defense, and the Comptroller General's office.

State Employment

State conservation departments use foresters in fire control, in management of state forests and game lands, in providing aid to private timberland owners (either directly through state programs or through the federal cooperative forest-management program), and in providing control against tree-destroying insects and diseases. They also provide planting stock for farmers and other landowners. Some of them give limited or substantial services to the wood-using industries. The activities covered and the conditions of employment vary widely from state to state. Some 28 states maintain a civil service system for all forestry employees. Standards may be comparable to those of the United States Civil Service Commission with retirement and other benefits in line with federal standards. At the opposite extreme are states in which foresters must obtain political endorsement before appointment.

Only a few states provide formal training courses for their employees, but a number of them do have one or more annual conferences. State forestry has expanded rapidly since 1945, and prospects seem bright for further expansion. Entering salaries in 1961 varied from about $4,000 to $6,000 and top salaries from $10,000 to almost $18,000, with the states having the larger programs tending to offer high salary ranges.[4] The individual state forester may be given wide latitude to plan and develop programs in the way he deems best. Tenure has been stable in a number of states. Service periods in excess of 30 years are not unusual.

The *esprit de corps* in state forestry organizations depends on freedom from political patronage and upon the decision, energy, and devotion of the administrative head. On the whole, men in state employ enjoy prestige equal to that of foresters in federal employ. The opportunities for service are equally great and the satisfactions the service brings are just as rich.

The state park services employ foresters and landscape architects. States are expanding their public outdoor recreational facilities rapidly and are drawing heavily upon landscape architects to plan and design the projects.

The state highway departments sometimes use foresters to plant roadside trees and hedges for snowbreaks, to help maintain tree growth along parkways, to stabilize embankments and road cuts, and to beautify the highways. A few highway departments have developed picnic areas and other public recreation grounds at strategic locations along the highways.

The state fish and game departments may employ foresters to manage state lands acquired for game production and public shooting grounds. They also employ forest biologists as wildlife managers. Frequently, foresters are used to handle the multitude of duties involved in protecting and furthering the abundance of wildlife. Employment in the state parks, state fish and game departments, and state highway departments is likely to be under conditions similar to those in the state forestry department.

State agricultural experiment stations, extension services, and colleges as employing agencies have been discussed in Chaps. 21 and 22.

Cities, Counties, and Communities

City foresters care for shade trees and parks. They handle tree planting, pruning, line clearance, cleanup after wind damage, spraying, and other activities. Municipalities having their own watersheds frequently employ foresters to manage these. A few cities have park and other properties outside the city limits that require services a forester can perform. Counties and communities in the aggregate maintain control over considerable areas of forest land. These furnish opportunities for foresters either by direct employment or by providing service through state or other employment.

Strong city governments, such as those of New York City and Buffalo, have large park departments with employment under civil service providing benefits similar to those in state service.

Small cities and counties offer variable employment conditions. Political sponsorship is sometimes required.

Private Industries

Employment of foresters by private industries has developed enormously since the Second World War.[2] The total employed in 1961 was in excess of 6,000. The fields for service, as well as the employing agencies, are broad. Agencies include the pulp and paper industry, lumber in-

dustry, veneer and plywood including wood-processing industries, wholesale and retail lumberyards, light-construction industry, and a growing
number of special industries that service the ones mentioned above or
that use wood or other forest products in their operations. Such industries vary from an owner-operated wood shop to huge pulp and paper
industries that are international in scope of activities. Employment opportunities and conditions vary just as widely as the industries themselves. Some have advanced personnel policies and elaborate recruitment and testing procedures for professional men. Others have none of
these. In general, the larger companies offer good careers for a college
man. The opportunities may, however, be equally attractive in family-
owned concerns of modest size wherein the owner takes a deep personal
interest in his employees.

The apprentice period for industrial foresters in large concerns paral-
lels that required in state or federal service. Thereafter, advancement is
likely to be rapid, particularly if the organization is expanding its land
holdings or intensifying its forestry practices.

The types of jobs to be encountered in industrial employment are
almost as varied as the types of employers. They actually vary from work
that a semiskilled laborer might perform to high-level managerial responsibilities and research. The past record for stability in employment in
private industry was disappointing. Today, the forestry divisions of large
corporations offer approximately the same degree of stability in employment that is afforded by any other division in the corporation. Industries
themselves fluctuate in output. This is particularly true of the lumber
industry and, to a lesser extent, the pulp and paper industry. The most
volatile is the light-construction industry, though this has enjoyed a high
degree of prosperity since the Second World War. The wood-processing
industries, generally, and particularly the furniture industries, fluctuate
with house construction. The small lumber manufacturing companies
have varied widely in stability of employment.

Opportunities for self-development and self-expression are very wide
for foresters employed by industry. The very fact that employment of
foresters has grown so rapidly in the past is indication that wide opportunity exists.

Private industries vary greatly in their retirement programs. Some have
generous ones; others have none other than those provided by public
social security programs.

The Pulp and Paper Industry

A pulp and paper mill requires the highest investment per employee
of any United States manufacture. It also requires around-the-clock

operation and an enormous supply of wood. Mills requiring from 200,000 to 400,000 cords a year are average in size. These must have approximately as many acres of forest land to draw upon as cords of wood required for annual operation. Their forestry departments have the responsibility of keeping the mill supplied with wood, whether it comes from company-owned lands or from private lands. In either case, the company is concerned with the future productivity of the land from which it draws its supplies; hence, it encourages good forest practice on all such lands. Many companies seek to attain a proper balance between woods they harvest from their own lands and those they purchase from private landowners within their supply area. The company foresters are usually available to supervise operations on both company and private lands. Corporations such as the International Paper Company, the Weyerhaeuser Company, Crown-Zellerbach Company, and many others number their professional foresters in the hundreds. Their employment practices are good, and the career opportunities offered by such companies are among the best.

The industry offers excellent careers for men trained in pulp and paper technology. Many have active recruitment programs with personnel officers visiting schools of pulp and paper technology to select men for their companies. Career ladders are good and lead to important managerial positions after some 10 or more years of experience. Beginning jobs are generally in the laboratory; intermediate jobs involve management of some section of the mill; advanced jobs include mill superintendent, general manager, and even vice-president in charge of production and sales. An increasing number of foresters and pulp and paper technologists have been reaching high-level administrative posts in recent years.

The Lumber Industry

Lumber manufacturers on the whole have lagged behind American industry in increase in output per worker, in expenditures for research, in innovation, in rate of expansion, and in stability of operation. This is an indication of opportunities that exist for better integration and better practice throughout the lumber industry. Men of energy, business acumen, ambition, and willingness to take a few chances can find in the lumber industry opportunity for exercising their skill. Beginning jobs are likely to be those such as scaling and cruising or various simple jobs on logging or milling operations. As men become skilled and show that they have an understanding of the output to be expected of loggers and millmen, they may hope to rise to positions of foremen and managers. The top jobs include woodlands managers and woodlands superintendents. Stability of employment depends in large degree upon the individual company and its policies with respect to a continuous timber supply.

Wood-processing Industries. Furniture factories, wood-turning mills, planing mills, sash and door mills, casket factories, and the many other plants that manufacture consumer goods from wood have been slow to employ men with technical training, particularly men with an understanding of the technical properties of wood. Some are becoming aware that wood technology is important in their business. A few employ technologists, notably the larger furniture companies, plywood companies, piano manufacturers, and others who process a considerable amount of wood and who must use good machining and gluing techniques to get satisfactory results. The opportunities in the wood-processing industry are wide, and these are expanding as research opens new fields for application.

Woodworking plants are generally small and are highly competitive. The technologist who enters employment in a plant must know how to fit into the organization as it exists and then how to prove his worth to the company by gradually suggesting technical advances that will pay off in the long run. This field, like that of logging, may be expected to absorb more foresters as young men with imagination and energy work their way up to top management.

As few wood-processing companies have an elaborate overhead organization, the technologist must often be his own cost analyst in considering changes in company processes. Versatility commands a premium. The opportunities for product improvement in appearance and service are great. Business and managerial skill are essential for advancement to a higher post.

Suppliers to the Wood-using Industries

Dry-kiln manufacturers, machinery manufacturers, adhesive companies, and others that serve the wood-using industries have been more prompt to employ the services of wood technologists and engineers than have the industries they serve. To be successful with such a company, a man should understand wood and the problems of the wood-using industries. The competition will come from men who know machinery or glue rather than from men who know what machines or glues are expected to do for the wood-fabricating industry.

Manufacturers of logging equipment and sawmill machinery employ demonstrators, salesmen, and research men. Men who understand the forest and forest work are in a position to specify the type of equipment needed to do a good job in the woods. Forest workshops have developed such important items as the Osborne fire finder and the Byram haze cutter, both of which are used by fire lookouts. They also developed the first bulldozer and the first integrated logging tractor and arch.

The Plywood Industry

The plywood industry is one of the rapidly expanding industries of the world. Closely related to it are the hardboard industry, insulating-board industry, and particle-board industry. All these industries manu-facture products for use by the construction industry, and all have experienced a growing market for their products primarily because they are relatively uniform in quality and large in size. Their use has con-siderably decreased the amount of labor required at the building site for house construction. All have technical problems that need the attention of properly trained technologists. All these industries have engaged in research or supported research in outside laboratories. Their technical sales force uses wood technologists. The opportunities in such industries are good because of their expanding markets and because they are sufficiently strong financially to employ technologists and to use them effectively.

The Light-construction Industry

The light-construction industry and the retail lumber business are in need of college-trained men, though most of the firms currently in the business are small and many do not recognize the need for modern technology. A number of foresters who have specialized in forest prod-ucts during their undergraduate years have found employment with the retail and wholesale lumber industry, and many have risen to high posi-tions in their individual companies. Others have gone into the light-construction business and have been successful in it. Opportunities are particularly good for men in the prefabricated-housing industry, in the mobile-housing industry, and in the industries that serve the light-con-struction industry, such as manufacturers of sash and doors, interior trim, and related items. Here, likewise, employment conditions and oppor-tunities vary widely from company to company.

Miscellaneous Industries

The railroad industry has employed foresters both as land managers and as agents to help solicit traffic along their rail lines. The Seaboard Air Line Railway was one of the first to launch a program of forest conservation with the expectation that by encouraging landowners to give better protection and care to the forests greater prosperity could be brought to the region and to the railway that served it. Companies mining coal and other products have also been owners of forested land and have employed foresters to manage their properties. Companies that purchase large quantities of wood such as railway ties or utility poles have employed foresters as purchasing agents. Utility companies sometimes employ foresters for line clearance. Miscellaneous wood-processing companies such as those engaged in the manufacture of shingles, cooperage, excelsior, and other products are potential employers of wood technologists.

Trade Associations

Regional and national trade associations of the pulp and paper, lumber, and wood-processing industries have offered openings for foresters. An outstanding performance was that of William B. Greeley, who left his position as Chief of the U.S. Forest Service to become forester for the West Coast Lumbermen's Association. Such associations offer wide latitude to the paid executive of the association to program his work and to seek ways in which to benefit the industry. Trade-association positions have been among the better-paying positions open to foresters and wood technologists. These positions require imagination, the ability to select and push worthwhile national and regional objectives, and the ability to find a common bond of purpose among the several competitive organizations that contribute to their support. The opportunities for industry-wide cooperation, particularly in the lumber and wood-processing field, to promote research and new methods of using wood have great potential and afford a real challenge to the imaginative forester and wood technologist.

Other Associations

A limited number of associations of landowners have employed foresters. These have the general purpose of helping the landowner to market his product to advantage. They may offer only advice or they may offer various sales services, such as marking timber, negotiating sales contracts, or even handling logging operations. The New England Forestry Foundation of Boston offers forester-supervised timber management on a cost basis to interested landowners. Conn-wood, a cooperative timber-harvesting and selling corporation, operates in Connecticut. Others have operated in Pennsylvania, Illinois, New Hampshire, New York, and other states. These associations have had a mixed record with a relatively high percentage of short-lived activity. Member interest and good management are vital to success.

Various local and national organizations such as the Audubon Society, the Izaak Walton League, the American Forestry Association, and state forestry associations have employed foresters as executive secretaries and managers. Some of these positions are very attractive and bring the secretary into touch with men of influence throughout the state and nation.

Self-employment in Forestry

Many experienced foresters have found that self-employment offers the widest opportunities for self-expression, the highest personal income, and the most fruitful overall field of service. The widest field of self-employment is consulting work.

Consulting Forestry. Since 1946, the number of men engaged in consulting forestry has increased rapidly. Consultants are found in almost all branches of forestry from nursery practice and arboriculture to timber appraisal, logging engineering, and wood technology. The Society of American Foresters has published each year since 1946 a directory of consulting foresters in the January issue of the *Journal of Forestry* (Table 20). The society list includes only a few of the consultants in

TABLE 20. SOCIETY OF AMERICAN FORESTERS' LIST
OF CONSULTING FORESTERS *

Date of publication	Number of firms listed	Estimated number of individuals employed
January, 1946......	40	45
January, 1950......	142	179
January, 1955......	231	336
January, 1960......	266	345
January, 1962......	297	407

* Published in the *Journal of Forestry* for the dates shown.

veneer and plywood, gluing, factory layout and design, design of products, pulp and paper technology, and in the cellulose chemical industries. Consultants are found in all these areas.

The relationship of a consultant to his client is confidential and must be conducted according to high ethical standards. The code of ethics of the Society of American Foresters includes several statements referring to this relationship. The consultant must use his expert knowledge to gain for his client the full financial and technical advantage to which he is entitled by the employment of the consultant. A consultant should reveal to his prospective employer any other retainership he may hold that might conflict with his serving the new client effectively.

A consultant should be one of the most highly trained foresters of all, for upon his advice others will locate plants, buy equipment, begin operations, and make other heavy financial commitments. The ideal training for a consultant would include a thorough knowledge of forestry with specialization in two or three fields, particularly in marketing, logging, and timber appraising. In addition, he should have an understanding of business law, trade practices, and markets.

A consulting forester must be prepared to build up his business over a period of years. Initial earnings are likely to be low. Once established, he may expect his income to increase in proportion to the value of his services and his success in attracting clients. A consultant's capital is his background of experience. His need for instruments, books, and working capital will be modest once his business is well established.

The outlook for consulting forestry remains bright. Any resource that can be counted on to appreciate in volume at the rate of 4 to 10 per cent compounded annually is certainly worth investigating from the financial standpoint. Value increments on forest properties can usually be made greater than volume increments through carefully planned forest operations. It is here that the consultant's true value comes in.

The average forest property produces a variety of products such as fuel wood, fence posts, poles, pulpwood, sawlogs, veneer logs, and also opportunities for hunting, fishing, trapping, and other forms of recreation. Through working out multiple-use arrangements, a consultant can often bring extra income to his client.

Landowner and Timber Operator. The ambition of many foresters is to own, manage, and operate their own forest property. Considerable capital is required to build up a large property. Foresters have purchased small tracts of land, done their own logging, plowed back earnings, and gradually built up a property. A few own as much as several thousand acres.

A forester is likely to be more successful in building up and managing such a property if he is in a position to do his own logging. For this reason it would be desirable to have logging experience before embarking on the venture. A property in a good location and added to progressively should yield a good livelihood and provide security for the future once it is well built up.

To build up a good timber property is not easy. Judicious purchasing and operating once the land is acquired are the basis for success in private timberland management.

Other forms of land management present possibilities. Christmas-tree growing has been extensively tried in some of the eastern states. Gross income may be as high as $100 per acre per year, which allows a reasonable margin for planting and shearing costs. Some imaginative land-owners have combined Christmas-tree growing with long-range forest plantations and use of their land by private clubs for recreation, hunting, and other purposes.

Timber and Sawmill Operator. A forester desiring to go into the timber-harvesting field can start as a logger and gradually build up his equipment for independent work. Contract felling and bucking with a chain saw may give him his start. Later a tractor for skidding, a truck for hauling, and a portable sawmill might be added to provide an integrated operation.

Wood Fabrication. A forester or wood technologist can engage in his own wood-fabricating operations. Many markets exist for special products. Such prosaic things as bed slats, the scantlings used to support the spring of an ordinary bed, have been the basis for an independent enterprise. Others have engaged in manufacturing small turned products, novelties, small-dimension hardwoods, small-dimension softwoods, custom-built furniture, baskets, veneered products, and a host of other commodities. These industries remain typically small industries. Toy manufacture and many other relatively simple wood-processing operations can be done with a minimum of elaborate equipment. The forester needs to be handy with tools, have some skill in designing, and, in particular, know where he can find adequate markets, if he is to make a success as a wood processor and fabricator.

Resort and Camp Operation. A few foresters operate children's camps and resort hotels for hunters, fishermen, and others. To succeed in this field, a forester must be enthusiastic, know how to provide reasonable comforts in outdoor surroundings, and, above all, have the capacity to make friends readily and to build up a permanent clientele.

A few camp operators with a deep feeling for the forest environment have been successful in building up splendid camps with a minimum of physical facilities and conventional camp programs. The man familiar with the forest and forest wildlife can capitalize on his knowledge. Swimming, boating, canoeing, hiking, mountain climbing, overnight camping, simple handicrafts, and woods lore can be drawn upon to popularize such a camp.

Landscape and Nursery Operations. Men with forestry training have become owners of small nurseries growing ornamental stock and have engaged in simple and even elaborate landscape and arboricultural activities. Competition in this field is well established. The business is stable and growing. Men wishing to embark in this field should be well trained in soils, silviculture, seeding, and planting and have some knowledge of landscape design as well as of business methods and operations.

A nursery requires a considerable investment in land, seed, equipment, and labor.

A forester may purchase stock at wholesale from nurseries and resell it to customers after making appropriate plans and designs and guaranteeing the success of his job. In this way a man can start in the business with little capital outlay other than that for his training and experience.

Regional Opportunities

Employment opportunities and working conditions for foresters are influenced by ownership of forest land, timber volume and growth rate, intensity of utilization, and general economic and employment conditions in the region. The North has intensive use of forests, the South rapidly growing forests, and the West the largest volume of standing timber. The West has unionized loggers and the highest wage. Workers here are also most productive and operations most highly mechanized.

Many industries tend to be grouped in certain regions. Pulp and paper manufacture is restricted chiefly to the Northeast, the Lake States, the South, and the Pacific Northwest. The shoe-last industry is centered in New York and Wisconsin, plywood on the West Coast. Even agencies are localized to some extent. The Forest Service and Bureau of Land Management have the majority of their lands in the West.

Trends in Regional Development

Employment opportunities tend to be more abundant and promotions more rapid in regions that are undergoing accelerated increase in population and industry than in industrially mature regions. Population changes from 1950 to 1960 show striking regional differences. For the United States as a whole, there was a population increase from 151 to 179 million, or 18.5 per cent. The Pacific regions showed a 40.2 per cent increase; the mountain area, 35.1; and the South Atlantic, 22.6. In contrast, the West–North Central Area had only a 9.5 per cent increase and the East–South Central, 5 per cent. When we consider with population increases the forest resources of the respective regions, the Pacific Coast and the South Atlantic regions stand out as particularly favorable.

Forestry is most active in those states that have large areas of forest land and well-developed forest-products industries. The states in which the largest number of members of the Society of American Foresters are located are those in which forestry opportunities are most widespread. As of 1962 the distribution of members among the states having 200 or more was as follows: *

* Data furnished by Society of American Foresters. 1962.

Oregon	1,341	Wisconsin	380
California	1,064	Virginia	378
Washington	870	Minnesota	372
Georgia	714	Idaho	349
Michigan	491	Montana	322
North Carolina	474	South Carolina	305
Louisiana	436	Mississippi	297
Pennsylvania	419	Arkansas	291
Alabama	392	Texas	237
Florida	390	Colorado	217
New York	383		

It is of interest also that the concentration of foresters in 1962 seemed to be heaviest in those regions such as the Pacific Coast and South Atlantic area where population growth had been rapid during the preceding decade.

Employment in the North. The North is characterized primarily by small woodland holdings, small timber operations, and relatively small wood-processing plants. Only a small amount of public forest land is found in the North. This region has a large number of the country's forestry schools and has had a longer period of forestry practice than the other regions. Forestry began early and has proceeded at a moderate pace.

Since the North is primarily an industrial and agricultural region, forest operations are secondary in the economy. The forest industries are relatively well developed in the North, though few of them are large in size. The North leads in furniture manufacture, in the manufacture of a wide variety of commodities that require wood of high technical quality, and in the use of lumber. In terms of potential employment it is obvious that the region offers substantial opportunities.

The opportunities for industrial employment in the North are promising because of the large number of industries and the intensity of use. Many manufacturers have small plants. In the years ahead, it is almost certain that both forest-management and industry practice will change a great deal and that this potentiality for change represents real opportunity. Active interest exists throughout the North in improved methods of timber harvesting and utilization, and a great deal of interest has been taken in improved practices on the land. The handicap of small, scattered ownership will continue to plague forest practice in the North for many years to come.

Employment in the South. The South is likewise characterized by agricultural development alongside forestry. Ownership of land is mostly in small holdings. Consequently, many of the lumber companies and wood-using industries are small. The pulp and paper industry of the

South, on the other hand, is big industry and is dependent upon the rapidly growing pine of the coastal-plain region. In the South also there is relatively little public land. Forests are mostly privately owned. The fact that timber grows rapidly in the South has encouraged many industries to engage in forestry on lands they own and to promote forestry throughout the territory from which they obtain timber.

Growing stock is inadequate over much of the South, and timber yields are correspondingly low. Wide opportunity exists for intensifying forest land management and, particularly, for increasing the intensity of industrial use of southern woods. The South probably offers the brightest opportunities for employment of foresters of any of the three major regions. Forest land has been increasing rapidly in value, and sustained-yield forestry has grown at a very rapid rate.[2]

Working conditions in the South Atlantic states are generally good and the companies tend to be progressive. Timber and the forest-products industries represent an important phase in the economy which seems destined to increase as a moderate decline in the demand for agricultural products takes place.

In the last two decades the southern people have taken vast strides to overcome local handicaps. Renewed efforts are being made to open up opportunities to develop the region industrially and to improve its use of resources.

Employment in the West. The West differs radically from both the North and the South. Vast quantities of virgin timber still exist. The timber is huge in size, and special logging equipment and highly trained woods operators are needed to exploit it. Public ownership of forest is a major factor in the economy and is destined to become even more important in the years ahead as the volume of timber standing on private holdings is further depleted.[6] The West has learned to cope with its rugged topography and the vast bulk of the trees harvested. This has required imagination, skill, and daring.

The Pacific Northwest remains the major lumber-producing area of the country. The forest-practice laws in these states and in California tend to encourage the employment of foresters. The large size of operations, the large size of timber, and the high degree of organization and mechanization of the timber industries of the Pacific Northwest mean opportunities for trained loggers and men trained in wood utilization. The veneer mills, pulp and paper mills, furniture factories, and other wood processors of this region employ men trained in either forestry schools or other colleges where technical knowledge is gained of wood fabrication and use (Fig. 88).

Industrial forestry has grown rapidly in the Pacific Northwest. Since the second-growth Douglas-fir forests grow rapidly, timberland owners are encouraged to hold the land. The industries of the Pacific Northwest are large in size, well organized, and, on the whole, well financed. They appreciate the need for technical knowledge and, consequently, are financing forest-products research. This, in turn, will open up new avenues for use of wood and new opportunities for trained technologists in wood utilization and related fields. A number of new products financed by industry research are already being placed on the market. Most of the major companies are building up timberland holdings with sustained yield in mind.

Integrated utilization is practiced in many communities. Industrialization of the region has proceeded at a more rapid pace than in the country as a whole. Both industrial leaders and the people realize that timber is a major product and are determined to safeguard future supplies and future markets for forest products.

Fig. 88   Seed-tree cutting in sugar pine. Umpqua National Forest. (*U.S. Forest Service photo.*)

Employment and living conditions are generally good. The companies have adopted a progressive attitude toward their employees.

Foreign Employment

Opportunities for American foresters to find employment outside the United States have increased greatly since 1945. This has been the result of three major forces: the technical activities of the Food and Agriculture Organization of the United Nations, the technical-aid programs sponsored by the United States government, and the expansion in investment of American capital abroad.

The American college youth of the 1960s would be provincial if he did not realize that our nation will have increasing interests abroad and that increasing numbers of American youths must prepare themselves for service outside our country. The success with which they meet such service will determine to a large extent the influence that our nation plays in world affairs for decades to come. Most who have engaged in foreign service find it a stimulating and satisfying life, even though it does demand forgoing the conveniences of life in America and requires a certain dedication to service of mankind on a world-wide basis. Those who approach such service with such an attitude of mind can expect responses from the people in the countries where they work that will reward them richly.

Moreover, there has been an awakening of interest in forestry in the many newly emergent nations throughout the world. These have come into being so rapidly and their ambitions for technological development are so great that they will need all the trained manpower they can obtain for decades to come. This does not mean that they as yet offer widespread employment opportunities for American college graduates. The new nations tend to be strongly nationalistic, proud of their independence, and unwilling to accept assistance other than on a basis of equality with the proffering nation.

Another development that may have even greater long-term significance is the linking of European nations together in a large common market area. The potentials of such organization are enormous. Within the European Economic Community a very rapid increase in industry and trade developed within the first few years. For the United States this poses increasingly keen competition in the world's markets. The long-term effects, however, seem likely to be salutary for the free world as a whole.

The Food and Agriculture Organization. The Food and Agriculture Organization has its headquarters in Rome, Italy. It has regional headquarters in Latin America, North America, Asia, the Far East, and Africa. The FAO offers technical aid to member nations throughout the world. Technical-aid missions are usually made up of nationals from several countries operating together under the aegis of the United Nations. Activities expanded rapidly in the late 1950s. As of 1962, it was expected that the FAO could place at least 50 men in Latin America.

Agency for International Development. The United States channels its technical-assistance programs through the Agency for International Development (AID). Technical missions operate in a number of countries, mostly on a temporary basis. Projects involving the survey of resources and the development of educational facilities are given priority. Because timber is one of the readily exploitable resources in many emerging nations, forestry projects are often requested of both the AID and the FAO.

Both organizations seek mature foresters for foreign technical missions. The opportunities for the newly fledged graduate are somewhat limited. In part as a recognition of this fact, but more for other reasons, the Peace Corps was established in 1961. This agency sends young Americans abroad to work with the natives of other lands on various technical projects. The pay is modest and the appeal is to the idealism of youth. Opportunities for a worthwhile forestry experience do exist through the Peace Corps. Young men interested in working abroad might well consider an assignment with this organization in order to become acquainted with the opportunities in foreign service as a career.

In 1962, forty-one United States foresters were working directly with the AID. At least five additional foresters were working on AID contracts with foreign universities, and 12 were employed abroad by the FAO of the United Nations. Others have been employed on short-term missions.

Other Foreign Employment Opportunities. Certain foreign governments also may employ foresters from the United States for specific tasks. These are usually of relatively short duration—one to two years—and require men of mature experience. Many import and export companies in the United States employ foresters for service outside the United States. Rubber companies, tropical dealers, and importers of chicle, cinchona bark, quebracho, tropical fruits, and nuts are all potential sources of employment for foresters. So also are the tropical-fruit companies, which frequently own considerable areas of land in tropical countries and require managers for the fruit, agriculture, and forest land which they own. Jobs with well-established companies usually provide good salaries and living conditions and reasonable opportunities for vacations in the United States.

Men who go into tropical work, however, should give it careful thought, as they cannot expect to attain a high degree of success in a short period of time. Tropical forestry is far more complex than forestry in the United States. Little research and experience are available to guide a man. It is truly a pioneering field. Men who are willing to devote their lives to tropical service can look forward to good opportunities for splendid careers.

Opportunities also exist to obtain employment directly in a foreign corporation. Young foresters should review the working conditions offered in such a corporation very carefully before accepting employment. In general, American foresters have been well treated by foreign countries and foreign companies that have employed them. They have been provided good living quarters and opportunities for travel to the United States to keep abreast of developments in our own country. The opportunities are probably greater in South America than elsewhere.

Men contemplating service in other countries should, first of all, learn the language of the country in which they are to work. It is equally important to learn the customs of the people, particularly the social niceties that the country expects of them. In many cases they will find living conditions in foreign lands more favorable for them than they are for foresters in our own country. They are likely to find themselves occupying positions of considerable importance to the nation and to the companies for which they work. Consequently, a high degree of integrity and fairness is demanded of them.

LITERATURE CITED

1. Allen, Shirley W. 1947. "Handbook of Information on Entering Positions in Forestry," 2d ed., Society of American Foresters, Washington, D.C. 56 pp.
2. Anonymous. 1950. "Employment Analysis Shows Industry Increase," *Journal of Forestry*, 48:444.
3. Commission on Organization of the Executive Branch of the Government. 1949. "Federal Personnel," U.S. Government Printing Office. 101 pp.
4. Guernsey, Roger L. 1961. "State Forestry in the United States, 1961," Memorandum to Ralph Wible, President, Association of State Foresters. 5 pp. mim.
5. Gulick, Luther H. 1951. "American Forest Policy: A Study of Government Administration and Economic Control," Duell, Sloan & Pearce, Inc., New York. 252 pp.
6. Guthrie, John A., and George R. Armstrong. 1961. "Western Forest Industry: An Economic Outlook," The Johns Hopkins Press, Baltimore. 324 pp.
7. Kaufman, Herbert. 1960. "The Forest Ranger," The Johns Hopkins Press, Baltimore. 259 pp.
8. Spero, Sterling D. 1948. "Government as Employer," Remsen Press, New York. 497 pp.

CHAPTER 25. *The Profession of Forestry*

On November 30, 1900, seven men met at the home of Gifford Pinchot to organize the Society of American Foresters.[1] The original constitution stated its objective: "To further the cause of forestry in America by fostering a spirit of comradeship among foresters; by creating opportunities for a free interchange of views upon forestry and allied subjects; and by disseminating a knowledge of the purpose and achievements of forestry."

Just as forestry is nationwide in scope, so also is the society with its 21 regional sections, its 10 subject-matter divisions, its many working committees, and its growing numbers of local chapters. These provide opportunities for young and seasoned members to meet on common ground in the service of the profession. The society's publications—the *Journal of Forestry*, the proceedings of meetings, and the several books that have resulted from society activities—furnish the chief means for recording professional advancement in education, research, and administration.

The society's membership in 1962 totaled more than 14,000 and its annual meeting attracted 1,500 people.

By invitation the society affiliated with the American Association for the Advancement of Science in 1913 and thus gained a voice in the council of this association. Since the formation of the National Research Council in 1917, the society has been represented in the Council's Division of Biology and Agriculture. It is represented on joint committees with the American Society of Mechanical Engineers and the American Geophysical Union. It is affiliated with the American Institute of Biological Sciences and the National Resources Council of America.

The society has sought to promote forestry by encouraging needed legislation, by protesting political sponsorship for forestry positions, and by upholding forest officers in the discharge of their duties against political pressure. It has set up requirements for society membership and, from these, established standards upon which schools of forestry and

419

their curricula are accredited. It makes studies of state administration of forestry upon requests by the states.

Although its members are loyal, the society is no supine, self-laudatory body. Healthy differences of opinion have characterized its meetings. Public regulation of private forest practice, public versus private forest ownership, state versus federal ownership, and other topics have been and remain live issues in debates in society meetings. The growing demands of recreationists on forests and the conflict between forest managers and wilderness exponents find champions for both sides among society members.

Code of Ethics for Foresters

In 1948 the Society of American Foresters adopted a code of ethics to guide professional conduct. This code is reproduced below.

Preamble

The purpose of these canons is to formulate guiding principles of professional conduct for foresters in their relations with each other, with their employers, and with the public. The observance of these canons secures decent and honorable professional and human relationships, establishes enduring mutual confidence and respect, and enables the profession to give its maximum service.

Professional Life

1. The professional forester will utilize his knowledge and skill for the benefit of society. He will cooperate in extending the effectiveness of the forestry profession by interchanging information and experience with other foresters, and by contributing to the work of forestry societies, associations, schools, and publications.

2. He will advertise only in a dignified manner, setting forth in truthful and factual statements the services he is prepared to render for his prospective clients and for the public.

Relations with the Public

3. He will strive for correct and increasing knowledge of forestry and the dissemination of this knowledge, and will discourage and condemn the spreading of untrue, unfair, and exaggerated statements concerning forestry.

4. He will not issue statements, criticism, or arguments on matters connected with public forestry policies without indicating at the same time on whose behalf he is acting.

5. When serving as an expert witness on forestry matters in a public or private fact finding proceeding, he will base his testimony on adequate knowledge of the subject matter, and render his opinion on his own honest convictions.

6. He will refrain from expressing publicly an opinion on a technical subject unless he is informed as to the facts relating thereto, and will not distort

or withhold data of a substantial or other nature for the purpose of substantiating a point of view.

Relations with Clients, Principals, and Employers

7. He will be loyal to his client or to the organization in which he is employed and will faithfully perform his work and assignments.

8. He will present clearly the consequences to be expected from deviations proposed if his professional forestry judgment is overruled by nontechnical authority in cases where he is responsible for the technical adequacy of forestry or related work.

9. He will not voluntarily disclose information concerning the business affairs of his employers, principals or clients, which they desire to keep confidential, unless express permission is first obtained.

10. He will not, without the full knowledge and consent of his client or employer, have an interest in any business which may influence his judgment in regard to the work for which he is engaged.

11. He will not, for the same service, accept compensation of any kind, other than from his client, principal, or employer, without full disclosure, knowledge, and consent of all parties concerned.

12. He will engage, or advise his client or employer to engage, other experts and specialists in forestry and related fields whenever the client's or employer's interests would be best served by such actions, and will cooperate freely with them in their work.

Relations with Professional Foresters

13. He will at all times strive to protect the forestry profession collectively and individually from misrepresentation and misunderstanding.

14. He will aid in safeguarding the profession against the admission to its ranks of persons unqualified because of lack of good moral character or of adequate training.

15. In writing or in speech he will be scrupulous to give full credit to others, in so far as his knowledge goes, for procedures and methods devised or discovered and ideas advanced or aid given.

16. He will not intentionally and without just cause, directly or indirectly, injure the reputation or business of another forester.

17. If he has substantial and convincing evidence of unprofessional conduct of a forester, he will present the information to the proper authority for action.

18. He will not compete with another forester on the basis of charges for work by underbidding through reduction of his quoted fee after being informed of the fee quoted by a competitor.

19. He will not use the advantages of a salaried position to compete unfairly with another forester.

20. He will not attempt to supplant another forester in a particular employment after becoming aware that the latter has been definitely engaged.

21. He will not review the work of another forester for the latter's employer without the other's knowledge unless the latter's connection with the work has been terminated.

22. He will base all letters of reference or oral recommendation on a fair and unbiased evaluation of the party concerned.

23. To the best of his ability he will support, work for, and adhere to the principles of the merit system of employment.

24. He will not participate in soliciting or collecting financial contributions from subordinates or employees for political purposes.

25. He will uphold the principle of appropriate and adequate compensation for those engaged in forestry work, including those in subordinate positions, as being in the public interest and maintaining the standards of the profession.

Rules of Construction

These canons of ethics shall be broadly construed in the interest of the public welfare and professional advancement.

They shall be deemed duties, obligations, and responsibilities of the professional forester to all those with whom he comes into contact in the course of his professional work and life.

These canons shall be construed so as to disregard any differentiation between professional foresters in public or private employ. The standard of professional conduct exacted by these canons of ethics from professional foresters makes no distinction as to place or kind of employment.

Because the foregoing canons consider the usual and foreseeable circumstances governing professional conduct only, experience may require modifications or additions.

Men entering professional work, therefore, enter into a covenant to devote themselves diligently to their chosen profession, adhere to its code of ethics, place public service above private gain, and strive to promote the good of the profession and to enlarge its services to mankind.

Obligations of a Forester

To be a forester is a privilege that carries with it obligations. The technical knowledge he acquires has been painstakingly built up by thousands of foresters since the beginnings of the profession. He is privileged to use this knowledge. It is his duty to pass it on more complete and better tested than he received it.

His education is provided largely at public expense in publicly supported or endowed universities. Training of a forester is costly compared with that of a teacher or graduate in liberal arts.

Foresters, as a group, have received a higher than average income. Mason [7] reported the average wage in the United States to be 60 per cent of the average salary and but 50 per cent of the average forester's pay. In 1949, a survey of alumni of a forestry school revealed their median salary to be higher than that of graduates of the same school who had left the profession of forestry. In 1960, graduates of one forestry college were receiving starting salaries averaging $5,000. Those with 10 years' experience had average earnings in excess of $8,000, and those with 20 years' experience had average pay of almost $12,000.[2]

Forestry flourishes only in those countries where it receives public support in whole or in part.

Men entering forestry colleges, therefore, accept an obligation to apply themselves diligently and to follow the profession as a life career, circumstances permitting. This means that they will devote their best efforts to the profession, follow its code of ethics, keep abreast of new developments in their field, and give generously of their time and effort to advance the profession by serving its society and helping new members to become established. It means also that they will place duty above personal convenience, especially when their duty calls for protection of life and property, and it means that they will be true to their professional ideals in the interests of ensuring abundant forests for posterity.

Age and Size of the Profession of Forestry

Forestry is a young profession in America but one that has now proved its value by more than 60 years of service.

The growth of the profession has been steady and rapid since 1900 (Table 21). Between 1900 and 1960 a total of 29,844 bachelor's degrees were granted by forestry schools. To this number should be added an

TABLE 21. ACADEMIC DEGREES GRANTED AT
SCHOOLS OF FORESTRY *

(Cumulative by decades since 1900)

| Year | Cumulative total by degree | | | |
	Bachelor's degrees	Master's degrees	Doctor's degrees	All degrees
1900	1			1
1910	211	264		475
1920	1,433	597		2,030
1930	3,835	1,080	34 †	4,949
1940	10,183	1,879	99	12,161
1950	17,701	3,120	212	21,033
1960	29,844	5,344	575	35,763

* Data from Markworth, Gordon D. 1961. "Statistics from Schools of Forestry for 1960: Degrees Granted and Enrollments," *Journal of Forestry*, 59:273–279.

† Cumulative total 1900 to 1931. Number for individual years before 1931 not available.

unknown number of men who took a master's or doctor's degree from a forestry college but not a bachelor's. Meanwhile, losses have occurred through deaths, retirements, and transfer to other lines of work. Also, a few men have entered the professional field who obtained their education in related fields such as biology, physical science, and engineering. The number estimated to be engaged as professional foresters in 1961 was 19,350.

Enrollments in forestry schools stood at an all-time high in 1960 with 8,439 candidates for the bachelor's degree, 604 for the master's, and 312 for the doctor's degree. Corresponding enrollments for the year 1951 were: bachelor's candidates, 4,799; master's, 344; doctor's, 137. The profession in 1961 was still expanding, with men holding advanced degrees in particular demand. The schools have responded to this demand by substantial increases in enrollment.

Closely Related Fields. Many men granted degrees from forestry schools find employment in fields closely related to forestry, such as wildlife management, park management, range management, ecology, wood-products technology, pulp and paper technology, and in teaching subjects basic to forestry. Several additional professional societies have been formed to serve their interests. Some of these had their origin as divisions of the Society of American Foresters. A description of some of those whose membership includes a substantial number of foresters follows.[6]

American Society of Range Management. This society was formed "to foster interest in the science and art of grazing land management, to promote progress in conservation and a maximum substained use of forage and soil resources; to stimulate discussion and understanding of scientific and practical range and pasture problems." The society publishes the *Journal of Range Management* and in 1961 had 3,700 members.*

Forest Products Research Society. The Forest Products Research Society was organized in 1947 to promote research in forest products and to interchange and disseminate information about forest products and to encourage increased use of wood and allied forest products. The membership for this organization totaled about 4,000 in 1961. The society publishes the *Forest Products Journal.* Its membership is made up largely of wood technologists, foresters, and engineers.

National Shade Tree Conference. This organization, made up mainly of men engaged in the nursery business and arboriculture, has the fundamental purpose of stimulating greater interest in the planting and preservation of shade and ornamental trees and fostering scientific investigation on tree care. The organization publishes *The Arborist News.* A

* Personal communication from John G. Clouston, Executive Secretary.

number of foresters who are interested in shade-tree work are members of this organization.

The Soil Conservation Society of America. Founded in 1941, this organization of some 8,000 members seeks to advance the science and art of good land use and to promote all phases of the conservation of soil and water resources. It publishes the *Journal of Soil and Water Conservation.*

Wildlife Society. The Wildlife Society was organized in 1947 and had in 1960 a membership of about 2,500. It seeks to establish professional solidarity and high standards among men engaged in wildlife management and research pertaining thereto. This society publishes the *Journal of Wildlife Management.* It numbers among its members foresters, wildlife managers, and game biologists.

The Technical Association of the Pulp and Paper Industries (TAPPI). This organization is made up of specialists in pulp and paper technology who seek to promote research in pulp and paper technology and the dissemination of the results thereof. The association meets annually in New York City during Paper Week, and also has a number of regional chapters. It publishes the journal, *TAPPI,* that is devoted largely to the technology of the pulp and paper industry.

Society of Wood Science and Technology. The Society of Wood Science and Technology was organized in 1958 "to establish qualifications for admission to the profession, to foster educational programs directed toward professional advancement, to establish standards of practice and ethics for the profession, to promote research in wood science and technology, and provide a medium of exchange of ideas and technical information relating to wood science and technology." It is also concerned with promoting use of wood. This society had 200 members in 1961.

American Society of Landscape Architects. This society is made up largely of men of professional competence in this field who seek to promote better understanding among their members and to create public respect for the work of the landscape architects. Foresters as such are not eligible to join this society, unless they have demonstrated competence in the field. As park administrators, however, foresters may join the American Institute of Park Executives, which seeks to improve standards of education for men who become professionals in the field of park management.

Employment in Forestry

Beginning Jobs. The forestry graduate may find his first job in any one of the fields discussed in the preceding chapters. Irrespective of field, beginning jobs are likely to involve hard physical work. Apprenticeship is essential before a man can assume full responsibilities. He must learn how to perform not only technical work but also much of the common routine work of laborers, mechanics, and artisans. His objective is to improve efficiency, safety, and overall performance. By participation he can best acquire the skill to train labor, prescribe safety regulations, inspect the work for compliance to standards, and compute the costs of the several operations.

Descriptions of various entering jobs in the land-management phases of forestry are given by Meyer.[8] Additional information has been given in Chaps. 23 and 24.

The science of forestry may be mastered in college, but skill in its use requires experience. The skilled forester can identify trees at a glance, without opportunity to examine leaves, buds, and twigs. He can use simple surveying instruments with surprising accuracy. He can select the proper tree to harvest without involved theoretical consideration. He can find his way in the woods with minimum reference to compass or landmarks. The acquisition of these skills and judgment is a part of the apprenticeship training. Not until they have been acquired can he efficiently perform technical forestry work and thereby demonstrate his competence as a professional man. He is only then in a position to compete successfully for assignments of supervisory responsibility.

Intermediate Jobs. Intermediate jobs are those of forest ranger, park ranger, farm forester, timber buyer, timber appraiser, superintendent of a small-sized logging operation or sawmill, lumberyard foreman, supervisor of a unit operation in a pulp and paper mill or a large sawmill or a woodworking factory, instructor in a college of forestry, and assistant to project leaders in research. It is in such jobs that men are called upon to exercise to the maximum their technical knowledge. They are also required to plan, organize, and supervise the work of others, and they begin to acquire a certain knowledge of the overall planning and operations of the agency or enterprise (Fig. 71).

Intermediate jobs in forestry require a substantial amount of individual initiative and judgment, as well as the ability to plan and carry on work with only general supervision. The tasks of such foresters require that they spend time dealing with men as well as with trees and physical improvements. Accomplishments here are measured by what the forester's unit accomplishes. Teamwork and leadership become important. Judgment and power of decision are developed.

Many men will find their greatest usefulness and satisfaction in such jobs. Save for a few staff specialists, research men and teachers, the national forest rangers and their equivalents in state and private forestry perform the real technical work in forestry. It is they who establish plantations, tend the forest crop, harvest its products, and provide for regrowth. Advancement beyond this level depends mainly on administrative skill in organizing and directing the work of others.

Advanced Jobs. Men in advanced jobs are called upon to deal with more than one specialty. Examples of such positions are those of supervisors of national forests and national parks, state district foresters, district foresters for pulp and paper or lumber companies, superintendents of pulp mills or paper mills, logging superintendents, managers of sawmills, managers of veneer manufacturing plants, city foresters or city park superintendents, consulting foresters, project leaders in research, and professional employees in colleges of forestry. These positions require up to 10 or more years' experience, a broad appreciation of overall objectives, ability to coordinate the work of two or more divisions, and the capacity to deal with the public and to interpret policies and programs to division chiefs. Or they require expert knowledge of difficult processes, which forms the basis for making important decisions governing the expenditure of large amounts of public or private money and the commitment of an agency.

Top Jobs. Top jobs in forestry include such positions as those of state foresters, United States regional foresters, directors of forest experiment stations, division chiefs and Chief of the U.S. Forest Service, top foresters in other federal agencies, secretaries of important associations dealing with forestry and forest products, professors and deans of colleges of forestry, world authorities on special subjects in forestry, top forestry positions in the Food and Agriculture Organization, and managers and presidents of large corporations engaged in forestry, timber processing, landscaping, and related work. These jobs require a maximum of ability to coordinate the work of others. Top administrators must deal effectively with the general public, high government officials, legislators, executives of other corporations, boards of directors, stockholders, and others. Executives are required to outline objectives and set the broad policies that guide the development of the organization, to delegate authority and responsibilities for major functions, to coordinate these major functions, to cooperate effectively with other agencies having related responsibilities, to plan long-range programs, to maintain high working morale, to draw out from the organization the best thoughts of all the workers, and to synthesize these into working procedures to improve effectiveness. High capacity for performing detailed work is useful, but not a necessity, for such men. It is their job to give general direction and to set the tone of the organization.

Jobs beyond the beginning positions in forestry usually present so many opportunities and such diversified tasks that they challenge to the utmost the ability of the most brilliant and hardworking forester. Always there are more tasks than can be performed and more opportunities for helpful service than there are funds or time to meet them.

Earnings of Foresters. In 1959, the Society of American Foresters made an extensive study of the income of professional foresters.[3] A questionnaire was sent to all members of the Society of American Foresters, to which 7,512 replied. Income was found to vary with years of experience, college degrees held, employer group, and field of employment. There was also considerable spread within classifications between the lower- and upper-decile income. How income increased with years of experience is shown in Table 22. It is significant that income in both the median

TABLE 22. MEDIAN PROFESSIONAL INCOME OF
FORESTERS BY YEARS OF EXPERIENCE [3]

Years of experience	Income, dollars		
	Median	Upper-decile	Lower-decile
0–1	4,800	5,890	4,110
2–5	5,710	7,000	4,720
5–10	7,010	8,920	5,580
16–20	8,900	14,630	6,460
26–30	9,750	14,960	7,170
36+	12,080	21,460	7,400
All years	7,310	11,610	5,110

and the upper-decile range continued to increase sharply up to 36 years of service and beyond, whereas lower-decile income reached a plateau after 20 years' experience, with only modest increases thereafter.

Men with the doctor's degree received more than 10 per cent higher incomes than those with only the bachelor's or master's degree. Between the last two, the holders of master's degrees had a slight edge. Among employing agencies the self-employed outstripped all others, with private industrial employment second. Men in educational institutions had higher income than federal employees, and the latter higher than state workers as a group. Type of work also influenced income, with men in technical sales leading followed by association executives and writers, teachers, consultants, and workers in administration.

The study revealed little difference in income for the several regions of the United States. There was a significant difference with field of specialization. Highest income came to specialists in forest products (median $8,990) followed by those in economics ($8,440), pathology ($8,180), range management ($8,120), logging ($7,890), and at the lower end by fire protection ($7,480), management ($6,800), scaling ($6,790), and photo interpretation for timber inventory ($6,170).

Eyre [4] made a brief comparison of the income of foresters with that revealed for scientists in general by a study of the National Science Foundation for the same year, 1959. Here we tend to be comparing income of foresters most of whom hold only the bachelor's degree with that of scientists, mostly holding the Ph.D. degree. In this study medicine ranked highest with median income of $14,000. Agriculture, including forestry, had a median income of $7,000. The median for foresters was $7,310. When all scientific fields were grouped, the median income for holders of the bachelor's and master's degrees was $9,000; for holders of the doctor's degree, $10,000. For foresters, bachelor's degree holders received $7,030; master's, $7,770; and doctor's, $9,710.

Earnings of men specializing in pulp and paper technology and in chemistry of wood tend to equal those of chemical engineers and to exceed considerably the earnings of foresters. Landscape architects, who reported lower earnings in the period 1945 to 1950 than foresters, had substantially higher earnings than foresters in 1961, with the outlook bright for further increases. Considerable shift can be expected in the future in income of professional groups, depending upon the character of the demand for their services and the supply of professionals available. The rather large spread in income among individuals is also likely to prevail in the future with those of high ability, constructive imagination, energy, and industry surpassing by a wide margin those content to look to others for job assignments.

Working Conditions in the Field. Men taking employment in forest land management should expect to fill positions that require a large amount of time in the woods. They will thus gain practical experience and develop an understanding of field problems that can be obtained in no other way and that are essential in the more advanced positions.

A variety of tasks may greet the forester on his first job. It is possible that he will be concerned with such work as cruising or marking timber, making range surveys, or reforesting denuded lands; or he may be detailed to conservation work in soil erosion or flood-control areas. If he takes a position with a private company, he may plan and build logging roads and camps, supervise cutting crews, carry on cost studies, act as a timber buyer, or scale logs at a sawmill. On most of these jobs he will live in the forest or in a small community.

If he shows considerable promise, the period of apprenticeship may be relatively short, but for most men it will occupy a number of years. As the number of foresters and competition increase, the training period will tend to lengthen. During the first years of professional work the young forester is apt to be moved from one place to another at rather short intervals. After a time he may expect to become more permanently settled as maturity brings advancement to a position of greater responsibility. Most foresters, however, find that a considerable period of each year must be spent away from home, generally in the field. Trips may be for a day, for a week, or for several weeks.

To urban dwellers a forester's life may appear idyllic. Much of it is spent out of doors working with nature. Surroundings are usually pleasant, frequently inspiring. In his daily work the forester may travel to remote places that city dwellers see only on brief vacation trips. Because the forester is trained to be a close observer of trees, forest animals, and plants, he finds much to interest him. His calling leads him to think in terms of resources, human welfare, employment, and industries. He sees the land, not only as it is, but as it was in the past and as it may become in the future. Foresters meet interesting people. Being members of a relatively small profession, foresters readily win each other's confidence and friendship. For most, their profession is both a means of livelihood and their chief hobby.

But there is another side to a forester's life. Fire fighting is grueling work. Smoke blinds the eyes and sears the lungs. Heat hastens exhaustion. Labor is likely to be unremitting from an hour or more before dawn until well into the night. Such is the forester's lot until the fire is brought under control, even though it may take weeks. Timber cruising, inspection of timber sales, planning logging layouts, and a host of other field tasks by foresters must be performed in fair weather or foul, in comfort or in discomfort.

The vigorous youth has a tendency to make light of such hardship, but he should learn that if he becomes a forester, he accepts these hardships and discomforts for a long time ahead. Standby fire duty on fair weekends, long workdays, and long work weeks must be expected. As long as he remains a forester, no one is entirely exempt from such duty. The fact that foresters in high positions may be called on to perform such tasks at widely spaced intervals only makes the hardship the more keen when it must be endured.

Wife and Family. Beginning jobs in field forestry frequently involve periods away from headquarters or isolated living on the part of the forester and his family. Men who enter the profession after they have already acquired a wife and family often do so with some handicap. Beginning jobs that will provide them sufficient time at home to meet the obligations family life entails may be difficult to find. Still, field training is essential for future success.

The inconvenience which the forester himself must endure is often less disturbing than that his wife may encounter. It may be her lot to live in remote places, to wait at home while her husband is away for long periods, to bear and train her children with limited household and community conveniences. She must look forward to spending many years in small communities where schools, hospitals, stores, and amusements may be meager. Keeping intellectually alert and finding congenial companionship are often more difficult for her than for her husband. She may, however, seek outlet for her sympathy and creative energies in service to her family and community. What it means to be a forester's wife is ably expressed in "The Pine Tree Shield." This book was written by Mrs. Flint, the wife of a man who devoted his entire career to forestry.[5]

The forester's wife who can reconcile herself to inconvenience, isolation, hard work, community service, and intellectual discipline can become an inspiration to her husband and friends. She can teach her children the essential values of land, water, trees, and grass and the importance of living a life devoted to more than narrow self-interest; and she can help her husband to rise in his calling to those higher jobs that involve the utmost in breadth of feeling, consideration for people, and devotion to the public interest. If she cannot face these responsibilities and these handicaps, neither she nor her husband is likely to be happy, and the careers of both of them are likely to fall short of their ambitions.

Although the foregoing applies particularly to the field-going forester, it applies more or less equally well to the forester engaged in logging, in sawmill operations, in small wood-processing plants, and in pulp and paper mills. The forest industries are mostly located near their source of raw materials. Frequently they are the major industry in the community, often the only industry. This places on technically trained men special burdens for community leadership and service in addition to a high standard of professional work.

Conditions have improved greatly since the days of which Mrs. Flint writes (Fig. 71). Moreover, neither government nor corporations are callous toward the needs of a forester with growing children, and they often arrange transfers in the interest of the family. The truly rugged forestry posts today are to be encountered more frequently in Alaska and in foreign service than in western mountains.

Satisfactions Offered by the Profession of Forestry

A career in forestry offers many recompenses other than monetary rewards. First of all is the privilege of working with living things, with trees, with wildlife, and with people. The forest is ordinarily free from the nervous tension of a noisy factory or a busy office. Life in the open is far less nerve-racking, and often it brings the forester in contact with scenery of outstanding beauty, with shy wild creatures, and with the open-forest environment in which our ancestors developed their vigorous faith in our country and love of freedom and democracy. Most satisfying of all, forestry is important work. The fact that foresters realize this and seek to increase the services of forests to mankind lends a dignity and a sense of inner satisfaction that may escape the industrial worker.

LITERATURE CITED

1. Allen, Shirley W. 1950. In Winters, Robert K., ed., "Fifty Years of Forestry in the U.S.A.," pp. 272–284, Society of American Foresters, Washington, D.C.
2. Armstrong, George R., and Marvin W. Kranz. 1961. "Forestry College —Essays on the Growth and Development of New York State's College of Forestry, 1911 to 1961," Syracuse. 360 pp.
3. Eyre, F. H. 1960. "Professional Income of Forestry—1959," *Journal of Forestry*, 58:952–956.
4. Eyre, F. H. 1961. "Professional Income of Scientists," *Journal of Forestry*, 59:437.
5. Flint, Elizabeth Canfield. 1943. "The Pine Tree Shield," Doubleday & Company, Inc., Garden City, N.Y. 251 pp.
6. Kauffman, Erle, ed. 1958. "The Conservation Yearbook 1957–1958." Published by Conservation Yearbook, Washington, D.C. 272 pp.
7. Mason, Earl George. 1944. "Functional Curriculum in Professional Forestry," Studies in Education and Guidance, Bulletin 1, pp. 1–100, Oregon State College, Corvallis, Ore.
8. Meyer, Arthur B. 1953. "Forestry as a Profession," Society of American Foresters, Washington. 9 pp.

CHAPTER 26. *Trends and Outlook*

FOR A RESOURCE that covers one-third of the land area of our country and 30 per cent of that of the world as a whole, the future is inevitably bound up with the future of the nation and of the world as an economic community. If our people live in a world torn by strife and with continuous threat of war, our economy will be affected differently than it would be if the world's resources were mobilized for peaceful collaboration.

At no time in history have changes in sovereignty over nations been more rapid. Often this has been accompanied by intense feeling on the part of peoples gaining their freedom. That violence was not more widespread has been due to the voluntary surrender of many colonial possessions by western powers. By 1962 few were left.

Needs of Newly Emergent Nations

Independence seldom brings immediate peace and prosperity to a people long subjected to domination by others. The daring, turbulent spirits that are most successful in plotting and leading insurrection to overthrow a colonial regime rarely display the tolerance, capacity for compromise, and patience needed to compose differences within the new country and prepare the way for democratic government. Still a new order must be established or the nation cannot survive. Economic need is tremendous. Aid will be sought wherever it can be obtained and on what seem to the nation's leaders to be the best terms offered.

The new nations will seek to exploit whatever natural resources they have to obtain foreign exchange for products they must import. In some nations timber is such a resource. They are likely to exploit their forests heavily to obtain food and other necessities and capital for economic development. They need mass communication, newspapers, books, magazines, and radios to weld their nation together. They need most of all education to open their minds to the adventure and responsibilities of self-government. And they need vast internal improvement—housing,

433

roads, and industries. They will sacrifice what they must to meet such basic needs if responsibly governed.

But emergent nations are not the only ones to experience the ferment of change. Great changes also have been taking place in Western Europe since 1955. First, the military alliance and, next, the trade alliance culminating in the European Economic Community have brought about a *rapprochement* among Western European nations. By 1961, this *rapprochement* had brought unprecedented prosperity to the nations involved. The stimulus of free international trade was then but in its early stages. Should it continue, and there seems strong reason for it to do so, Western Europe will build an economy second to none in the world. Its productivity can be expected to outstrip that of the Soviet powers and will be an increasingly serious challenge to the trade position of the United States. With the United Kingdom looking toward the common market, an economic confederation of Western Europe seems assured. If the United States, Canada, and the nations of Latin America can develop an appropriate working relationship with this European confederation, an economic power combination should be produced that the Communist world could never hope to match.

The United States in 1962 faced its own economic problems. One of the foremost was how to continue a substantial foreign-aid program. The United States, since the close of the Second World War, had suffered a tremendous drain in its gold supply. This was due perhaps in major part to the cost of maintaining expensive military establishments abroad and to the costs of aid given to foreign nations from which the United States received limited economic returns. The economic aid the United States furnished prostrate Europe and Japan following the Second World War was astonishingly successful. These countries have become among the most prosperous in the world. A method needs to be found to make the aid being extended to the emergent and underdeveloped nations likewise yield returns to the United States commensurate with its cost. The United States, powerful as we may be, can never become the major producer that supplies goods without recompense to all underprivileged peoples and nations. Only by helping other nations to develop their own physical, human, and spiritual resources can we develop freedom-loving allies with the hope, faith, and courage to resist aggression.

The United States, though having a favorable trade balance in 1961, seemed definitely to be challenged in the world markets by the growing economic strength of Japan and the common market countries of Europe. It is important to the prosperity of the Western European countries as well as that of the United States that a strong economy be maintained in both. If the United States rises to meet this new world situation, it will of necessity enter upon a period of prosperity greater than that at any previous time. This will place heavy demands upon all the resources of our nation, particularly our human resources and our natural resources.

Future Demand for Forest Products and Services

The general trend in population growth, economic growth, scientific research and development, and the position of the United States in world affairs all pointed toward a substantial increase in resource use in the decades ahead. Moreover, the projections of future United States economic development that have been made since 1950 have proved to be conservative for the most part. The astounding development that has occurred in Western Europe since the Second World War and particularly following the trade agreements of 1955 make the United States' rate of development appear modest. However, the free exchange in technology and professional personnel between our country and Western Europe almost assures a mutual sharing of the benefits from social and scientific advance.

Reference has already been made to forecast of the future demands for wood, water, wildlife, recreation, forage, and other products from America's forests. The latest projection available at the time of writing was that prepared in a preliminary report on the land and water resource policy for the U.S. Department of Agriculture in January, 1962.[1] This projected a decline in cropland from 458 to 407 million acres between 1959 and 1980. It projected a 20-million-acre increase in pastureland, a 7-million-acre increase in commercial forest land, and a 4-million-acre decrease in noncommercial forest land.

The timber requirements projected for the year 1980 were 16 billion cubic feet, or about one-third above the consumption in 1961. The projected timber growth needed to meet this requirement was 68 billion board feet, or 44 per cent above production in 1961. It was expected that the actual growth will fall short of that needed by at least 14 per cent unless there is a significant improvement in current forest practice.* Land devoted to recreation and wildlife was expected to increase from 62 to 85 million acres by 1980 with forest land contributing 34 of the 85 million acres. Water use was expected to increase much more rapidly than timber use. The use in 1960 was 338 million acre-feet. For 1980 it was

* An independent and more extensive projection of resource needs appeared in "Resources in America's Future" by Hans H. Landsberg, Leonard L. Fischman, and Joseph L. Fisher, The Johns Hopkins Press, Baltimore, 1963, 1017 pp. Their medium-level projection of timber use for the year 1980 is 17.2 billion cubic feet and for the year 2000, 30.8 billion cubic feet. Projections of needs for water and recreational use of land are also given.

estimated that the use will be 835 million acre-feet. The total renewable annual supply is but 1,326,000 acre-feet, so by the year 1980 we should be pressing closely on the total water resources available.

Outdoor recreational use was expected to increase markedly. The Forest Service reported 102 million visits to the national forests in 1961, expected 300 million visits by 1980, and expected 635 million by the year 2000. The National Park Service expected a similar increase in visits to national parks. In 1960 there were 79.2 million visits, and by the year 2000 they expect 400 million visits. State parks in 1959 accommodated 255 million visits, but no projections have been made for future use of these parks. The total acreage of public lands available for public recreational use in 1960 was approximately 240 million acres, of which 60 million acres were considered as primarily for recreational use. Private lands also are extensively used for outdoor recreation, and this use is expected to expand rapidly by the year 1980. More than one-third of the households in the United States have one or more members who engage in hunting or sport fishing. In 1960 some 30 million indulged in these sports. By the year 1980 there will probably be 50 to 60 million hunters and fishermen, almost twice the number in 1960. States have been acquiring a great deal of land for fishing and public shooting grounds, and there is every prospect that this activity will continue.

The program proposed by the Department of Agriculture in 1962 included substantial increase in intensity of the management of the national forests. It proposed blocking up ownership through exchange and purchase but no major change in overall national forest ownership. It proposed a substantial change in farmlands. This included a reduction in cropland by some 50 million acres, an increase in pastureland, and the use of land on farms for recreation, wildlife development, and forestry. The report recognized that many farms are too small in size, at present, to be suitable for commercial agriculture. A program of farm consolidation was, therefore, proposed. A similar program of consolidation of small woodland holdings was a part of the program. The adjustments will involve substantial outlays by individual landowners; therefore, the program envisages certain public assistance in the form of long-term credit and actual payments for conservation practices.

President Kennedy in March, 1962, recommended to Congress a $1 billion program in conservation to activate proposals of the Outdoor Recreation Resources Review Commission. Another specific proposal was to establish a Youth Conservation Corps. He urged Congress to speed up action on pending conservation legislation and called a White House Conference on Conservation to plot a course for future action.

The Food and Agriculture Act of 1962 provides public aids and long-term loans to enable farmers and associations to carry out many of the land-use changes proposed. The Area Redevelopment Act of 1961 provides for similar aids for industrial development in areas having high rates of unemployment.

These and other proposals are for the most part in line with developments that are taking place in any case. We can expect, therefore, by the year 1980 to need about one-third more timber than we were consuming in 1960, about $2\frac{1}{2}$ times more water, and accommodations for twice as many hunters and fishermen and for about three times as many outdoor recreationists. All the timber, most of the water, and the accommodations for a high percentage of the recreationists, hunters, and fishermen must be provided from our forest lands. This will mean that multiple use should be invoked wherever this is consistent with the major use to which the land must be dedicated, and it means more intensive use of all forest lands. We can expect that a part of this increase in use intensity will occur on farm woodlands. The major portion, however, must be met from public forests, industrial forests, and private nonfarm forest holdings.

The increased forage requirement for domestic animals is likely to be met mainly from nonforested lands. There seems to be opportunity in the eastern section of the United States for increasing substantially the volume of forage produced on cultivated lands and pastures. At the same time, the western ranges are being restored to increased productivity so that the demand upon the forest for forage for domestic animals will increase only moderately. To the extent that domestic animals are withdrawn from productive range, wildlife tends to take their place. We can, therefore, expect a substantial increase in the wildlife population of the forests. This will enhance the value of the forest for recreational use and will provide sport for millions of hunters and fishermen. The problem of maintaining private land open to public hunting seems destined to become increasingly acute in the next few decades.

Evolution in Land Use

The position of the United States in world politics and economy, the great expansion of modern technology, and the avid desire of the American citizen to enjoy the best life our country can provide are together causing a substantial change in our use of the land. At no time in our nation's history has this shift in use been more pronounced. Since 1920, the use of land for agriculture has been declining, and this trend seems likely to continue at least to the year 1980. Since our nation was founded, use of land for urban development has increased, and this increase will be pronounced between 1960 and the year 2000. During this time the total population of the nation is expected to double. Suburban development will grow even more rapidly. How much of this will be preceded by orderly planning and how much will be haphazard depends on our wisdom and foresight. Haphazard growth, on the whole, is wasteful inasmuch as unplanned development often leads to the necessity of shifting from one use to another with consequent destruction of homes, commercial establishments, and other improvements that man has made.

Efforts at county and regional land-use planning that were pushed vigorously during the 1930s have not been followed up. There is, however, a resurgent interest in planning. A number of cities have already set about reconstructing their blighted areas. These are being cleared and huge civic and commercial structures are replacing them. The changes that are occurring in agriculture are equally dramatic. Farms are being increased in size, capital improvements on the farms are occurring, and the total capital investment necessary for a successful farm operation is increasing. The good soils are being more intensively cultivated and the poorer soils are being retired to pasture and forest. In this process, many farms are going out of operation or being consolidated with existing farms. If the program proposed by the Department of Agriculture is activated fully, the farm will acquire some of the amenities of the country estate providing, in addition to agriculture, ponds for

Fig. 89 Park naturalist giving tests to junior naturalists. (*National Park Service photo.*)

swimming, boating, and fishing; forests; wild areas for hunting; and clear water for downstream use. There will, however, be fewer farm families on the land, but substantially increased total agricultural production (Fig. 89).

The Shifting Role of Governments

The federal government is an important forest landowner and is likely to continue to be so for the indefinite future. There seems little prospect, however, of substantial expansion in public ownership of forest land, except for recreational use. The federal government can be expected to increase the intensity of management on its national forests and other forest holdings. Certainly the public will wish to look to the national forests as a source of the large-sized and higher-quality materials that may be uneconomic for the private owner to grow.

The federal government will be the major force behind international programs whether these are sponsored by the United States through the Agency for International Development or through the United Nations Food and Agriculture Organization. This service seems likely to increase substantially during the period 1960 to 1980. International forestry, therefore, will become a significant role of our federal government. The federal government will cooperate with the individual states in regional development planning where this involves substantial rehabilitation of both urban and rural areas. It is important that governmental aid for such development carry with it certain standards that will ensure proper planning and bold execution.

The federal government is expected likewise to continue to play a major role in forest research in both the land-management and the forest-products fields. These activities as well as the management of the national forests and the state-aid programs of the federal government will give it a catalytic role in promoting forestry activities by the states and private industry. The future role of the federal government in forestry, therefore, is likely to be considerably greater than it was in 1962 and to require the services of some of our nation's most capable foresters.

The Role of the States

The states can be expected to play the major role in acquiring land for parks, wildlife and game refuges, and general recreational use. The states will be the main agency for helping the landowners with their individual forestry programs. The states will undoubtedly have an increasingly important task to perform in watershed management and in regional development planning. The states are currently the major agency engaged in professional education in forestry. Aids to private landowners, whether financed by federal or by state funds, will be administered largely by state agencies. How far such aids may increase in the future is still uncertain. It is becoming clear, however, that a number of forest practices will not be carried out on a sufficiently large scale by small private owners without public aid. This is particularly true of planting, restoration of brushlands to forest, soil-improvement measures such as fertilizing, swamp drainage, and many other practices that will yield returns in increased timber growth but barely pay expenses to the landowner unless the public helps. Should the public recognize and compensate the landowner for his production of wildlife, water, and other products from which he currently receives little or no income, such recompense would probably be channeled through the state forestry agencies.

The granting of subsidies to individuals to carry out practices on their own lands from which they personally will benefit is always open to question as a public policy. If the states and the federal government are to continue to expand such subsidies, it would seem entirely appropriate that they extend their aid only where realistic benefits can be derived from doing so. Little public good can be anticipated from indiscriminate aid to small uneconomic units.

Private Agencies

Main expansion in forestry activities during the next few decades is expected to occur on lands in private ownership and in the privately operated wood-processing industries. Certainly industries using substantial quantities of wood will seek to expand their forest holdings sufficient to assure them a permanent and steady wood supply. This does not mean that they will attempt to become self-sufficient in timber needs. Many will find it prudent to own no more than one-half the land necessary to supply their needs and to look to other forest landowners for the remainder. This tends to increase their strength in the local community and to provide a certain versatility in operation and freedom from heavy costs for land ownership and management that they might otherwise be obliged to incur. It seems probable that the industries will continue to build up goodwill among the landowners by offering forestry services.

Pulp and Paper Industry

The pulp and paper industry seems destined to continue its rapid expansion. This is true because of the versatility and wide use of paper and paper products including paperboard and of the vigorous research program of the industry to keep their products competitive with those manufactured from other raw materials. The paper industry also has possibilities for expanding into international trade with the newly developing countries and for the establishment of operations in these new countries. One of the major roles of American industry in the next two decades may be the establishment of plants in the newly developing countries wherever sound financial arrangements can be made.

Plywood Industry

The plywood and building-board industry, generally, is expected to expand at a rate comparable to that of the pulp and paper industry. There is great need for plywood by the construction industry. This, together with various fiberboards, including particle board, has wide use in construction and in general manufacturing. The industry, moreover, has launched a substantial research program which should help it to maintain a strong position in the future.

Lumber Industry

The outlook for lumber is less certain. There will be undoubtedly a substantial increase in housing and rural and urban development that will make heavy demands on construction materials of all sorts. Lumber will be used to the extent that it is competitive with other available materials. The lumber industry has been promoting increased use of wood and is also developing research programs that should open up new markets for wood and help to regain old ones. Many of the major difficulties, particularly organizational, remain still to be solved. Hence, lumber is likely to continue to lose markets to other structural materials though the general upward trend in construction needs will probably mean substantial increase in lumber use.

Integrated Industries

The trend toward integration among wood-using industries will probably continue in the decades to come. This may take place through one corporation's engaging in lumber manufacture, plywood manufacture, secondary manufacture, and pulp and paper manufacture. It may also occur through the pulp and paper industry's furnishing a market for chips to sawmills and wood-processing plants. One type of integration that seems destined to develop very rapidly will be integration between paper and plastics, or rather the use of plastic materials as additives and coatings on paper.

Whether or not integration of wood-using industries will take the form it has in Scandinavian countries where one huge company may manufacture several grades of paper, lumber, plywood, prefabricated houses, furniture, turned products, and other specialties is uncertain. Of the major companies in the United States, one that achieved dominance in the lumber industry also entered upon the manufacture of plywood, pulp, and paper. Another company having extensive paper-manufacturing facilities purchased a large lumber company. A few modest-sized lumber companies have sought to use all products from their land; hence, they have built pulp and paper mills and wood-distillation plants. The trend has not been general. In fact, there is little in common in technology or sales organization between lumber manufacture and pulp and paper manufacture. Recognizing this, several pulp and paper companies have established a policy of selling sawlog timber to lumber manufacturers and purchasing chips from them rather than attempting operations in the two separate fields.

Integration within the lumber industry itself would seem to offer greater possibilities of economies and efficiency, though these may be more apparent than real. It would seem that the lumber industry might appropriately expand operations to include planing-mill products, furniture blanks and other small-dimension products, prefabricated or precut wall panels, and even prefabricated light-construction units such as garages, summer camps, and even dwellings. Such integration could result in much more complete use of raw material and would place the lumber manufacturer in the consumer market where he could capture intermediate profits. However, few lumber companies have either the resources or the technical competence to cover this wide field. The large companies that do have such resources have not met with such degree of success as to tempt others to follow their lead.

Nor has the light-construction industry as such felt the need to enter the field of raw-material manufacture. The dispersal of operations and markets, the bulky nature of the materials and product, the limited degree of standardization of sizes and structural parts, and the need for various species for different functions within a structure have all discouraged the builder from becoming a forest landowner and sawmill operator.

With growing concentration of housing developments in the future, larger building operations will become possible and profitable. These may seek to establish contacts with primary suppliers that will short-cut some of the organizational structure that currently exists. However, there seems reason to expect that the lumber wholesaler and retailer will survive for a long time to come by continuing to supply services that neither the builder nor lumber manufacturer can provide economically. The complex subcontracting within the light-construction industry itself also will probably continue for decades.

Research and Development

The greatest force for directing the future use of wood and the forests will be research and development. We can anticipate substantial changes in equipment for harvesting trees. The timber-harvesting machines that were in use in 1961 and 1962 were probably but crude prototypes of those that can be expected by the year 1980. Research on the chemistry of cellulose and lignin seems destined to lead to a host of new products and new uses of wood. The development of graft polymers is but one of many techniques that may transform cellulose into a product differing radically from its natural state. Solid-state physics offers another approach to modifying cellulose and wood products. Pulping methods have been improved greatly within the period 1950 to 1961, and the research effort now going into this work seems destined to improve it to an even greater extent during the coming decades.

We are rapidly developing new insight into wood technology that can lead to much more efficient use of wood in the future. This opens up new opportunities for design in wood, a field in which the prospects seem unlimited. Each advance in wood technology carries with it a potential advance in design of products to be made of wood. The relative mobility of our population places special demands on housing. Also the need for housing of varying sizes as the family increases to its maximum size, then shrinks when the children leave home, makes it prudent for many couples to make three or more moves during their lifetime even

Fig. 90 Foresters look to the future. (*U.S. Forest Service photo.*)

though they may reside in the same community. When this is linked with transfers to other cities, it is obvious that consideration does need to be given to building homes into which a family can move with a minimum of disruption to normal activities. The designer here is faced with the possibilities of making homes compact, yet suited to family harmony, entertainment of friends, and individual privacy.

All these are challenges to the research efforts of foresters, wood technologists, pulp and paper technologists, landscape architects, architects, builders, and the industries which employ these people. With the rate at which research is expanding, it can confidently be forecast that new technology will make a major impression on forestry and forest products within the next few decades (Fig. 90).

Employment

The employment outlook seems bright for decades ahead for graduates in pulp and paper technology because of the continued growth of the industry and its expanding world-wide outlook. Moreover, the growing use of products made from paper and plastic combinations ensures a bright outlook in the domestic market.

The tremendous expansion in outdoor recreation, in highway development, and in urban and suburban renewal and development presents a very favorable outlook for landscape architects. Jobs will be abundant for as many men as existing schools can educate.

Wood technologists also have a vast service to perform. It is less certain, however, if the industry will actually have jobs for them in the abundance expected for landscape architects and pulp and paper technologists. Sooner or later this field, too, will open for college-trained men, and when it does it will be a large one. Meanwhile, many openings can be found with lumber manufacturers, planing mills, wholesale and retail lumberyards, builders, and wood-processing industries.

There remains the broad field of forest land management for wood, water, wildlife, forage, and recreation. The needs for all are growing, and with this the need for scientific management. With the U.S. Forest Service alone anticipating a need for 550 new foresters annually, and with other agencies combined using far larger numbers, the long-range outlook for employment seems bright. This does not mean that there will be no years when jobs are scarce because of business or government curtailment, nor does it mean that all men, irrespective of ability or motivation, will find lucrative employment upon graduation. But with the bright general outlook both at home and abroad, there should be little waiting to find jobs by men well educated in the profession.

The chief tasks of the colleges of forestry, therefore, will be to attract in sufficient numbers men having the basic talents needed to respond well to the increasingly complex forest science of the future. Once their students are enrolled, the colleges must give them an education well grounded in the basic sciences and forest technology and a vision of the service opportunities they will face. No man of talent and a high sense of public service need shrink from electing a forestry career.

LITERATURE CITED

1. U.S. Department of Agriculture. 1962. "Preliminary Report: A Land and Water Resources Policy for the United States," Washington. 228 pp.

Index

446